Francis William Newman

A History of the Hebrew Monarchy

From the administration of Samuel to the Babylonish captivity

Francis William Newman

A History of the Hebrew Monarchy
From the administration of Samuel to the Babylonish captivity

ISBN/EAN: 9783337243784

Printed in Europe, USA, Canada, Australia, Japan

Cover: Foto ©ninafisch / pixelio.de

More available books at **www.hansebooks.com**

A

HISTORY

OF

THE HEBREW MONARCHY

FROM

THE ADMINISTRATION OF SAMUEL TO THE
BABYLONISH CAPTIVITY.

BY

FRANCIS WILLIAM NEWMAN,

FORMERLY FELLOW OF BALLIOL COLLEGE, OXFORD.

Third Edition.

LONDON:
N. TRÜBNER & CO., 60, PATERNOSTER ROW.
1865.

[The right of Translation is reserved.]

PREFACE TO THIRD EDITION.

In this third edition I have omitted many controversial notes, which seem no longer needful.

To avoid any mystery, and prevent future misconception, I will say plainly that I hold in my hands a letter from the late Editor of the North British Review, which fixes on the late Archbishop Whately the responsibility of a certain article, by which I was much aggrieved. But as it is not likely to be now read, I am glad to say no more about it.

A few general remarks may assist the reader to understand the point of view from which the following pages were written.

1. I did not start from the assumption that "miracles are incredible;" but from the earlier axiom, that "the more strange the thing attested, the more cogent is the proof needed." Under the application of this very cautious principle, it is gradually discovered that the great majority of alleged miracles have really no better evidence than have ghosts, magic, and stories of fairies. In Hebrew history, as in that of Greeks and Romans, the miraculous element disappears in proportion as we obtain historical attestations: thus the belief is undermined by the growth of knowledge and of criticism.—Others may now start from a more advanced principle; that "after the researches of the last 100 years we have a right to *presume* mistake in every pretended miracle." But I believe this

to be a result which has been earned by much research, not an original first principle of philosophy. At any rate, I never started from it myself.

2. So far am I from renouncing a Divine Element in Hebrew history, that I see a Divine Element in all history. God is in Nature and in Man. There is no contrast of the natural and supernatural; for natural agencies are divine, and divine influences are in the human heart. No one who venerates Hebrew history and literature can be offended at my believing this. I cannot consent to desecrate all other history in order to consecrate that of the Hebrews.

3. The work of refuting error is strictly necessary, if truth is to be advanced. The negative side of every question is as essential to truth as are the shadows in a picture. Unless rubbish be cleared away, and all its miasma purged, no firm and healthy building can rise. Apostles and prophets were emphatically idol-breakers in their own day, and often very harsh ones. While we must strive never needlessly to wound men's susceptibilities, it is neither kind nor profitable to practise suppression, lest the utterance of truth give pain.

4. I assume that God is unchangeably perfect, ever like Himself, and that His judgment of human conduct cannot vary with mere time and place. According to the words ascribed to an apostle, "He is no respecter of persons; but in every nation those who work righteousness are approved by Him." Any sentiments to the contrary found in early writers are treated by me as errors incident to their age and nation. Whatever is our highest moral attainment, from it, as from our best elevation, we must try to survey ancient as well as modern events.

CONTENTS.

CHAPTER I.

THE LAND AND TRIBES OF ISRAEL.—AGRICULTURAL AND OTHER SOCIAL INSTITUTIONS.—THE BORDER COUNTRIES.

PAGE

Land of Israel. — The Jordan and the Eastern Tribes. — The Northern Tribes.—The Central Tribes.—The Southern Tribes. — Mosaic Agriculturalism. — The Levites. — Polygamy. — The Neighbouring Nations   1

CHAPTER II.

ADMINISTRATION OF SAMUEL AND REIGN OF SAUL.

The Philistines.—Hebrew monotheism.—Administration of Samuel. —Early Hebrew psalmody.—Exterior marks of the Prophet.— Modes of divination.—Foreign dangers of Israel.—Appointment of Saul.—Romantic Philistine campaign. — Ammonite inroad.— Enmity with Amalek.—Massacre of the Amalekites.—David, anointed by Samuel. — David, Saul's armour-bearer. — David, Saul's son-in-law.—David, a freebooter.—David with Achish of Gath —David reinforced from Israel.—David's return to Ziklag. —Battle of Mount Gilboa   21

CHAPTER III.

REIGN OF DAVID.

David, king in Hebron.—Battle near Gibeon.—Murder of Abner.—Jerusalem.—Capture of Jerusalem.—The ark conveyed to Jerusalem.—State of Hebrew industry.—Conquest of Moab.—First war with the Zobahites.—Conquest of Edom.—Prosperity of David.—Ammonite war.—Destruction of the Ammonites.—Career of Absalom.—Death of Absalom.—Disgrace of Mephibosheth.—Immolation of Saul's descendants.—The pestilence.—Conspiracy of Adonijah.—Death of David 65

CHAPTER IV.

REIGN OF SOLOMON.

Foreign commotions.—Political executions.—Solomon's trade by the Red Sea.—Trade over the Syrian Desert.—Visit of the Queen of Sheba.—Gold vessels of the Temple.—Building of the Temple.—Bondmen in Israel.—The Temple worship.—The Decalogue.—Dowry of an Egyptian princess.—Solomon's idolatry.—Hostilities against Solomon.—Death of Solomon.—Chronology of the Kings.—Chronological table 107

CHAPTER V.

FROM THE DEATH OF SOLOMON TO THE ACCESSION OF OMRI, B.C. 955—901.

Division of the Monarchy.—Calves of Dan and Bethel.—Jeroboam's neglect of Levites.—Invasion by Shishak.—Later years of Rehoboam.—Massacre of the house of Jeroboam.—Power of Damascus.—War of Baasha and Asa.—Asa's later reign.—Massacre of the house of Baasha 141

CHAPTER VI.

THE HOUSE OF OMRI, B.C. 904—864.

Building of Samaria.—Phœnician worship in Israel.—Miracles of Elijah.—Syrian chariot warfare.—Syrian campaigns west of Jordan.—Benhadad at Ramoth Gilead.—Greatness of Jehoshaphat.—Joint war of Ahab and Jehoshaphat.—Doctrine of lying spirits.—Combined war against Moab.—Siege of Samaria.—Revolt of the Edomites.—Second battle at Ramoth.—Naboth's vineyard.—Massacres of Jehu.—Massacre by Athaliah 163

CHAPTER VII.

THE PERIOD OF THE HOUSE OF JEHU, B.C. 864—762.

Priests and Levites in Jerusalem.—Revolution conducted by Jehoiada.—Regency of Jehoiada.—Reigns of Jehu and his son.—Dispersion of Judah and Israel.—Repairs of the Temple.—Prophecy of Joel.—Peace is bought of Hazael.—Invasion of Idumæa.—Decline of Damascus.—Victorious career of Jeroboam II.—Internal state of Israel.—Prophecy of Amos.—Uzziah's long prophecy. Internal state of Judæa.—Genealogies of the High Priests 197

CHAPTER VIII.

FROM THE CONQUESTS OF JEROBOAM II. TO THE FALL OF SAMARIA, B.C. 762—721.

City of Nineveh.—New parties in Israel.—Disorganization of Israel.—Zechariah's Prophecy.—League against Judæa.—Sufferings of Judah.—Isaiah encourages Ahaz.—Fall of Damascus.—Religious character of Ahaz.—Sargon and the Philistines.—First invasion of Shalmaneser.—Revolt of Judah and of Ephraim.—Final transplanting of Israel.—Anticipations of Isaiah and Micah.—Decline of prophecy in Israel.—Rough dates of certain prophecies 232

CHAPTER IX.

FROM THE FALL OF SAMARIA TO THE DEATH OF JOSIAH,
B.C. 721—609.

PAGE

Assyrian siege of Tyre.—Hezekiah's passover.—Invasion by Sennacherib.—Ethiopian embassy.—Submission of Hezekiah.—New complication of affairs.—Renewal of hostilities.—Disasters of Sennacherib.—Hezekiah's illness.—Isaiah's prophecy concerning Egypt.—Zenith of Hebrew prophecy.—Character of Manasseh.—Paganism and persecution.—State of the Assyrian power. Rise of scholastic learning.—Scythian irruption into Media.—Rise of the Chaldees.—Final ruin of Nineveh.—Renewal of prophecy.—Josiah's reform.—Recency of Deuteronomy.—Peculiarities of Deuteronomy.—The Pentateuch a gradual growth.—Uncritical proceedings.—False prophets in Judæa.—Contemporary Egyptian affairs.—Battle near Megiddon 267

CHAPTER X.

CLOSE OF THE HEBREW MONARCHY.

Popular election from the Dynasty.—Jehoahaz and Jehoiakim.—Defeat of Necho at Carchemish.—Jeremiah's Political Prophecies.—Babylonian invasions.—First deportation of Jews to Babylon. Rebellion of Zedekiah.—Destruction of Jerusalem.—Gedaliah the Babylonian Satrap.—Prophecies against Egypt.—Later School of Prophecy.—Function of the Jewish Nation   324

HISTORY

OF

THE HEBREW MONARCHY.

CHAPTER I.

THE LAND AND TRIBES OF ISRAEL—AGRICULTURAL AND OTHER SOCIAL INSTITUTIONS—THE BORDER COUNTRIES.

FEW nations which have put forth a wide and enduring influence upon others, proclaim themselves to have been indigenous[1] on the land of their celebrity. Tradition for the most part points back to a time at which they dispossessed earlier inhabitants, who, as hereditary enemies, are sure to be drawn in unfavourable colours, whether as unfaithful allies, brutish savages, ferocious giants, or again, as impure, heretical, or atheistical unbelievers. Where the country consists of extensive plains, with no frontier difficult to pass, its older occupants more readily migrate under the pressure of an enemy, and the whole nation may really disappear. But in this case, the resistance is generally less lingering and the traditions of wars vaguer. In a hilly or mountainous country, on the contrary, the invaders seldom succeed in doing more than driving the former possessors of the soil into their natural fastnesses; where, after long maintaining themselves in independence,

[1] The great civilized nations, which, from the absence of all earlier traditions, we vaguely name *indigenous*, are principally the Egyptians, the Indians, and the Chinese. What Strabo says of India might as truly be said of all,—that they have neither received nor sent out colonies; though Indians and Chinese emigrate largely as individuals. Masses so great have inevitably affected the barbarous tribes around them; yet their external influence has been small in proportion to their means. China has subdued Mongolia only by being subdued.

nothing is commoner than that they should finally be blended with the victorious nation, and having adopted its manners, its religion, its tongue, should boast of its triumphs as their own, and moralize over the utter extirpation of the tribes whose lineal descendants they themselves are.

Many of these phenomena may be observed in the history of the Hebrew nation, whose origin was[1] referred to their great ancestor Abraham, a Chaldee by birth and language, and progenitor not only of Israel but of the Hagarenes and Edomites; while from Lot, his nephew and associate, were derived the contiguous nations of Ammon and Moab. But the history of the Israelites is distinguished from that of their neighbours by their early migration to Egypt and their eventful return; in the course of which an entirely new impress is supposed to have been left upon them under the agency of Moses, as the peculiar people of JEHOVAH. The tongue of Canaan or of Chaldea had been carried with them to Egypt; but in that country they were reduced to miserable bond-slaves, so mixed up with the Egyptian population, that even in birth their infants were liable to be murdered by their oppressors. If this account can be at all trusted, it is difficult to avoid the inference, that, like other slave populations, they lost their own language, and therefore brought back with them into Canaan the Egyptian tongue.[2] Be this as it may, at any rate the invaders either kept or in course of time gained a Canaanitish speech, not untinctured by Egyptian words. The other Canaanites named them *Hebrews*; a word which the Alexandrine translators of Genesis seem rightly to connect with the idea of being or coming *across a river*;[3] nor is it unreasonable to be-

---

[1] I decline the task of discussing these genealogies minutely. They may be true: yet no stress is to be laid upon them, since from the nature of the case they cannot be *proved*. The details concerning Lot's incest are so evidently an invention of national enmity, as to throw some discredit on the rest of the genealogy.

[2] This opinion is maintained by the Rev. Dr Giles in his Hebrew Records, p. 173. The conclusion may be reasonably doubted by any who regard the tale of Hebrew bondage in Egypt to be much exaggerated in the details of the book of Exodus; yet to balance the probabilities is to me exceedingly hard.

[3] Gen. xiv. 13, *the Hebrew* is rendered τὸν περάτην. The Hebrew and Arabic root "*Eber*, whence the national name "*Ebri* (Hebrew) comes, means, *to cross* or *to be across a river*. In the later geography of Palestine the east

lieve that they first obtained this name, when their proper seat was conceived of by the Canaanites as on the east of Jordan. As their numbers were by no means such as to be able to occupy the country on both banks, they had no sooner obtained an adequate settlement in its various parts, than peaceful tendencies began to prevail over the aversion which religion excited in at least the principal leaders of Israel; and coalitions, which were generally reprobated by a distant posterity, arose between the armies of Jehovah and the families of Canaan.

The land over the fairest parts of which they had spread themselves, was critically situated in the ancient world, and had remarkable peculiarities of its own. It was the highway for armies between Egypt and all the great countries of Western Asia; a fact, the importance of which was not felt in the earlier stages of Hebrew history, but which, from the time that Assyria rose into power, mainly influenced the whole external destiny of the nation. The land itself is naturally very deficient in facilities for general communication, and in any well-marked frontier; and except when grasped in some more widely-spread dominion, it appears calculated to foster numerous small principalities or republics. The sea-coast on its western side runs nearly northward, though inclining to the east: two sets of highlands range north and south, between which is the valley of the river Jordan, a very remarkable depression. The streams run off from both sides of the western highlands, into the sea and into the Jordan, but are nowhere navigable nor of any magnitude. Nor did the coast afford many harbours able to accommodate even the little vessels of early navigation, until it reached the immediate neighbourhood of the Phœnicians, whose experience taught them beyond what point they must not covet its possession. The district theoretically assigned to the tribe of Asher[1] runs north as far as Sidon, including

bank of Jordan was called ἡ περαία, which significantly confirms the belief that the people of Moses, when settled on that district, were called for the same reason Hebrews by their western neighbours. Those who suppose *Abraham* to have been called a Hebrew, as the book of Genesis represents, must interpret the word of his having crossed *the Euphrates :* but this was not a present visible fact, to impress the people's imagination, and lead to a name. The Jewish notion that Abraham specifically was so called from his distant ancestor Heber, merely shows how undiscriminating in these matters is popular opinion.

[1] The words in Gen. xlix. 13 greatly need elucidation : "*Zebulon* shall be a

Tyre with all its villages; but in fact neither Zebulon nor Asher seems ever to have possessed even the important city and harbour of Accho (*Ptolemaïs* or *Acre*), south of which, the bay of Accho, bounded by Carmel, belonged to Zebulon. Yet it is probable that the Tyrians did not grudge to them either the mainland or the havenless shore, but were satisfied to maintain themselves in fortified seaports, and keep up peaceful relations with the agricultural Asherites. The sea-coast allotted to Dan and Simeon, from Joppa southward, was yet to be conquered, though maritime Danites are once alluded to (Judges v. 17); so that with trifling exception the Israelitish nation was shut up on to the continent.

The Jordan, which gives to Canaan so peculiar a character, might have seemed the natural centre of the whole country; since the warmth and fertility of its well-watered basin, and the ease of keeping up communication along it, appear to award its possession to a single power, and to give to that power large home-resources. But in fact it rather separated than united the children of Israel. The tribes to whom its eastern side was conceded found the open highlands very favourable to pasturage; and having brought with them out of Egypt the habits of shepherds, would not renounce that independent, roving, and marauding life to become laborious tillers of fertile plains, whose crops must always be exposed to the inroads of their pastoral neighbours. A sharp line of division, which affected the whole subsequent history, was thus drawn between the western agriculturists and the eastern or grazier tribes of Israel. These were, the Reubenites on the south; the Gadites above them; and, still farther to the north, the half-tribe of Manasseh, which, though warlike and adventurous, seldom took any eager interest in the welfare of Israel at large. Our narratives ascribe their easy and complete possession of their land to the fact that Israel entered Canaan from that side, and by united force conquered Sihon king of Heshbon, and Og king of Bashan. Indeed, from a knowledge of the later history alone, a speculator might imagine that all Israel had resided or

haven for ships, and *his border shall be unto Zidon.*" It is said that "Zidon" means Phœnicia; but if this is admissible, the words still are far more appropriate to Asher.

roved for some generations on the land of the eastern tribes; and when their numbers increased, had gradually crossed the Jordan in parties, with far inferior force to that which had overrun the eastern shore.

Another physical circumstance is not to be neglected, as probably affecting the dwellers on the banks of the Jordan, little as we could expect it to be understood or distinctly noticed in early times. Although the Jordan flows from the low grounds of Mount Hermon,—the lofty peak which terminates Anti-Libanus on the south,—it descends so rapidly, that, when it reaches the small lake called by the Jews "the Waters of Merom" (*Samachonitis*, *Bahr el Huleh*), it is already on the level of the Mediterranean Sea; and the lake of Gennesareth, which next receives it, is now known to be about 330 feet below that level. Out of the latter lake it issues with a most violent course, precipitating itself along what is more peculiarly called the basin of the Jordan (Arab. *El Ghor*, the hollow), by so steep a slope, that the surface of the Dead Sea, in which it is swallowed up, has been estimated by the latest inquiries as nearly 1000 feet lower than that of the lake of Gennesareth. If instead of 1312 feet below the Mediterranean, we adopt the earlier and more moderate computation of 600, we can still have no doubt that the Indian heat of the valley is caused by this singular depression. In the flood season ("the first month," 1 Chron. xii. 15) the Jordan appears ordinarily to have overflowed its banks, adding fertility to the soil, but not health to the climate. On the plain of Jericho, which lies west of the Jordan, at the head of the Dead Sea, the palm-groves grew with an exuberance celebrated by the ancients; and the oppressive, often-steaming atmosphere of the entire district, whatever vigour it may impart to certain vegetation, seems to be exactly that in which the human frame becomes unstrung. The natives of such a dell were not likely to keep up a superiority over the inhabitants of the table-land, which on the western side ranges at two thousand feet and upwards above the Mediterranean, without considering its hills; and the actual rulers of the country appear at every time to have dwelt on the higher grounds.

A little below the lake of Gennesareth the Jordan receives from the east the waters of the Jarmuk[1] (*Hieromax, Sheriat el Mandhur*), which runs down in numerous branches from the elevated country of Hauran, and passes near the very ancient city Ashtaroth Karnaim. There was on this side no frontier to separate the Manassites from their neighbours. Close at hand lay Bashan, a rich grazing country north of the Jarmuk and east of the Jordan, which was free from the stony districts characterizing the upper Hauran, and must have been such a prize to pastoral tribes, that it would naturally often change its masters. The Hebrews held it to be a land of giants. Although the northern bank of the Jarmuk had been nominally Hebrew ever since the defeat of king Og, yet after the many disasters of Israel the sixty cities of Argob in Bashan ("fenced with high walls, gates and bars, besides unwalled towns a great many") might well need to be recaptured by Jair the Manassite. But the exploits of this hero are obscurely and enigmatically reported. According to the most probable interpretation, he won only twenty-three "small towns" in Bashan. We incidentally learn (1 Chron. ii. 23) that the Geshurites and Syrians afterwards recovered the towns of Jair and many others beside, "sixty cities" in all; and (Josh. xiii. 13) that the people of Geshur and Maachath lived in friendly commixture with the Israelites, no doubt after alternate conquests and lingering struggles. The achievements of Jair, echoed down from distant times, took also another form, according to which he was a "Judge" of all Israel for twenty-two years, and gave to his thirty sons, who rode on thirty young asses, thirty cities in the land of Gilead.[2]

[1] *Yarmuk* appears like a modern corruption of *Hieromax*; yet as *max* has no Greek meaning, and *Yar* (river) is an old Hebrew or Egyptian term (as in Jordan?), it is at least as possible that *Yarmuk* is the old name, and *Hieromax* an attempt to reduce it to Hellenism. The name, it is believed, is not found in the Hebrew books.

[2] The most recent, and perhaps also the most ancient, application of the name of Gilead (*Djelaad*), is to a mountain or table-land south of the river Jabbok, which falls into the Jordan many miles below the Jarmuk. But the word Gilead in the Hebrew geography extended much farther to the north, perhaps as far as the Jarmuk. In Joshua xiii. 25, 31, "all the cities of Gilead" are given to Gad, and "half Gilead" to Manasseh. It is probable that the Manassite district was shared between two names, Bashan and (northern) Gilead. The apparent extension of the name Argob in Deut. iii. to the whole country northward as far as the borders of Geshur and Maachath, is another perplexity. We may imagine the Geshurites and Maachathites to have been

The simplest general result of the various accounts would seem to be this: Gilead and southern Bashan were held firmly by Israel before they could permanently keep northern Bashan. After long contests a compromise took place with their Geshurite neighbours, which on the whole left the Manassites with a decided advantage.

The land of the Hebrews west of the Jordan is narrow on the northern end, where the two tribes of Naphthali and Asher are depicted on a small territory, with Zebulon and Issachar to the south of them; all in the later GALILEE, and therefore to the north of Carmel. This ridge, commencing from the sea at the southern point of the bay of Accho, runs at first south-east, having on its northern declivity the fine plain of Jezreel (*Esdraelon*), along whose slope the brook of Kishon falls, parallel to the mountain, and enters the bay of Accho. The line of Carmel at length bends due east, and terminates above Succoth, where it sees the mountains of Gilboa fronting it on the north, with the city of Beth Shean (*Scythopolis*) at their feet, on the basin of the Jordan. The district of these four tribes was not called by the collective name of Galilee until after the return from Babylon; and the "Gentile Galilee" of Isaiah was a smaller territory on the Phœnician frontier. From the earliest times a Gentile influence pervaded this whole country. Few, if any, names are found in it of ancient holy seats connected with the wanderings of the Hebrew patriarchs, or otherwise sacred; and (whether cause or effect) no strong zeal for the national religion, either in its prophetical or its priestly development, came forth out of Galilee.[1] But it was in every external sense a most favoured country; physically, if also mentally, the *Bœotia* of Palestine. "The Galilæans," says Josephus, "are warlike from infancy, and always numerous; the land is all fat, and good for grazing, and planted with every sort of tree, so as by its exuberance to invite even the least industrious husbandmen. At least

a united people, who until a late time held nearly all Gaulonitis; that Argob, or the kingdom of Og, reached not far north of the Jarmuk; and that Bashan, in a large sense, comprised Gaulonitis and Argob together. But the village Argob was about fifteen miles west of Gerasa (on the northern bank of *the Jabbok*): Euseb. apud *Winer*.

[1] This was also true of the eastern tribes, but when their country had been long heathenized, no peculiar reproach fell on it.

it is all fully tilled, and no part of it is left idle. It has thick-set cities, and multitudes of flourishing villages, holding from 500 to 1000 inhabitants each. In short, though in size it is inferior to the Peræa [or the land beyond Jordan], yet it is superior in power, for it is entirely turned to service, and everywhere productive." Although in the earlier times it was naturally less peopled and less fully tilled, and a great change of population afterwards took place, we may safely abide by this general description as a clue to its earlier state. The rebellious disposition ascribed to the Galilæans was a necessary result of their bravery and love of independence. Satisfied with their own soil, they aspired at little beyond what it supplied, and made domestic independence their chief aim. The contiguity of Tyre on the north must undoubtedly have called out their agricultural industry, and greatly reconciled them to the foreigners with whom they were intermixed at home.[1]

Yet the Galilæan Hebrews were twice, in very early times, put foremost in battle for the independence of Israel. The first danger was from a petty potentate, called by the high-sounding title, Jabin, *king of Canaan*,[2]—more properly king of Hazor near the waters of Merom,—whose military successes threatened with subjugation the whole country to the west of Jordan. He was defeated by Barak of Kadesh Naphthali, with the forces of Naphthali and Zebulon. The other tribes either held aloof in suspense and anxiety,[3] or were content with sending "princes" to

[1] In Judges i. the following Canaanitish nations are recorded as permanently dwelling in the Galilæan territory: 1. in the tribe of Asher, the inhabitants of *Accho*, of *Zidon*, of *Ahlab*, of *Achzib*, of *Helbah*, of *Aphik*, of *Rehob*; 2. in the tribe of Naphthali, the inhabitants of *Bethshemesh* and *Bethanath*, who however at length became tributary; 3. in the tribe of Zebulon, the inhabitants of *Kitron* and *Nahalol*, also made tributary; 4. in the tribe of Issachar (theoretically in that of Manasseh, Josh. xvii. 11), Bethshean and her towns, Taanach and her towns, Dor and her towns, Ibleam and her towns, Megiddo and her towns. These tribes were made tributary only at a late æra. Besides the Canaanites, who drew notice by remaining independent so long, great numbers more must have been silently incorporated with Israel from early times.

[2] *Canaan* is by many interpreted "the low country," as opposed to *Aram* (Syria), "the high country:" and the name *Canaan*, as applicable to the dwellers of the coast, was perhaps primitively given to the Phœnicians: whence also the word meant "a trader." Possibly therefore "Jabin, king of Canaan" stands for "Jabin, a Phœnician potentate."

[3] Judges v. 14—18. "Zebulon and Naphthali, in the high places of the field, jeoparded their lives unto the death."—"On the brooks of Reuben were *great*

Deborah—as ambassadors, it would seem—by way of promising succour. On the second occasion the Midianites were the foreign enemy, and Gideon the Manassite was the Hebrew champion. It is remarkable that *both* contests took place on the broad slope of Jezreel, ever the great battle-field of this country; and,—as Gideon's troops were gathered from Manasseh, Asher, Zebulon, and Naphthali, —we may infer that he was a *western* Manassite, and that the danger threatened Galilee peculiarly. After the defeat and flight of the Midianites,—who (if we can trust the interpretation of an enigmatical phrase, Judges vii. 3) had come with "Amalekites and children of the east" *from Mount Gilead*,—Naphthali, Asher, and Manasseh distinguished themselves in the pursuit. It is reasonable to believe that the inroads of such marauders, whose cattle year after year destroyed the crops (Judges vi. 1—6), must have helped to unite the Hebrews and the older inhabitants. The latter doubtless suffered from the invasions equally with the former, and can hardly have refused to join their armies in driving off the common enemy. Israel in the mass was in those days wholly destitute of repulsive religious zeal, and would warmly have welcomed all assistance.

South of Mount Carmel begins the central portion of western Palestine, afterwards named SAMARIA. Its northern district was assigned to part of the tribe of Manasseh, and the southern and more important to Ephraim. A large proportion of the whole is table-land, diversified with hills, in ridges and numerous knolls. The soil, according to Josephus, was soft to the plough and fertile; less watered by streams than Galilee; but all the water was peculiarly sweet, and the grass such as to give an unusual abundance of milk to the cattle. In early times, it is probable that Samaria, as compared to Galilee, had a greater advantage in population than afterwards; or the energetic ambition of the Ephraimites more rapidly reduced the Canaanitish natives, and forced them to coalesce with Israel. The only city in the tribe of Ephraim which was not subdued

resolutions" (De Wette).—"Gilead [i. e. the Gadites] abode beyond Jordan: why was Dan a stranger on shipboard? why sate Asher on the sea-shore, and abode in his bays?"—The song is almost too obscure to extract trustworthy history from it.

was Gezer, on the western border between them and the tribe of Dan. First an Amorite town, it afterwards was the most northern fortress of the Philistines, and retained its independence (subject, at most, to tribute) until the reign of Solomon, when it was captured, not by Hebrew, but by Egyptian force. The energy which the Ephraimites showed in the very first period of Israelitish history, may be referred to the fact, that the celebrated leader Joshua belonged to this tribe. Among them also, at Shiloh, for many generations, the tabernacle of Jehovah with the sacred ark was fixed; and at once in a local, a political, and a religious sense, became the centre of the Hebrew nation. Their extreme pride was shown in their insolent conduct to Gideon and to Jephthah; of whom the former pacified them by gentleness, and the latter retaliated by a cruel massacre, which appears for a long while after to have humbled their pretensions. Their principal town was Shechem (*Neapolis, Nablus*), where Jacob had dwelt; and they pointed to the well of Jacob and to the tomb of Joseph. From them arose Deborah, a woman, yet the earliest prophet of Israel; whose word called forth Barak as champion against Jabin. Finally, it was in Shechem that Abimelech, a son of Gideon by a woman of that town, set up a monarchy, which lasted three years, "over Israel" (Judges ix. 22); by which we are perhaps to understand Israel west of the Jordan.

No natural division exists between the regions called in later time Samaria and JUDÆA. The latter, which is immediately to the south of the former, contained the district assigned to be conquered by the four tribes of Dan, Benjamin, Simeon, and Judah. But Dan and Simeon were always insignificant, and could not overcome the Amorites. A portion of the Danites migrated to the extreme north, and treacherously attacked Laish or Leshem, a town "dwelling carelessly, *after the manner of the Sidonians*, quiet and secure." Having massacred a peaceful and industrious population, they established themselves in their place; and as if to warn the modern reader that no zeal for the Law prompted the atrocity, they forthwith set up a graven image, under a priest of the tribe of Manasseh, whose children continued to officiate until the day of the captivity of the land (Judges xviii. 30). This is the well-known town of Dan, which, in contrast to Beersheba, so long marked the extreme northern point of Israel. The rest of the Danites, in common with the Simeonites, soon had to struggle with a yet more dangerous enemy—the Philistines, against whom the marvellous hero Samson, of the tribe of Dan, so often entered the lists; but at length Dan seems to have lost its existence as a tribe in these parts. Neither could the Simeonites win the cities assigned to them by lot, some of which at a much later period were acquired by the tribe of Judah. Such was Ziklag, which David afterwards received from Achish, king of Gath; such too was Beersheba, which in the time of Ahab (1 Kings xix. 3) was reckoned as Judah's. Simeon nevertheless continued to hold various less important places until the time of the kings (1 Chron. iv. 31, 42), and so late as the reign of Hezekiah two strange migrations of this tribe are named.[1] It is uncertain how the rest of them disappeared; but so thoroughly does the tribe seem to have been afterwards forgotten in Israel, that at the time when the song of Moses was penned, Simeon was entirely dropped out of the list. Dan, on the contrary, is named, but only as in proximity with "Bashan," where the town of Dan lay.[2]

Benjamin had his portion on the north of Judæa eastward, close beneath the tribe of Ephraim, in an inland district small in extent, but great in sacred and legendary interest. Jerusalem on the table-land, and Jericho deep in the basin of the Jordan; Bethel, where God appeared to Jacob; Gilgal, perhaps,—where twelve stones recorded the passage of Jordan by the twelve tribes,—and Mizpeh, whither from the earliest times (Judges xx. 1, etc.) the tribes were accustomed to assemble before Jehovah;—all lay in the lot of Benjamin. The Benjamites are represented as originally superior in numbers to the Manassites,

---

[1] It is surprising that "*sons of Ham*" are described as dwelling at Gedor, in the centre of the tribe of Judah, between Hebron and Jerusalem, in the days of Hezekiah; when they are expelled by a colony of Simeonites. That another colony should migrate into Idumæa is also singular.

[2] Some of the Christian fathers have imagined that Antichrist is to be of the tribe of Dan, apparently because the name of Dan is omitted in the list, Rev. vii.

notwithstanding the vast disproportion of the tract allowed to them. But in a most extraordinary civil war,[1] they had been almost extirpated by their Hebrew brethren, their numbers being reduced to 600 adult males, and every woman and child destroyed. After this, it seems not wonderful that the land of the Benjamites proved large enough for them. It must be added, that it was judged to be more fruitful even than any part of Galilee. The plain of Jericho, which it included, was looked upon as a sort of earthly paradise, and the hills admitted of artificial culture up to their very tops. Jerusalem however, with the fertile tract around it, never fell into the hands of Benjamin;[2] for by reason of the extreme strength of its position, they could not drive the Jebusites out of the city. After years of hostility, peaceful relations were established, if at least we may so interpret the words: "The Jebusites dwell with the children of Benjamin in Jerusalem unto this day" (Judges i. 21). However, until David captured the fortress of Zion, the Jebusites continued independent.

South of all Israel lay the land of the tribe of Judah, including Hebron, or Kirjath Arba, and Beersheba;—places consecrated by the traditions of Abraham and Isaac. The country is described as equally fertile with Samaria, and very similar; but this must be understood of its favourable portions. It is more mountainous, and its whole eastern side is a wilderness of limestone; on the south-west also are wide wastes. Indeed at present the deficiency of water[3] and soil in the entire district is so great, that none

[1] The other tribes had sworn to Jehovah to give no wives to the Benjamites; but the oath was evaded by slaughtering the Jabesh-gileadites in mass for *not* having helped to exterminate Benjamin, and by then giving 400 Jabeshite maidens as wives to the survivors of that tribe. As these did not suffice, the "rape of the Sabines" was anticipated at a feast of Jehovah near Shiloh, and 200 wives more were captured from the sacred dances. The whole narrative has so little to accredit it as history, and the statement that Phinehas was still the high priest is so suspicious (xx. 28), as to abate our confidence in the assertion that Mizpeh was used as a gathering-place before the days of Samuel. Whatever may be judged of the general tale, we cannot doubt that the description of savage manners and barbarous religion had its counterpart in reality.

[2] In Judges i. 8, it is stated that the men of *Judah* took Jerusalem, slaughtered the inhabitants, and burnt the city. How it was recovered by the Jebusites is not explained.

[3] Some countries have become drier by the destruction of forests; but we do not hear of forests except in lofty mountains from the early Hebrew annals: and no cutting down of timber would have laid the rock bare of soil except where the showers were of immense violence.

are able to account for the fertility ascribed to it by all the ancients, except by the elaborate system of cultivation which was carried on while it was in the hands of small native proprietors. The tribe of Judah rivalled that of Ephraim in spirit and in ambition; and as the Ephraimites boasted of their Joshua, so did the men of Judah of their Caleb; who, to justify his defiance of the Canaanites, demanded of Joshua as his portion the unconquered city and mountain of Hebron, where the dreadful giants the Anakim dwelt. Under the inspiring genius of Caleb, the tribe of Judah single-handed conquered not Hebron only, but numerous other cities, among which are named Gaza, Askelon, and Ekron; all of them afterwards chief seats of the Philistine power, and none of them within the lot of Judah. In the theory of the conquest, Ekron was to belong to Dan; Askelon and Gaza to Simeon; but those tribes, as we have stated, proved unsuccessful and feeble. From Judah moreover is said to have proceeded the first "Judge" of Israel, Othniel, the nephew and son-in-law of Caleb; which virtually denotes that Othniel, the antagonist of Chusan Rishathaim, was the first successor to Joshua. That the tribe of Judah should have been eminent in the war against Chushan Rishathaim (who is rather mysteriously called king of the distant country of *Mesopotamia*), is the more remarkable, since of all the tribes Judah was the most distant, and the last to suffer from such an enemy; yet a long time passed before circumstances arose which could give to this farthest tribe any enduring primacy over Israel at large.

Such was the land of Canaan, and such the distribution of the tribes over it: beyond Jordan, a pastoral people, of which the northern part had been engaged in lingering warfare with powerful neighbours, and had earned an energetic character and extensive territory; west of Jordan, in Galilee on the north, a brave but unambitious race, easily coalescing with the older inhabitants: in Samaria the central power of Israel lay, and the most decisive triumphs, west of Jordan, were first won: in Judæa, a large part of Israel was driven out, first by the Amorites, then by the Philistines, while the tribe of Judah itself with difficulty stood its ground, and lost many of its conquests. It is possible that the early and complete successes of the Ephraimites, leaving them little to contend against, gave them more pride than warlike experience; while the long and painful struggles of Judah were preparing that tribe for ultimate pre-eminence.

The chief political idea prominent in the institutions which we ascribe to Moses, was to constitute a people of small independent landowners; a state of things highly conducive to national virtue, equably-spread and moderate abundance, personal bravery, and sober stable republicanism; but adverse to great wealth, commerce, intellectual development, standing armies, and royal or oligarchical power. In regard to the eastern tribes, the Mosaic system gave way altogether; for they chose and adhered to a pastoral life: but west of Jordan the agricultural constitution was fixedly established. The most remarkable law was that which forbade the sale of land beyond the year of Jubilee; a regulation intended to hinder a man, to whom a life-interest only in his estate was given, from defrauding his posterity. It was, in short, the *Mosaic law of entail*;[1] which aimed, however, not to keep landed property together in large masses, but to prevent accumulation; nor was there any mode of cutting off the entail by agreement between father and son. The practical result was, that no permanent aristocracy could arise west of the Jordan; and that during the earlier period of the national existence, each tribe acted for itself except at moments of great exigence from powerful foreign enemies.

But we here touch on a delicate subject, which may need more detailed and cautious remark. The law of Jubilee is not to be conceived of in a literal sense, since we know that if it was ever so much enacted in writing, no means of expounding or enforcing it were at hand in the early times of violence. But as the Dorians who conquered Laconia, so the Hebrews who possessed themselves of Canaan, had a traditionary feeling, that the land, having been primitively apportioned to families, ought to remain as a fixed property of the same families. It must have been forbidden *by usage* to sell that patrimony in which the present holder had only a life-interest; and it is pro-

---

[1] A peculiar marriage law, which had its counterpart in Athens, was directed to uphold the law of entail:—the man *nearest of kin* was bound to endow *or to wed* a portionless maiden: Ruth iv.

bable that sales were never made except for a fixed and very limited number of years, after which the land reverted to the children of him who sold it. Out of this the idea of a Jubilee may have at length shaped itself in later ages; but it appears certain that no law of jubilee can have had its first origin in the later times, without such usage preceding : for after the return from Babylon, land was in too great abundance for the people, and no one could have then first conceived such a law; and if, during the time of the kings, land had habitually been sold for ever, the idea of Jubilee could not have established itself at all. We infer therefore, that national feeling and usage really kept up small landed properties west of Jordan from the earliest times.[1]

Yet it is not to be supposed that the Israelites on that side the river became at once and exclusively agricultural. The transition from a state of pastoral rovers to that of agriculturists was probably gradual, and spread over many generations; and in fact the Simeonites (1 Chron. iv. 41) may seem to have remained mere wandering shepherds until the latest period, until (as may be suspected) they were swallowed up in the Amalekites of those parts. Great diversities of wealth in cattle will soon arise among men who at first are equal, and those who have too many cattle for their land buy leave to pasture them on the fields of those who have too few. The rich man virtually in such case becomes the tenant, and the poor the landlord, who receives yearly a small quit-rent for the use of his land; and though it may be called his, yet after a time he fears to expel his tenant and take the land into his own hands, if this would inflict a severe inconvenience on one powerful to resent it. Although Englishmen may not possess land in Turkey, modes of evading the law are easily found, so as to prevent the legal owner from ejecting his tenant except by extreme effort; and it is quite consistent with a general system of small landed properties, that an oligarchy of rich men should practically spread beyond their nominal estates. The example of Gideon, who could afford to rear seventy sons in princely station, and whose son Abimelech aspired to regal dignity, shows that there existed means of retaining great wealth and in-

[1] To this the story of Naboth and Ahab agrees.

influence; and as the wealth cannot have accrued from yearly taxation, it must have been in cattle or in land, or in both. Nevertheless, such rich men were probably few, or at any rate did not constitute a permanent aristocracy. They were not a recognized *order*, and could not easily act in conjunction. Birth and age were chiefly regarded in selecting the ordinary elders or heads of families and tribes; and it is probable that riches, where the limits of land were so narrow, seldom continued long in the same family. A rallying centre for the parts of the nation was wanting; and when this arose in the person of a king, the royal power was liable to become despotic from the absence of an interposing aristocracy. Not that this was wholly wanting; for (besides what was just said), among the tribes east of Jordan, men not only of great but of hereditary wealth in cattle and visible substance arose;—wealth accruing in part from legitimate increase under clever management, in part probably from the plunder of neighbours. The wealthy chieftain in these parts must often have combined the marauder with the grazier, and have been able to gather a considerable force of men around him. But it was only to a weak or unpopular king that these chiefs could dare to offer resistance; especially as they had no constitutional organs of their own, and no support from this side Jordan. Yet a check to the regal power grew up at last in Judah, as we shall see, out of the priestly body, which had no organization or public efficiency in the ante-Davidical æra.

It might have been imagined that the Levites, spread over the whole country, would cement the tribes together; but the causes of their failing so to do are easy to find. Whether they ever actually enjoyed the cities in theory allotted to them is highly doubtful. If it be even allowed that Joshua put them in possession, it is evident that they must have been expelled ten times over from many districts, by the series of invaders who domineered over part or the whole of Israel. When lands are once lost by religious bodies, it is exceedingly difficult in the most religious countries of modern Europe to recover them; and it is clear that no Levitical spirit existed in early Israel which should assist restitution. As for ecclesiastical tithes, to collect them when crops are liable to be burnt by an enemy, is a hopeless affair: and those were days (as we are repeatedly told) when "every man did what was right in his own eyes." In short, whatever Joshua did for the Levites, might as well not have been done, as regards any permanent result. We start with the history of the Kings, as if no Levitical *order* existed.

Not but that there were Levites scattered through the land; and there were certainly some priestly towns: but, as in early Greece, each religious establishment rested on its own basis and was wholly isolated from the rest. A bishop in the Middle Ages of Europe differed from a temporal prince in bearing a sacred character; but he equally needed the aid of men, arms, and horses, to sustain his official position; and so was it with the Aaronites[1] who came to Hebron to install David as king. We may safely infer that their exterior was not less warlike in the turbulent period which had preceded; but as nothing is heard of priestly authority, except in connexion with the name of Eli, they cannot have exerted any wide-spread influence. The only specimen which we have of the primitive life of a Levite, represents a young man who bore that name to have been consecrated as a priest of Jehovah, by Micah, a man of Mount Ephraim; as though any man had power to make a priest for himself: moreover the Levite is said to have been of Bethlehem and "of the family of *Judah*," (Judg. xvii. 7); which implies that "Levite" was not then understood to imply descent from Levi, but simply occupation in a certain routine of religious observance. Previous to the arrival of the Levite, Micah had consecrated one of his own sons; and the Danites at Laish in like manner made a descendant of *Manasseh*,[2] priest in their city. The Levite was to Micah (what we should call) *a family chaplain*; and agreed to receive his clothes and food and ten shekels of silver every year. The simplicity of Micah's self-congratulation,—"Now know I that Jehovah will do me good, seeing I have a Levite for my priest,"—so comes forth from the popular heart, as to convince us that this was a widely-spread feel-

---

[1] Zadok, the most eminent of them, was "a young man mighty of valour," 1 Chron. xii. 28.
[2] He is called, "Jonathan *son* of Gershom *son* of Manasseh." *Son* is expounded to mean Descendant.

ing; and that the Levites of those days were a family appendage coveted by the more wealthy, but not an independent, much less an organized, body. No definite statements inform us, whether any of them as yet performed the functions of "scribes;" either as clerks, registrars, attorneys, or as literary teachers; but whatever insight we can get into the spirit of the age, tends to show that nothing of the sort was as yet needed or sought after. Bargains were made in Israel,—whether the purchase of a field or the purchase of a wife (Ruth iv. 3—10),—by a man's plucking off his shoe and giving it to his neighbour before the elders of the town, in the gate.

Although the laws of Moses, as we read them, definitely permit and regulate polygamy, the custom nowhere existed in the body of the nation. The freedom of the Hebrew women, married and unmarried, is utterly opposed to the polygamic spirit; and in such a state of things to suppress the evil practice would seem so easy, that one might wonder why it should be sanctioned; especially when it is at once child and parent of despotism, and thereby in direct contravention to the whole genius of the Hebrew institutions. It must nevertheless be remembered, that when the safety of a tribe depended on its population, the law of marriage could hardly be the same as when the moral influences of that state are chiefly looked to: and when a certain public disgrace is incurred by leaving no representative in one's social position, *both* of the married parties would sometimes become desirous of a deviation from strict monogamy. Concubines (or wives of lower rank) seem to have been reputable, even during the lifetime of a wife, when no heirs of a family had arisen. Thus was it that Abraham took Hagar, and Jacob took Bilhah and Zilpah, *at the request of the wives;* but it was only by fraud[1] that Jacob had two sisters as wives imposed upon him. The first eminent example of oriental polygamy was in the chieftain Gideon, who had seventy sons; whose example was followed by the Judges named Ibzan, Abdon, and Jair, as we may infer from the number of their chil-

---

[1] If any one regard the fraud practised on Jacob as a popular fiction to save the patriarch's credit, it will not the less, but even the more, prove that it was popularly discreditable to have two equal wives. In fact, to have two sisters *at once* is expressly forbidden in the Pentateuch.

dren.[1] More singular, as in a private household, would be the case of Elkanah, father of Samuel, who had two equal wives, Hannah and Peninnah; only that the long barrenness of Hannah is probably the explanation. But with royalty, wives rapidly multiplied. The first king had one concubine; the next had at least eight wives; the third 700 wives and 300 concubines (as the numbers in the book stand); the fourth had eighty sons. As under the monarchy the practice was fixed, and could no longer be got rid of, the national law would then at least be forced to sanction and would seek to regulate it, though often in vain as regards the sovereigns. The miserable results of it will appear in the history.

The nations bordering on Israel must now be concisely noticed. Egypt was widely separated by the desart, and until the time of Solomon had no dealings at all with them. On the south-west but within the frontier lay the Philistines, concerning whose power and hostility more particular details will be presently needed. On the south of Judah dwelt or roamed various tribes of the Amalekites. Although this was their more peculiar district, it may be suspected that the name, like that of Midianites and Ishmaelites, was often used improperly of any people of the desart dwelling in tents. Such neighbours are of all others most vexatious to agriculturists; and the Amalekites were viewed by the tribes of Israel with an abhorrence felt towards none of the " seven nations " of Canaan. Immediately to the south of the Dead Sea the territory of Edom (*Idumæa*) began, and ran along a remarkable mountain valley called Mount Seir (*Shera*), till it reached the gulf of Akaba, the eastern branch of the Red Sea. The Edomites appear always to have maintained peaceful relations with the Hebrews, until assailed by the kings of Israel. Their territory is admirably defended by nature, has parts of moderate fertility, and is not without commercial advantages.

East of the Dead Sea, and as far north as the river Arnon, the Moabite people lived, whose wealth was in flocks.[2]

[1] Some may hesitate to build upon the concise notice of these judges: the thirty sons of the variously celebrated Jair appear such a natural appendage to the cities won by the father, as to make historical conclusions exceedingly dou¹tful.
[2] 2 Kings iii. 4. Contrast 2 Chron. xxvii. 5.

Formerly their limits had extended much farther to the north; so that the "Plains of Moab," so called, lie opposite to the plains of Jericho, on the lower Jordan. But Sihon king of Heshbon drove them back to the Arnon; and when he was himself defeated by Israel, this portion of Moabite territory passed over to the Reubenites. Once only were the Moabites in conflict with Israel, under their king Eglon, who was assassinated by Ehud: at all other times they seem to have been friendly; and the simple tale of Ruth the Moabitess exhibits the nation in a pleasing light. To the east of the Gadites lay Rabbath Ammon, the chief city of the Ammonites; in a small district, with no apparent advantages over that of Moab: but as the Ammonites were agricultural, their soil was probably more fertile. *They* also remembered that their territory had once extended to the Jordan[1] (Josh. xiii. 25), and though Israel had taken it from Sihon, not from them (Judg. xi. 13—26), they at length recovered it by war, and kept it eighteen years; after which, falling then into conflict with Judah, Benjamin, and Ephraim (Judg. x. 9), they brought on themselves the resentment of all Israel. Jephthah meanwhile expelled them by the help of the eastern tribes alone, and incurred the anger of the Ephraimites for acting without them. This is the only recorded breach of peace in early days between Ammon and Israel. North of the Ammonites, the half-tribe of Manasseh stretched its pretensions over an inordinately large district. Its neighbours east of Gilead seemed to have been called Hagarenes; we meet also the names of Jetur, Nephish, Nodab. But the formidable enemy was Damascus, whose pretensions easily interfered with the ambition of the Manassites. Maachath also and Geshur appear to have been states of respectable force, with settled institutions, and blocked up the progress of Israel northward. On the north-west lay Sidon and Tyre, peaceful and valuable neighbours, who constantly preserved a good understanding with Israel.

Such were, on the whole, the character and the relations

---

[1] We cannot reconcile the claim of the Ammonites to the land from Arnon to Jabbok along the Jordan, with the other statement about the Moabites, except by supposing that the district had been temporarily possessed by both Moabites and Ammonites.

of the land, which is so eloquently described as a land of brooks of water, of fountains and depths that spring out of valleys and hills, a land of wheat and barley and vines and fig-trees and pomegranates, a land of oil-olive and of honey, a land whose stones are iron, and out of whose hills one may dig brass.[1] Its wealth however was not of such a nature as to supersede human industry, as the vague phrase "flowing with milk and honey" might suggest : it needed, as much as any other, secure possession and firm government, to prevent a large part of it from being a desert. It neither possessed great navigable rivers, and a broad extent of alluvial soil on their side, as Egypt, Mesopotamia, India, China, and all the countries in which civilization gained its earliest start ; nor had it a well-indented sea-coast, numerous ports and convenient islands, as Greece and the Eastern Archipelago,—countries formed to appropriate and transmit whatever of material or mental cultivation has been earned in wealthier territories. But the land of Israel, for so very small a tract, possessed an unusual self-sufficiency for all physical well-being. On the eastern side, its natural defences were very imperfect even against rude enemies; elsewhere its frontier was generally good; and though it must not be compared to mountain-fastnesses, yet it was (better than most equally fertile countries of like extent) suited to a people which was "to dwell alone, and not be reckoned among the nations."

CHAPTER II.

ADMINISTRATION OF SAMUEL AND REIGN OF SAUL.

In the twelfth century before Christ, the tribes of Israel can be dimly discerned as occupying the districts which have been above described; and although by no means animated by any deep consciousness of unity, yet beginning to coalesce into a single nation. In the long years of their residence in Canaan, a silent revolution had taken

[1] Deut. viii. 7, etc.

place by the gradual absorption of the Canaanite population
into the name and sympathies of Israel. There was in
fact so little to separate them, that time only was needed
to insure the result. To judge by the existing records
and laws, the concubinage of Israelitish warriors with
conquered Canaanite maidens must have been practised
on an enormous scale. The mixed race inherited the
mothers' tongue, but adopted the fathers' ambition; and
if the people of Moses talked Egyptian, their language
was obliterated long before Canaan was all conquered. All
the races alike were circumcised; the Hebrews had as yet
no importunate zeal for monotheism, but on the contrary
were perpetually prone to adopt the superstitions of
Canaanites, Moabites, or Ammonites. The few specimens
given of Hebrew proceedings indicate to us a people probably more ferocious and energetic than the townsmen
of Canaan, and, we may readily believe, free from
those vices which luxury engenders; but not superior to
the Canaanites in sensitiveness of conscience or spirituality
of heart. It has been already suggested that the inroads
of roving tribes would sensibly tend to unite all the
settled inhabitants of the country; and it may be observed
that all the severer struggles between Israel and Canaan
seem to have preceded the first war against a foreign
enemy, Chushan Rishathaim; for Jabin, though called the
King of "Canaan," was almost beyond the northern
frontier. The great complaint transmitted to us by the
more zealous part of the Hebrews is, that their people
were *too friendly* with the Canaanites, after the first excitement of the invasion was passed; and since, on the
whole, the invaders proved the stronger, their name and
institutions at length swallowed up all others.

One small nation alone, of all which dwelt on the land
claimed by Israel, permanently refused to amalgamate itself with the circumcised peoples,—namely, the uncircumcised Philistines. They occupied the lots which ought to
have been conquered by Dan and Simeon, and had five
principal cities, *Gaza, Askelon, Ashdod, Gath,* and *Ekron,*
of which the three first are on the sea-coast. Ashdod and
Gaza were places of great strength, capable of long resisting the efforts of Egyptian and Greek warfare. The Philistines cannot have been a populous nation, but they were

far more advanced in the arts of peace and war than the Hebrews. Their position commanded the land-traffic between Egypt and Canaan, and gave them access to the sea; hence perhaps their wealth and comparatively advanced civilization. Some learned men give credit to an account in Sanchoniathon, that they came from Crete,[1] whence Tacitus erroneously stated this of the Jews; and that the name *Cherethites* retains a trace of this origin. In the times of Nehemiah, a distinction of language between Philistine and Jew was noted; but this may have been no greater than between Dorian and Ionian Greek. The Philistines appear to have been intelligible to their neighbours; and as the Phœnicians, like them, were uncircumcised, obvious probabilities would refer them to the same stock of population. Some of their towns are described as possessed by the Amorites at the time of Joshua's invasion; and were not the Philistines[2] alluded to as an impediment to the Israelites marching out of Egypt by the coast of the Mediterranean, we might even be tempted to believe that they were more recent occupants of the country. They have given their name to the whole land of Canaan under the form of *Palæstina*, owing to the accident that the Greek merchants were familiar with the inhabitants of the sea-coast long before they could have intercourse with the interior; and the very fact suggests that the Philistines would in early times be familiar with the best armour and weapons of war which the coasts of Asia or of Greece could furnish. Be this as it may, the Danites and Simeonites who came to subdue them, found before long that they were on the contrary themselves turned into tributaries and vassals. The Philistines, who lived in walled towns, permitted the vagrant shepherds to pasture their herds and flocks in the open country, just as the Egyptians had done,—no doubt demanding some tithe of their cattle,—but carefully deprived them of warlike weapons and of all use of iron. In the Mosaic, as in the Homeric times, "brass" alone was used in the manufacture of spears and swords; the metal denoted being a mixture of copper and tin, very

[1] Winer, *Philister*. They may have been Cretan Phœnicians.
[2] This is possibly an anachronism, especially since when Judah conquered Gaza, Askelon, and Ekron no mention was made of Philistines.

hard, but also very brittle. When working in iron and steel was invented, a warlike superiority soon rested with the people which exclusively possessed the improved weapons; and it is easy to believe that the Philistines, blocking up access to the sea and to Egypt, would be able to withhold iron spears and swords from the shepherd tribes.[1] A similar prohibition of iron was laid upon the Romans by Porsena, under circumstances in which enforcement was far more difficult. From this thraldom the Israelites were delivered by the bravery of Shamgar, son of Anath, who, at the head of a host of 40,000 men, without shield or spear (Judg. v. 6—8),—if we rightly interpret an ode of triumph,—contended successfully against the armed enemy. A national tradition embalmed his exploit under the mythical form, that *with an ox-goad* he had alone slain 600 Philistines (Judg. iii. 31).

Whatever the result of Shamgar's victories, the Philistines were not ejected from their towns; on the contrary, they pressed their fortresses forward,—probably from feeling the ambition and strength of the Hebrews,—and possessed themselves of *Gezer*, a strong Amorite town on the frontier of Ephraim and Dan. How soon they set garrisons in *Geba*, on the northern frontier of Benjamin, and in *Bethlehem* of Judah, cannot be decided; but all such garrisons must have been strictly defensive, and have entailed great expense on this spirited but naturally peaceful people. Their uncircumcision was intensely resented by the Hebrews, whose conscience in these days is not ill typified by that of their tribal ancestors, Simeon and Levi,—men who were too scrupulous to form affinity with an uncircumcised tribe, though they shrank not to massacre all its males in cold blood, because the youthful passion of its chief had too rapidly precipitated the course of honourable love. It may seem remarkable, that at a period in which the institutions which we call Mosaic had so little force, the Israelites should have been bigoted to the single ceremony of circumcision. But it must be remembered, that "uncircumcision" was the sarcasm cast by the Egyptians against everything unclean (Josh. v. 9),

[1] Reasons will afterwards be given for believing that the statement in 1 Sam. xiii. 19—22 really belongs to the days of Shamgar, not of Saul. Nor is it to be imagined that *all* the tribes were under this dominion.

—a reproach which the nation from its very birth had been accustomed to dread. The neglect of this institution needed not Levites and Priests to punish it, for the very Canaanites of the interior who surrounded them would treat the uncircumcised as unclean. In modern Abyssinia, equally as among Mohammedans, it is well known that intense prejudice exists on the part of the circumcised against marrying with uncircumcised families; thus, we may believe, small as the matter may seem in itself, an effectual barrier was interposed against the amalgamating of the Philistines with the Hebrews.

The same cause kept Israel separate from the Phœnicians on the north-west; but this people—whether from their more exclusively maritime spirit, or because their continental rights were better respected, or from whatever other cause—continued on excellent terms with their circumcised neighbours. The Philistines on the contrary with the growth of strength, spirit, and unity in the Hebrew confederation, appear to have become more inveterately hostile. Under Eli the priest, the twelve tribes began to coalesce into a united nation, fearing no Canaanite enmity from within. We know not what brought on new war with the Philistines, farther than the constant claim of Israel to take away their country from them: a severe defeat however was suffered, in which both the sons of Eli were slain, with (it is said) 30,000 Israelites. After this, the Philistines may have increased their garrisons; but to occupy and subdue the country was impossible for so small a people, even if they had been disposed; and the Hebrews were only panic-struck and crushed for the time, not conquered. Meanwhile, a new personage had come forward in Israel, destined to impress an entirely fresh character on Hebrew history, and practically to identify the earthly greatness of the people with its zeal for the worship of a single unseen and moral God.

SAMUEL the seer may with no small justice be called a second Moses. The results of his ministry were greater than any which can be traced to Moses, and his institutions far more permanent. Reared under Eli the priest, he saw with indignation the old man's sons practise Pagan impurities, and display insolent greediness towards the worshippers at Shiloh. By bold remonstrances against

vice he first became known as a "seer of Jehovah."
His fame spread through all Israel; and when of Eli's
family none remained but infants or minors, Samuel naturally stept forward into high consideration. A singular
event had awakened the Israelitish people to unusual sensitiveness. In the great defeat recently suffered, the ark
of Jehovah had been captured and carried away by the
Philistines; and although superstitious imaginations soon
induced them to restore the booty, it proved almost as
unwelcome to the Hebrews as it had been to their enemies. Fifty thousand and seventy men of Bethshemesh,[1]
it was believed, had been struck with death, because some
of them, while it lodged in their town, had looked into
the holy ark. So unlucky a deposit was gladly left with
the first city which had courage to accept it, and for many
years[2] it remained in obscurity at Kirjathjearim, instead
of conferring sanctity and glory on Shiloh or Gibeon.
Perhaps also a real pressure of the Philistine power was
now felt. It is highly probable that the Hebrews were
heavily taxed to keep up the garrisons, and that symbols
of their vassalage in many ways met the eyes. The more
pious part of the nation were struck with humiliation and
with unusual longings. It seemed that for their sins the
presence of Jehovah was withdrawn, and they eagerly
sought counsel of Samuel how they might regain the
favour of their offended deity.

With the spirit which ever afterward distinguished the
Hebrew prophets, Samuel broadly announced the great
principle essential to all acceptance with Jehovah their
God; namely, to put away the worship of *all other* gods.
This is constantly denoted by the phrase, that "Jehovah
is a *jealous* God;" and out of it arose the perpetual metaphor of the prophets, in which the relation of God to his
people is compared to a marriage, the daughter of Israel
being his bride or wife, and he a jealous husband. Thus
also every false god is a paramour, and the worship of
them is adultery or fornication. But we must not confound the worshipping before symbols, at least in this

---

[1] They were by race Canaanites. Beth Shemesh means, "house of the Sun;" no doubt an idolatrous name.
[2] The narrative says *twenty;* but it was much longer before its final re-
moval by David.

stage of the Hebrew mind, with idolatry in the offensive sense. Just as it has been for ages customary in Christendom to venerate a crucifix or a picture with adorations alleged not to be idolatrous, so did the Hebrews worship Jehovah himself by help of images in human form, called *Teraphim;* in adoring which they believed themselves irreproachable. The seers themselves appear to have sanctioned this; indeed, even at a later time, a startling passage in the only extant prophet of northern Israel mentions images and Teraphim as part (it would seem) of the desirable apparatus of a religious state (Hosea iii. 4, 5). Fuller experience at length, or clearer insight, showed to the leading religious authorities in Judah, that *idols* (that is, sensible images or symbols of the Divinity) must be totally forbidden, if *idolatry* is to be extirpated. But the zeal of the earlier prophets did not attack statues or emblems, as such: they were satisfied with denouncing all honour paid to a foreign god, and with securing that, under whatever outward rites, Jehovah alone should be the professed and felt object of reverence.

Ancient Polytheism was always tolerant of collateral polytheistic systems; and he who venerated numerous deities was naturally ready to believe that other gods existed, unknown to him, yet equally deserving of worship. The pure monotheistic faiths on the contrary, whether of Zoroaster, Moses, or Mohammed, have been all marked by an intolerance which in that stage of the world could not be separated from the interests of truth; and on this cardinal point the unity of Israel was to depend. A noble and pure soul looked with disgust on the foul errors entangled with Canaanitish and Syrian superstitions; and in maintaining the exclusive honour of the national God of Israel,—the Lord and Creator of Heaven and Earth,—was guilty of no such mean-spirited sectarianism as might fairly be imputed to one who contended for a Neptune against an Apollo, an Adonis against a Neith. The prophet of Jehovah was in fact striving for the pure moral attributes of God,—for holiness against impurity,—majesty and goodness against caprice or cruelty,—for a God whose powers reached to the utmost limits of space and time, against gods whose being was but of yesterday, and whose agencies thwarted one another. Nevertheless, the

Hebrew creed was not monotheistic, in the sense of denying the *existence* of other gods. It rather degraded them into devils, and set the omnipotence of Jehovah into proud contrast with their superhuman yet limited might, than exploded them as utterly fabulous.

How Samuel preached and exhorted and warned his countrymen, no writing has recorded; but those who have read how Scotland and Bohemia were worked up to resist Popish idolatry and foreign tyranny, may well imagine the union of patriotic and monotheistic zeal with which the Israelites burned under the exhortations of Samuel. Of the events which followed we have no details; but we learn in general, that by the energetic union of the whole people the Philistines were defeated in the field and national freedom was proclaimed. The period that follows is called the administration of Samuel, who, in the character of "Judge," presided over Israel, principally in the three towns of Bethel, Gilgal, and Mizpeh. All of these seem to have been in the tribe of Benjamin, and are supposed to have had local sanctuaries in early times. Samuel himself was of Ramah (Ramath or Arimathæa), where he continued to live, not far from Mizpeh. His father is called *an Ephrathite*, or as scholars of the first rank have interpreted the word, *an Ephraimite* (1 Sam. i. 1); but as he had grown up from childhood under the care and patronage of Eli, his parentage can have had little to do with his authority or connexions. It may be conjectured that his original influence had been most deeply rooted in the neighbourhood of Ramah, and that for this reason it was expedient to hold his courts in the tribe of Benjamin. Mizpeh, as nearest to his home, and as the place to which all Israel had assembled when first he called them to the worship of Jehovah and to liberty, was the most natural centre of his administration; but for the sake of speedy communication with the tribes beyond the Jordan, he came to meet them so far as Gilgal, on the low plain of Jericho, where twelve stones typified the union of the twelve tribes; while, to please perhaps the powerful and jealous Ephraimites, he visited them at Bethel, which was on their very border, if indeed it was not at that time considered to be their possession. To a people recently emerged from foreign vassalage, among whom also great uncertainty of property and of law must have existed, an upright and patriotic judge was of high political importance: but in Samuel's case the decisions of the judge derived weight from the veneration paid to the prophet; and in turn the influence which was honourably won by intelligent, disinterested, and laborious judicial activity, redounded to the honour of the doctrine that Jehovah exclusively must be worshipped by Israel. Unlike most of those called " Judges " before him, the influence of Samuel was founded on moral superiority to his countrymen, and was confirmed, not by warlike exploits (although he had encouraged them to a successful war of liberty), but by a steady administration of civil justice. By him accordingly was laid the foundation of Hebrew nationality, as it actually unfolded itself, and of that Hebrew prophecy to which all Christendom owes an endless debt. To him in fact is justly ascribed the establishment of the " schools of the prophets," which at least cannot be traced back to an earlier era.

The prophets must on no account be confounded with the "priests." How little Samuel affected the latter character, is manifest from the chief-priesthood remaining with the family of Eli, whose son Phinehas left a son Ahitub. That Ahitub enjoyed the highest sacerdotal honour is scarcely questionable, since we find his two sons Ahiah and Ahimelech referred to familiarly as discharging that revered office (1 Sam. xiv. 3, 18; xxii. 9). Priests must no doubt have been all but coeval with the existence of the nation; and at this time they probably lived in knots at particular towns, where certain sacerdotal families happened to have multiplied, since the character of the priest was generally *hereditary*. His business was one of routine,—to sacrifice, or to burn incense; to light lamps, to offer show-bread, or perform some other of the ceremonies with which ancient religion abounded. It is a striking fact, that during all Samuel's administration no one ventured to remove the ark from Kirjathjearim; nor do the priests seem to have been concerned to take charge of it. But " *the men* of Kirjathjearim sanctified Eleazar son of Abinadab to keep the ark of Jehovah;" and under the care of the same house it is found in the beginning of David's reign at Jerusalem (2 Sam. vi. 3). This however is but one out of numerous proofs that the ceremonial system only gradually grew up, and was as yet exceedingly immature.

Except where lands had been attached to some sanctuary, the priest must have lived by the sacrifices and other offerings, and only in very rare cases exercised, or sought to exercise, any influence which can be called spiritual. But no man became a *prophet* by birth : he needed some call for the office, with exercise and teaching; nor did the prophets often concern themselves with mere ceremonies, although they occasionally introduced symbolic actions of their own, suited to impress the public senses. Their characteristic emblem was some musical instrument, and their highest function to compose and sing solemn psalms of religious worship or instruction. Unlike to the minstrel of the Greeks, who devoted his powers to flatter chieftains and amuse the crowd; or to the later lyrist, who composed laudatory odes for pecuniary recompense; —more like in some respects to a patriotic Tyrtæus, or to a Welsh bard;—the Hebrew prophet differed essentially in this, that his first and great aim was to please and honour GOD, believing that from obedience to Him the highest good of man would assuredly follow. In the extremely difficult problems presented by Hebrew criticism, it becomes a matter of great doubt how many of the psalms still extant may be confidently assigned to the era now under consideration ; but perhaps we cannot be wrong in accepting the ninetieth psalm in the Psalter (the heading of which arbitrarily assigns it to Moses) as a specimen of composition full as old as Samuel. It gives us a good sample of the depth and purity of religious feeling at work among the prophets, which imparts to their psalms a majesty peculiar to themselves, and no small portion of poetical beauty.

> 1. Lord, thou hast been our refuge in every generation.
> Ere ever the mountains were born,
> Ere thou hadst rounded the earth and world,
> From ages to ages thou art God.
>
> 2. Thou turnest mortals to the dust;
> Again, thou callest back the children of Adam.
> For a thousand years, in thy sight,
> Are but as yesterday when it vanishes,
> And as a watch in the night.

Thou sweepest them away, and they are as a dream,
Or as the grass in the morning, which grows afresh,[1]
In the morning it flourishes and grows afresh,
In the evening it fades and withers.

3. For we are consumed by thy anger,
And by thy wrath we are afflicted.
Thou hast set our sins before thy eyes,
And all our secrets in the light of thy countenance.
In thy displeasure all our days vanish,
And, *swift* as thought, we bring our years to nothing.

4. Our days of life are seventy years,
Or by reason of strength, eighty years:
Yet is their pride but labour and sorrow;
It hastens over, and we fly away.
Who knoweth the might of thy anger?
As are thy terrors, such is thy displeasure.
Our days therefore teach us to number,
That we may attain a wise heart.

5. Return, O Jehovah! how long first?
And take pity on thy servants.
Early with thy mercy satisfy us,
That all our life we may joy and be glad.
Gladden us as many days as thou hast bowed us down,
As many years as we have seen adversity.
Show to thy servants thy deeds,
And to their children thy glory!
And let the grace of Jehovah our God be upon us,
And the work of our hands, establish thou it,
The work of our hands, establish thou it.

Yet it must not be supposed that the poetry of that day was confined to these solemn and contemplative subjects. Israel lived in the midst of poetical nations, and from the earliest times must have been accustomed to hear from Canaanites and Amorites songs of no mean beauty, well-fitted to cultivate several species of composition. Israelitish war-songs arose at a very early period. As one very ancient specimen, we may here produce the song of triumph which celebrated the conquest of the plains of Moab by Israel from Sihon, king of Heshbon, who had himself taken them from the Moabites (Num. xxi. 27).

1. Come into Heshbon!
Built and fortified be Sihon's city!
For out of Heshbon a fire is gone,
A flame out of Sihon's city,
Which has devoured Ar of Moab,
And the dwellers of the heights of Arnon.

---

[1] We have here followed Winer's Simonis and our current English Version, in preference to De Wette and Ewald.

2. Woe to thee, Moab!
Thou art undone, people of Chemosh!
He[1] has made his sons to be runaways,
And his daughters captives to the Amorite king, Sihon.

3. We have shot at them!
Heshbon is perished, even unto Dibon.
We have laid them waste even unto Nophah;
There is fire as far as Medeba.

The satirical congratulation of Sihon and pity over Moab give a grand irony to the short and energetic conclusion, which in its very abruptness characterizes the unartificial and primitive style.

Nevertheless, the Hebrew prophets were not free from various tinges of fanaticism, which generated also affectation. That they often worked themselves into a religious frenzy (as in the wild Asiatic ceremonies which the Greeks called *Orgies*), may be inferred from the same verb in Hebrew[2] meaning "to prophesy" and "to be mad." The extravagance ascribed to Saul, that in prophesying he stripped off his clothes before Samuel, and lay down bare of raiment all day and all night,—whatever doubt may rest on the narrative from its being a duplicate of a similar story,—must have been borrowed from the manners of the age, and is mentioned without surprise or censure. Even later prophets are recorded to have walked naked[3] and barefoot, or to have lain upon one side sometimes for years, like the religious madmen of the East; and some proceedings yet more ambiguous are ascribed to them.[4] The

[1] He,—the god Chemosh.
[2] Euripides (Baech. 299) says: " Frenzy has in it much divination; " a sentence which seems allusive to the Greek idea that *mantis* (diviner) is derived from *mania* (frenzy).
[3] I have been censured for using the word *naked*. I am told it means, " without one's jacket," as John xxi. 7. I have but innocently followed the received English version, and do not pretend to know exactly what it means, except that to the Hebrews themselves it appeared unseemly and more than undignified. My immediate allusion was to Isaiah xx. 2—4, where it says: " Loose the sackcloth from off *thy loins* " (which, I confess, suggests to me nakedness of the most shameful kind), and adds: " naked and barefoot, *with buttocks uncovered, to the shame of Egypt.*" So in 2 Sam. vi. 20, Michal remonstrating with David on his religious dancing, complains that he " uncovered himself *in the eyes of the handmaids*, as one of the *vain fellows shamelessly uncovereth himself.*" I do not know how these expressions affect other minds. To me it is truly hard to imagine, that they imply no more than stripping the upper part of the body as a workman to relieve heat.
[4] Many commentators have wished to explain such deeds as done *only in vision*, but their sole argument seems to be, that we ought not to believe anything

habit of wearing a single coarse garment originally perhaps arose from real indigence; but it gradually grew into an affectation, like the austere dress of monks and friars; and in the later times of the monarchy, men who are stigmatized as "*false* prophets" are accused of assuming for unworthy ends the sanctified exterior of poverty. In fact, even concerning those who are regarded as true prophets we hear occasionally of fanatical acts, which are not without analogy to the practice of the priests of Baal, who cut themselves with knives to assist in prophesying. For instance (1 Kings xx. 35, etc.), a prophet orders a man to wound him, and pronounces a solemn curse on him because he refuses; and having induced another to obey, goes thus wounded to address the king of Israel. It might even seem (from Zech. xiii. 4—6), that wounds inflicted on the hands were, equally with the rough garment, an ordinary emblem of the prophet.

So strong was the tendency of the vulgar to seek to prophets rather for a knowledge of the future than for religious instruction, that it was scarcely possible to get rid of Divination in all its forms; which nevertheless the prophets endeavoured to reduce to those few which had most moral dignity. Against the various modes of enchantment and necromancy, to which the neighbouring religions were addicted, they protested vehemently, as against a concealed idolatry. To consult the spirit of a dead man, or to watch the flight of birds, was at best to seek to the creature instead of the Creator; and led to an indiscriminate adoption of other foreign superstitions. But they did not treat with the same severity all desire to penetrate into the secrets of futurity, provided that the Being consulted was none but Jehovah himself. We hear of four principal modes in which Jehovah was supposed to give responses (1 Sam. x. 20; xxviii. 6)—*by dreams, by Urim, by lot*, and *by prophecy*. (1.) It has always been a specious and favourite idea that the human soul during sleep passes into closer contact with the world of spirits, and is better fitted than in waking hours for receiving divine communications. Nice distinctions indeed were

so outrageous of those holy men as the literal interpretation states. Yet this appears to be hardly an adequate ground for rejecting a plain assertion, which does not in itself suggest that the transactions are visionary.

drawn between *dreams* and *visions* by most early nations; but it is manifest that they can have had no very trustworthy criterion for judging to which of the two classes a particular appearance belonged. The learned Jews in later times have with one voice declared, that the highest species of prophecy was that, in which the divine spirit influenced the soul without throwing it into sleep or impairing its natural energies: nevertheless, visions seen in sleep were always recognized as one undoubted mode in which Jehovah made known his will and laid open the future; and though it is probable that divine dreams were not regarded as confined to prophets, yet none were so eminent in this sort of revelation as they. (2.) *Urim* and *Thummim* was the name of a peculiar breastplate of precious stones worn by the High Priest, and employed by him to ask counsel of Jehovah. The imperfect explanation given of this apparatus in the Hebrew books, is in part cleared up by a collateral ornament employed by the Egyptians. We know from Diodorus (i. 48, 75), that the Chief Judge of Egypt carried on his breast an image symbolic of TRUTH, with its eyes shut,[1] formed of precious stones, and hung from his neck by a golden chain. The stones are said by Ælian[2] to be of *sapphire*. As the words Urim and Thummim are rendered by the Alexandrian translators Δήλωσις καὶ 'Αλήθεια, Manifestation and Truth, and indeed the Egyptian word is *Thmei*, we cannot overlook the similarity. According to the learned Alexandrian Jew Philo, the sacred breastplate of the Hebrews contained "images of the two virtues (or powers);" which he is likely to have inferred in part from Egyptian analogies: but how it was used to obtain omens, we are wholly ignorant. Two things may be alleged concerning this method. First, that the prophets felt no jealousy whatever against it, as in the slightest degree compromising the honour of Jehovah, who was professionally consulted by it. Secondly, that it cannot have been free from a large admixture of that, which *we* (surveying it from a higher point of view) are

[1] See Gen. xli. 42. This appears to be the original of *Justice* with her eyes handaged; but the Hebrew conception may rather be, that the priest saw more distinctly with the inward eye, when his bodily eye was closed. (Compare Num. xxiv. 4.)
[2] Schweighaeuser in loco Diodori. The root *Thumm* is Hebrew and Arabic. Egyptian *Thmei* suggests also Greek Θέμις, Justice.

forced to regard as Superstition. The priest, when seeking for an oracle, first put on the sacred tippet, called the Ephod; then looked to the twelve precious stones which he wore on his breast; and according to Josephus, found in the brilliancy of some of them an intelligible omen. (3.) The *lot* is recorded to have been used on many solemn occasions; and down to the latest times of the existence of Israel it was firmly believed that God made replies by means of it. (4.) Finally, the people resorted to the prophet, not merely as a moral teacher, but as a soothsayer, who would tell them of goods lost or stolen, and other convenient matters; and from this lower point of view (as it would seem) they called him a *seer* rather than a *prophet*.[1] In the times preceding Samuel the prophetical spirit had put forth so little influence on the nation, that the prevailing tendency with the ignorant was to view Samuel himself as only a *seer*; and whatever degree of historical weight we attach to the events connected with Saul's looking after the asses of Kish, it is clear that the story could not have originated, if it had not been a familiar belief that the seers were useful persons to consult on such affairs. From this time forth however they were gradually to assume a higher national importance. Their advice was asked on topics of great public moment, nor did they refuse it; but their mode of seeking for a divine reply was not ceremonial or superstitious, however tinged with a high enthusiasm. The prophet either played on the lyre himself or (to judge by one distinct example) called for a minstrel to do so, and wrapt himself in pious meditation on the subject of inquiry; until, gaining an insight into its moral bearings and kindled by the melody, he delivered a response in high-wrought and generally poetical strain.

Such is the best general idea which we can get of the position and agency of those prophets, who from Samuel downwards imparted to the history of Israel nearly all its peculiarity and all its value. Samuel himself indeed is more prominent in the history as Judge; but in this character his influence, however beneficial, was only temporary :

[1] Yet a *seer* is a man who has *visions*, like Ezekiel: thus in contrast to Nathan the prophet we have Gad the seer and Iddo the seer (who saw visions against Jeroboam), 2 Chron. ix. 29.

he could not imbue his successors with his own spirit. In fact, whether through a natural but unwise fatherly partiality, or from a real difficulty in continuing the government by any other than the hereditary principle, Samuel put forward his own sons Joel and Abijah as his successors in the judicial office. That they were in name his assistants only, may be inferred from the seat of their tribunal. It was the town of Beersheba, on the southern frontier, which could never have been chosen as the chief place of administration. Nevertheless, their want of principle soon produced disastrous effects which were felt to the extreme north. Vexed perhaps to observe how long a life of service their father had given to his nation without being able to bequeath to his family any monuments of material greatness, they rushed into a headlong career of bribery and perverse judgment. Fresh sufferings, which happened to be simultaneous, if indeed not a result of their misconduct, gave edge to the national resentment. Public enemies became once more formidable, and a new war of resistance seemed to be necessary.

It is difficult from our existing materials to extract a distinct and congruous narrative of these transactions. If it be true that when Saul commenced his reign, the Israelites had been forbidden by the Philistines to work at the smith's trade, it is manifest that they were under a severe bondage to them; and the statement (1 Sam. xiii. 20) that "all the Israelites went down to the Philistines to sharpen every man his share, his coulter, his axe, and his mattock," implies that the slavery was of some duration. Nevertheless our account (vii. 13, 14) here says broadly, that the Philistines were driven out from the Israelitish towns which they possessed in the south, and had no power over Israel "all the days of Samuel." Moreover, all the transactions which follow, prove that Israel was now in possession of complete internal independence; as will presently be more fully urged.

It is however possible that the Philistines were making preparations which excited alarm; and still more likely that attack was foreseen from the side of the Ammonites. During the long peace which had been enjoyed under Samuel, the nation had been coalescing into unity and strength: the repose had been exceedingly important to it, but the disuse of martial exertions had also its present inconvenience. Samuel himself was in declining years, and had never borne any military character. The nation could not trust his sons to head them in a new and dangerous enterprise; and the discontent felt against their malversation now assumed a practical form. The elders of Israel headed a deputation to Samuel, representing their grievances in plain terms, and making the entirely new demand, that he would appoint over them a *King*, as a military leader against their hostile neighbours.

The demand appears to have been equally unforeseen and unacceptable to Samuel, whose favourite idea had been, that Israel, resting under the protection of Jehovah and guided by his prophets, would not need to be governed like the heathen, and would be able to escape the evils of military rule. If Samuel in his own administration had discovered anything of the pride, the covetousness, and the domineering spirit of a hierarch, or if he had invested an organized priesthood with supreme power, there might be room for the imputations which some modern writers have cast upon him. But, according to the statements transmitted to us (none of which appear in any way unlikely), there is no ground for impeaching the simplicity of his conduct. Nor need we suppose that he undervalued national independence; for if the independence of Israel was to turn on their unity and their unity on the exclusive worship of Jehovah, the advantage of a king, whose more imperious sway might force them to gather for battle, would be dearly bought, should he happen to be lax in religious principle. Moreover, without assuming that Samuel actually spoke in detail the speech assigned to him (1 Sam. viii. 11—18,)—which may seem to have gained edge from the experience of a somewhat later age, we know that he must have heard of Jephthah and Samson, to say nothing of Abimelech, the son of Gideon,[1] whose cha-

---

[1] Samson's career is too overclouded with mystery to comment on; he is represented as a hero of invincible strength, but without the slightest claim to any moral or intellectual superiority. Jephthah was a leader of freebooters, who engaged in civil war with the tribe of Ephraim, and perpetrated on them a dreadful massacre in cold blood; who also, in pursuance of a heathenish vow, offered up his own daughter as a sacrifice to Jehovah. Under Gideon, the Israelitish nation presented something of the appearance of Oriental monarchy. Gideon had a large seraglio of wives and seventy-one sons; of whom one,

racters might well make him adverse to elevate mere strength and military prowess into supreme authority. After a useless resistance to the national cry, he was at length convinced that the tide ran too strong for him to oppose; and (according to the later narrative) he then at last received a positive and direct instruction from Jehovah, not only to comply with the general desire, but also as to the individual whom he was to invest with the kingly office, —SAUL, the son of Kish. He ordered a series of lots to be cast among the people; whereupon the lot, miraculously guided, picked out Saul from the myriads of Israel to be their King.

That there is some great error in the still current belief of this transaction, is clear from its being impossible to harmonize the beginning and end of the narrative. The event shows that the choice had fallen on a wrong person, and that Saul was anything but the man whom God approved. Yet his whole character must have been seen from the beginning by the Allwise Ruler of Israel, with whom it is not conceivable that the election of so unfit a king can have originated. It becomes therefore highly doubtful whether Samuel, any more than Jehovah, ought to be regarded as chargeable with this erroneous choice. The general course of the history leads strongly to an opposite view, viz. that Saul was forced upon Samuel by public enthusiasm, seconding the opinion of the elders of the tribe of Benjamin. That tribe had probably of late been gaining an unusual influence in all national movements, owing to the fact that the three towns in which Samuel conducted public affairs all belonged to Benjamin; which would give to their elders a superior organization and great facilities of communication with all Israel. That they should be disposed to bring forward as king a man of their own tribe, was natural; and that they should select him for his bodily size and beauty, rose almost necessarily out of the circumstances. In those days the king was the leader in war, and, as such, was expected to excel in personal strength, agility, and boldness. That battles

Abimelech, slew sixty-nine of his brothers, and made himself king for three years, when he was slain in an insurrection.

were decided by individual prowess, is evident in the accounts of David's heroes, and cannot have been less true a generation earlier. A king was wanted, whose very presence would kindle the warlike enthusiasm of the nation; yet as Israel had for some time been without armies and without heroes, there was no old and celebrated warrior on whom it would be natural to fix. They selected therefore a young man of remarkable beauty and stature,—a whole head taller than the common size of men. Saul, the son of Kish, of the tribe of Benjamin, had hitherto known no loftier occupation than that of superintending his father's estate. This however was an office in high esteem; and no sooner was he displayed to the collected multitudes, than the very sight of him satisfied all of his fitness for the royal duties. However little convinced by this argument Samuel may have been, and however painful his misgivings, it would have been the height of imprudence to bring forward a rival candidate. He probably tried to hope for the best, smothered his own doubts, and finally presented the new king for the people's acceptance in the most honourable manner, enforcing his claims by the only topic which the case allowed,—his noble personal appearance.

The first meeting on this subject between Samuel and the elders of Israel was at *Ramah* (or Arimathæa), where was Samuel's own house: the second, at which he presented Saul to the great assembly as king, was gathered at *Mizpeh*. Samuel however was careful to counteract the opinion, that the new king was to possess unlimited authority. He publicly expounded to the people the royal rights and privileges; and not satisfied with this, committed the same to writing, and laid up the manuscript "before Jehovah:" by which we are probably to understand, that he committed it as a sacred deposit to the custody of some leading priest. It is not probable that writing or even reading was at this time a common accomplishment; but there is no ground for questioning, that there was already sufficient knowledge among the more educated few to make this act important to men's feelings. Thus Saul, the first Hebrew monarch, commenced his reign as a constitutional king, freely chosen by the nation, sanctioned by the prophets of Jehovah, and responsible to the animadversions of both prophet and priest, if he transgressed the limits assigned him.

In pursuing his reign into its details, although our materials are multiplied, the difficulty of using them is great, owing to their fragmentary character. Some of the documents appear to be duplicates of others, representing events in substance the same, but with variations sufficiently notable; others involve incongruities which cannot always be removed by help of transposition. In short, we are by no means as yet in the region of contemporary and clear history.

On the very face of the narrative as above given, a question obtrudes itself:—Why does an air of independence pervade the whole transaction of choosing a king; without a single fear implied, that armed Philistines would come down and break up the unarmed assembly? If their dominion was at this time so overwhelming, as to be able to enforce the rigorous prohibition of sharp weapons, the assembly cannot have taken place in spite of them, or without their knowledge. Many reasons combine to make us suppose that the passage in 1 Sam. xiii. 19, out of which the inconsistency arises, has unwittingly attributed to these times, what can only have been true at an earlier æra, and of a small portion of Israel. A later generation, grateful for the military services which Saul really rendered, or seeking to justify Samuel's supposed choice of him, may have unawares exaggerated the difficulties with which in the opening of his reign he had to contend.

The very first event recorded is an expedition against the Ammonites (ch. xi.), which is represented as pacifying a partial discontent at the election of Saul, and ends by confirming him in the kingdom. The narrative is so compacted as quite to resist such a dislocation as would be needed, if we wished to delay the Ammonite campaign until after chapters xiii. and xiv. Moreover, the date assigned to the defeat of the Philistines (chap. xiii. 1) is explicit. It was in Saul's *second year*: which makes it clear that the writer who finally wove the narrative together, intended the Ammonite invasion to be in the first year. Nevertheless, it is manifest in the battle with the Ammonites that the Israelites were well-armed, though in the later transaction they are described as having been for some time disarmed by Philistine policy.

On closer examination we find abundant grounds for regarding chapters xiii. and xiv. to be of inferior historical value to those which precede them. These two chapters in fact make a whole in themselves, bearing almost an epical character, with little that marks sober history. The narrative has all the vividness and detail which characterizes romance, but cannot be reduced within the limits of reality. It opens with assigning to Saul an army of three thousand men, without hinting that they were mere bowmen or slingers; yet afterwards it states that no one of them all, except Saul and Jonathan, had either sword or spear. The host of the Philistines which opposes such a motley crowd is clearly unhistorical,—" thirty thousand chariots, and six thousand horsemen, and people as the sand which is on the sea-shore in multitude." The passage (xiii. 8—14) which describes the quarrel of Saul with Samuel appears to be a duplicate of a transaction in ch. xv., with which it is not easily compatible. Moreover, the offence which Samuel is represented as taking at Saul's offering sacrifice is not merely unreasonable, but unintelligible; and as a ground for so serious a schism at such a time, frivolous if not factious and infatuated. To sacrifice was as much the right or duty of Saul as of Samuel, who affected not the priestly office; and to elevate a petty ceremonial affair of this sort into the basis of Samuel's feud with Saul, indicates the misconception of a later time, when the priestly power had given far greater weight to such matters, when kings had ceased to officiate at the altar, and when it had become a cherished notion that Samuel was a Levite. Nor could Saul have been " a choice young man and a goodly'"[1] when elected to the throne, if his son Jonathan had been a formidable warrior in the very next year. That Jonathan and his armourbearer, two men, should storm a Philistine garrison with much slaughter,—that a great earthquake should follow,— and that hereupon the Philistines, instead of resisting their assailants or simply taking to flight, should begin,

[1] This description evidently implies *youthful beauty*. Soldiers are no doubt called " young men" in many tongues, as long as they retain full activity for running: but such an interpretation is here out of place.

both in the garrison and in their vast army, to slay one another, until Saul and his people, coming up, continued the massacre with whatever weapons they had,—is a story on which criticism would be wasted, considering that it is of unknown authorship and date. The romantic curse of Saul on all who should taste food that day, and the involuntary breach of it by Jonathan, who dipped his cane into some wild honey, is evident poetry. That Jehovah should sanction Saul's curse, and in displeasure at Jonathan should refuse to give any oracle, and, when Saul discerned that some one had "sinned," should then guide the lot to fall on Jonathan,—all this gives a view of Jehovah's moral attributes, in which it might seem impossible that any Christian should acquiesce. The closing summary of Saul's successes "against Moab, Ammon, Edom, *the kings of Zobah* and the Philistines," are apparently borrowed from David's reign, and at least cannot have been true of Saul, who was feeble against the Philistines, and utterly unable to compete with the distant and formidable Zobahites.[1] In short, the more these two chapters are studied, the less historical value do they seem to have. We cannot then in deference to their authority believe what draws after it so many difficulties, as that Israel was under any such subjection to the Philistines at the commencement of Saul's reign as these chapters state.

We have seen that the first great danger broke out against Israel, not from the Philistines, but from the Ammonites; whose king Nahash marched up against Jabesh in Gilead with a very superior force. The tribes east of the Jordan were probably always safe from the attacks of the Philistines; but they were proportionably exposed to the Moabites and Ammonites, and could seldom hope for zealous succour from the western tribes, whom they often deserted in the hour of danger. Now however, finding that Nahash demanded conditions outrageous and unbearable, they sent to ask speedy help of Saul; and it appears more than probable, that this was the very danger

---

[1] Another statement, which is very positively made, is of suspicious accuracy. It is said that "the ark of God" was at this time with Saul in the camp, under the care of Ahiah, son of Ahitub; which does not naturally harmonize with other accounts.

to avert which the election of a king had been determined on. Saul received the messengers of Jabesh in his own house at Gibeah; and learning the urgency of the case, performed a barbarous but expressive ceremony. Having with his own hand hewed two oxen in pieces, he sent morsels of their limbs into every part of Israel, with the threat, " Whosoever cometh not forth after Saul and after Samuel, so shall it be done unto his oxen."¹ From the urgency with which Saul thus commanded every man who could bear arms to assemble against the Ammonites, we may safely deduce that there was no pressing and immediate danger from the Philistines. The men of Jabesh Gilead are represented as having deluded the Ammonites by a stratagem of war. Saul had assured them of succour "to-morrow, by the time that the sun is hot." Accordingly, they promised the Ammonites at that very time to come out and surrender at discretion; it being understood that a truce of seven days which had been made was to continue until then. While however the Ammonites were intent upon the townsmen, expecting their surrender, they were attacked from behind by three companies, and were utterly routed, so that no army at all could be kept together.²

After this easy and sudden success there could be no question of Saul's being received as king. The eastern tribes had effectually been won over. A cry next arose to punish all who had opposed his election, but he had the prudence or magnanimity to crush this spirit at once; and with the sanction of Samuel his kingly rights were now confirmed at Gilgal. The prophet however took care to add a new protest against tyranny and irreligion, under the form of a solemn appeal to the people as to the example

¹ The narrative proceeds to state, that the whole host of Israel which actually assembled was 300,000, "and the men of Judah 30,000." This distinction of the tribe of Judah here and elsewhere, denotes that the account was penned at a later time, when the tribe of Judah was elevated to the place of royalty. The Vatican LXX. has 600,000 and 70,000. Josephus says there were 700,000 without the men of Judah, who alone were 70,000. The round numbers of themselves betray that it is all theory; and in fact, credulity on this matter was perpetually on the growth, in proportion to the distance of the writer from the facts.

² If Nahash was king of the Ammonites in the first year of Saul, and his son Hanun succeeded him in the middle of David's reign, we can scarcely allow more than twenty years for the reign of Saul. Yet we cannot perfectly trust the name of Nahash.

which he had set during his own administration. The energetic exhortation with which he closed, is not likely to have pleased the haughty Saul, already, it is probable, puffed up with his successes; more especially if we can rest on the letter of the statement, that Samuel plainly declared the people " to have committed a great sin against Jehovah" in desiring to have a king. The extreme imprudence and utter uselessness of such a statement at such a time, may make us pause before we attribute it to the aged and experienced prophet: and it is, in fact, a speech more likely to have been written after the event, when Saul had become an avowed enemy of the priesthood. It is nevertheless in every way probable, that as Samuel saw through the vainglorious and empty king, so the latter already felt that he was anything but a favourite with Samuel. While outwardly concordant, the sparks of a fierce feud were already burning between the two.

The annalists of these events were persuaded, that at first Samuel selected Saul by free preference or divine order; hence they seem to have been driven to speculate on some definite act committed by Saul, which changed the prophet's mind. One tradition said, that it was because Saul sacrificed on a certain occasion at Gilgal, when Samuel failed of being punctual to the day he had appointed. Another ascribed it to Saul's disobedience in an affair concerning the Amalekites. It is requisite to narrate the latter distinctly, difficult as it is to ascertain how much of it has been correctly represented.

The Amalekites, as was said, dwelt and roved along the southern border of Israel. According to the description of the text, their abodes were "from Havilah to Shur" (1 Sam. xv. 7), which agrees with a part of the region over which the Ishmaelites encamped (Gen. xxv. 18). They are generally regarded as a branch of the Edomites, but their name is as old as Abraham: their chief locality must at any rate have been between Idumæa and Egypt. Though they reached to the south of the Philistines, they penetrated into immediate contact with the tribe of Judah; and in fact, the town of Arad and the whole southern portion of that tribe, seems originally to have belonged to the Amalekites (Num. xiv. 45; xxi. 1—3). It was remembered, that great opposition had been offered

by Amalek, when the Israelites, coming out of Egypt,
endeavoured to enter Canaan. A simple and probable[1]
account (*l. c.*) represents them as repulsed by the Amalekites on their first attempt to enter; and from the repulse, in indirect consequence, a tedious and disastrous
delay in the wilderness. A burning hatred is alleged to
have been left behind, a first result of which was a voluntary and savage vow of exterminating the population of
that district (Num. xxi. 2, 3), which was hence named
Hormah, or Desolation. A second result was, the genesis[2] of new tales of Amalekite wickedness, such as should
justify this cruel retribution. One of these is found in
Exod. xvii., where the Israelites are attacked at Rephidim,
in the heart of Mount Sinai, by an army of Amalekites.
The latter are nevertheless discomfited by Joshua, and a
solemn curse of JEHOVAH against Amalek is then recorded,
with His equally solemn vow that HE (and therefore His
people) will have war with Amalek from generation to
generation, and will blot out the remembrance of him from
under heaven. The fictitiousness of the details is trans-
parent. At Rephidim, we are told, the Israelites would
have perished from thirst, but for a miraculous supply of
water from the stony rock: yet the Amalekites voluntarily
march through this desert to assail them, at a great distance from their frontier. The host of Israel came out of
Egypt unarmed, yet now they destroy Amalek "with the
edge of the sword." Joshua also is named as their leader;
yet, according to the tenor of the rest of the narrative,
Joshua was undistinguished and unheard of until a later
time. The miraculous tale loses all moral greatness,
through the clumsy machinery of prayer, not more spiritual than that of a Tartar prayer-mill. Moses, it is said,
was so tired of holding up his hands, that Aaron and Hur
were forced to help in supporting them, with a view to

[1] Since scattered portions of the Amalekite nation, or tribes *called* Amalekites from having similar habits, moved about the desert between Palestine or
Idumæa and Egypt, it is likely enough that collisions took place between them
and the Israelites during the wanderings of the latter. If the host of men,
women, children, and beasts was a tithe of the received account, its approach
to the springs and pastures of the Amalekites would be resented as an injurious
robbery. Affrays rising out of such matters may have furnished a hint for the
accounts in Exod xvii. and Deut. xxv.

[2] Some of my critics need to be told that *genesis* does not mean wilful and
conscious forgery, but a growth out of the national heart.

ensure the victory to Israel. Finally, the curse pronounced on generations of Amalekites yet unborn, on account of a sin committed by *relatives of their ancestors*, is quite out of character with the true Jehovah, "the Father of mercies and God of all comfort." Another tale against Amalek is found in Deut. xxv. 17, which recounts his unavenged cruelty,—"How he met thee by the way (out of Egypt), and smote the hindmost of thee, even all that were feeble behind thee, when thou wast faint and weary; and he feared not God." The moral however is the same,—a positive command "*not* to forget" or forgive, but to "blot out the remembrance of Amalek under heaven," whenever Israel should have the power.

That time was now arrived. As our accounts state, Samuel stirred up Saul to attack the Amalekites, adding the strict charge that he should destroy all their cattle, as well as all the human population. Saul partially obeyed. Having advised the Kenites[1] to withdraw from among the Amalekites and not to share their evil lot, he fulfilled to the letter the murderous command against the people of Amalek, but saved their king Agag, and the best of their cattle. Upon this Samuel uttered against him the bitterest rebuke; scornfully rejected his excuse that he had saved the cattle for sacrifice to Jehovah; and when Saul humbly confessed his sin, and begged for pardon, gave him no milder reply than, that, as he had rejected the word of Jehovah, Jehovah had rejected him from being king over Israel. All this is described as passing in private: afterwards, to keep up appearances with the people, Samuel joined Saul in a public sacrifice. This finished, the prophet sent for the Amalekite king, and with his own hand "hewed him in pieces before Jehovah in Gilgal."

This account has nothing in it very difficult to believe, except that it gives a much harsher and darker view of Samuel's character than the general narrative justifies. It may be urged:—If the unknown writer of this account could admire the conduct here attributed to Samuel, why may not Samuel himself also have thought it wise, noble, and merciful so to behave? The possibility of it cannot be denied; yet there are circumstances which may modify this view. First, it is manifest from later events that the

[1] The tribe of Jethro, father-in-law of Moses.

Amalekites were *not* all destroyed by Saul. Indeed, this nation, destined so solemnly to extirpation, shows great tenacity of life: for in ch. xxvii., some twenty years later, David, when living with Achish at Gath, has again utterly to destroy the neighbouring Amalekites, in spite of which they are presently strong enough to retaliate on Ziklag (ch. xxx.); and when a second time defeated by David, "there escaped not a man of them, *except* four hundred young men which rode upon camels," (v. 17). If 400 was a small fraction, it is evident that the army was a powerful one; and that Saul's invasion, however murderous in intent, effected its object very partially. Again, unless we knew that Samuel himself had penned the narrative, we could have no strong ground for receiving as certain the conversation which went on *in private* between him and Saul: while, that the account comes from a later hand, may appear from the enumeration of the host of Israel (v. 4)—"in all 200,000 men, of whom 10,000 belonged to Judah."[1] This careful attention to Judah denotes that the tribe and house of David was already in the ascendant; and if so, it is beyond reasonable doubt that the address put into the mouth of Samuel has been highly coloured by the writer's knowledge of the after-events. Such language indeed might have stirred up Saul to an awful crime against the prophet's life, but could have no tendency to benefit him. Splendid though it be as a piece of rhetoric, it is eminently unlikely to have proceeded from a wise and aged man, experienced in public concerns; while it is exactly such a speech as a zealous lover of the Levitical law might compose for Samuel in the leisure of the closet at a later time. This may lead us farther to doubt, whether the expedition against the Amalekites was at all originated by Samuel's urgency; since even if he was merely passive in it, the writer's zeal would probably attribute to Samuel as an honour, that he was Jehovah's instrument in exciting Saul.

On the whole, it is credible that the following more tame account comes nearer to the truth. The Israelites had often been engaged in petty hostilities with their

[1] We do not insist that such a host must have starved, if absent from home more days than they could carry provisions for. The numbers in the Vatican LXX. are 400,000 and 30,000; but Josephus makes the latter 40,000.

roving Amalekite neighbours, and Saul now undertook "a religious war" against them, intending their thorough extirpation. Samuel's sanction to the expedition was given, with the proviso that the cattle should be slain as well as the human beings; since this was the best guarantee that mere cupidity should not assume religious or patriotic zeal as its cloak. Saul however would not or could not prevail on his people to execute this condition; and the Amalekite cattle were preserved as a valuable spoil, to the very manifest and stern displeasure of Samuel. Nor only so; but when Saul had spared Agag the king, and none beside, the prophet looked on this as a germ of union between the king of Israel, as a king, and foreign monarchs; and was intensely jealous lest Saul should think more of his *order* than of his *nation*. In the same spirit do we afterwards find a prophet threaten Ahab for his tenderness towards the king of Syria (1 Kings xx. 42), whom he had styled "brother." That under such a feeling Samuel should "hew Agag in pieces before Jehovah," however opposed to the merciful spirit of Christ's religion, had nothing in it to shock the sensitiveness of the Jew, more than of the Greek or Roman. The deed nevertheless was a distinct public proof that the king had forfeited the confidence of the prophet. Thenceforth Samuel kept apart from the royal counsels; while Saul became low-spirited and suspicious, fearing that the influence of the prophet would now be turned against him.

This was in fact the case, if we accept our narrative in its obvious sense; nor was there any flinching from the last step of that which is politically called Treason.[1] Samuel is represented as proceeding straightway to elect and anoint as king, though in domestic privacy, a youth of the tribe of Judah,—David, son of Jesse the Bethlehemite. Nevertheless, no practical result followed, and the act, if performed, was a barren type. The brothers of

[1] It may seem too obvious to remark, that if the deed was not in itself justifiable, it cannot be justified by pleading the command of Jehovah. The whole theory is self-contradictory. Jehovah had made Saul *king*, and not a mere underling to Samuel; and "the Strength of Israel is not a man, that he should repent." Samuel would never have felt the repugnance which he testified to the electing of Saul, if he had been only choosing one who was to be to him what Joshua was to Moses.

David did not guess at any superiority conferred by it on him. The youth himself, although devoted to the prophetical influence, appears long after wholly unconscious that this high authority has invested him with regal power; on the contrary, he both expresses and shows a devoted loyalty to Saul. If therefore Samuel ever anointed David, it must have been in such a way that no one imagined the act to have the meaning which was afterwards assigned to it. Nay, in the earlier days of David's intercourse with his royal patron, no one appears to have whispered against the young man, that Samuel had anointed him as Saul's rival. We must therefore in reason exculpate Samuel of having intended to excite regal hopes in David or loyal feelings in others towards him; and if so, it becomes more than doubtful whether he at all performed so useless a ceremony. Afterwards indeed, when David had set aside the pretensions of Saul's sons, nothing would be easier than the propagation of a belief that the authority of the holy Samuel had been given to the youthful David;—an authority so much the more revered, when the distant report of his tranquil and successful administration was contrasted with the recent sad experience of Saul's declining years. In short, therefore, whether there was any connexion (at least at this time) between Samuel and David, is extremely problematical.

When the breach between the prophet and the king had become public, a change in the royal policy might have been easily anticipated. In the beginning of his reign Saul had acted the part of a zealous Jehovist, in so far as to put to death the wizards and witches, and all pretenders to divination by foreign gods. Upon his eldest son he bestowed the name *Jonathan* (or, Jehovah hath given). His second son is variously called *Ishui* and *Abinadab*, and his third *Malchishua*; names which suggest no particular remark. But his youngest legitimate son received the name of *Eshbaal* (or, the man of Baal?), while the only son of Jonathan was called *Meribbaal* (or, the contest of Baal?). That these appellations were looked on with disgust by the Jehovist party, may be inferred from their ordinarily changing them into *Ish-bosheth* (the man of shame) and *Mephibosheth* (perhaps, the mouth or opening of shame); it being the habit of later times to change the name *Baal* (lord) into *Bosheth* (shame).[1] We may with high probability infer that Saul's later policy was to foster the worshippers of foreign deities, as a counterpoise to the influence of the prophets, which was now turned against him. With the progress of events, he fell into a still more deadly feud, as we shall see, with the priestly body.

The first introduction of David to Saul was brought about by the young man's skill as a minstrel; and since this was after Jonathan was grown up, it is clear that we have no record whatever of about the first fifteen years of Saul's reign, except his battle with the Ammonites and his war against the Amalekites. Beyond a doubt there had also been obstinate warfare with the Philistines, although we have nothing extant concerning it except the echo contained in the 13th and 14th chapters of the 1st book of Samuel. Another eminently epical chapter (ch. xvii.) has described their formidable array; and especially how their champion, Goliath of Gath, a giant six cubits and a half high,—whose spear's head[2] weighed 600 shekels of iron and his coat of mail 5000 shekels of brass,—defied the host of Israel day by day. It is in many ways manifest that the Israelites and Philistines,—as the Homeric Greeks, and as the Persians in purely historical times, or the Europeans during the Crusades,—fought as individual warriors, the art of tactics being unknown. A general was little more than a very brave and sturdy soldier, whose single prowess was feared by every one of the adversaries; and if he slew an opposite champion, it often produced consternation in the whole hostile army. By inroads at various times, the Philistines had exceedingly alarmed Israel, and had disquieted the mind of Saul; who saw that the high object for which he had been elected, remained unfulfilled. Israel was not delivered by his hand; and the chief of the prophets had withdrawn from him. His vainglorious mind sank into despondency through ill-success, as easily as it had been puffed up by victory; and

[1] Thus in 2 Sam. xi. 21, *Jerubbaal* is turned into *Jerubbesheth*; and in Hosea ix. 10, *Bosheth* (shame) is used, where *Baal* seems to be intended.

[2] The *sword* of Goliath is afterwards spoken of (in sober prose) as not too heavy for David's use. This, no doubt, is the truer account.

superstition or remorse began to prey upon him. To relieve his fits of melancholy, a minstrel was sought out; and this was no other than the son of Jesse: a youth whose susceptibility to music was doubtless closely connected with his devotion to the religion of Samuel, and with his own generous kindling nature. He soon attracted the personal affection of Saul, and as he added martial accomplishments to his harper's skill, it was clear that he was destined for high promotion. Saul, in fact, requested to have him as his constant attendant, and made him his armour-bearer.

In following the steps of David's elevation, we enter upon the legend just alluded to; his slaughter of Goliath in single combat. The chapter which describes this, bears in many respects the marks of romance, and is quite irreconcileable with the rest of the history. It gives a totally new and incompatible account of his first introduction to Saul. It makes him to be a stripling unpractised in arms and unused to the weight of armour; whereas he was before described as "a mighty valiant man and a man of war." It further states that David carried the head of Goliath to Jerusalem; a city which for many years after was in the hands of a hostile people, a branch of the Jebusites:[1] showing that the account was first penned long after David had made Jerusalem the sacred city of Israel, and that there was abundant time for oral tradition to generate a mere romance. Nevertheless, although the details appear to be fabulous, it is credible enough that David may have slain with his own hand the Philistine champion Goliath, the belief of which runs through the record. That he slew him with sling and stone may seem to have been a deduction from the rumour that David was at the time a simple shepherd. Be this as it may, from this moment the whole narrative of Saul's reign is merged in the fortunes of David; than which there cannot be a more decided proof how fragmentary and doubtful are our materials for a history of this king. No reverential tenderness was felt towards the fallen

---

[1] The Vatican LXX. has recourse to the desperate method of cutting out large parts from the text in order to reduce the narrative to coherence; but even this has by no means been successful. English critics once tried large transposition; but that method is as hopeless, and seems now to be abandoned.

dynasty by the chroniclers who lived under the house of David; and if documents were extant which might have illustrated the reign of Saul, they were neglected, except so far as they tended to honour David or to justify the exclusion of Saul from the throne. The solitary exception is found in the victory over the Ammonites, by which Saul was confirmed in the kingdom; which seems to be regarded as exculpating Samuel's choice of him. Under such circumstances, we are forced to follow our meagre materials, and briefly to sketch the early career of David during the reign of Saul.

When David had engaged and slain the formidable Philistine champion, the hostile army was as usual panic-struck and fled. Much slaughter ensued; David distinguished himself in the pursuit; and on his return, as if to ascribe to Jehovah the honour of his victory, he laid up the sword of Goliath with Ahimelech, then the head of the priestly family descended from Eli. He was welcomed with the warmest admiration by Saul, and with affectionate friendship by Jonathan, Saul's eldest son; and from this time forth he became more and more prominent among the champions of Israel. But the brilliancy of David's achievements soon kindled jealousy in the king, who foresaw too distinctly that if David won for Israel the liberation from Philistine attack, for which Saul had striven in vain, the reigning house must be very unsafe, especially when the prophets were disinclined to it. The affection of Jonathan for David only exasperated the monarch's fears, who looked on his son as one who was madly throwing away his own prospects of the crown. Nevertheless, the popular favour towards David could not be rudely stemmed. Saul therefore debated, whether he might not gain David as a prop to his family by uniting him to his elder daughter Merab. Through irresolution he broke off this plan, when it had already transpired; and again perhaps meditated craftily to degrade David. But as the youth continued to win all hearts, the king adopted a still more insidious course, of offering him (it is said) his younger daughter in marriage, on the chivalric condition of his slaying 100 Philistines in battle. David promptly overdid the proposal, and having slain 200, laid

his proofs[1] of the fact before the king. Hereby he earned
Michal as his bride, but with her, the implacable and
deadly enmity of her father.

After this, we enter on a new period of uncertainty;
that of David's persecution by Saul. The only account
which we have is in many respects questionable;[2] if how-

---

[1] The barbarity, to us so disgusting, of exhibiting the *foreskins* of Philistines in proof of the reality of slaughter, has its parallel in the *scalps* of the North American Indians and *skulls* of many savage tribes. It seems to indicate the intensity of national feeling, with which this war of independence was prosecuted by the Israelites. At the same time, it is a pretty good proof that the Philistines were the *only* uncircumcised nation in those parts; else the test would have been delusive.

[2] Three separate attempts to assassinate David while sitting at table are ascribed to Saul, in nearly the same words (ch. xviii. 11; xix. 10), as if a man whose life had been thus sought, would so expose himself again. The attempt in ch. xviii. is so manifestly premature and a duplicate account, that it has been freely expunged by the Vatican LXX. Notwithstanding this, and other more inveterate efforts to arrest David's person (xix. 11, 20, 21), Jonathan is immediately after wholly incredulous that his father has any evil designs against David (xx. 3); and Saul is surprised to find that David does not occupy his usual place at the new moon (v. 26, 27). Finally, Jonathan *first* discovers his father's deadly intentions, by the latter hurling his javelin at David's empty seat (v. 33). Not only does this imply no overt attack on David's life to have been previously made; but we have here a probable indication, that the story of the thrice-attempted assassination is a mere exaggeration of the last-named display of malice. Various *duplicate* accounts also occur in this portion of the narrative. A new version is given us of the story of Saul's prophesying, which, it is said, gave rise to the proverb, "Is Saul also among the prophets?" (Contrast 1 Sam. x. 12, with xix. 24.) Since both of these accounts cannot assign the correct origin of the proverb, it is possible that neither may. Another credible source of it is exhibited inadvertently in 1 Sam. xviii. 10, where Saul, when enraged against David, is said (in the English version) to have "*prophesied* in the midst of the house." Beyond a doubt the Hebrew word here means *he raved*; but as in later times this sense was almost unknown, the idea of Saul's "prophesying" may have risen out of some misunderstanding on the subject. A double and inconsistent account is found of David's abode at the court of Achish king of Gath (xxi. 10—15, and xxvii.), of which the former seems to be wrong in chronology. Twice also it is told how David spared Saul's life under circumstances peculiarly romantic and unlikely to recur (xxiv. and xxvi.). Each event is preceded by an attempt of the men of Ziph to betray David; each is followed by a solemn reconciliation; and in the former, David makes oath by Jehovah that when he shall become king he will not cut off the seed of Saul (xxiv. 21, 22); an oath wholly unknown to a writer of a later part of the history (2 Sam. xxi. 7—9). Strange to say, the latter reconciliation and the solemn blessing of Saul on David (xxvi. 25) does but make David despair of safety and determine to leave the land of Israel entirely (xxvii. 1); so disjointed is the whole account. Immediately after his first flight from Saul, David is described as betaking himself to Samuel at Ramah; whereupon Samuel and he leave Ramah and take up their dwelling at Naioth. The narrative then states (xix. 18—24) that Saul's messengers and Saul himself were thrice miraculously foiled in an attempt to seize David there. Nevertheless,

over we try to gather up the trustworthy points, we may perhaps find the following to be historical. Michal suspected that Saul harboured evil designs, and warned her husband (xix. 11) not to trust himself to Saul's messengers, when they came with peaceful pretensions; upon which David withdrew into retirement, and possibly sought the counsel of Samuel and other prophets. Jonathan however could not be persuaded that there was any danger, and besought David to return to court; which the latter refused. When Saul inquired why David was not in his seat at table on the first and and second day of the new moon, Jonathan pretended that he was accidentally absent in consequence of a feast at Bethlehem; at which Saul, whose conscience told him that this was not the true reason, was so enraged as to dart his javelin at the empty seat. The truth was now manifest to Jonathan, who sent word to David to beware. The latter had already for some time had a peculiar body-guard,—those perhaps who were chiefly round his person in battle, as he was both a general and the king's son-in-law: with these he proceeded hastily to Ahimelech,[1] the chief priest, at Nôb, on his way to the strongholds of the hill-country of Judah, where the authority of Saul was weak, and the border tribes within easy reach. His first care was to carry his parents over into the Moabite country, and commit them to the good faith of the Moabite king, whose people seems for a long time to have kept up a friendly connexion with Israel. That he did not stay in Moab himself may show that from this moment he had determined, if not to contest the kingdom with Saul (which his friendship for Jonathan forbad), yet to measure force against him and reduce him to some secure conditions of peace. Yet it is also credible that the king of Moab may have feared to involve his people in war by protecting David himself. Be

the miracles appear to have been very partially effectual; for David instantly leaves Naioth as if insecure.

[1] Our account states that none of his men were armed; which excited the surprise of Ahimelech; and that David was glad to borrow for himself the sword of Goliath. Why or how this should be, is not explained. We may at any rate infer that Ahimelech had been previously used to see him attended by an armed guard.

About this time it is credible that David composed the 11th Psalm, as applicable to his forlorn state. It seems to be his earliest extant composition, and gives a beautiful view of his resigned self-possession.

this as it may, David now undisguisedly assumed the character of a freebooter, and invited all to join him who could strengthen his little army. According to the narrative in 1 Sam. xxvi., Abishai, son of David's sister, and probably Joab, his brother, came at this time of distress to David's side, if indeed they were not previously in his body-guard. Moreover, " every one who was in distress, or in debt, or discontented," flocked around him ; and he had soon a band of 400 men, which gradually swelled into 600. He employed them in protecting the cattle on the wild and open country from the hostilities of marauding neighbours—Amalekites, Hittites, Jebusites, and others ; and as his reward, received tributes of food and other necessaries from the sheep-masters, which were generally paid with good will, but when otherwise, were summarily enforced (xxv. 34).

Meanwhile, Saul regarded him as no longer a domestic rival, but as a robber and public enemy; and proceeded to treat all who harboured him as traitors. His first dreadful wrath fell upon Nôb, where Ahimelech had given provisions to David's retinue, using the sacred *show-bread* for this purpose. Nôb, at a very short distance to the north of Jerusalem, was at this time the chief town of the priests, where the customary ceremonies to Jehovah went on day by day, in spite of the absence of both ark and tabernacle.[1] In Nôb the head of the house of Eli enjoyed the priestly veneration which Samuel had not sought to appropriate; and by the public liberality directed to this centre of worship, a large number of priestly families were enabled to live together. Saul now resolved to terrify all from the cause of David by a tremendous example, and ordered a general massacre, not of the priests only, but of every living thing within the town. No true-born Israelite could be found to obey; one man only (as our account declares), Doeg the Edomite, executed the atrocious command; and slew in that day eighty-five " persons who wore a linen ephod," besides " all the men and women, children and sucklings, oxen, asses, and sheep," in the town of Nôb.

[1] The ark seems to have remained at Kirjathjearim, with the family of Abinadab, " who dwelt on the hill." The ridge ended in the greater elevation of *Gibeon*, where also was the tabernacle and the high altar of burnt-offering.

This statement seems to need comment. Taken to the letter, it is physically impossible that one man can have perpetrated such carnage; although he might certainly have slain eighty-five priests in chains, if the Israelites had so far obeyed the king as to chain them. We have already seen in the case of the Amalekites a credulous exaggeration of massacre; and there is nothing in the whole book which justifies us in supposing that Doeg was leader of a *band* of Edomites serving under the king, whose united force might have been used. Here, as elsewhere, a monarch who was cut off in unsuccessful battle, and whose dynasty fell with him,—mainly through his own follies and crime,—has probably had still more imputed to him than the reality. Yet we cannot doubt that at this time he slew Ahimelech and many other leading men among the priests; under the idea that by this vigorous policy—(for so worldly-minded and short-sighted statesmen often denominate cruelty)—he would cut off all support from David. Nor did Saul's anger stay here. By a later allusion we find that "he slew the Gibeonites;" which must have been a continuation of his feud against the priests. The Gibeonites intended are not the inhabitants of Gibeon in general, but a class of inferior ministers of the high altar at Gibeon, whose duty was to supply water and firewood for religious services. At present the tabernacle also was at Gibeon; and we may conjecture that the priestly families there showed some sympathy with their brethren of Nôb, sufficient to offend the king, who could no longer stop at half-measures. Whether he slew any priests at Gibeon, as well as the "hewers of wood and drawers of water," is uncertain. But the murder of the latter is specially commemorated, because they were a kind of sacred slaves, whose lives were guaranteed, as tradition told, by the oath of Joshua; when, being Hivites, they had surrendered themselves, though with fraudulent concealment that they belonged to that nation. This remarkable story may seem to show that the high altar had been at Gibeon from the time of Joshua, though the tabernacle was then placed at Shiloh.

But Saul's cruelty produced the very reverse of what he intended. The priestly body over the whole land was made inveterately hostile, and began to look out for security and revenge; moreover, Abiathar son of Ahimelech fled to David, and instantly gave a new colour to his position. With the representative of Eli in his camp, who wore a high priest's ephod and consulted Jehovah by Urim, David now appeared as the champion of the priests in a sacred war of vengeance.

Upon this the king looked on the rebellion as sufficiently important to need his personal presence with an armed force; and having marched out with as little delay as possible, he hunted his active adversary from stronghold to stronghold, though never able to intercept him. Saul's own company was no doubt composed of heavy-armed warriors, while David's were half-armed, and in large number slingers and bowmen. No force of cavalry existed in Israel, and perhaps it could not have been efficient in the precipitous and rocky wildernesses of Judah, where David and his men took refuge. The king nevertheless so often found active aid from the zeal of those who sent him word concerning David's places of retreat, that concealment was not long together possible; and the outlaw was sometimes betrayed even by those in whom he had put confidence. A psalm has come down to us (the 7th psalm), composed on such an occasion. A Benjamite named Cush, if we may trust the superscription, was the immediate subject of it. Having won the confidence and friendship of the generous warrior, he used it only to entrap him; and this perhaps was the turning-point of David's career; for so inveterate was the perseverance of the jealous and enraged king, that David at last found it impossible to preserve his footing on Israelitish soil; and betook himself to the desperate and unpatriotic resource of offering his services to the Philistines, who were at this very time engaged in lingering and inactive war with Israel. The chieftain on whose hospitality he determined to throw himself, was Achish, king of Gath.

What length of time elapsed between the first march of David to Ahimelech, and his escape out of the land, we do not know; yet some domestic circumstances imply that it was more than a few months. Having heard that Saul had given away Michal in marriage to another man, David found no difficulty in replacing her by two wives, who can hardly have been taken in very close succession. Ahinoam of Jezreel (perhaps in the mountains of Judah, Joshua xv. 56) was the one, but of her nothing is known: the other was Abigail of Carmel, near Maon in Judah, widow of the wealthy Nabal, who appears to have brought to her new husband all the possessions of the deceased, and thus enabled him to appear in greater splendour and importance before king Achish.[1]

How savage had been Saul's pursuit of David, can have been no secret to the Gittites; and they may well have thought that David's resentment would now make him as useful an ally as he had before been a dangerous enemy. Achish was well-disposed to receive him; and David took the favourable opportunity of making his terms, which were nothing less than to demand under a civil and humble pretext, the possession of a castle for himself, where he and his men might be safe from the Philistine population. To this Achish consented, and bestowed on him the fortress of Ziklag; another step of elevation, which almost converted him into an independent prince. Our narrative proceeds to make statements which surpass all belief: how Achish used to send him out on marauding excursions against the Israelites; and how David used craftily to attack some other tribe instead, and feign that he had executed the orders; and how he extirpated all the population,—Philistines and wicked Amalekites,—so that not a soul remained to bring the tidings to the ears of Achish. The simple king was so lulled into infatuation, as to congratulate himself on his success in committing David to implacable feud with his fellow-Israelites.

Such a tale may perhaps be translated as follows. The Philistines were not yet assembling for active conflict with Israel (this appears by xxviii. 1); yet war was im-

[1] An earlier flight to Achish is narrated (xxi. 10—15), with circumstances scarcely compatible. Achish *then* distrusted David—naturally, it may be said, because his feud with Saul was not as yet publicly developed; but if on that occasion David was so afraid of Achish as to feign madness, it is not likely that he would now have selected him as his patron. Moreover, whether Achish still believed the madness to be real, or had since discovered it to be feigned, in neither case was it probable that he would put much trust in David; and a consciousness of this would have kept the latter aloof. The writer seems unaware that Achish has been before named, and the obvious probability is that the two stories have grown out of one.

pending. Meanwhile, various neighbouring tribes, whose incursions vexed the Gittites, were chastised by David's arms; and on some of them a very promiscuous slaughter was perpetrated. In the districts where Israelites were mingled with foreigners, David may have carefully avoided conflict with his own people, and this may have been the nucleus of the preposterous representation above delivered. Yet we cannot pretend to divine, and merely suggest the above as probable.

Certainly this was no time for David to risk the loss of his countrymen's hearts: for at this very crisis, while he was occupying the stronghold of Ziklag, he received most important reinforcements of Israelites. A long list has come down to us (1 Chron. xii. 1—22) of more or less eminent persons, who through dissatisfaction with Saul became voluntary exiles and staked all their prospects on David's cause. The list opens with members of the tribe of Benjamin, " Saul's own brethren;" at which we may the less wonder, since Samuel's authority must have been deeply felt in that tribe. The venerable prophet would seem to have just died, having been spared the misery of seeing the confusions of his people; and we are left to conjecture whether he had given any opinion as to the duty of true Israelites. The Benjamites at this time were celebrated for the use of the sling and bow,[1] and all who now joined David had these weapons. Besides these came Gadite captains, full-armed warriors formidable in close fight, eleven in number, with a considerable army of banditti. Of these men we are abruptly informed that they had crossed the Jordan in its flood season, and had chased away all the inhabitants of the river valley on both banks. This indicates that Israel was already suffering the miseries of a civil war, the pastoral tribes spurning restraint and plundering their agricultural brethren at pleasure. We accidentally learn an important circumstance which throws fresh light on their behaviour. During the reign of Saul, the Reubenites, Gadites, and half-tribe of Manasseh made war on their own account against their

[1] They appear especially to have aimed at slinging with the *left hand*, since this struck a shielded warrior more easily on his undefended side. Ehud, a Benjamite, is particularly stated to have been left-handed, in the earliest times, Judg. iii. 15.

neighbours the Hagarenes, with whom are joined the obscure people of Jetur, Nephish, and Nodab (1 Chron. v. 10, 18—22). Meeting with entire success, they seized all the cattle of these people and appropriated their pasture grounds, which they retained as a permanent possession. After this, it is not likely that they felt constrained to respect Saul's authority, who in his later contests with the Philistines seems to have had no assistance from beyond Jordan.[1] Nor only so, but the spirit of enterprise and freebooting had so spread among them, that Gadite captains of great power lived by pillage; of whom it is rather obscurely said, "the least of them was over a hundred, and the greatest of them over a thousand." Now, however, the fame of David drew them to swell his retinue at Ziklag, and he profited by Saul's misfortunes as well as by his crimes.

As power generally tends to its own increase, new accessions soon followed on the last. A trained force of Benjamin and Judah marched out to Ziklag, of whom the chief captain was Amasai,— perhaps the same man as Amasa, son of Abigail, a sister of David. Their arrival at first created apprehension, which however was instantly dissipated by Amasai, and David added them to his army.

To this succeeded the gathering of Philistine forces for the war against Saul, and Achish required the co-operation of his new ally. Whether David would have had any compunction to engage in the war cannot now be decided. At a later period "there was long war between the house of Saul and the house of David" (2 Sam. iii. 1), which may imply that the latter would not have shrunk from personal collision with Saul's armies at present. He was however saved from the trial by the jealousy of the other Philistine princes, who were startled to observe how large a body of Hebrews under David had posted itself in their rear (1 Sam. xxix. 2), when the army was drawn up near Jezreel. Accident may have suggested to them that treachery was intended; at any rate, so powerful a Hebrew force, it might be argued, was dangerous. At the same

[1] Although the rescue of the body of Saul and his sons by the men of Jabesh Gilead proves that a sentiment of loyalty was far from extinct in Gilead, still the circumstances rather suggest that these Gileadites were not in the fatal battle. Their spirit is that of unconquered men, who are stirred to anger by the indignity put on their fallen king.

crisis a troop of Manassites deserted from Saul and joined David (1 Chron. xii. 19), and this may have increased the suspicion that there was a secret understanding between the king of Israel and his late son-in-law, and that David was intending to purchase forgiveness by betraying his Philistine allies. In vain did Achish try to reassure the other princes, who insisted that David should withdraw. On his journey home to Ziklag the fortunate Hebrew was joined by seven more Manassites (who are entitled " captains of thousands "), with their bands (1 Chron. xii. 20) : and he was soon to need their aid. The Amalekites, whose country he had devastated, had taken advantage of his absence to attack Ziklag. Far more merciful than Saul or David (if the massacres ascribed to these chieftains are not undeserved but well-intended eulogies), the Amalekites had only burned the town of Ziklag and carried captive all the women and children (among whom were David's two wives), but they put none of them to death. The narrator from whom we quote (1 Sam. xxx.) appears to regard David's army as consisting solely of the six hundred men with whom he originally came to Achish ; which is certainly in direct opposition to the record in a later book (1 Chron. xii. 21). Hence some doubt might seem to be cast on all that has been said concerning the accession of force received by him in Ziklag, were not this[1] confirmed by internal evidence. That David was still looked on as but the creature and organ of the wild men who served him, appears from the cry which now arose to stone him, as a punishment for having left their wives and daughters undefended. But at this crisis the self-possession of David was eminent, as also (we cannot doubt) his sincere faith in a higher power. " He encouraged himself in Jehovah his God," and sending for Abiathar the priest, ordered him solemnly to consult the sacred Urim whether he should pursue the enemy. Obtaining permission, he set out with extreme rapidity, and came upon them while they were at ease and encumbered with spoil, supposing that David was fully occupied in the Philistine host. Thus

[1] I do not mean that I regard the *numbers* as trustworthy, here or anywhere else; but that the accession of force in Ziklag is not an arbitrary fiction. See the Note in the next chapter on the forces which came to David in Hebron.

surprised, they could offer no resistance. Not only was everything recovered, but all the booty which they had collected from a wide marauding excursion, fell to David's troops. The behaviour of the conqueror was at once generous and politic. To the precedent now set by him was traced the principle thenceforward established in the Hebrew army, to divide the spoil fairly among the whole host, whether employed in defence or offence, instead of the barbarian practice that each soldier should keep what he could snatch. By the customs of border warfare, a large fraction of the spoil fell to David personally, which he immediately sent in presents to the "elders" of numerous towns and villages of Judah, and to all the places where in former days he had received kindness and support. As a result of his policy,—to use the emphatic language of the chronicler, which, accepted as poetry, may be substantially true,—"from that time, day by day, men came to David to help him, until it was a great host, like the host of God."

In part, these accessions may have come from the Gittites themselves; for David must here first have formed the band of Gittites, which long afterwards, under his friend Ittai, continued to do him so faithful service. But the greater part probably fell to him from the unhappy Saul, whose forces had wasted away, so that he had lost half of his kingdom west of Jordan before a blow was struck. Having no support, it would seem, in the southern tribes, he had been forced to cross the frontier of Galilee, in the region of Mount Gilboa, whither the Philistines had followed and encamped on the slope of Jezreel. In vain did he call on priest and prophet[1] to give him an oracle from Jehovah: their reply was uniform, that Jehovah answered not. His superstition demanding some relief, he proceeded to consult one of the enchantresses, or female necromancers.[2] Such a woman was

[1] He sought a reply *by dreams, by Urim,* and *by prophets.* If *Urim* was at this time confined to the chief priest, Saul had made a new chief priest in place of Ahimelech or Abiathar. But the words are possibly a mere formula.

[2] It is a striking illustration of the intensely Jehovistic but *unmoral* spirit of the book of Chronicles, that it records Saul to have been slain, and his dynasty to have fallen, not because he massacred the priests (which morally,

found at Endor, and Saul went by night to ask her to bring up Samuel from the dead. It seldom happens that we can obtain the details of such adventures at first hand, or penetrate the cloud which shrouds them. The current belief of Israel,—which has been preserved for the reverence or perplexity of Europe,—was, that the woman's art really succeeded beyond her own expectation, in bringing up Samuel himself out of the ground, in the form of an old man wrapt in a mantle, who proceeded to utter an awful prophecy against Saul, in the name of Jehovah, predicting with unsparing truth the judgments impending on him. In fact, it needed no magician to see that Saul was in evil case, nor could the decisive battle be long averted. It took place by Mount Gilboa, and the Hebrews were soon put to flight. Saul and his three eldest sons disdained to accompany them, and were all slain: but, as happens in such cases, there was some uncertainty as to the mode of Saul's death. One account told that he fell upon his own sword. Another was reported by a young Amalekite, who professed that he had, at Saul's urgent request, performed the service of slaying him. The only interest attaching to this variation is, that the young man was himself slaughtered by the order and under the eyes of David, for having claimed the merit of the deed; a high-handed manifesto of loyalty, with which it is hard for Christian or modern feelings to sympathize, but which was probably much admired by his countrymen when executed on the cheap body of an Amalekite. The action was politic, as proclaiming the sanctity of kings; and by the death of Jonathan David saw the way to kingly station open to him. Yet we may believe that impulse had a larger share in the act than calculation. Although David had not attained the Christian virtue of loving enemies, he burned with indignation that an Israelitish king should be killed by a dog of an Amalekite; and any personal resentment he may have felt against Saul vanished at once when his death was ascertained. The generous feelings had full sway, and real tenderness burst out in David's soul at the untimely fate of his friend

politically, and religiously was the true reason), but "because he inquired of a necromancer and not of Jehovah." (1 Chron. x. 13.)

Jonathan. The simple and touching ditty in which he lamented their loss still survives to testify not only his grief, but how Hebrew a heart he had maintained while dwelling among the Philistines.

1. O Israel, on thy heights the gazelle is slain!
   Fallen, alas! are the heroes.
   Tell it not in Gath, publish it not in the streets of Askelon;
   Lest the daughters of the Philistines rejoice,
   Lest the daughters of the uncircumcised triumph.

2. O mountains of Gilboa, let there be upon you neither dew,
   Nor rain, nor crops of first-fruits;
   For on you was the shield of heroes cast away,
   The shield of Saul, as though not an anointed king.

3. From the blood of the slain, from the prime of the heroes,
   The bow of Jonathan turned not aside,
   And the sword of Saul came not back empty.
   Saul and Jonathan were lovely and pleasant in life
   And in death they were not parted:
   They were swifter than eagles, stronger than lions.

4. Daughters of Israel, weep over Saul,
   Who clothed you in scarlet delightfully,
   Who put ornaments of gold on your apparel.

5. Fallen, alas! are the heroes in the battle.
   On thy heights is Jonathan slain.
   Ah, Jonathan my brother, I am grieved for thee.
   Very sweet unto me wast thou;
   Marvellous thy love to me, beyond woman's love.
   Fallen, alas! are the heroes
   And perished the weapons of war.

As for the victorious army, it temporarily occupied the neighbouring towns, which were deserted by the Israelites. On finding the royal corpses next day, the Philistines retaliated on Saul what David had inflicted on Goliath, carrying away his head as a barbarous trophy. His trunk and the bodies of his sons they fastened to the wall of Bethshean, and bore off his armour to hang up in the temple of Astarte. The men of Jabesh Gilead however, grateful for the deliverance from the Ammonites which Saul had won for them in his first year, carried away the bodies by night and buried them at Jabesh. So ended the career of Saul, first king of Israel.

CHAPTER III.

REIGN OF DAVID.

THE prince on whom the hopes of the Hebrew priesthood were fixed, was at the death of Saul only thirty years old. He possessed exactly those qualities which rallied round him every influential element of the nation, and he had most carefully conciliated the good will of the elders of his own tribe. With coarse and wild men attending upon him, he maintained not only warm-hearted gratitude and spontaneous generosity, but a delicate susceptibility which made tears over a fallen rival natural to him. Whatever hardship was endured by his faithful band was shared by David, of which a pleasing anecdote has been preserved in a passage evidently of great antiquity (2 Sam. xxiii. 8—23). David was in the cave of Adullam, and the Philistines had set a garrison in Bethlehem. When suffering from thirst, remembering the sweetness of the water from the well of his native town, he inadvertently expressed his longing for a draught. Three of his bravos who caught the words, went boldly through the Philistine host, and having drawn water from the well, brought it to David; but when it arrived—forestalling the deed of Alexander the Great in the desart of Gedrosia,—" he poured it out before Jehovah," declaring that he would not drink the blood of his men. This can only be a specimen of the generous arts by which he won their attachment. During his sojourn at Ziklag, he appears to have established a certain gradation of ranks in his motley army, depending entirely on that personal prowess which soldiers honour in their comrades without envying. The three chief warriors of his band were named Josebbassebeth[1] (or, Jashobeam) the Hachmonite, Eleazar son of Dodo, and Shammah son of Agee. The first of them was said to have slain 800 men in one

---

[1] The LXX. renders it 'Ιεβοσθέ or *Ishbosheth*. The words " Adino the Eznite" in 2 Sam. xxiii. 8, are corrupt for "lifted up his spear;" as appears by comparing 1 Chron. xi. 11; and so De Wette has translated.

5

battle; and the other two to have done exploits almost as marvellous against the Philistines. A second valiant trio is imperfectly named. Abishai, son of Zeruiah, David's sister, was its chief; he is stated to have slain 300 men, yet not to have attained to the first three. Benaiah, the son of Jehoiada, was the second: he had slain a lion. The third was perhaps Joab, son of Zeruiah. Besides these,[1] 31 eminent captains are named, among whom was Asahel, brother of Joab, and Uriah the Hittite. As Joab's armour-bearer, Nahari, was also one of them, Joab can scarcely have been excluded from them himself.

It is needless to insist that the exploits of slaying 800 and 300 men are clearly fabulous. This does not affect the register of the ranks assigned to them; and it must be observed that as no superiority is here given to Joab, and as Asahel was yet alive, the date belongs to the very beginning of David's reign.[2] Even so a difficulty is met; for Benaiah appears as if in the vigour of life when Solomon ascends the throne, just forty years later. If Benaiah's name in this rank belongs to a later date, it will follow that David continued afterwards the same arrangement in his army; three chiefest heroes, three heroes of second rank, and thirty of honourable prowess. Nor is it improbable that the gradations of honour established by him at Ziklag should have been adopted as a perpetual rule.

On learning of Saul's death, after solemn mourning for the event, David's first care was to consult Jehovah,—by Urim, we must suppose,—whether he should go up to any of the cities of Judah. Having obtained leave, he asked again, To which of them? and the reply was, To Hebron:

[1] The enumeration which we are told to expect is,—*three* chief heroes, *three* second in prowess, and *thirty* inferior to these. On the contrary we have, *three*, *two*, and then *thirty-one*; who are finally said to be *thirty-seven* in all. There is evidently something incomplete. Shammah the *Hararite*, one of the first three, appears to be repeated in the list of 31 (which ought to be 30? see vv. 13, 23) under the name of Shammah the *Harodite*: for the difference of *r* and *d* (ר and ד) is a very common error of transcription.

[2] This might make it seem necessary to refer the battles against the Philistines, and their garrisoning of Bethlehem, to the reign of Saul; for David had no war with them between his first escape from Saul and the death of Asahel. But in truth it is vain to criticise this document as if we had in it the authentic and uninterpolated words of a contemporary. It probably received its present form from one who did not trouble himself about smaller points in chronology.

—the city of Abraham. This was the strongest place in Judah, and central to the tribe; and to march up to it and quarter his army on the surrounding towns was virtually to take military possession of the district. The elders understood the hint, if their minds had not previously been decided; and assembling at Hebron, they there anointed David "king over the house of Judah."[1] It was natural for him to hope that the rest of Israel would follow the example; especially, if the powerful and spirited Manassites beyond Jordan could be won, there would be little doubt of the result. He accordingly sent a kind message to the men of Jabesh Gilead, which ran thus:—" Blessed be ye of Jehovah, that ye have showed this kindness to Saul your lord, and have buried him. Now may Jehovah show unto you kindness and truth, and I also will requite you this kindness. Therefore let your hands be strong, and be ye valiant; for though your master Saul is dead, yet the house of Judah have annointed me king over them." Since many Manassites (perhaps from Bashan and Gilead) were in his army, this communication might have had the desired effect, had not a great man, whom we have not yet mentioned, anticipated David's projects. Abner, the son of Ner, was first cousin of Saul,[2] and had long been chief captain of Saul's host. He enjoyed high respect in all Israel, and now took a decisive step for securing the kingdom to the family of Saul. Judging perhaps that the eastern tribes would turn the scale, he crossed into Gilead with Ishbosheth, the surviving son of Saul; and there, at Mahhanaim, not far south of Jabesh Gilead, proclaimed Ishbosheth as king. His title was quickly recognized by all Gilead, and by western Israel, beginning with Benjamin,

[1] The compiler of the "Chronicles" is here guilty of a fraud, which from the recurrence of many similar cases, we must ascribe to a dishonest love of exalting an orthodox king. He represents the elders of *all Israel* as assembling *at Hebron*, and anointing David king over *all Israel* immediately upon the death of Saul (1 Chr. xi. 1—3). We afterwards learn (xxix. 27) that David reigned seven years in Hebron; but no one could discover from this book that it was a reign over one tribe only; much less that David carried on a civil war against the other tribes.

[2] In 1 Sam. ix. 1, Kish, the father of Saul, is son of Abiel; and in xiv. 51, Ner, father of Abner, is also son of Abiel. Thus the fathers of Saul and Abner were brothers. In the Chronicles Ner is twice called father of Kish (1 Chron. viii. 33; ix. 39); but this is directly contradicted by ix. 36, where Ner and Kish are made sons of Jehiel.

northward. Thus the tribe of Judah only was left to David. But Ishbosheth was king in little more than name: the mainstay of the government was in Abner. The tenor indeed of the narrative would persuade us that the new king was quite a youth, and had on this ground been absent from the fatal battle at Mount Gilboa. Yet the text distinctly calls him *forty* years old.[1] As he was a younger brother to Jonathan, and probably youngest of all Saul's sons, such an age puts far too great a discrepancy between Jonathan and David for the romantic friendship which subsisted between them. If for *forty* we substitute *fourteen*, it may seem nearer to the truth.

Abner (it might seem) had forthwith to rally the undefeated forces of eastern Israel, and present such a front of war to the Philistines as they would not desire to oppose. Of this no record remains; but in fact the Philistines retired, without an effort to increase their territory after their great success. This is very similar to the course of events after their capture of the ark, and certainly suggests that they were, like the Tyrians, unambitious of continental empire and probably too few in number to think of upholding government over Israel. They pertinaciously held by their own cities and territory, not understanding by what right the Israelites could claim to expel them; but their martial efforts seem to have been limited to mere self-defence. They kept their own town of Gezer, on the border of Ephraim, and probably strengthened it; but as far as can be learned, this continued to be their northern limit. Towards David, as long as he should be in opposition to the house of Saul, they had a friendly feeling. Not displeased to see the tribes of Israel divided against themselves, and satisfied that David would not molest their territory while he had

---

[1] *Forty* is known to be a fatal number in these records. A ludicrous example is where Absalom tarries forty years in his house at Jerusalem (2 Sam. xv. 7). [*Forty* (say some who do not know when a cause is lost) *is a round number in Hebrew*. But a specific and a small number is here needed. A hundred is a round number in English; but no critic would justify writing "Absalom tarried a hundred years, &c." Round numbers are a confession of ignorance, not a vehicle of infallible and perfect knowledge.] A second error of a number is found in this very verse, 2 Sam. ii. 10, in which it is said that Ishbosheth *reigned two years*. This disagrees with the "long war" between him and David, and with the reign of David "*over Judah* in Hebron" seven years and a half (iii. 1, and ii. 11).

to contend against Abner on the north, they withdrew to peaceful occupations, and remained quiet during the seven years that David was king at Hebron.

After this Abner concentrated a force near the sacred hill of Gibeon, threatening the territory of Judah. Whether defence or offence was his object, is not clear; but an army came forthwith from David to meet him, and stationed itself at the other side of the pool of Gibeon. Its general was Joab, son of Zeruiah, David's sister, whose rude energy was already beginning to exert a predominance among David's warriors, although hitherto he had been surpassed in feats of battle not only by the three great heroes, but by his own brother Abishai. Abner hereupon made a proposal, the intent of which is obscurely indicated; but if we interpret it by other times of chivalry, it was—that in order to save bloodshed, the quarrel should be decided by twelve Benjamites fighting against twelve of David's men. According to our account, the whole twenty-four were slain by contrary wounds. More agreeably with the common course of real events, the two armies, instead of abiding by the decision, whatever it was, rushed into the combat. After a severe struggle, the troops of Abner gave way, and he himself was so keenly chased by the swift Asahel, youngest brother of Joab, as to be forced in self-defence to turn round and slay him. Three hundred and sixty of the Israelites are stated to have been cut down in the fierceness of pursuit; while only nineteen men, with Asahel, had fallen on the opposite side. By an appeal to Joab's better feelings, Abner induced him towards evening to recall his men by the trumpet; and marching all night long with the survivors whom he had gathered, stopped not until he had crossed Jordan and regained Mahanaim. The details of this battle have been carefully recorded, only, it may seem, because the death of Asahel gave Joab an excuse for remorseless treachery towards the honoured Abner.

David meanwhile had taken another step which shows him not to have disdained the resources of common politicians. We have already mentioned the Geshurites, whose territory bordered on the Manassites in Bashan, and who, in spite of a contest for the towns of Jair, lived on good terms with them. Geshur was at present subject to a king, whose name was Talmai, son of Ammihud; and David, although he had two wives already, made successful suit to Talmai for the hand of his daughter Maacah. The friendship of this monarch at such a time must have been much to be coveted as influencing the men of Asher and of Bashan, by fear or by good will, towards David; and after the event of the battle near Gibeon, less zeal in behalf of Ishbosheth was likely to be shown by any of the tribes. A lingering civil war did indeed continue, but the cause of the house of Saul was evidently declining, and the experienced Abner was forced to feel that he was labouring in vain.

When Saul had been dead about seven years,[1] Ishbosheth imprudently cast on Abner a reproachful accusation, which determined the latter no longer to uphold his throne. Whether passion or calculation moved Abner, or possibly both, is left uncertain: but it would seem, that he now saw Ishbosheth to be likely to expel him from his hard-earned honours as chief captain, and he accordingly resolved to make the best terms he could with David. But David at once saw the advantage which he had, and made a very unexpected demand as prerequisite to all negotiation;—that Abner would deliver up to him as a wife Michal, the daughter of Saul, who had been living full ten years in contented union with Phaltiel son of Laish. After becoming son-in-law of Talmai, David had taken to himself three other wives,—Haggith, Abital, and Eglah. He had now a seraglio of six around him, and each of them had given him a son in Hebron. It was evidently therefore no love for Michal which led him now to rend open new wounds under pretence of healing old ones: his design was to add to his person one more claim to the kingdom over Israel, by appearing in the character of Saul's son-in-law, and renewing the memory of the days when he had led Saul's armies to victory. Abner executed the unkind commission with as much civility as the case allowed; and Phaltiel went weeping behind the wife who was being torn from him, till they reached Bahurim in the tribe of Benjamin, near the frontier of Judah. When she had been given into David's hands,

[1] If Ishbosheth reigned only two years, this date must be incorrect; but see the note on the age of Ishbosheth.

Abner proceeded to conciliate the elders of all Israel, and especially of Benjamin, to the cause of David; after which he was entertained with a guard of twenty men by David in Hebron, and definitely engaged himself to gather deputies from all Israel who should publicly recognize David as king of the twelve tribes.

But when Joab, on returning to Hebron, learned what was going on, he perceived that Abner, so aged and esteemed a leader, must necessarily supersede him as captain of the host of Israel. With all the freedom of one who remembered the time when David had been an outlaw, his rude nephew coarsely rebuked him and imputed treachery to Abner. Then having enticed the unsuspecting warrior back on pretence of further conference, he assassinated him on the spot with his own hand.

At this bloody deed the heart of David fainted. It was his first taste perhaps of the misery of possessing royal power, purchased by the aid of such comrades as Joab. Besides the natural horror which he must have felt at the violent death of one whom he had so much reason to respect, he seemed to have lost the hopes which Abner's mission was to have confirmed, and to be in danger of incurring hatred with all Israel as implicated in the treacherous murder. Although Joab was his sister's son, it is probable that David would have executed summary justice on him if he had dared; but Joab's cause was now upheld by Abishai his brother, and both gave out that it had been a just retaliation for the death of Asahel. Their influence in the army at Hebron was too formidable to oppose; and David could not sacrifice Joab without making Abishai also his mortal enemy. His indignation and disgust vented itself in grievous curses against Joab; and to avert the public odium of the deed, he made an ostentatious display of grief. Not satisfied with public fasting and solemn procession to the grave of Abner, he wept publicly with loud crying, and recited a simple ditty,—perhaps extemporaneously poured forth:—

> Why needed Abner to die the death of the impious?
> Thy hands were not bound:
> Thy feet were not put into fetters:
> As a man falls by the sons of malice, so didst thou fall.

But this calamitous event did not practically delay the

accession of David to the throne of Israel. Abner had lived to do the work he had undertaken, and it had become notorious that all was ripe for a revolution in favour of David. Two brothers, captains of bands under Ishbosheth,—by name Baanah and Rechab, sons of Rimmon,— aiming to forestall favour with the expected sovereign, murdered Ishbosheth on his couch at noon, and carried his head to David. It was the fortune of this prince to be relieved by others from the perpetration of crime; and although he at length became corrupted by power, he was always spared its worst temptations. Ishbosheth had died without issue: Jonathan had left a son Mephibosheth, but he was lame, and was now about thirteen years old. Saul's surviving sons were born of a concubine,—Rizpah daughter of Aiah,—and were not regarded as politically legitimate. Thus, as husband to Michal, David would in any case have had a near claim on the succession; nor ought the murderers to have calculated on a gracious reception from the brother-in-law of their victim, even if they did not know how the Amalekite was treated who professed to have slain Saul, David's personal and inveterate foe. Without hesitation David ordered them both to be killed on the spot, their hands and feet to be cut off, and hanged over the pool in Hebron. The head of Ishbosheth was buried with all respect in the sepulchre of Abner at the same place.

David had reigned seven years and a half in Hebron over the tribe of Judah alone. He was now solemnly installed as king by the elders of all Israel, and "made a league with them before Jehovah in Hebron."[1] This was equivalent to what we now call a "coronation oath," and denoted that he was a constitutional, not an arbitrary monarch. The Israelites had no intention to resign their liberties, but in the sequel it will appear, that, with paid

[1] According to 1 Chron. xii. 23—40, an army of more than 340,000 men marched from all Israel to Hebron to welcome David to the throne. The numbers are an evident exaggeration characteristic of the whole book, yet their proportions are not without interest, as indicating the ideas once current concerning the relative strength of the tribes in David's reign. The men of Judah are few, perhaps because David was at home with them. The numbers assigned to the Danites are surprising, also the small ratio which Ephraim bears to Zebulon, Naphthali, and Asher. The separation of Aaronites from Levites, who are all treated as fighting men, the prowess ascribed to Zadok the Aaronite, and the remarkable detail that 200 chiefs of Issachar came *without troops*,

foreign troops at his side, even a most religious king could be nothing but a despot.

Concerning David's military proceedings during his reign at Hebron, we know nothing in detail, though we read of Joab bringing in a large spoil, probably from his old enemies the Amalekites. David had an army to feed, to exercise, and to keep out of mischief; but it is probable that the war against Abner generally occupied it sufficiently. Now however he determined to signalize his new power by a great exploit. The strength of JERUSALEM had been sufficiently proved by the long secure dwelling of Jebusites in it, surrounded by a Hebraized population. Hebron was no longer a suitable place for the centre of David's administration; but Jerusalem, on the frontier of Benjamin and Judah, without separating him from his own tribe, gave him a ready access to the plains of Jericho below, and thereby to the eastern districts; and although by no means a central position, it was less remote from Ephraim than Hebron. Of this Jebusite town he therefore determined to possess himself.

Jerusalem is situated on, and in the midst of, round or square hills; the ravines on three sides of it make a natural defence. The brook Kidron winds round it on the north and east along the valley of Jehoshaphat, which is flanked by cliffs taller and steeper towards its southern end, near which is the flat-topped hill of Moriah. To the south-west of this is the larger and higher hill of Zion,

while the Manassites came "expressed by name," appear like real history, at which this is an elaborate effort, and no arbitrary invention.

Judah	6,800
Simeon	7,100
Levi	4,600
Aaronites	3,700
Benjamin	3,000
Ephraim	20,800
Western Manasseh ..	18,000
Zebulon	50,000
Naphthali	37,000
And Captains ..	1,000
Danites	28,600
Asher	40,000
Issachar chiefs	200
Eastern tribes	120,000
Total	340,800

divided from it by a ravine, which forms a steep descent
to the pool of Siloam and valley of Jehoshaphat. The
western and southern sides of Mount Zion are lofty and
abrupt, and at their bottom lies the narrow Valley of
Hinnom,[1] called in Hebrew *Gehinnom:* a word which has
strangely changed its meaning, both in Hebrew and in
Arabic. Towards the north-west the descent from both
hills is more gradual, yet each of them is defended by a
depression of moderate depth, which art would easily con-
vert into a fortification available against the modes of attack known to the Hebrews. The entire breadth of the
table-land across the top of Zion and the skirt of Moriah,
to the edge of the valley of Jehoshaphat, little exceeds
half a mile; and was not too great for a moderate force to
defend. The hills which look down on Jerusalem from the
north-east, south-east, and south, probably explain the
abundance of spring-water for which Jerusalem has been
celebrated: for in the numerous blockades which it has
endured, the besiegers are said to have been often distressed for want of water, the besieged never.

The Jebusites were so confident of their safety, as to
send to David an enigmatical message of defiance; which
may be explained,—that a lame and blind garrison was
sufficient to defend the place. David saw in this an opportunity of displacing Joab from his office of chief captain,
—if indeed Joab formally held that office as yet, and had
not merely assumed authority as David's eldest nephew
and old comrade in arms. The king however now declared, that whoever should first scale the wall and drive
off its defenders, should be made chief captain; but his
hopes were signally disappointed. His impetuous nephew
resolved not to be outdone, and triumphantly mounting
the wall, was the immediate means of the capture of the
town. After this, Joab's supremacy in the king's army
could not be shaken off: for thirty-two years more this
bold and bad man continued to hold high authority in the
court of the pious king. Painfully different often are the
aspirations of devotional hours from the necessities im-

[1] The northern end of this valley is also named the Valley of Gihon, and contains the pool of Gihon. *Gihinnom* or *Gehennem* has taken the sense of Hell; because in later times this valley was the scene of the cruel superstition which made children to pass through the fire to Molech.

posed by political life: for, probably, very soon after, David composed the 101st Psalm, declaring his resolution not to promote or endure the presence of wicked men. The Psalm[1] is thus translated:—

1. Of Goodness and Righteousness will I sing:
Unto thee, O JEHOVAH, will I play (on the harp).
2. I will attend unto guiltless ways.—
O, when wilt thou come unto me,
That I may walk in my house with guiltless heart?
3. No wicked thing will I set before my eyes:
I hate to use evil agency:
It shall not cleave unto me.
4. The falsehearted shall be far from me;
I will not know a bad man.
5. I will uproot him who secretly slandereth his neighbour;
The man of haughty eye and proud heart I will not endure.
6. My eyes shall be on the faithful in the land, that they may dwell with me:
He that walketh in a guiltless way shall serve me.
7. He that worketh deceit shall not stay in my house;
He that telleth lies shall not stand in my sight.
8. I will watch to pluck up the wicked of the land,
That I may uproot all evildoers from JEHOVAH'S CITY.

Although David's resolutions rose high above his practice or his power to perform, his practice would have fallen far lower had not his aspirations been so high; nor were the sincerely good intentions with which he entered the captured place wholly in vain. *Jerusalem* is henceforth its name in the history; in poetry only, and not before the times of king Hezekiah, is it entitled Salem, or *peace;* identifying it with the city of the legendary Melchisedek. David's first care was to provide for the security of his intended capital, by suitable fortifications. Immediately to the north of Mount Zion, and separated from it by a slighter depression which we have named, was another hill, called *Millo* in the Hebrew, ἄκρα (or citadel?) in the Greek. In ancient times this seems to have been much loftier than now; for it has been artificially lowered. David made no attempt to include Millo (or *Acra*) in his city, but fortified Mount Zion separately; whence it was afterwards called, The city of David. Mount Moriah

[1] The 15th Psalm and the first part of the 24th, which have no internal marks of being composed by a king, have many similarities of expression to the 101st. Ewald regards the 15th as not quite so old. It is credible that the psalmists and prophets of those days had certain current sentiments and phrases, which make it impossible to say what has been *imitated* from what.

also was left outside to the north-east, since great works were needed in preparing a royal palace and treasure-house, besides the outer wall; and he was anxious to strengthen as speedily as possible that which he destined as JEHOVAH's CITY, before foreign war should distract him.

In fact this was impending. The Philistines, who had maintained an honourable peace as long as David had been engaged by civil broils, were alarmed as soon as he became king of all Israel; and his sudden attack on Jebus showed them what they had to expect for Gezer and their other towns, even if they were not moved by any alliance with the Jebusites. They marched out in force and encamped on the high plain of Rephaim, on the south or south-west of Mount Zion, from which it is separated only by the valley of Hinnom. David now anxiously consulted Jehovah by Urim whether to attack the Philistines; and having obtained leave, he succeeded so far as to repulse them and capture the images of their gods, which the Hebrews burned. It does not appear whether these were attached to military standards, like the Roman eagles; but the fact deserves remark, as the first intimation that David was making war against idolatry. The Philistines, however,—it would appear with increased forces,—resumed their position on the same lofty plain, and the priest, after consulting the Urim, forbade David to assail them in front. We may probably infer that they were emboldened to detach a body of men for the support of Geba; for, as we learn, when the signal was heard for which the Urim had bade David to wait, the Hebrews who had fetched a compass round them attacked their flank, and they fled "from Geba to Gezer." In Geba, northward of Jerusalem, they had had a garrison in Saul's days, which probably still remained, and Gezer, which contained a Canaanite population, seems to have been their own town to which they would flee for refuge.

These events appear to have been of no farther importance than to show the Philistines that they could not contend single-handed against David; and whatever the danger of allowing him to grow strong, peace was at present their wisest or their only policy. But a remark is needed on David's consulting of the Urim. He did not seek divine counsel whether to attack Jebus; apparently because his mind was clear that the enterprise was advantageous. But when Ziklag had been burned by the Amalekites, and now, when a dangerous army is at hand, he is glad of such advice. It would appear that he regarded it as a divine aid in times of perplexity,[1] but only to be sought for in such times. He had no idea of abdicating his duties as military leader, and putting the movements of his army into the control of the priest. Hence perhaps it is that, as his confidence in his troops and in his own warlike experience increased, he ceased altogether to consult the sacred Urim, for we hear no more of it in his later wars.

He was now at liberty to carry out his intention of making Jerusalem a sacred city for all Israel, and binding the tribes together by a new centre of interest. With this was coupled his wish to exalt the honour of Jehovah and destroy in Israel all foreign superstition. The tabernacle, it will be remembered, was at Gibeon,[2] and the ark at Kirjathjearim. Later times treated these as natural and proper companions; and if David had shared the feelings of Nehemiah, it is probable that he would have brought *both* of them to Jerusalem. No one can certainly say why he resolved on what may seem a very capricious course,—to bring the ark to Jerusalem, but instead of putting it into the ancient tabernacle, to erect a new tabernacle for it himself.[3] It is possible that his new pavilion was superior in size and beauty; and in any case we may conjecture that he wished to provide a double priestly establishment for the rival pretensions of Zadok and Abiathar. Zadok was left to minister at Gibeon,[4] and was perhaps already David's favourite; but Abiathar was the representative of Eli and of the priests whom Saul had massacred. Yet the theory of a single High Priest was alien to David's policy. His own rise by priestly aid had shown sufficiently what a united

---

[1] Socrates, in Xenoph. Memor. I. 1. 6—9, takes this view of divination.

[2] This is mentioned by the "Chronicler" *only;* on which account some critics doubt whether there was any old tabernacle at all. To me it seems, that if it were a fiction of sacerdotal vanity, that vanity would have displayed itself in something more than the dry statements of 2 Chron. i. 3, 13.

[3] 2 Sam. vi. 17; 2 Chron. i. 4.   [4] 1 Chron. xvi. 39.

priesthood could do against the crown; and while warmly patronizing religion, he would not make its officers too powerful. All through his reign Zadok and Abiathar[1] continued as joint and co-ordinate authorities, although Abiathar, as the representative of Eli, took precedence of the other. Numerous circumstances will open upon us in the course of the history which will warn us not to assume that David's ecclesiastical proceedings were modelled according to the Pentateuch.

It will be remembered that the tarrying of the ark at Kirjathjearim was ascribed to the extreme danger of mortal plagues proceeding from it while it was exposed to vulgar curiosity. A new calamity was now reported which impeded its travelling. When on the way to Jerusalem, escorted by David with 30,000 men and numerous musicians, it was jolted on its cart by the oxen which drew it; and when Uzzah, the son of Abinadab, who was in charge of it, put forth his hand to save it from falling, the anger of Jehovah was kindled against Uzzah, and smote him so that he died on the spot. Such was the belief of the later Jews, and such has been the belief of Christians: we therefore are not justified in doubting whether David too could lie under so palsying a superstition. He dared not to bring the ark any farther at the moment, and it halted three months at the house of Obed Edom the Gittite. The chief interest of this to us is, that it shows us a man of Gath, not only established in Israel, but invested with a religious charge. However, the three months' tarrying was believed to have brought a blessing to Obed Edom, and David took fresh courage. He came down again in person with a great multitude, and offered sacrifices as soon as the ark was in motion: finally, it was brought into the city of David with the sound of the trumpet; musicians and singers accompanied it, singing (according to the most probable criticism) the whole, or the close only, of the 24th Psalm:—[2]

[1] In 2 Sam. viii. 17, 1 Chron. xviii. 16, *Abimelech son of Abiathar* is erroneously put for *Abiathar son of Ahimelech*. See 1 Kings ii. 26. in proof that the Abiathar disgraced by Solomon is he whose father, Ahimelech, was slain by Saul.

[2] The song ascribed to David on this occasion by the "Chronicler" bears internal evidence of much later origin.

> Lift up, O ye doors, your heads:
> Lift them up, ye ancient gates:
> Let the glorious King come in!
>
> Who then is the glorious King?
> 'Tis Jehovah, strong and mighty,
> 'Tis Jehovah, lord of battles, etc., etc.

While the ark was proceeding towards its new tabernacle, the king himself danced before it in a priest's linen vest. He had evidently no idea that priests were to monopolize religious ministrations, or that the joy of a worshipper might not manifest itself in the modes familiar to his country. Perhaps this little incident might have been suppressed, as an invasion of sacerdotal functions, by the narrow formality of a later age, had it not been preserved to us by a result in which the priestly enemies of Saul rejoiced. Michal was displeased at David's public dancing, inasmuch as the sort of nakedness which it involved (the lower gown or robe being laid aside,—to gain activity, we presume) seemed to her degrading to a king, and she did not spare to reproach her husband for it. He on his part, not wanting in spirit, took care to let her understand that it was to Jehovah and His cause, not to her name, that he was indebted for his kingdom, and that he would not be controlled by her influence. To this altercation the old historian imputes it,—whether by a divine judgment or by the disgust with which it inspired David,—that the daughter of Saul had no children to the day of her death.

Soon after his peaceable establishment in Jerusalem, David took measures for building himself a palace. The arts of the mason and the carpenter were exceedingly rude among the Hebrews; but the Tyrians[1] were excellent neighbours and skilful workmen, and an alliance of commerce now commenced between the nations, which was of extreme importance for developing the industry of the ruder and poorer people. Although little or nothing is recorded concerning the tillage of the land under Saul, we may judge that there must have been frequent insecur-

---

[1] The Chronicler says, "*Hiram* king of Tyre." But Hiram is still on the throne in the middle of Solomon's reign, forty or fifty years later. This seems merely a mark that no earlier king's name at Tyre was known to the writer; just as the Ammonite king at Saul's accession is called *Nahash*.

ity, little stimulus from foreign trade, and no good supply of agricultural implements. With cultivation, *wheat* and *wine* in abundance,—and, almost self-produced, *oil* and *honey*,—could be exported from the land of Israel to Tyre; and there can be no doubt that a more diligent production of these staple articles began from the period of David's first commerce with his Tyrian neighbours. As little question can there be that every species of manufactured implement, especially weapons of war and superior armour, would be obtained abundantly from Tyre, as soon as tranquil and steady industry became possible. And as far as our sources of information are available, it would seem that at this crisis there was a considerable interval of peace. For a long time previous the Philistines alone had been dangerous or troublesome enemies; and respite being now gained, both from *their* attacks and from civil war, the industrious arts began to receive a development before unknown; and by interchange of raw produce with the Tyrians, the wealth of Israel at large and of the king's treasury must have obtained a great accession. How long this repose lasted, we cannot tell; but as no enemy set foot on the land during David's reign, and no complaint is recorded against the king's taxes, it must be believed that a steady increase of wealth and population went on during the whole period. It is not likely that he meanwhile relaxed any of his old martial exercises. We learn incidentally that 600 men "had followed him from Gath,"[1] whom we find at a much later time as part of his bodyguard. Since they must have been with him from the beginning, we cannot but see in the fact a nucleus of military despotism, and that, as all other despots, he preferred to trust to foreigners the care of his person. These troops were, no doubt, kept in constant training; and as his treasury filled, he was able to increase his standing army.

The first consequence of his increase of strength was a voice from the holy Urim, suggesting to him to undertake the conquest of Moab, Philistia, and Edom. At least, a fragment of his poetry which has come down to us imbedded in two different Psalms,[2] represents him as contem-

[1] 2 Sam. xv. 18.   [2] Psalms cviii. and lx.

plating this threefold enterprise, while elated by a voice from the sanctuary. He names Judah *his lawgiver*, perhaps to denote the more strictly constitutional rights under which he was bound to his own tribe; against which he had never contended in war, and from which he had first received the kingly power.

> God hath spoken in his holy place; and I rejoice.
> I divide Shechem, and mete out the valley of Succoth:
> Gilead is mine, Manasseh is mine:
> Ephraim also is the strength of my head:
> Judah is my lawgiver.
> Moab is my washpot: over Edom will I cast out my shoe:
> Over Philistia will I triumph.
> Who will bring me into the strong city? who will lead me into Edom?
> Wilt not thou, O God, etc. . . . ?

From this it might appear that Edom was the country which he destined first to attack. Yet according to the order stated in the concise summary preserved to us, David commenced his career of encroachment by an invasion of Philistia, which might seem to be justified by their aggressive movement when he ascended the throne of Israel. His success is vaguely spoken of as complete, but the only definite result named is his taking from them the fortress Metheg-Ammah (or, the Bridle of Ammah), which we may infer, was important for keeping them in check. But it is not stated that the Philistines became tributary.

This however was followed by a far more deadly war against the Moabites, who were previously known as a very friendly people. To the king of Moab, it will be remembered, David had committed his parents at the time of his great danger from Saul; thus he had personal, as well as national, grounds for maintaining with them peaceful relations. No causes are assigned for the attack which he now made on them, which ended in his putting to the sword[1] two-thirds of the unfortunate population, and subjecting the rest to tribute. Treatment so ferocious could hardly have proceeded from mutual exasperation, else some other striking facts would have been recorded, such as perfidy and cruelty on the part of the Moabites. It is therefore rather to be ascribed to policy, and perhaps to the greediness of the neighbour-tribe of Reuben to ap-

---

[1] Such seems the meaning of the words, 2 Sam. viii. 2: "with two lines measured he to put to death, and with one full line to keep alive."

propriate their pasture-grounds; but it must not be forgotten, that in this fierce massacre, even if dictated by pure avarice and ambition, David would not want the express permission of the great Jewish lawgiver,[1] if we could persuade ourselves that Moses wrote the book of Deuteronomy. At any rate the Hebrew king did nothing which the later bards and priests of his own nation, or the statesmen of Rome, would have censured as cruel or unjust.

Thus far we have contemplated David as warring against his immediate neighbours; petty nations, inferior each of them in numbers and resources to united Israel, though occasionally superior by arts or by accident. But about this time, new events threw the Hebrew prince into conflict with a far greater potentate, whose person, people, and dominion are alike dimly descried by us; nevertheless, what we do know about him, is both negatively and positively of great importance. If we could believe the vulgar tradition of an old Assyrian monarchy, beginning with Ninus and Semiramis in an extreme antiquity, Nineveh was in the time of David the seat of a wide-reaching empire, the power of which was felt in Egypt and Phœnicia, in Lydia and in Media. But the Hebrew annals would in themselves suffice to show that this is an exaggeration. All that we can distinctly assert is, that about this time a branch of the Syrian nation called *Zobahites* (or, the house of Zobah) had risen to great eminence in Northern Mesopotamia and Syria. The later Syrian tradition represents *Nisibis* in Mesopotamia as their head-quarters; while the Jews place them at Aleppo. Probably Zobah itself, like Israel, Seljuk, Othman, was the name of a patriarch rather than of a place. Whether the Zobahites at this period were all under one king, we do not know; but a great leader of them, called Hadadezer son of Rehob, had made himself celebrated by his wars in Syria, and appears to have been keeping the city of Damascus in dependent alliance. Toi, king of Hamath, is specified as one who had had painful proofs of Hadadezer's prowess. The *city* of Hamath was called Epiphaneia by the Greeks. Since however Hamath is often treated as

[1] Deut. xx. 10—15.

FIRST WAR WITH THE ZOBAHITES.

touching Israel on the northern frontier,[1] we are forced to infer that its *territory* included the remarkable plain to the south of the city, which was called *the Hollow Syria*, from its position between the vast mountain walls of Libanus and Anti-Libanus. Moreover, if at the æra of which we are treating some other power than Hamath had possessed this district, we must of necessity have heard of it in the war with Hadadezer. He had great strength in cavalry and in chariots of war, a species of force in which the earlier Assyrians excelled: as cavalry indeed has at every time distinguished all the great empires of Asia. By occupying Damascus and its territory, the king of Zobah in a manner flanked all the dominions of Hamath; and as either his direct sway or his national connexions reached over into Mesopotamia, his resources made him a most formidable neighbour to every state in Syria.

The circumstances which threw him into collision with David are very obscurely explained:[2] nor can it even be made out from the statements whether the war was offensive or defensive on David's part, nor whether the first meeting took place on Israelitish ground or so far off as the bank of the Euphrates. As however king Toi immediately afterwards appears in friendship with David, the nature of the case itself seems almost to force us on some such interpretation as the following.

The king of Hamath, impelled by the danger which threatened him from the growth of the Zobahite power, and learning of the spirit and high success of David in various wars, solicited him to attack Hadadezer, thus placing the Zobahites in Damascus between opposite enemies. It was agreed that Toi should intercept all communications with Mesopotamia by occupying or overrunning the Syrian bank of the Euphrates; and while Hadadezer was engaged in recovering his posts and connexions in this quarter, David fell upon him in the more immediate neighbourhood of Israel. The part of the Zobahite army

---

[1] Num. xxxiv. 8, etc.
[2] 2 Sam. viii. 3. "David smote him, as *he* (Hadadezer?) went to recover his border at the river Euphrates." Who had taken it away? David? That appears inconceivable. Was it not Toi, king of Hamath? and was not David only his ally, and secondary in the war?

most feared consisted of cavalry and chariots; but we may infer that it had injudiciously ventured in rugged and enclosed country, where it could not act to advantage. Meeting with brave resistance, not from infantry only, but, we need not doubt, from David's archers and slingers, it was miserably discomfited and a great number of the horses were captured.[1]

Hadadezer was too much accustomed to conquest tamely to submit to this repulse, and called out to his aid an army of Damascenes. But this only increased his disasters. The troops of Damascus fought with little spirit in behalf of their foreign master, and were totally routed by the well-trained bands of David, now flushed with conscious prowess and mutual confidence. The Hebrew king followed up his advantage sharply, and entered Damascus as a conqueror. No native government was organized to withstand him, and as the Zobahites were forced to withdraw, he easily stept into their place as suzerain of the district. The Damascenes without a struggle consented to change their master; paid homage and tribute to David, and received garrisons from him into their critical fortresses. It would have been morally impossible for all this to have been brought about so easily if the Zobahites had themselves held the castles with a powerful infantry, or if the Damascenes had been independent and struggling in a national cause.

Nor was this the end of Hadadezer's reverses. The king of Hamath undoubtedly took full advantage of his weakness, and helped himself freely out of Hadadezer's resources. The advantages he gained may in part be inferred from his gratitude to David, to whom he sent, by the hand of his son Hadoram, vessels of silver, gold, and brass, as gifts of honour. Never before had such splendour been seen in Israel. Regarding his success in the war to have been of Jehovah, the pious king dedicated all these vessels to religious uses, instead of displaying them in personal pride. Yet at the same time, and from the same victories, valuable metals, as spoils of war, now began to pour themselves into David's coffers. One of

[1] David is said to capture 1000 chariots, 700 horsemen, and 20,000 footmen. The Chronicler says 7000 horsemen. No credit whatever is due to his estimates of numbers.

Hadadezer's bands is said to have had shields of *gold*, which the Hebrews captured: even if we adopt the reasonable interpretation of *shields adorned with gold*, it is sufficiently indicative of the pomp and wealth of the enemy. But a far greater booty must have been the abundance of brass which David got from the plunder of Betah and Berothai, cities of Hadadezer; of unknown site, but not likely to have been far from Damascus.

These and other accessions of valuable metal gave rise to a new scheme in David's contemplations. It was at least propagated and believed afterwards that he had designed to build a splendid temple for the ark of God, instead of the pavilion of curtains in which it had hitherto lodged; but that the prophet Nathan, who had at first encouraged the scheme, received a nightly revelation from Jehovah that it was not his will at present;[1] but that *a son of David* should build the house of Jehovah, and that his seed should reign for ever on his throne. This very remarkable message undoubtedly in its first intent pointed at Solomon, son of David; and it deserves attention, as the commencement of new political and prophetical thoughts of immense moment. For the *oath* which on this occasion Jehovah made to David through the prophet was perpetually celebrated by the psalmists of Israel, as indeed by David himself in his last words of poetry. By the deep hold which the idea took on the national mind, it saved the royalty to the house of David for several centuries; and when it failed at last, bequeathed to posterity a new and mystical interpretation of still grander import.

But the Hebrew monarch was now himself in turn started on a career of conquest, which must naturally have alarmed his immediate neighbours. To hold Damascus and its territory with garrisons, needed a constant increase of his army in the north; and the necessity of drawing away his forces from the south may possibly have laid him

---

[1] In 2 Sam. vii., as 1 Chron. xvii., no reason against it is assigned but old precedent. In 1 Kings v. 3, it is said that David *could not find time* by reason of his wars; but as this seemed insufficient to sacerdotal zeal, the Chroniclers (1 Chron. xxii. 8) discovered a new reason—that David *had shed much blood*. The date of Nathan's message is imperfectly given. It was *after Jehovah had given David rest from all his enemies*, 2 Sam. vii. 1; which may point to his latest years.

open to attack from the Edomites in that quarter. Indeed, if we may abide by an old tradition,[1] David's main army was still occupied by the Syrian war, when he was forced to detach Joab to repel the Edomites, who undoubtedly had been made hostile ever since the exterminating conquest of Moab. David's general and troops had learned to trust one another; extreme promptitude was his only rule of action (for *tactics*, in a modern sense, cannot be thought of); and long habits of warfare had given them great superiority over brave neighbours. It is not stated whether the Edomites needed to be driven off from Hebrew ground, or whether Joab's rapidity anticipated them; a severe battle however was fought in the Valley of Salt, a remarkable place in Idumæa, just south of the Dead Sea, afterwards the scene of a still greater battle under King Amaziah.[2] The enemy was defeated with great slaughter,[3] and had to receive Hebrew garrisons into their cities.

But this was only the beginning of atrocious vengeance. Joab,[4] when the troops returned from the Syrian war, stayed in the country for six whole months with an overpowering force, and deliberately attempted to kill every male Edomite. His battalions roved far and wide, and drove out those whom they could not catch. Hitherto Selah or *Petra* in Mount Seir had been the great centre of the Edomites; but perhaps from this massacre the city of *Teman* to the east, and the much more[5] distant *Bozra* to the north-east, began to increase in Edomite population. The burying of the slain was itself a great labour: after which it devolved on David in person to regulate the future government of the empty land and miserable fraction of the nation whom policy at length spared. From this blow it was long before Idumæa could lift up its head.

[1] Superscription of Ps. lx.   [2] 2 Kings xiv. 7.
[3] In 2 Sam. viii. it is 18,000 men slain; only 12,000 in the Superscription of Ps. lx. Knowing what we do of the *land* of Edom, we cannot unhesitatingly receive even the smaller number. If a hostile army was *popularly estimated* at 12,000, and if it was totally dispersed, an ode of triumph would easily represent 12,000 as actually slain. Let this be understood in future, in regard to the more moderate numbers in the books of Kings.
[4] 1 Kings xi. 15, 16.
[5] There is great uncertainty as to the site of this city; and the objections of many learned commentators to the Bozra of our maps appear to be well founded.

For thirty or forty years after, the Hebrew ascendancy was in full vigour there; and for a century and a half no national movement to throw it off could arise. The district, although generally rocky and barren, is not destitute of valleys, which (in comparison to the rest) have been called fruitful. We may presume that it was rich enough in sheep and goats to repay the trouble of rudely governing it. Yet it was ambition and uncontrolled ferocity, not greedy calculation, which dictated a violence for which Judah in future generations was dearly to pay. But of that nothing was then dreamed. The conquest raised Joab to high distinction, which only his brother Abishai[1] shared with him. Praises, no doubt, in abundance were offered up to Jehovah, God of battles; and the people in general joyfully deduced from the whole the same moral as the historian:—"Jehovah preserveth David whithersoever he goeth."

About this time, it may be believed, some prophet attached to the court (if not Nathan himself), addressed to David a solemn hymn, congratulating him alike on his victories and on his sacred character as a psalmist of Jehovah and a devout upholder of religion.[2]

1. Jehovah said unto my lord [David],
    Sit thou at my right hand, till I make thy foes thy footstool.
    Jehovah sendeth out from Zion thy mighty sceptre;
    Rule thou in the midst of thy foes.
2. Jehovah sware, and will not repent:
    Thou art a *Priest* for ever, after the order of *Melchisedek*.
    Jehovah, at thy right hand, strikes through kings in his day of wrath.
3. [David] executes judgments on the nations, and fills them with carcases;
    He wounds the heads over many countries.
    He drinks of the brook in the way;
    Therefore does he lift up the head.

The star of David, in fact, was now culminating. Nothing had occurred to bedim its brightness, and according to the religious theory of those days, he was eminently the beloved of Jehovah. Another pause of war took place, during which it is briefly recorded that he "reigned over all Israel and executed judgment and justice." When the same individual was chief administrator of war and peace, such a rest was signally needed, to provide for the

[1] 1 Chron. xviii. 12, attributes the battle in the Valley of Salt to Abishai.
[2] Psalm cx.

government of his extended dominion. Now perhaps it was that more systematic arrangements were made concerning the crown-lands and the royal bailiffs, who were twelve in number, according to the later narrative:[1] over the treasury; over the country stores; over the tillage; over the vineyards; over the wine-cellars; over the olive and sycamore trees; over the oil-cellars; over the herds in Sharon; over the herds in the valleys; over the camels; over the asses; over the flocks. At this same time we have the following list given us of David's cabinet by the older historian:[2] Joab, son of Zeruiah, was captain of the host; Jehoshaphat, son of Ahilud, was recorder; Zadok, son of Ahitub, and Abiathar, son of Ahimelech, were the two chief priests; Seraiah was the scribe; Benaiah, son of Jehoiada, was captain of the Cherethites and Pelethites: of whom also David's sons were chief officers. This Benaiah has already been named as a man of great valour who had slain a lion. His father may have been that Jehoiada, chief of the Aaronites, who came to David at Hebron; and a little latter he is recorded as one of David's chief counsellors.[3] The son, like the præfect of the prætorians under the Roman emperors, would naturally become the second person in the kingdom, and, as we shall see, ultimately supplanted Joab.

His troops, the Cherethites and Pelethites, are now mentioned for the first time, and it is contested whether their names indicate their foreign extraction or their office. Yet as the Cherethites are certainly a nation neighbouring to the Philistines,[4] the former opinion seems more probable. They do not include the 600 Gittites, of whom Ittai was the captain. It is reasonable to conjecture that David had employed Hebrew troops to garrison the foreign territories,—Damascus, Moab, and Edom, —and then, to augment his available army, had taken into his pay formidable numbers of the southern barbarians, here called Cherethites and Pelethites,—whom he would support by the tribute derived from foreign sources, without pressing on his own people. Thus he became more and more beyond the reach of constitutional con-

---

[1] 1 Chron. xxvii. 25—31.   [2] 2 Sam. viii. 16.
[3] 1 Chron. xxvii. 34.   [4] 1 Sam. xxx. 14; Ezek. xxv. 16; Zeph. ii. 5.

trol.¹ A slight circumstance gives us a rough date for these events. The sons of David (it has been mentioned) were " chief officers,"—apparently of the Cherethites and Pelethites,² which implies that he had sons of manly age, and was far advanced in his reign.

David now felt himself too strong on the throne to be jealous of the house of Saul, and for the first time remembered his friend Jonathan enough to bestow kindness on his representatives. One son only lived, by name Meribbaal; whom later times contemptuously called Mephibosheth. This young man, being lame, could not be suspected of aspiring to the kingdom in a warlike age and against such a warrior as David. The king now restored to him all the private estate of Saul, and admitted him to a permanent place at his own table. Mephibosheth³ was only five years old when his father Jonathan was slain; but at the time of which we are treating, he had already, it is intimated, a young son named Micha, of whom at present no jealousy was felt by David.

It may be here well to remark on the change which had been for some time going on as to the names⁴ which the Hebrews gave to their children. In the earlier times the word God (*El* and *Eli*) had been a very usual component.⁵ In the name *Israel*, as in *Jezreel*, *Ammiel*, *Penuel*, and a hundred others, we see an ending which is common to the Hebrews with the tribes around them. From the time of Samuel onwards, the name *Jehovah* or *Jah* appears to become a more favourite element of names. We have already named *Jeho*shaphat and *Jeho*iada as counsellors of David; Zeru*iah* was David's sister; Bena*iah* and Ur*iah* among his captains. Under Saul even the names Eshbaal and Meribbaal appear; but from the time of David Jehovistic names gain a marked predominance.

---

¹ The details given us in 1 Chron. xxvii. concerning David's standing army cannot be received with any confidence, considering the prodigious credulity of that book in regard to figures. It however is there estimated that 288,000 men were kept constantly under training, of whom 24,000 were every month taken into more direct service by rotation.
² 2 Sam. viii. 18. ³ 2 Sam. iv. 5.
⁴ Ewald, in Kitto's Biblical Cycl., Art. NAMES.
⁵ In fact, most ancient nations show this tendency, as in the Chaldee *Nabo*polassar, *Nebu*chadnezzar, and the Greek *Dion*, *Poseidonius*, *Apollonius*, etc.

It is remarkable that Athaliah, daughter of Jezebel, received a Jehovistic name.[1]

The peace which followed the extirpation of the Edomites was first disturbed by a strange event out of which many disastrous consequences arose. Nahash, king of the Ammonites, a former friend of David, died; upon which the Hebrew monarch sent an embassy to condole with Hanun, the new king; but the ambassadors were suspected to be spies,—not unnaturally, when the Ammonites looked to their conquered neighbours, Moab and Edom; and Hanun sent them away with gross and characteristic insult.[2] Fearing then retaliation from David, Hanun plunged at once into hostilities and hired aid from two branches of the Syrians,—the Rehobites[3] and Zobahites,—also from the king of Maacah in the immediate north of the Hebrew territory, and from Ishtob or the Hauran. A coalition against David might in any case have been expected; but this had broken out prematurely through the precipitation of the Ammonites, who ought scarcely to have volunteered being principals in the war, while Hadadezer of Zobah was still powerful. The defence of Israel was again entrusted to Joab, for David appears now to have given up military for civil duties. The Hebrew army was enclosed between the Syrian confederates from the north, and the Ammonites from the east; Joab therefore took a picked body with him against the Syrians, and sent his brother Abishai with the rest against the Ammonites. The hired army soon gave way before Joab and fled; upon which the Ammonites were discouraged and retreated, seeing that Joab was coming up to join his brother against them. The Ammonites did not wish to risk farther loss, but shutting themselves up in a fortified place, endeavoured to re-assure and excite afresh their northern confederates; and it is probable that this time they were successful in stirring up Hadadezer to a serious effort on his own account; for we read of no farther payment for the Syrian troops, and Hadad-

[1] Bishop Colenso (vol. v. p. 276) maintains "Jehovah" to be of *Phœnician origin*. It is, none the less, with the Hebrews, the watchword of high monotheism.
[2] He shaved half their beards and cut off the lower part of their garments, so as to leave them half naked.
[3] The Rehobites are immediately on the northern frontier of Israel.

ezer gathered a new and very formidable army of chariots and horsemen from Mesopotamia as well as Syria. Joab on his part thought the danger so threatening, that he repaired to Jerusalem to concert measures and increase his forces: and David himself now marched out in person, taking with him a general levy of all Israel. He crossed over Jordan, and made a long march beyond the Hebrew limits; whether in order to save his own land from the ravages of the Syrian cavalry, or to engage it before it could form a junction with the Ammonites. In a battle which took place at Helam (an unknown spot), he was once more successful, and as usual, an exaggerated account is given of the number of slain.[1] This was the last blow needed by Hadadezer. He vanishes from the narrative, and his tributary chiefs in the neighbourhood of the Hebrews made submission to David.

Internal evidence may incline us to believe, that about this time the twentieth Psalm was composed, as an address and encouragement to David in warring on the side of Jehovah.

1. Jehovah hear thee in the day of trouble;
The name of Jacob's God defend thee:
Send thee help from the sanctuary,
And strengthen thee out of Zion:
Remember all thy offerings,
Accept thy burnt sacrifice,
Grant thee according to thine own heart,
And fulfil all thy counsel!

2. We will rejoice in thy preservation
And in God's name set up our banners.
Jehovah fulfil all thy petitions!

3. Now know I that Jehovah saveth his anointed.
He heareth him from his holy heaven,
With the strong aid of his right hand.
Some trust in *chariots*, some in *horses*,
But we will trust in the name of Jehovah our God.
They[2] are brought down and fallen;
But we are risen and stand upright.

4. Oh Jehovah, help thou the king!
Let him hear us when we cry to him.

For the next campaign Joab was despatched against

---

[1] 2 Sam. x. 18. Forty thousand horsemen, and the men of seven hundred chariots. The Chronicler increases the chariots to seven *thousand:* 1 Chr. xix. 18.

[2] Namely, the Zobahites?—Ewald regarded this Psalm by its Hebrew style to be of the Davidical age.

the Ammonites, and after desolating the country, laid siege to their chief city. Meanwhile David, now reveling in success, was smitten at Jerusalem by the beauty of Bathsheba, wife of Uriah the Hittite, one of his leading warriors. After gratifying his guilty passion, and finding that he would not be able to conceal it from the injured husband, he was base enough to order Joab so to expose the brave Uriah in battle, as to assure that he would be slain by the Ammonites. Joab obeyed without scruple, and by succeeding added one link more to the chain by which he held the infatuated king.

The war lingered on; but the enemy was still shut up in his walls, and, receiving no aid from Syria, was at length reduced to helplessness. The chief town appears to have consisted of two separate fortifications, of which one was the royal palace, called also the Water-City, probably from its commanding access to the supply of water. This was actually captured by the Israelites, who thus had the enemy at their mercy. But the conqueror of Edom was prudent enough not to encounter the royal jealousy, by winning for himself the new name of conqueror of the Ammonites. He therefore sent and urged David to come down in person and take possession of the city, which was no longer able to resist. The Hebrew monarch felt the importance of the occasion; and revenge, as well as pride, was now to be gratified. The Ammonite king had rejected his friendly offices with insult, had plunged into hostilities, and kindled a flame against him which reached beyond the Euphrates. True, this had only displayed and increased the might of Israel; yet it was not the less needful, signally to manifest to subject nations that that might was not to be assailed without the most terrible retribution. David accordingly gathered an imposing host, and having marched without delay, captured the city immediately on his arrival. The crown of the Ammonite king (which is stated to have weighed a talent of gold, and to have been set with precious stones), was with all form placed upon David's head, and all the valuables of the city were seized as public spoil. After the cold-blooded execution inflicted on the Moabites, and the deliberate effort to extirpate the whole nation of Edom, it was perhaps to be expected that a still more horrible doom would fall upon the Ammonite people. Not those only who were found in the *Rabba* (or chief city), but the inhabitants of all the towns of Ammon were brought out and executed by various modes of torture,[1] which are specified as "putting them under saws, and under harrows of iron, and passing them through the brick-kiln." No enumeration is attempted of those who thus suffered, but the vagueness of the language implies that such tortures were inflicted on all who could be caught.

By this dreadful triumph the military supremacy of David seemed to be finally confirmed, and with it his despotic authority over his own people. If about this time the twenty-first Psalm was composed in his honour (as the English reader easily persuades himself),[2] the praise was destined shortly to become as a cup of gall to the miserable man. He returned home from his public display to suffer the pangs of a guilty conscience on the matter of Uriah and his wife. With a haste that barely observed the most necessary rules of decorum, he had publicly espoused Bathsheba, as soon as the days of mourning for Uriah were completed. This probably indicates only one full month.[3] Even if David could have better dissembled his passion, his guilt could not have been kept secret, and the prophet Nathan was bold enough to rebuke and denounce his deed. The self-condemned monarch had too much susceptibility left to resent the interference. He had not been hardened in iniquity by a series of petty unrepented sins, but had plunged headlong into one complicated and enormous crime. Happily for himself, he now confessed his guilt; but the past could not be recalled, and the rest of his reign was sullied by domestic shame, misery, and confusion.

[1] Many respectable critics think that *hard labour* only is intended; and it is possible that a mistake has been made. The Arabic translation has: "He *sawed* them with saws . . . , and *cut* them with knives, etc. . . ."

[2] The substance of the *meaning* agrees better with this period in the time of David, than with the reign of Jehoshaphat, which is the next best place for it. V. 4 is the usual oriental hyperbole; compare Ps. cx. 4, and Dan. ii. 4, iii. 9. If v. 3 ought not to be referred to the Ammonite crown, yet vv. 8—11 excellently agree with punishment of that people. Ewald however thinks the style of Ps. xxi. too polished and soft to be Davidical.

[3] Such was the time allowed to a beautiful captive, in Deut. xxi. 11; and was also the time of mourning for Moses, Deut. xxxiv. 8.

The first outbreak of retribution came upon him from the unbridled passion of his eldest son Amnon. This young man, having conceived a love for his half-sister Tamar, by the advice of his cousin Jonadab[1] entrapped her into his chamber and brutally ravished her. Great as was the rage of the king, remembrance of his own crime withheld him from punishing his son, and Absalom, whose full sister Tamar was, undertook to avenge her himself. At his next sheep-shearing he invited all his brothers to a banquet, in the course of which his servants assailed and slew Amnon. As for Absalom, he instantly fled to his grandfather Talmai, king of Geshúr, who was likely to applaud his deed; while David, torn in pieces between sorrow for Tamar and Amnon, and love for Absalom, for three whole years took no further step in the matter.

The subtle Joab, who narrowly watched the king's mind, perceived that he was desirous of Absalom's return; and the cautious steps by which he proceeded to move for it, indicate the oriental despotism now reigning in David's court. He suborned a woman of Tekoah to act the part of a mourner, and tell a fictitious tale calculated to arouse the paternal affection of the king; after winning his ear and his favour, she ended by entreating him to "fetch home his banished." David perceived that it was Joab's contrivance, but assented to the suggestion. Absalom was accordingly brought back to Jerusalem, but the king refused to set eyes upon him for two full years more. This was a sore trial to the young man, who was already looking forward with impatience to the day when he should succeed his father on the throne. He perhaps had still an elder brother, Chileab,[2] born of Abigail the Carmelitess; but his own birth of a king's daughter seemed to give him the preference. Nevertheless, this must depend upon David's favour; and he was uneasy to see his brothers occupied in public offices, and moving freely in the king's court, while he was himself shut up in a private station. By a strange and violent stratagem,[3]

---

[1] Jonadab was son of Shimeah, David's brother. The extreme improbability of his giving such advice may lead to many surmises: but no sharpness of thought will enable even contemporaries to pierce through the dark deeds which oriental harems hide.
[2] It is not certain that Chileab was still alive.
[3] By burning Joab's barley-field.

he forced Joab to introduce him to David's presence, and an apparent reconciliation took place. The king (it is said) "kissed Absalom;" but the result shows that Absalom's ambition was only stimulated, not gratified. He discerned perhaps that David's heart only, and not his judgment, was moved in his favour, and that while he loved Absalom best, he might still choose another son for his successor. No time was to be lost, it seemed, and Absalom plunged into a headlong career.

Of his own personal accomplishments he was doubtless fully conscious. The same remarkable beauty and winning manners which excited his father's fondness, drew also the admiration of the people, who are likely to have forgiven his brother's murder, considering the enormity of the provocation; and he flattered himself perhaps that the odium under which the old king lay on account of Uriah the Hittite, would aid his attempts. Having gained at length the right of presenting himself freely at court, he now used his position there to seduce, by blandishments, promises, and seditious insinuations, the suitors who came from various parts; and in order to make a semiregal display, he equipped for himself chariots and horses (a new luxury in Israel) with fifty outrunners. Under pretence of paying a vow in Hebron, he repaired thither with 200 men; and after seizing that strong town,—David's original seat of government,—he had himself proclaimed king by sound of trumpet, in many parts of Israel simultaneously. David was confounded both by the unexpectedness of the event, and by the fear that it implied general disaffection. In this exigence, when news came of fresh and fresh revolt, he could trust none but his foreign troops, the Cherethites, Pelethites, and Gittites, with all of whom he marched out of Jerusalem, utterly uncertain whither to betake himself.[1] Zadok however and Abiathar, and the whole priestly body, held firm to him, and were willing to have carried out the ark of God to accompany his flight; but he remanded them to Jerusalem, and recommended his faithful counsellor Hushai to join the party of Absalom and undermine by craft the

[1] It is judged by Ewald to be a true tradition, which states that David in his present distress composed the third Psalm. That he does not name Absalom is not to be wondered at.

crafty advice of Ahithophel,—an unprincipled but very able man who had espoused Absalom's cause. Ahithophel well understood that for a son who conspires against his father there can be no half-measures; and he urged Absalom to take public possession of his father's concubines,[1] —as an indisputable demonstration of deadly feud; advice upon which Absalom forthwith acted. Ahithophel moreover pressed him instantly to chase David with an overwhelming force, and slay him before he could recover himself. But Hushai now interfered with specious reasons, and spoiled the counsel of Ahithophel, who forthwith went home and hanged himself. At the same time David received tidings of his danger through Hushai and Zadok, and with no farther delay crossed the Jordan to the city of Mahhanaim, where Ishbosheth had reigned. Here he received abundant supplies from three men, whose names have deserved record. The first was no other than Shobi, son of the Ammonite Nahash, perhaps become David's viceroy on the deposition of his brother Hanun; the second was Machir of Lodebar, who had acted as host and father to Mephibosheth, until David took notice of him: this man was in all probability a warm friend of the house of Saul. The third was the aged and blind chieftain Barzillai the Gileadite. In this pastoral district wealth consisted chiefly in cattle and food: brave men abounded, who at the call of their leaders flocked round their legitimate king, and a powerful army was soon assembled.

Absalom had pursued his father over Jordan into Gilead, taking as the captain of his host Amasa, son of Ithra or Jether the Ishmaelite, and of Abigail,[2] David's sister. A decisive battle was fought in a place called the Forest of Ephraim (a name which might mislead us into the belief that it was west of Jordan), and David's people were victorious. Absalom is said to have met with a most singular fate. In riding through the forest in violent haste, his head was caught by the boughs of an oak, and he was left dangling in the air by the escape of his mule. On receiving news of this, Joab made haste to slay him before the king should be able to interfere; for David had

[1] David had probably taken his *wives* with him.
[2] Whether Abigail was *mother* or *step-mother* to Amasa, is left doubtful in 2 Sam. xvii. 25; but 1 Chron. ii. 17 is distinct.

solemnly commanded all to spare his son's life. In any other man than Joab this might be called patriotism and loyalty; nor in fact can we doubt that it was substantially sound judgment. A son who had waged war so implacable on his father could never again be wisely trusted. In open battle Joab had earned a just right to slay this youth, whose life was so dangerous to his father, his father's friends, and the peace of the nation; and David himself, when his first grief was past, would praise his zeal and his prudence. The immediate effect however was the very opposite. David displayed a public and tumultuous grief for his son's death, which was undoubtedly most unseemly after so many brave men had fallen in defending the king from his attack; and when Joab boldly remonstrated against his proceedings, he with difficulty suppressed his disgust.

A new doubt embarrassed him. So easy had been Absalom's success at Hebron, as to make the attachment of David's own tribe of Judah highly questionable; and he feared to return, unless brought back by their voluntary zeal. In hope of exciting it, he sent to Zadok and Abiathar, distinctly calling on them to escort him home; and by another highly imprudent message to his nephew Amasa, Absalom's captain, promised to make him chief-captain in place of Joab. A senile imbecility, it may be suspected, had already stolen over the king, whose conduct, ever since the announcement of Absalom's revolt, had been unaccountably weak. He could hardly expect that Abishai,—who with Joab and Ittai the Gittite had commanded the forces against Absalom,—would endure to have disgrace put on his brother at such a time and from such a cause; and if he thus trifled away the affections of the men who had just risked their all for him, it would be a poor consolation that he had bought by bribes the momentary allegiance of those, who, but now, had armed against his life. In fact, he was still in the hands of Joab and his brother, and needed their aid to escape a new and immediate danger.

In the late revolt, the unshrinking impiety of Absalom had led many of his party into courses for which they despaired of forgiveness: disaffection was of necessity widely spread, and a quarrel which arose between the men of

Judah and the rest of the Israelites, on the occasion of David's return, inspired new hopes in the seditions. Sheba, the son of Bichri, observing the disgust felt by the rest at the fierce assumption of the men of Judah, set up a new standard of revolt, and was presently followed by formidable numbers. The king gave orders to Amasa to assemble the forces of Judah in three days, and pursue Sheba before the movement should grow into actual revolution; but, from whatever causes, Amasa was longer than the time appointed, and David was forced to commission his other nephew Abishai to put down the alarming conspiracy. This was enough for the two sons of Zeruiah, who went both together, though one only had been sent. They fell in with their cousin Amasa at Gibeon, and Joab without hesitation murdered him in the highway, just as, many years before, he had murdered Abner. Then resuming the pursuit of Sheba, he shut him up in Abel Bethmaachah; where the people of the town, to escape a siege, cut off Sheba's head and threw it over the wall.[1] Such was the end of this tragical commotion, which left behind it many serious feuds, and damaged all parties concerned. We must here name some particulars which affected the family of Saul.

Ziba, the servant of Mephibosheth, immediately upon Absalom's rebellion, slandered his master to David, as now filled with hopes of getting the throne for himself; and David, in such a time of trial, credulously receiving the statement, bestowed upon Ziba (so far as his royal word still had power) all the estates of the son of Jonathan. On David's return, Mephibosheth presented himself in person, and complained of his servant's calumny; alleging (it would seem) that Ziba had taken to himself the credit of the presents which Mephibosheth had sent by his hand to David, and that nothing but lameness had prevented Mephibosheth from following the king in his flight. That David felt he had been precipitate and unjust, is clear by his conduct:—he ordered Ziba to restore *half* of the estate to Mephibosheth. It cannot be doubted, that since it had become manifest how little the king retained the hearts of his people, a new jealousy of the house of Saul

[1] This is the most probable crisis of David's life for his composing the 18th Psalm.

had come over him. The son of Jonathan was indeed lame; but *he* had a son, Micha, who might in a few years prove a troublesome aspirant, as the legitimate representative of Saul's eldest-born. Besides, Sheba, the late rebel, was a Benjamite: and Shimei of Gerar, a near relative of Saul, had cast stones, and still more cruel curses, at David; and though, on his way towards Jerusalem, the king would not permit Abishai to punish Shimei, and pronounced over him a public solemn pardon, a later event would prove (if we could trust the statements), that this was merely ostentatious policy, and not Christian forgiveness. A jealous fear now dictated to cripple all the family of Saul, as far as it could be done under forms of justice, and Mephibosheth accordingly was doomed to forfeit half his estate. This was the more ungracious, inasmuch as Mephibosheth's old friend and host, Machir of Lodebar, had been so eminent in generosity towards David and his destitute army in the late deplorable rebellion.

It would have been well if this had been all; but a darker and bloodier plot was to follow, suggested by the occurrence of a three years' famine. It is now well understood, that, as in the frequent tossing up of a crown-piece there will occur periodically (what are called) "runs of luck" on the side of the heads,[1] so the seasons, which commonly vary within narrow limits, at distant times exhibit more prolonged series of very good or very bad weather. When poverty, improvidence, or the ravages of civil war aggravate the calamity of several bad seasons, real famine arises, which an ignorant age imputes to a divine judgment. In the case before us, there possibly *was* a divine retribution of a certain kind; for the recent convulsions may truly have had much to do with the famine. But it was very undesirable that the nation should think thus, and some other reason was needed. David inquired solemnly of Jehovah (we may suppose, by Urim and Thummim), what was the cause of the calamity.

[1] This whole argument, *and the phraseology*, was taken by me from an article in the Penny Cyclopædia, which seeks to illustrate the subject without the remotest idea of theological controversy. Yet it has drawn upon me the grave rebuke of the British Quarterly, which feels "lively regret" that my religion "has not taught me *tolerance of speech* for the views taken by others." Forsooth, I am to expound the doctrine of chances, without alluding to anything so vulgar or trivial as the tossing of a penny or casting of a die!

Common conscience might perhaps have replied :—it is on
account of our impious civil war ; or for Absalom's fratri-
cide and incest ; or for Amnon's brutal lust ; or for David's
murder of Uriah and adultery with Bathsheba ; or (if
national deeds could have been thought of) for the tortured
Ammonites, for the slaughtered Edomites and Moabites.
Far otherwise ran the priestly response, in the name of
Jehovah : *It is for Saul, and for his bloody house, because
he slew the Gibeonites.*

How Saul massacred the priests at Nôb, is distinctly recorded ; concerning his slaughter of the Gibeonites, who
waited on the tabernacle, we know nothing ; but as it
cannot have been more atrocious than the former, it is
impossible to help feeling that the vengeance here in name
exacted for the one crime, was in fact demanded for the
other. But whatever the guilt of Saul, his grandchildren
were innocent. Most rude nations have approved of cutting off the children of a traitor simultaneously with the
father ;[1] and if the priestly party had murdered Saul and
all his family in the crudeness of passion, no one could
criticise it. But when he had been some thirty years in
his grave, when his legitimate sons also had perished,
and all their children except Mephibosheth,—then to lay
on his daughter's sons the sin of a grandfather, was an
iniquity so shocking to common feeling as to need no
Ezekiel to rebuke it.[2] Such however was the course of
events :—David asked the Gibeonites what atonement
would satisfy them, and they demanded seven male descendants of Saul " to hang up before Jehovah " on Saul's
own estate of Gibeah. The king remembered his romantic attachment to Jonathan,[3] and spared that branch
of the family ; but he devoted the five sons of Merab,[4]

[1] The law of Moses, as we now read it (Deut. xxiv. 16), especially forbids it : but we shall do very ill to assume, that David had the book of Deuteronomy at his side.

[2] Ezek. xviii., whole chapter. In short, v. 20, " The son shall not bear the iniquity of the father."

[3] The narrator (2 Sam. xxi. 7) attributes David's exemption of Mephibosheth to *the oath of Jehovah* between David and Jonathan. But there was, according to the account, a similar oath between David and Saul, 1 Sam. xxiv. 20, 21.

[4] *Michal* in the common version, for *Merab*, is undoubtedly an error. See 1 Sam. xviii. 19, where it appears that Merab was given in marriage to Adriel the Meholathite, the father of these five innocent victims. One of the two sons of Saul by Rizpah, daughter of Aiah, was called Mephibosheth, as well as the son of Jonathan.

daughter of Saul, and the two sons of Saul's concubine Rizpah. These seven men the Gibeonites took, and hanged them, as they had proposed. The bereaved Rizpah, says our narrator, " spread sackcloth for her on the rock, from the beginning of harvest until water dropped upon them out of heaven, and suffered neither the birds of the air to rest upon them by day, nor the beasts of the field by night." This indicates that even their burial had been forbidden; as if a mother's heart were not sufficiently wrung by the slaughter of her innocent sons, unless their corpses also be treated with contumely. It is a melancholy thing, that Christians can so ill read the lessons of *both* their Testaments, as to believe that God could approve of this human sacrifice.

But this did not suffice. It was requisite to obliterate every monument of Saul's reign, and to impress as deeply as possible on the public mind that this guilty family was for ever to be degraded into a private station. Accordingly, the bones of Saul and Jonathan were disinterred from Jabesh Gilead, and conveyed to the sepulchre of Kish, Saul's father. After this, it was believed, the pollution of the land having been removed, God was appeased, and fruitful seasons returned.

It was to be expected that such internal convulsions would excite the oppressed foreign nations to revolt. Of these, none bore the yoke so ill as the Philistines, who not only remembered how recently they had been superior to the Hebrews in arms as well as in arts, but who, by living in towns under civic constitutions, had become accustomed to municipal independence. The Edomites and the adjoining nations had been too much weakened by enormous destruction to make head against Israel as yet; and besides, it mattered less to them to be subject to a Hebrew instead of a native king, if the former were moderate in his demands: but the more republican Philistines, like the Phœnicians and the Greeks, ill endured any foreign dominion, and panted for freedom. About this period four severe battles are recorded, which resulted from the attempts of the Philistines to shake off the Hebrew yoke. In the first, David was nearly slain by a Philistine champion, but was saved by his heroic nephew Abishai. In each of the four battles one gigantic Philistine is said to have been killed, which throws an unhistorical air over the details. In fact, it is manifest that these are erroneous; for a *brother* of Goliath, who was a man in full strength when David was a youth, is represented as a Philistine hero, in a battle fought when David was enfeebled with age, and no longer allowed to expose himself to the enemy (2 Sam. xxi. 17, 19). Abishai also must have been growing old.

One notable event is recorded, apparently in the later years of this prince, but without a date :—the occurrence of a pestilence. Error inevitable in that age ascribed it to some definite sin nationally incurred : a trespass had to be found. David had done what every prudent king will do, and (we may add) what every ruler who wishes to do his duty must do; he had taken a census of his people. Of course, in his long reign of internal prosperity, the numbers of the Hebrew nation had greatly increased;[1] which would be to all a subject of congratulation and pride. When therefore a pestilence occurred, by which (it was estimated) 70,000 persons died, this was looked on as a punishment for his having numbered the people. Such is the only historical view which we can take of the transaction. The Jewish records however represent Jehovah as sending Gad the seer to David, and allowing him to choose one of three miseries; seven years of famine, three months of defeat by enemies, or three days' pestilence. Of these, David chose the last; and when the plague was ended, propitiated Jehovah by burnt-offerings and peace-offerings at the threshing-floor of Araunah the Jebusite,[2] where David *had seen the destroying angel standing*, when Jehovah bade him to withhold his hand.

[1] The numbers in 2 Sam. xxiv. 9 are, 800,000 fighting men of Israel, and 500,000 of Judah ; while in 1 Chron. xxi. 5, they are 1,100,000 of Israel, and 470,000 of Judah. Strange to add, 1 Chron. xxvii. 24 says that the enumeration was never completed. The very distinction of Israel and Judah may warn us that the estimates belong to a later period ; for in David's reign, *Judah* was a word which excluded *Benjamin*, and was opposed to the *eleven* tribes (or to the twelve, including Levi), not to the *ten*. It is absurd to imagine that Judah was, to all Israel beside, in the ratio of 500 to 800, or even as 470 to 1100, which seems to be a corrected estimate. In 2 Sam. xix. 43 is a similar anachronism ; where the men of Israel say they have *ten parts* in the king as compared to the men of Judah.

[2] David buys the floor of Araunah for fifty shekels of silver in 2 Sam. xxiv. 24, but for six hundred shekels of gold in 1 Chron. xxi. 25. Such exaggerations are throughout characteristic of the Chronicles.

Yet the whole idea that the pestilence was a judgment on David, was perhaps of later origin. If, as there is some ground to think, Psalm xci. was composed by David on occasion of a pestilence, this must apparently have been the æra: the Psalmist there appears wholly unconscious of guilt, and full of a noble faith. Time had doubtless assuaged the deep wounds of David's spirit, and his calamities had not been without their profit. To a late period of his life we may probably refer the fine 32nd Psalm, which breathes high confidence and confirmed wisdom in the midst of its penitence; and reminds us how imperfectly we can judge of the secret workings of men's hearts, whose political actions alone we know. The last piece written by David is also preserved (2 Sam. xxiii.), but its beauty is dimmed to us by its great difficulty and consequent imperfect translation. The centre stanza contains its main object, which is, to hold up a high ideal of a good ruler, which he confesses he has not in his own administration realized.

> A righteous ruler over men, ruling in the fear of God,
> Is as morning light when the sun arises,
> As a morning without clouds,
> As the green blade from the earth by sunshine and by rain.

It ends by lamenting that worthless men cannot be ruled by gentleness, but must be constrained by weapons of war.

After the Philistine outbreak was ended, the increased weakness of the aged king had become evident, and new uneasiness concerning the succession to the throne broke out among his sons. Of his second son, Chileab, we know nothing: Amnon and Absalom, the first and third, were slain; the fourth was Adonijah, son of Haggith, who, like Absalom, had many personal attractions, and had been a favourite of his father. He was now perhaps the eldest son, and hardly believed that his father could mean to give the kingdom to any of the younger ones. Bathsheba however, the widow of Uriah, continued to hold a great ascendency over David. She must have been much younger than the mothers of his elder children; and her son Solomon, as a son of old age, was likely to win the susceptible mind of a prince, whose power of decisive action was exceedingly weakened by his time of life.

Adonijah thought it the safest plan to seize the kingdom, and so forestall Bathsheba's intrigues; and he found a certain part of David's own cabinet ready to aid him. Joab had probably been disaffected ever since David endeavoured to supersede him as captain of the host; and his influence with the army might seem to promise all that Adonijah could wish from that quarter, when Joab joined his cause. Of Abishai we hear no more, and perhaps he had recently died. But the priest *Abiathar* was another important ally. He was grandson of the grandson of Eli, tracing his genealogy by Phinehas, Ahitub, and Ahimelech; and as his father and family were all murdered by Saul for David's sake, it may be suspected that he made larger claims on David's gratitude than were permanently admitted. With the details we are not acquainted; but we find indications that Zadok, who at first was appointed over the tabernacle at Gibeon, was also admitted to minister before the ark in Jerusalem, jointly with Abiathar, though still the chief rank rested with the latter. It is possible that Abiathar thought, by joining Adonijah, to secure for himself and his male posterity the pre-eminent position which he was in danger of losing through Zadok. With the head of the army and the head of the priesthood to aid him, Adonijah now, like his brother Absalom, went out in royal style, "with chariots and horsemen and fifty outrunners," and having made a great sacrifice at the stone of Zoheleth near Enrogel, invited all the king's sons except Solomon, with the chief men of Judah, to a public banquet, at which he intended formally to assume the honours of royalty. He had kept clear of inviting those who were known to be of Solomon's party; these are specified as Nathan the prophet, Zadok the priest, Benaiah commander of the foreign body-guard, and "the mighty men;" by which we are to understand the celebrated warriors who fought round the king's person in battle.

Judging by the analogy of other despotisms, we may believe that the king had come to lean more and more on his foreign body-guard. We have seen that in the revolt of Absalom he was able at once to count on the fidelity of the Cherethites, Pelethites, and Gittites, when the allegiance of the general army was doubtful and divided. This must have taught a lesson not to be neglected ; and considering the very flourishing state of the finances, we can hardly doubt that Benaiah's troops were at present the most effective and perhaps the most numerous part of David's standing army. Benaiah had thus become a more important person than Joab; and his force now obtained the empire for Solomon. Bathsheba first broke to David the unpleasant secret, and with the help of Nathan induced him to take immediate measures for securing the succession of the throne. Benaiah marched hastily with his guards and surprised Adonijah while yet at the banquet. The guests were dispersed, and Solomon was proclaimed king. No immediate notice was taken of the chief actors in this conspiracy. Solomon indeed publicly pardoned his brother Adonijah for the past; nevertheless it is certain that, together with Joab and Abiathar, he was from that day devoted to ruin.

Soon after these events the strength of David sank rapidly. With his last breath he charged Solomon to remember gratefully the services of old Barzillai the Gileadite, and admit his sons to the royal table; but to find some pretext for putting to death Joab son of Zeruiah, and Shimei the Benjamite, whom, some ten years before, he had ostentatiously pardoned for cursing him. So at least our record states ; but it is very credible that David was more sincere in his forgiveness, and that his charge to Solomon against these two persons is no more true than the charge of Augustus to Tiberius Cæsar to put to death his daughter and her son. The despot who slays for his own policy shifts the crime on to the memory of his predecessor.

David, the son of Jesse, after a reign of forty years, closed his eyes to all mortal ambition, and slept with his fathers. Of him we may say, as of some other very eminent persons, it would have been well had he died before absolute power had corrupted him. The complicated baseness involved in his murder of Uriah so casts his honour in the dust, that thenceforth we rather pity and excuse than admire him. All the brilliancy alike of his chivalry and of his piety is sullied, and cold minds suspect his religious raptures of hypocrisy. But we cannot wonder at sins of passion in a despotic and victorious prince.

David was not indeed an Antoninus, an Alfred, or a Saint Louis; yet neither was he one of the vulgar herd of kings. The polygamy in which he indulged so injuriously must in part be laid to his personal weakness, when we observe how restrained (in comparison) was his predecessor Saul.[1] Nevertheless, as a man, he was affectionate and generous, sympathetic and constitutionally pious : as a king, his patronage of religious persons was highly judicious, and his whole devotional character of permanent importance to the best interests of his people and of mankind; as a warrior, he taught Israel a mutual confidence and common pride in Jehovah their God; and first elevated his countrymen into a ruling and leading race, whose high place it was to legislate for and teach the heathen around. His career may serve to warn all who are wanting in depth of passion or enlarged knowledge of human nature, that those on whose conduct society has relaxed its wholesome grasp are not to be judged of by their partial outbreaks of evil, but by the amount of positive good which they habitually exhibit. Compared with the great statesmen of the educated nations of Europe, David's virtues and vices appear alike puerile; but among Asiatics he was a great man; and of his own posterity, though several, who were happily subjected to greater restraints, were far more consistent in goodness, there is none who more attracts our interest and our love than the heroic and royal Psalmist.

[1] Saul, as far as we know, had only one wife and one concubine, Rizpah; and it is quite possible that the wife was removed by death before the concubine was espoused, since Rizpah's children are named in company with their nephews, as if much younger than Saul's legitimate sons. A concubine, in ancient times, was only a wife *of inferior rank*, and the union was just as permanent as with a wife.

CHAPTER IV.

REIGN OF SOLOMON.

SAUL and David had each of them been installed in the throne of Israel by the solemn act of the elders, as kings accepted by the free voice of the nation, and bound to respect its liberties. But Solomon was elevated to the supreme authority by his father's will and by the aid of the irresistible body-guard;[1] not indeed without the sanction of Zadok the priest and Nathan the prophet; yet the helplessness of Abiathar, the elder priest and the representative of Eli, showed clearly enough that the swords of Benaiah were now the decisive influence. Israel in fact had for years been accustomed to address David with unmanly servility; and although the old king's popularity had been thoroughly worn out, the nation was ready to welcome his youthful son with a credulous loyalty. In young princes, as yet uncorrupted by power, and guiltless

[1] The Chronicler not merely passes over the conspiracy of Adonijah, and the prompt military proceedings of David by which Solomon was made king, but introduces an account intended to glorify the constitutional decorum and religious spirit of the whole proceeding (1 Chr. xxviii. xxix). David (says he) assembled all the princes of the nation, civil and military, and told them of the earnest desire which he had felt to build a temple to Jehovah; but *Jehovah* had forbidden him, as having been a warrior, but *had now chosen his son Solomon to succeed him* and build the temple. David then delivers to Solomon an exact "pattern" of the temple and all its furniture, with all the materials of precious or common metals, precious stones and marble, and requests the princes to contribute to the same sacred object. Of course they contribute with a zeal very edifying to the people of Nehemiah. Then follows a thanksgiving by David, of such eminent beauty, that for the sake of it we can almost pardon the fabulous history in which it has been imbedded. Afterwards is a sacrifice of 1000 bullocks, 1000 rams, and 1000 lambs, preparatory to the final object of the whole meeting, *the free election of Solomon by the assembly to be king*, in confirmation of his election by Jehovah. The untrustworthiness of the whole is strongly marked in its last words—that the congregation simultaneously *elected Zadok to be priest*. This is directly opposed to the book of Kings. Abiathar continued to be the priest until after the death of Adonijah. The Chronicler did not like to confess that Zadok was indebted for his sacred pre-eminence to the mere will of a despotic prince, who broke the hierarchical succession. In the Chronicles, not only is the disgrace of Abiathar omitted, but no notice of him occurs in the history except the formal statement that " Abimelech son of Abiathar" was colleague of Zadok, 1 Chr. xviii. 16, which is an error reproduced from 2 Sam. viii. 17.

of the evil deeds by which it was won, the common people enthusiastically believe a superhuman virtue to exist; and as the administration passed into Solomon's hands before death surprised his aged father, the new reign commenced without any shock or felt internal jar.

There appears nevertheless to have been some commotion among the foreign nations now subject to the Hebrew sway. They might naturally expect feebleness in a young king who had never headed an army, and they may have reckoned on some internal disorders to aid them. Our accounts of this reign are too defective as to all foreign affairs to allow of appeal to historical details; but an echo has been preserved to us of certain attempts to throw off the yoke, in a celebrated psalm (Ps. ii.) composed in honour of Solomon's empire by a prophet of the day, who seems to put the words into the mouth of Solomon himself.

1. Why rage the peoples? and why do the nations plan things vain?
Why assemble the kings of earth, why plot together the rulers,
Against Jehovah and his anointed one?
Saying, "Let us break their bands asunder,
Let us cast their cords away from us."

2. He that sitteth in the heavens shall laugh,
Jehovah shall mock at them.
Then he shall say unto them in his wrath,
(And vex them in his sore displeasure,)
"Behold! I have set up my king,
On Zion, my hill of holiness."

3. I[1] will rehearse the decree which Jehovah hath uttered to me:
Jehovah hath said unto me: "Thou art my Son;
This day have I begotten thee.
Ask of me, and I will give thee the nations for thy inheritance,
The uttermost parts of earth for thy possession.
Thou shalt break them with a rod of iron;
Thou shalt dash them in pieces like a potsherd."

4. Be wise now therefore, O ye kings;
Be instructed, ye judges of earth.
Serve Jehovah with fear;
Rejoice with trembling.
Worship in purity,[2] lest he be angry,
And ye perish straightway, should his wrath be a little kindled.

5. Blessed are all they that put their trust in him.

Whatever disturbances were threatened among Philis-

---

[1] I, Solomon.

[2] This word in good Hebrew cannot mean *a Son*. The LXX. renders the clause Δράξασθε παιδείας, "lay hold of instruction." We have nearly followed Ewald.

tines, Moabites, or Damascenes, were presently quelled with no serious effort by the unimpaired vigour of David's armies; and as far as can be ascertained, no farther attempt was made to shake off the yoke until the later days of Solomon. The young prince was therefore fully at leisure to devote himself to his internal affairs, and first of all to that first object of interest, the secure establishment of his own title to the crown against all competitors.

Four great political offenders had been ostensibly, but not sincerely, pardoned:—Adonijah brother of Solomon, Joab the king's first cousin, Abiathar the priest, and Shimei the kinsman of Saul who cursed David. The ruin of all four was resolved upon, and Solomon was only waiting for a specious pretence. Nor was one long wanting. David in extreme old age had received into his harem, by the superfluous zeal of his courtiers, a young damsel of remarkable beauty, Abishag the Shunamite. If it be true that they sought far and wide, and picked her out of all Israel, it cannot be wonderful that her brilliancy attracted the love of Adonijah; who engaged the interest of Bathsheba, mother of Solomon, to make his suit to the king for the hand of Abishag. But no sooner had the unsuspicious Bathsheba preferred her request, than the king felt or affected great rage, alleging that this was a plot for dethroning him; and forthwith sent Benaiah with his myrmidons, who murdered the king's brother on the spot where they found him.

So flagrant an act of despotism had not been seen in Israel since Doeg the Edomite massacred the priests at Saul's command. It was at least politic of Solomon to follow up the deed by commanding the death of Joab as a partner in the imagined new conspiracy. Joab fled to "the tabernacle of Jehovah" (which here perhaps means the tent in Jerusalem, in which the ark was kept), and caught hold of the horns of the altar. When he would not come forth, Benaiah hesitated to attack him in the holy place, until he had been re-assured by Solomon, who reminded him of the double assassination which Joab had perpetrated. Then at last Benaiah broke through all scruples, and with his own hand laid the hoary criminal dead at the foot of the altar.

Neither was the old Abiathar altogether to escape, although his life was spared, in remembrance of his long sufferings as David's early comrade. He was ordered to confine himself to his own private estate at Anathoth, and was deposed from all his dignities and emoluments as priest to Jehovah. This was clearly done by the simple will of the king. A later generation softened to its own feelings the harshness of an act so unconstitutional, by the belief that this ejection of Abiathar and his descendants from the priestly office was a fulfilment of the denunciation of Jehovah, uttered against the house of Eli by the mouth of the boy Samuel. Be this as it may, such was the *political* coincidence which deprived Israel of one of its two great priestly families, and left Zadok and his posterity as the most distinguished representatives of the house of Aaron.

As Zadok was promoted to the place of Abiathar, so was Benaiah to the captaincy of the host vacated by Joab. But more work of the same odious kind still remained for Benaiah. Shimei had given no excuse for pretending that he was an accomplice of the three great victims; and an arbitrary device was needed for entangling him. The king ordered him to build a house at Jerusalem, and not to set foot out of the city on pain of death. Three years later, two of Shimei's servants ran away from him into Gath; upon which Shimei pursued, overtook them, and brought them back. On his return Solomon upbraided him with his disobedience, and having bitterly reminded him of his curses on David, commanded Benaiah to hew him down. The order was obeyed in the style of military despots who disdain the sanctities, the decencies, or the hypocrisy of a civil tribunal. So at length, it may seem, King Solomon was able to breathe freely and to forget all domestic jealousies.

From the reign of David onward historical documents were carefully kept, and select accounts compiled by contemporaries. Nathan the prophet and Gad the seer were the chief authorities known to a latter age concerning the life of David himself: for the Acts of Solomon reference is made to the same Nathan, to Ahijah the Shilonite, and in part also to Iddo the seer.[1] Nevertheless it must

[1] 1 Chron. xxix. 29; 2 Chron. ix. 29; 1 Kings xi. 41. As the Phœnicians possessed an alphabet and spoke a Hebrew dialect, while the Egyptians afforded

be confessed that we know very indistinctly the chronology of Solomon's life, and we are driven to write concerning it rather as in a book of antiquities than in the consecutive manner of a history. There are few marked events to divide this reign into portions. It glides by like a dream of prosperity, so dazzling the mind that we take no note of time, until the calm breaks up with a storm, and the unhealthiness of the brilliant pageantry manifests itself.

Young Solomon ascended to his enviable position with the usual aspirations of young princes, and something more. Undoubtedly he desired to reign in glory and magnificence, but he also wished his magnificence to be displayed signally in the honour of his father's God, and he had already a clear conception that though arms might win empire, policy and wisdom must preserve it. As a basis for all his other greatness, he endeavoured to order his finances well, and to open to himself by commerce various new sources of gain. We shall therefore first give such account as we are able of his traffic and his wealth.

I. The delusiveness of the *numbers* transmitted to us has often been remarked upon, and it is utterly vain to endeavour to found upon them any estimate of the wealth of Solomon. It is enough that we know the land of Israel itself to have been highly productive in wheat, barley, honey, oil, and wine, in wool, hides, and certain kinds of timber; for all of which the Phœnicians afforded markets close at hand, and gladly repaid the Israelites in every sort of manufactured and ornamental work, or, in part, by the precious and the useful metals. In hewing timber for elegant uses, the Israelites were indeed unskilled, and want of roads was an impediment, except where the choiceness of the wood permitted its carriage by animal strength. In such cases the Tyrians themselves aided in the hewing. But Solomon had two other projects, neither of which he could execute without Tyrian aid,—maritime traffic by the way of the Red Sea,

papyrus, the seers and prophets of Solomon's day were at no loss for the means of writing. Yet prose composition was quite in its infancy; and the Chronicles of the Kings are likely to have been concise and dry facts, like those of the Middle Age chroniclers.

and land traffic across the Syrian desart to Babylon and Media, of which the latter was not carried out till the middle of his reign. The ports of Edom on the Red Sea had long been barren possessions in his father's hand. To build in them a fleet of ships suited for the navigation of that difficult coast was certainly an arduous and spirited enterprise, which indeed, if we were to judge solely by the accounts of modern travellers, might seem simply impossible. Nevertheless, by his excellent understanding with Hiram, king of Tyre, the fleet[1] was not only built but duly manned with a mixed crew of Hebrews and Tyrians. On the details of its voyages whole treatises have been written. That it sailed to Sheba, the southernmost angle of Arabia, no one can doubt. The celebrated *Ophir*, the most distant point of the course, was possibly in the province of Oman in Arabia, where Seetzen has pointed out the name as still existing. Although it was outside of the straits of Bab el mandeb, the *three years* allowed for the voyage was long enough to enable the navigators to wait quietly for the month in which they could safely commit their frail vessels to the Indian Ocean. The return merchandise which the Hebrews regarded as characteristic of Ophir, —gold and silver, ivory, monkeys, and peacocks,—do not all agree equally well with Arabia; and were not Ophir generally named by the Hebrews in connexion with places in that great peninsula, this might make us incline to the opinion that it was on the east coast of Africa. But we have no proof that the ivory was produced round Ophir: it may have come thither from India. The chief wealth however which this traffic conferred, depended on a power of selling again such as the Phœnicians possessed. Spices in great abundance, whether from India, Arabia, or Africa, were to be had in the marts of Sheba; and in

---

[1] It is called *a fleet of Tarshish*, but there is no doubt that this means a fleet of ships *similar to those in which* the Tyrians sailed to Tarshish, or Tartessus, in Spain. This has been often illustrated by supposing an Englishman to say, that "a fleet of *Indiamen* was built to sail to the coast of New York." The words in 1 Kings x. 22, "a navy of Tarshish *with the navy of Hiram*," are obscure, and 2 Chron. viii. 18 makes the matter worse,—"Hiram *sent ships* by the hand of his servants, and they went with the servants of Solomon to Ophir." But the chronicler is in hopeless confusion about Tarshish, Ophir, and the Red Sea, 2 Chron. xx. 36.

the whole basin of the Mediterranean the consumption of incense for religious worship was enormous. To the carriers of this commodity a good profit always accrued; and although the Egyptians[1] perhaps made their full share of it, as certainly did the land caravans of Syria, Solomon and Hiram also found their account in the trade. Ivory, almug[2] and other scented woods, precious stones,—besides gold, in which Sheba was very abundant in those times,—received a new value by being transported into the Grecian seas.

We have less distinct information as to the results of the trade across the Syrian desert. One thing is not to be omitted,—that it could not be established without fresh conquests, which are so named in our later record, as to imply that they were made in the middle of Solomon's reign, after he had finished the temple and his own palace. He then marched, perhaps in person, and conquered the district called Hamath-Zobah, a name not found elsewhere, but which we may gather to be the outlying country to the north-east, bounded by the Euphrates, for which the kings of Hamath and Zobah contended. It would appear[3] that Solomon now possessed himself of the city of Tiphsah (or Thapsacus) on the Euphrates, and fortified Tadmor (or Palmyra) in the desart. We also hear of *store-cities* which he built in Hamath, undoubtedly to hold his north-eastern merchandise, which must have been carried upon the backs of camels. As the heavy produce of Palestine cannot have been sent out by such a conveyance, we are left to conjecture that Solomon's caravans carried those Phœnician or Egyptian light and elegant manufactures, which were unrivalled by the home-productions of the countries visited. To direct such operations, the knowledge and experience of the Tyrians was essential; and as we hear little further of it, we cannot be sure that they here zealously assisted, or whether the results were alike satisfactory to Solomon's revenue

---

[1] We do not know how far the Egyptian prejudice against sea-voyages may have crippled them.
[2] The *almug* wood came from Ophir; 1 Kings x. 11. The Chronicler speaks of *algum* trees in Lebanon, 2 Chron. ii. 8: but this is probably an error. The wood intended is supposed to be the red sandal-wood.
[3] 1 Kings iv. 24; ix. 18, 19; 2 Chron. viii. 1—6.

as to his pride. It may even have been a losing trade, and have contributed to his later humiliation.

In estimating its returns, it must be remembered that the vast expense of garrisoning and provisioning these distant cities in the midst of hostile nations ought all to be deducted from the profits. Besides Thapsacus and Palmyra, Baalbek (or Heliopolis) was very probably among the cities which he held, and may be included among the "store-cities of Hamath,"[1] even if it be not denoted by the name *Baalath*,[2] about which there is controversy.

The late date which the Chronicler appears to assign to Solomon's conquest of Hamath-Zobah, and consequent establishment of the north-eastern trade, decidedly favours the suspicion that in this whole scheme his ambition overreached his judgment. For it is clear in the history, that in his later years this king oppressed his subjects grievously by taxation; which strongly implies that his mercantile profits were no longer what they had been.

A matter of no small importance is stated to us very drily—the dissatisfaction of Hiram king of Tyre with the recompense which Solomon made to him after receiving twenty-four years' aid. The recompense consisted of twenty towns in the land of Galilee; which so little pleased Hiram, that he named the district Cabul (or *disgust*), and refused to occupy it. We may conjecture that the towns were too far inland, and with too insecure a frontier, for him to protect and hold. Strange to add, Solomon re-occupies and fortifies them,[3] and is so far from giving any compensation to Hiram, that he *receives* from him 120 talents of gold. There is evidently something suppressed here. It is difficult to avoid suspecting that a breach took place between the two powers at this time, and that Hiram prudently yielded, though with much disgust, to Solomon's superior might by land; and that when the Hebrew king proceeded to conquer Hamath-Zobah, and endeavoured to monopolize the north-eastern trade, he had no aid from Tyre, and in the result met with damaging losses. But all such topics are

---

[1] 2 Chron. viii. 4. [2] 1 Kings ix. 18.
[3] 1 Kings ix. 10—14; 2 Chron. viii. 2.

glibly passed over in the narrative, although the hiatus cannot be concealed.

With Egypt also the king opened a commerce previously unknown. Particular mention is made of the *linen yarn* thence imported (perhaps chiefly for re-exportation), and of the horses and chariots. In passing, we learn an interesting fact,—that princes of the Hittites still existed in social independence in the midst of the Israelites, who bought the Egyptian horses and chariots, as also did many of the princes of Syria. The Egyptian breed, it may even be judged by paintings, was particularly fine, being, in appearance, only a more powerful Arab. Africa however was probably the native land of this horse. The same paintings show us the compact, light, yet solid fabric of the Egyptian chariot; the building of which, when springs were not yet thought of, was a peculiarly difficult art. Solomon had the means of paying for his Egyptian merchandise by the native wine and oil of Palestine. The old Greeks in general believed that the Egyptians had none but *barley*-wine, and *toddy* made from the palm-tree. Herodotus positively says that they had no vines in their country : and this may have been true of *Lower* Egypt. The error is accounted for by the very active importation of Greek and Phœnician wine into that country, which proves that the native Egyptian wine was either very inferior or very deficient in quantity : probably both. The hills of Palestine are suited to rear vines of a superior quality, though little wine is now made of them, in deference to the scruples of the Turks. As for *oil*, a later prophet [1] alludes to the carriage of it into Egypt. The olive to this day grows and flourishes almost without care in any corner of rock [2] round Jerusalem, where it might seem to have no soil; and yields oil abundantly. Considering the enormous use of it under an African sun for the purposes of soap, butter, and tallow, the olive-grounds of Judah, with Egypt for the market, must have been a more valuable possession than mines of gold. *Honey* was probably another article for

---

[1] Hosea xii. 1.
[2] The beautiful poetry of Deut. xxxii. 13 is at the same time sober prose: "Jehovah has made Jacob *to suck honey out of the rock*, and *oil out of the hard flint.*"

export of first importance, since sugar was unknown; but *corn* was not wanted in Egypt.

On the whole, it must be remembered that the foreign trade of Solomon was carried on by himself as an individual merchant,—in fact, as the only merchant of the community. Private Hebrews could not build themselves ships at Elath or Eziongeber; and probably they either were not allowed to send their own camels and goods with the king's caravans, or had to purchase the permission by a heavy payment. The celebrated commerce of Ophir is likely to have been far less profitable than that with the nearer countries, Egypt and Tyre; but the distant traffic struck men's imaginations more. The royal demesnes in Israel possessed by David were considerable, and the accumulated treasure bequeathed by him very large; and since foreign tribute, paid in kind,—added to the ordinary tribute of Israel,—was probably enough to defray the general expenses of government, the king found a large balance in his own hands which he could apply as mercantile *capital*. Indeed, the nature of the result shows that this was certainly the case. By the potent aid of monopoly he became, at least in the first half of his reign, a most successful merchant, and soon attracted the wonder and envy of foreigners.

The most renowned stranger who visited the court of Solomon was the queen of Sheba. Her proper territory was in the extreme south of Arabia, having a coast on the Indian Ocean as well as on the Red Sea; yet in the time of Strabo, this government or people was regarded as reaching along nearly the whole Arabian coast of the Red Sea, till it met the Nabathæans. It is evident that the people of Sheba inherited a very ancient civilization, with many advantages and some peculiar enormities. Among the last must be reckoned the revolting institution of *polyandry*,[1] or (in practice) the marriage of several brothers at once to a single wife, which is known still to prevail in certain districts of India and Thibet. This may seem to ally the people of Sheba to an Indian stock. Their language however, though widely different from the Arabic of literature, is supposed to class them with Arabs

[1] Strabo, xvi. ch. 4. He imputes the practice, apparently, to the Nabathæans also.

and Hebrews. Since at a later period the Jewish faith became very powerful in Sheba, insomuch that some of its kings are called Jewish, it is interesting to find at this early date the impression made by Solomon and his monotheistic religion on his royal visitant. Her valuable presents show the close intimacy which was arising between the two states by reason of the commerce; and had it been continued, it may seem credible that a greater extension of the Jewish faith would have taken place than was ever afterwards possible. For as yet, only the moral doctrine of Jehovah was declared; narrow Levitism had not grown into a dominant power; vexatious ceremonies had no prominence; there was no repugnance felt towards foreigners; intermarriage with them was easy. Circumcision indeed was insisted on; but this, however offensive to Europe, was a natural and comely practice in the judgment of Egypt, Arabia, Africa, and perhaps of the distant Indian islands. The simple-minded queen found nothing in Solomon's court to repel or annoy her, and she returned (as at least our annalist believed) blessing Jehovah on Solomon's account, and congratulating the people who had such a king.

In consequence of his traffic with Egypt, Solomon was naturally induced,—partly for pomp, partly for service,—to set up a new species of military force, that of horses and chariots. He is stated to have had 1400 chariots and 12,000 horsemen. But this gave decided offence to the more religious portion of his people. It was remembered how gloriously his father, without horses, had vanquished the pride of Hadadezer's chivalry; and how all the honour had been ascribed to Jehovah, with whom a horse is but a vain thing, and who loves by weak instruments to confound the mighty. The feelings of the pious boded no good to Israel from the innovation; and when, in the next reign, Egypt proved a victorious enemy and the cavalry a useless arm of defence, it probably became a fixed traditional principle with the prophetical body, that this proud force was outlandish, heathenish, and unbelieving.

II. From the sources of Solomon's wealth we proceed to his principal use of wealth,—in building. The edifices which deserve to be here noticed are the following: the

Temple, his own Palace, his Queen's Palace, his Piazza (for walking and recreation?), his Porch of Judgment, or law-court, and his house of the forest of Lebanon.[1] The last, it has been conjectured, was so called from the great quantity of cedar used in its construction. Besides these peaceful buildings, Solomon fortified the *Millo*, or citadel of Jerusalem, and added largely to the walls. Various other towns[2] are likewise named, which he had occasion to fortify.

With regard to the splendour of the Temple, a certain moderate caution of belief,—not to say scepticism,—appears to be called for by the circumstances of its history. In the very next reign it was despoiled of all the wealth which could be carried away, by its Egyptian conqueror: this opened to the national regret a wide door for supposing that still more had been lost than really was. That much credulity was here at work appears from collateral facts. The temple was stripped of its principal treasures six times over,—by Shishak king of Egypt, by king Asa, by Jehoash king of Judah, by another Jehoash of Israel, by Ahaz, and by Hezekiah. After the death of Josiah, the king of Egypt could only get one talent of gold out of all Judah. Yet when Nebuchadnezzar soon after captures Jerusalem, it is imagined that he carried off "all the vessels of gold which Solomon had made in the temple of Jehovah;"[3] and although it is added that Nebuchadnezzar "cut them all in pieces," Ezra believed that Cyrus restored these identical articles, 5400 in number.[4] Since at the later period the golden vessels of Solomon certainly existed only in the imagination of the narrator, we cannot feel any great confidence as to the details asserted concerning such points of magnificence 400 years earlier.

We have seen that David, after his first war with Hadadezer, dedicated gold and silver vessels and large quantities of brass to the service of Jehovah, all of which were undoubtedly used for the temple of Solomon. Out of this fact has arisen a long account in detail, how David

[1] In Isaiah (xxii. 8) we find "the house of the forest" alluded to as an arsenal for arms within the city of David.
[2] Hazor, Megiddo, Gezer of the Philistines, one or both Beth-horons, Baalath, and Tadmor in the wilderness.
[3] 2 Kings xxiv. 13: contrast 1 Kings xiv. 26. [4] Ezra i. 11.

left to Solomon a pattern of every part of the house, and an account by weight of every vessel that was to be made, with a splendid estimate of the total weight of metal (which however is not consistent with itself),[1] and of the additional contributions made by the princes of Israel. David is even alleged in one fragmentary passage to have prepared the hewn stones, the cedar wood, and other matters, by help of the Tyrians and other foreign artificers; but this is clearly an anticipation of the proceedings of Solomon.[2]

It will be remembered that by the displacement of Abiathar, Zadok his successor naturally gave up all connexion with the tabernacle and high altar at Gibeon; and it now became a question, whether to retain the separate establishment at Gibeon or not. And this was easily decided. It was impolitic and a needless expense (unless two rival priests were to be purposely upheld) at so short a distance to maintain a second altar. The analogy of monarchy dictated centralization, and it was determined to remove the old tabernacle and the sacred Gibeonites[3] with it. An honourable pretext for this was found in the erection of a temple at Jerusalem, which was to supersede both tabernacles; and thus was laid the foundation of a more vigorous sacerdotal order, which should in time become independent of the now dominating imperial power.

For constructing this sacred edifice, Solomon still needed the help of the Tyrians, both to hew timber from Lebanon, to square the blocks of stone, and (what was still more essential) for all the curious works in brass. The work was begun early in Solomon's fourth year, and took seven years to complete. That no very satisfactory description of the building, as a whole, can be attained, may perhaps be inferred from the great discordances be-

[1] All this is from the Chronicler, not from the book of Kings. In 1 Chron. xxii. 14, David bequeaths to Solomon for the temple 100,000 talents of gold, and 1,000,000 talents of silver. In ch. xxix. 4, it is only 3000 talents of gold and 7000 of silver, to which the princes add 5000 talents and 10.000 *darics* of gold, 10.000 talents of silver, 18,000 of brass, and 100,000 of iron. *Darics* were a Persian, and quite a later coin. Even the 8000 talents of gold is an incredibly large sum.

[2] 2 Chron. ii. 3, makes Hiram to have built a cedar-palace for David also.

[3] The word *Gibeonites* at length gave place to that of *Nethinim*, which is interpreted ἱερόδουλοι, sacred slaves.

tween learned commentators. Nevertheless, a part of their diversities is ascribable to the undue weight which some have given to the arbitrary assertions of the Jewish historian Josephus; and another part, to the endeavour to harmonize the fictitious additions of the "Chronicler" with the simpler account given in the book of "Kings." It is perhaps impossible to attain any more exact ideas than the following outline will give. The general ground plan of the three principal compartments was oblong, and ran 70 cubits in the clear from east to west, but only 20 cubits in breadth, from north to south. From the eastern end was cut off a porch, or ante-chapel, which occupied only 10 cubits of the entire length. Of the rest, the first 40 cubits made the principal sanctuary, and the remaining 20 was the secret "oracle" or most holy place; which was thus an apartment 20 cubits square. The height of the whole is called 30 cubits; yet the oracle is elsewhere distinctly said to be but 20 cubits high;[1] so that it appears to have been lower than the central hall. Many of the pillars were made of the precious *almug* wood. Within the ante-chapel also stood two highly ornamented pillars of brass, called Jachin and Boaz, the work of a man of Naphthali, whose father was a Tyrian. This clever artificer bore the same name as the king of Tyre,—Hiram, who sent him to the service of Solomon. He wrought likewise a large tank of brass, ten cubits in diameter, supported by twelve oxen; and ten large baths of brass richly ornamented, and very many other curious works. Among the ornaments are specified lions, oxen, and *cherubim*. What the last were is now pretty well ascertained, by comparing the descriptions in Ezekiel with Persian or Assyrian sculptures and Egyptian paintings, where we find figures which may be denoted as winged oxen with human faces, and as angels with eagles' heads. Within the "oracle" or crypt were also two cherubim of olive wood, each ten cubits high, and having ten cubits for the span of the wings; and the walls and doors of the house were carved everywhere with cherubim, palm-trees, and open flowers. It is incredible that when such animals and such symbols were freely made in brass, as suitable decorations to the interior of the temple, there can have been

[1] Kings vi. 2, 20.

any such aversion to images of hewn stone and sculptured ornaments of the altar, as the modern Pentateuch inculcates. Against each side of the house there rested a lower structure, affording chambers for the priests. The windows also were lofty and narrow; and if Josephus had any valid tradition for his belief of the very disproportionate height of the porch, the whole building had a strong general resemblance in form to a very small European cathedral, having a lofty tower at its east end, and a chancel, lower than the central building, at the west. Moreover, the preparation of the foundation of the temple on the top of Mount Moriah, on the threshing-floor of Araunah the Jebusite, was in itself an elaborate work, as the *substructions* of the Roman temple to Jupiter Capitolinus. But on this we have no details from our more trustworthy authority.

The size of the building thus described is extremely moderate, even if we assign to the cubit its greatest length, of one foot nine inches English. But when we are told that the wonder of the building consisted in the prodigious quantity of gold which was lavished on it; that it was an edifice such as a traveller might expect in El Dorado; that the whole house, in short, was *overlaid* with gold;—we may believe the last assertion in the letter, but must deny it in the spirit. Such is the ductility of gold, that even in the earliest developments of art, gilding was a comparatively unexpensive process; nor is there any reason to question, that not only the olive-wood cherubim, but the general carved work within the temple was superbly *gilt*. This is quite in the spirit of antiquity,[1] and did not exceed the means of a wealthy, though third-rate, power. But if the gold on the wood-work had been thick enough to yield anything worth carrying off by cutting or scraping, we can scarcely think that even king Shishak in the next reign would have left any of it standing; or at least when later plunderers broke in, much would be heard of the valuable gold wainscoting and tables which they carried off. In short, the real magnificence of the Temple consisted in its hewn stones, its noble cedar-

[1] The learned reader may be reminded of the palace of Deïoces in Ecbatana, which had seven circular walls of different colours, the two innermost having their battlements covered respectively with silvering and with gilding.

beams, its curious carvings, and its skilful works in brass; not in the profusion of gold and silver, however speciously it may have been gilt: and even so, considering its very small dimensions, its grandeur must be understood by comparison with all that had preceded it. Side by side with an Egyptian temple, or even with the cathedrals of Christendom and mosques of Islâm, it shrinks into insignificance. In every way there was much room left for improvement by his successors. Hezekiah, for instance, overlaid the doors and pillars with gold; a fact which we should not have learned, had he not accidentally been forced to cut it off again, as a propitiation to the king of Assyria.

The hewing of the cedar from mount Lebanon discloses to us an important fact, that in the heart of Israel there existed a nation of bondsmen or vassals, liable to perform public works for king Solomon, just as of old the Israelites for Pharaoh. The words of the older compiler are extremely distinct. "All the people which were left of the Amorites, Hittites, Perizzites, Hivites, and Jebusites, which were not of the children of Israel; their children that were left after them in the land;—upon those did Solomon levy a tribute of bondservice *unto this day*. But of the children of Israel did Solomon make no bondmen; but they were men of war, and his servants, and his princes, and his captains, and rulers of his chariots and his horsemen." The number of these strangers liable to bondservice is estimated at 153,600 (in a book[1] indeed prone to exaggeration), and 30,000 is given as the number actually kept at work at once. Our earlier and better authority[2] may seem on the whole to confirm this, in reckoning the Hebrew overseers of the labourers as 550. While the same word is used concerning the taskwork of these slaves as concerning the Israelitish service in Egypt,[3] and they were manifestly at the mercy of their conquerors, it is still uncertain what was the actual pressure of suffering upon them. But unless we could imagine

[1] 2 Chron. ii. 17.
[2] 1 Kings ix. 23.
[3] The word is *Mas*; 1 Kings ix. 21, and Exod. i. 11. It is explained in Winer's Simonis, " tribute paid by the body, that is, servitude, *Frohndienst*;" or soccage paid by a serf to his landlord. It occurs also in 2 Sam. xx. 24, in enumerating *David's* revenues and administration.

Jewish rule to be far milder than that of Christendom, a conquered class,—strange in religion,—subjected to public task-work,—without political rights,—below the sympathies of the dominant race,—without moral relations to definite families and patrons,—forced to work under public overseers, who must of necessity have been armed with the whip,—such a class can have had little in their lot to prefer to the exceeding bitter bondage of Israel in Egypt. As we read of certain Hittite *princes* (apparently in Israel), it is possible that some chieftains of these races made favourable terms with David and Solomon, and retained their domains and rank. The conquest and subjugation of the rest seems to account for the ample territorial domains of David and his son; for the land of the conquered was doubtless confiscated to the crown. No Moses arose to rescue them; and no modern writer can express sympathy for them[1] without exciting indignation. So capricious and sectarian are religious partialities; so slow are Christians to enlarge their hearts in pity to Pagans, or deplore the permanent degradation of a whole caste of men. Yet the well-known phrase *"unto this day"* indicates that the bondage (under whatever modifications) lasted down to the time when the book of Kings was compiled.

It would be needless to employ moral criticism on Solomon's much-celebrated undertaking, were not the whole affair habitually represented in a false light. The kings of Egypt and the republics of Greece, equally with the great sovereigns, barons, or archbishops of Europe, were urged by a comfortable combination of pride, piety, and architectural taste, to erect magnificent sacred edifices. Where so many motives conspire, it is absurd to dwell on the religious zeal of the projectors: the temples indeed of Selinus or Ephesus would probably have eclipsed that of Jerusalem. Instinct generally guides the founders to a work, the end of which they most imperfectly know; and so, we believe, it was with this of Solomon.

[1] In my first edition I gave great offence by the following words: "Their persons, being reduced to slavery, formed the hapless multitude, whose unnoticed groans supplied the raw material of Solomon's glory." Perhaps I should have said *serfdom*, not *slavery*. I withdraw the words from the text, chiefly because I find I am supposed to intend a personal and peculiar blame against Solomon more than other ancient kings.

His father David had bequeathed to him a great institution, of signal value, in the *singers and musicians* annexed to the worship of the tabernacle. In rank and in remuneration inferior to the priests, in spiritual position they were as much higher as the preaching curate than the ordaining bishop. No preaching indeed or teaching or reading of the Law existed as yet; but the very fact made the singing of psalms and hymns so much the more important. They were the only spiritual, intellectual, and elevating part of the service. To the priest, on the contrary, belonged mere punctilious ceremony and gorgeous parade, defining and atoning-for external pollutions, consulting of Jehovah by Urim, burning of incense, and vain slaughter of beasts, alike foreign to the genius of the prophets, as to the real demands of the only true God. The first composers of hymns were undoubtedly regarded as prophets; and when it became the duty of a particular corporation or hereditary class to collect, keep, and sing them, a traditionary taste was cultivated; commoner productions dropped into neglect, and the most purifying or elevating odes claimed their rightful superiority. Hence the attendance at divine service in Jerusalem, which from David's day onward beyond a doubt was celebrated at least every Sabbath, became a spiritual service, dear to the heart of every true worshipper of Jehovah. With this the priest himself was imbued, and his dreariest routine gained some relief by an allegorical spiritualism infused into it. With the progress of time, none are so likely to have become composers of new hymns as the Levites, whose chief business was in singing and keeping copies of them. At last the principal literary culture lay with them, and they were prepared to become religious instructors of the nation. By their care the Proverbs written by Solomon were also likely to be preserved and copied, and the archives of the temple to be kept.

But Solomon's splendour brought in, over and above, a material attraction to those who had no affinity for things spiritual. Every Hebrew desired at some time in his life to go up to the famous temple, if only for mere curiosity; and the same principle which in modern days has enforced pilgrimages to Jerusalem and Mecca, must have begun to work on Israel very early. The shortness of the distance made many visits in one life an easy undertaking; and there were Three great Feasts from this time celebrated with peculiar solemnity, when king Solomon officiated in person[1] at the high altar, by burning incense and offering victims to Jehovah. These feasts are nearly identical with those celebrated among all ancient nations, at the First Fruits, after the general Harvest, and after the Vintage or Ingathering; but, at least in course of time, they were blended with associations drawn from the early history of the Hebrew race. At such celebrations in particular it was natural for crowds of country people to flock into Jerusalem; and, certainly at a later period, the priests diligently inculcated the duty of this, in order to bring the whole land within the influence of the central sanctuary. There is no question that the magnificence of the Temple and the institutions connected with it, imparted to the priesthood an ever-growing authority, the deeper because it was unseen and gradual in its encroachments. Little by little it worked itself into the political constitution, and ultimately became a check upon the power of the king, whose authority indeed it outlasted by centuries. Without this, Judah would have been as Israel; great prophets might have arisen, but their words would probably have perished with them; or perhaps, if preserved, would be judged by us the racy but harsh fruit of uneducated zeal, neither refined by traditionary culture nor sweetened by the influences of tranquil domestic life. In the sacerdotal and Levitical system of Jerusalem we see the nidus, in which the germs of prophetical genius were fostered, expanded, and preserved:—yet the time at last came when ceremonialism froze into lifelessness, and presented that formal, narrow, and repulsive front which we name Pharisaism.

Not that the idea was admitted either by the nation or by any king of Judah earlier than Hezekiah, that "in Jerusalem alone men ought to worship." The most pious kings, before Hezekiah, in common with the mass of Israel, continued to uphold the worship of Jehovah (but of Jehovah alone) on the High Places, without any suspicion that they could be offending; nor did Jehoiada, the

[1] 1 Kings ix. 25. As the following kings disused the practice, it came at last to be looked upon as impious; hence the Chronicler's story against Uzziah.

regent-priest, forbid it. In fact, it was no priest nor prophet, but Solomon himself, who consecrated the temple at Jerusalem, and removed the tabernacle from Gibeon; and although a new doctrine grew up in the sacerdotal circles, an Asa or a Jehoshaphat felt within himself full authority (had occasion required) to build and dedicate new temples in new places. The Ark itself was opened, and in it was found neither the rod of Aaron which budded nor the golden pot of manna, but only two tables of stone. This we know on the authority indeed of a compiler[1] who wrote four centuries later; but as he had access to contemporary documents, and can have had no bias in such a statement, there is no ground for doubting its truth.

It is difficult to avoid speculating concerning the two tables of stone, whether they were ever turned, or meant to be turned, to practical use; whether successive high-priests ever dared to examine them, and to compare the inscription with the professed copy in their books. In the absence of the tables, we are driven to the books alone, and there encounter two very different versions of the inscription. The Decalogue (as it is called), which is contained in the 20th chapter of Exodus, is too well known to cite; and the copy of it in Deuteronomy deviates from it only in regard to the Fourth Commandment. But in the 34th chapter of Exodus a very remarkable diversity meets us, which is uniformly overlooked by divines. Moses had broken the first pair of tables in indignation at the idolatry of the people; and ascends Mount Sinai a second time with a second pair of blank tables, on which Jehovah inscribes Ten[2] Commandments, nearly as follows. (The first, third, and sixth Commandments are here shortened.)

The Words of the Covenant—the Ten Commandments.
[FIRST TABLE?]
I. Thou shalt worship no other God than Jehovah; for Jehovah whose name is Jealous, is a jealous God.
II. Thou shalt make thee no molten gods.

---

[1] 1 Kings viii. 9. Contrast Heb. ix. 4, Num. xvii. 10, Exod. xvi. 34.
[2] Exod. xxxiv. 10: " Behold, I make *a covenant;* 11. Observe what *I command* thee;" 27. Write thou *these words,* for after the tenor of *these words* have I made *a covenant* with thee and with Israel. 28. He wrote upon the tables *the words of the covenant, the Ten Commandments.*

III. The feast of unleavened bread shalt thou keep, and dedicate all firstlings unto me: but the first-born of thy sons thou shalt redeem. None shall appear before me empty.
IV. Six days shalt thou work, but on the seventh day thou shalt rest: in ploughing time and in harvest thou shalt rest.
[SECOND TABLE?]
V. Thou shalt observe the feast of Weeks, Firstfruits of Wheat-harvest, and the feast of Ingathering at the year's end.
VI. Thrice in the year shall all your males appear before the Lord Jehovah, the God of Israel.
VII. Thou shalt not offer the blood of my sacrifice with leaven.
VIII. The sacrifice of the feast of the Passover shall not be left to the morning.
IX. The first of the firstfruits of the land shalt thou bring into the house of Jehovah thy God.
X. Thou shalt not seethe a kid in his mother's milk.

If we abide by our present book of Exodus, these are clearly the commandments which were written on the tables of stone; for those which are found in the 20th chapter were spoken indeed by the voice of Jehovah, but are not said to have been written on the tables. It is only Deuteronomy which contradicts Exodus,[1] but Exodus is herein consistent with itself. This circumstance might lead some to imagine that we have here the genuine Mosaic decalogue, and that the other is a modernized improvement. While we regard this as a plausible opinion, nothing ought confidently to be held until the matter has been more fully discussed; for a little consideration will suggest other possible theories, as well as objections to this view.[2] In fact there are so many other phænomena to be reviewed, that a summary conclusion is impossible. Of these one only can here be noticed,—the apparent occurrence of a mutilated *third copy* of the Decalogue in Exod. xxiii. 10—19; where however it is not marked out as such, but concludes a small book of law. The Second Table is there only verbally different from what has been already quoted; but the First Table seems to have only three Commandments:

I. Six years shalt thou sow thy land, and gather in the fruits thereof, but the seventh year shalt let it rest and lie still.

---

[1] Deut. v. 22, x. 4, sanctions the popular opinion, which is opposed to Exod. xxxiv.
[2] The absence of a precept of *circumcision*, in the midst of these ceremonial precepts, suggests that (as with the Arabs) this practice was originally only a national custom, common to them with the neighbouring nations, though it gradually became a precept of religion.

In like manner shalt thou deal with thy vineyard and thy olive-yard.
II. Six days thou shalt do thy work, and on the seventh day thou shalt rest.
III. To all things that I have said unto you be ye attentive, and make no mention of the name of other gods, neither let it be heard out of thy mouth.

If this first table were perfect,[1] it might have a claim to still greater antiquity, on the ground of its being less spiritual than the other. Yet it is by no means always true that the earliest views are the least spiritual, or the latest the least ceremonial; and if we could ascertain ever so accurately which was the most primitive Decalogue, we might be no nearer to ascertaining which was inscribed on Solomon's tables.

The Ark having been solemnly brought into the temple by the priests, Solomon made a public speech to the congregation and a very long prayer in front of the altar; after which he performed sacrifices[2] on the greatest scale of magnificence, and joined with all the people to dedicate the house of Jehovah. A great festival was held for a full fortnight, at which (as it is hyperbolically stated) *all* Israel, "from the defile of Hamath unto the brook of Egypt," were assembled. Nor is it likely that at any other time during the whole monarchy there was ever a greater concourse of visitors in Jerusalem.

His own palace and that of his queen, though less celebrated than the temple, were more extensive structures, and occupied more years in finishing.[3] In fact, with the growth of his seraglio Solomon must have needed increased domestic accommodation, so that it was difficult to find an end of building: thirteen years however is

---

[1] The imperfection is caused by merging in one what are the 3rd and 6th of the other system. The 6th orders the observance of three feasts, and the 3rd gives *special details* concerning the *first* of the feasts, at which all firstlings of beasts are to be dedicated, and firstlings of men to be redeemed. This law of firstlings is omitted in the imperfect table.

[2] 1 Kings ix. 63: it says, 22,000 oxen and 120,000 sheep. This was probably a theoretical estimate of what *must* have been eaten by all the assembled males of Israel, who, according to the legal presumption, were regarded by the author of this estimate as present. Even so, the number of cattle here given is extravagant, unless we suppose it to take in the fortnight's festivity.
The Chronicler says that they dispersed on the 23rd day of the seventh month. This is intended to identify it with the *Feast of Tabernacles*.

[3] It scarcely belongs to history to register the details of a king's luxury and pomp. His ivory throne, overlaid with gold, having six steps and fourteen lions upon it; his 200 targets and 300 shields of beaten gold; his harps and psalteries made of almug wood; have been carefully recorded.

given as the estimate. The queen, for whom a peculiarly splendid abode was erected, was a daughter of the king of Egypt; and with her Solomon received a very singular dowry. The Egyptians, we may infer from their paintings, from the earliest times had had great experience in sieges, in which it is certain that the Israelites were very unskilful, from the low state of the mechanical arts among them. Gezer, inhabited by Canaanites, had continued to defy the forces of David and Solomon; but Pharaoh marched against it through the territory of his son-in-law, and having captured it, presented it to his daughter, Solomon's wife. This transaction strikingly indicates the good understanding which at that time subsisted between the two powers.

III. We are now naturally led on to another phænomenon, which, from the magnitude of its scale and its peculiar results, draws attention in this reign,—the harem of the prince. It would be a matter of interest to learn in what order of time his numerous wives and concubines were taken. The remark that "when he was old his wives turned away his heart," might suggest that only in his later years, when he had exhausted the enjoyments of pomp and pride, voluptuous weakness stole over him. The seven hundred wives and three hundred concubines ascribed to him, amounting together to an exact thousand, indicate something unhistorical; yet the cumbrousness of his matrimonial establishment remains unquestionable. One marriage-song survives to us, which, from its peculiar applicability to Solomon's nuptials with some eminent princess, we can better believe to have been written for him than for any other Hebrew monarch. It appears to have been sung during the marriage procession which conducted the royal pair to their palace. In one or two passages there is an abruptness, which either indicates corruption of the text, or savours of antique rudeness which had not yet been rubbed off.

PSALM XLV.

1. My heart boils up with goodly matter.
I ponder; and my verse concerns the King.
Let my tongue be a ready writer's pen!

2. Fairer art thou than all the sons of men.
Over thy lips delightsomeness is pour'd:
Therefore hath God for ever blessed thee.

3. Gird at thy hip thy hero-sword,
   Thy glory and thy majesty:
   And forth victorious ride majestic,
   For truth and meekness, righteously;
   And let thy right hand teach thee wondrous deeds.
   Beneath thy feet the peoples fall;
   For in the heart of the king's enemies
   Sharp are thy arrows.

4. Thy throne divine ever and always stands:
   A righteous sceptre is thy royal sceptre.
   Thou lovest right and hatest evil;
   Therefore hath God, thy God, anointed thee
   With oil of joy above thy fellow-*kings*.
   Myrrh, aloes, cassia, all thy raiment is.
   From ivory palaces the viols gladden thee.
   Kings' daughters count among thy favourites;
   And at thy right hand stands the Queen
   In gold of Ophir.

5. O daughter, hark! behold! and bend thy ear:
   Forget thy people and thy father's house.
   Win thou the King thy beauty to desire;
   He is thy lord: do homage unto him.
   So Tyrus' daughter[1] and the sons of wealth
   With gifts shall court thee.

6. Right glorious is the royal damsel:
   Wrought of gold is her apparel.
   In broider'd tissues to the King she is led:
   Her maiden-friends, behind, are brought to thee.
   They come with joy and gladness,
   They enter the royal palace.

7. Thy fathers by thy sons shall be replaced;
   As princes o'er the land shalt thou exalt them.
   So will I publish to all times thy name;
   So shall the nations praise thee, now and alway.[2]

It will be observed, that the practice of a favourite wife receiving rich presents to engage her influence with the king, is here alluded to, without any disapproval, as a natural privilege of her station. Under despotism and polygamy it could not be otherwise; and in spite of Solomon's wisdom and diligence in his porch of judgment, no small item of public discontent is likely to have arisen from this cause. In regard to the *number* of his wives, our knowledge of the modern[3] court of Persia has

[1] In the Heb. idiom, *Daughter* of Tyre means only *the Nation*. In the passage before us it appears to be a mere type of a wealthy people.

[2] There is a difficulty in supposing, as Ewald suggests, that the king here celebrated was a successor of Jeroboam. None of them had a sufficient pretence of religion, to make it decorous for a Jehovistic prophet to write this ode: nor is it easy to think it could then have been incorporated with the sacred Psalms.

[3] Indeed Cambyses in Herodotus, desiring a hostage, demands the daughter of the king of Egypt as a wife, and makes war when deceived.

furnished an ingenious suggestion, that Solomon took them as virtual hostages for the good behaviour of their fathers;—chieftains of the Moabites, Ammonites, Edomites, Sidonians, and Hittites. This idea is not entirely to be rejected, as applicable to a fraction of the whole; but it will not account for their great multitude, and much less for the concubines. Two far more powerful passions must have been at work,—an ever-increasing love of the pomp and pageantry which a royal wedding involved, and a depraved taste for perpetual novelty in the partners of his bed. Both of these are so degrading to the soul, that we cannot wonder to find Solomon's reign to become more inglorious, more pernicious, and more overclouded with danger, the longer he lived.

IV. The particular manifestation of evil, which most struck the imagination and heart of the religious persons who recorded his reign, was the public idolatry which he sanctioned and supported in his wives. Whatever may be urged on the side of mere toleration, this active patronage was both a grave and a gratuitous mischief. He had been under no necessity to multiply idolatrous wives, and therefore could not plead necessity for introducing their superstitions. It must be remembered also that these pagan religions were not a simple conviction cherished in the heart and conscience, which ought to be sacred, but were a public and obtrusive display of much that was corrupting, even where they did not involve practices of cruelty. It was therefore no narrow bigotry or gloomy fanaticism which filled the prophets and priests of Jehovah with dismay, when king Solomon built on a high hill before Jerusalem altars, images, and the whole apparatus of heathen worship for Chemosh and Molech, the idol-divinities of Moab and of Ammon; and celebrated the rites of the Sidonian goddess Astarte, and of the other gods of his wives.

If a mere politic and worldly-minded despot chose to patronize such paganism, no one would feel surprise. It is only when we contemplate Solomon as the author of the early portions of the book of Proverbs, that we are indignant at his maintaining these indefensible abominations. Of what avail was it that he warned young men against foreign harlotry,—a vice which was stealing into

Jerusalem with the influx of strangers and of luxury,—
when the royal preacher himself established the far more
hateful and disgusting impurities connected with the rites
of Astarte?[1] Or of what avail that he enjoined precepts
of parental and filial duty, when he encouraged the bloody
religion of Molech, in which children were immolated by
their natural protectors? We could almost disbelieve the
plain statement of our historian, as mere prejudice and
mistake, did not Solomon's extravagant polygamy warn
us that he had become a besotted voluptuary, in whose
favour we must not do violence to the clear depositions of
one who loves to extol him.

V. The old prophet Nathan and Gad the seer must have
died ere this. Whether any of their successors had the
boldness to confront and oppose the king, or whether his
self-will and habitual despotism made them all shrink from
it as from a hopeless enterprise, has not been recorded.
But the horror and disgust of the prophetical body vented
itself in another way, most pernicious in the result to the
monotheistic cause which they were aiming to advance.
One man alone indeed was the agent or organ; and as he
undoubtedly believed himself to be only the minister of
the Most High Jehovah, it would be an error to assume
that there was any definite and conscious conspiracy among
the monotheists. It is rather to be believed, that the
sentiment which actuated them all burst out from the lips
of one. All felt that the son of David was following the
downward path of Saul, and was no longer the king whom
Jehovah could approve and love. It was high time therefore, that, as David superseded Saul, so for Solomon a
worthier substitute should be found.

At this period the prophet Ahijah, who was in some
sense a successor of Nathan,[2] commanded great popular
reverence. Burning with indignation against the king,
he set his eyes on a young man named Jeroboam, who had,
under Solomon, the important charge of the tribe of
Ephraim,[3] and was eminent both for valour and for energy

---

[1] 1 Kings xv. 12; 2 Kings xxiii. 7; and elsewhere.
[2] The acts of Solomon are described (2 Chron. ix. 29) as written by Nathan the prophet, Ahijah the Shilonite, and Iddo the seer.
[3] The text says, the house of *Joseph*; but this probably means *Ephraim* only.

in the discharge of duty. In him perhaps Ahijah saw a second David. Having met him in a solitary place, he made an energetic address to him, the scope of which was to declare that God should rend away the kingdom from Solomon and give it to him; in token of which he tore off the garment from Jeroboam's back.[1] This deed became noised abroad, and soon brought forth bitter fruit. The jealousy of Solomon was too surely stirred up, and Jeroboam's life was no longer safe. On this he escaped into Egypt, having been gratuitously turned from a loyal and valuable subject into an outlaw, a rebel, and a dangerous foe. What change of policy, or even of dynasty, had come over the court of Egypt, we do not know; but the new king, who is called Shishak in the Hebrew annals, was no longer Solomon's friend. He received Jeroboam with open arms, and probably gained from him much valuable information; whether this king was already planning the invasion of Judah, which he soon after executed, or whether it was wholly of Jeroboam's suggestion.

At the same court in the former reign, there had been living another dangerous and inveterate enemy of the Hebrew monarch, by name Hadad, of the royal family of Edom. He was an infant at the time when Joab with his relentless bands had made promiscuous slaughter of all the males in Idumæa; but having been saved into Midian and Paran, he was at length received at the Egyptian court; and when he was grown to manhood, won great favour with the king, who gave to him in marriage his own queen's sister. As *this* Pharaoh was in close alliance with Solomon, whose father-in-law he had become, Hadad carefully concealed from him his intentions, while begging leave to return to his own country.[2] On reaching it, he soon commenced a harassing petty warfare against the Israelites, which Solomon was unable to repress. This must have been a sore vexation to the traffic of the Red

[1] Our reporter gives details which have the appearance of being added after the event,—that Jeroboam was to have only ten of the twelve tribes, and this, not until after the death of Solomon.

[2] There is a chronological difficulty. It seems to be implied (1 Kings xi. 21) that Hadad returned to Edom as soon as David and Joab were dead; yet as his hostilities are regarded as a punishment on the idolatry of Solomon's old age, they need to be deferred some twenty years after the death of Joab. And until this later period, Hadad can hardly have become dangerous.

Sea, since all the merchandise had to pass through Idumæa, on the backs of camels. Thus, while the court and government had become habitually expensive beyond all proportion to the magnitude of the territory, the sources of revenue began to be cut off.

On the northern side also a troublesome enemy appeared. How long the garrisons of David were kept up in the fortresses of Damascus, we do not know; nor whether they were voluntarily withdrawn, or were forcibly expelled. It cannot be imagined that without them the Hebrew dominion over Thapsacus, Tadmor, and the cities of Hamath could be upheld, or the north-eastern traffic be secure: yet the difficulty of maintaining them must have been very great. At any rate in Solomon's later years, Rezon, who is described as a revolted servant of Hadadezer, made himself master of Damascus and its district, and founded a kingdom which was soon to become exceeding formidable. His power entirely shut Solomon out from the trade across the desart, at least by its natural channel; and the activity of two such adversaries as Rezon and Hadad must have awakened the slumbering enmities of Ammon and Moab, which, as well as Edom, had fearful wrongs to avenge.

Thus clouds were gathering over the late splendid Hebrew empire. The secret began to transpire among the enemies of the house of David, that the lofty statue of Hebrew ascendency before which they had crouched in homage, was nothing but a gaudy gigantic doll. The veterans of David had passed away, and as no new wars of importance or continuity had arisen to train up successors to them, the very instrument of dominion had been seriously impaired; nor was military exertion in accordance with Solomon's tastes and habits. The embarrassments in which he was involved were in part bequeathed to him by his father; for empire begun by prowess and established by massacre is certain to breed smothered enmities, which at last blaze out in retaliation. But another still more formidable danger rose out of his own pomp and voluptuousness. These could not be supported simultaneously with the large expenses of his over-grasping empire, from the ample revenues of his own domains, of his exclusive trade, and of his foreign tribute; and it had become requisite to lay heavy taxes on his own people. They had discovered that his wealth was their poverty; and, having no constitutional mode of remonstrance, waited with impatience for the commencement of a new reign, hoping then to exact some conditions from the prince, and not allow him to ascend the throne in as arbitrary and unformal a manner as Solomon had done. To men in such a temper, the declaration of Ahijah the Shilonite in favour of Jeroboam fell as spark upon tinder. The house of Ephraim, over whom Jeroboam was placed, accepted Ahijah's address as a protest against the king personally, and as a sanction given to Jeroboam, to whom they were favourably disposed; while Solomon's immediate persecution of him must assuredly have increased his popularity.—Once more; the lavish display of wealth in which the Hebrew monarch indulged, excited the cupidity of neighbouring powers. While his army was in its prime of strength, such conduct may have been not impolitic; but when he had been seen unable to repress the attacks of petty potentates, like Rezon and Hadad, his temple and his treasures were but a mark to the spoiler, and presently lured the powerful king of Egypt against the land.

It was well for Solomon that death overtook him before this calamity and disgrace overwhelmed Jerusalem. His career had come to its natural termination, when the primitive impulse of prosperity had been spent. In spite of his much-vaunted wisdom, there had been no vitality or reproductive power infused into the national finances. All were sensible that the public weal was decaying; and when he died very few regretted him.[1]

The sagacity attributed to him seems to have been threefold: wisdom in the administration of justice,—which consisted chiefly in cleverness to discover truth, when the evidence was insufficient, doubtful, or contradictory; wisdom in general government,—as to which the actual results prove him to have been most lamentably deficient; and wisdom of a more scholastic kind, such as was evidenced in the writing of proverbs and books of natural history. Of his merit in the last, no means of judging exist; but those chapters of the Proverbs which are regarded as his genuine writing, are the production of no

[1] B.C. 955. See Appendix.

common mind, and explain how, in that age, he was regarded as intellectually towering above other kings.

There is a marked contrast between the tone of the authorities on which we are dependent for the lives of David and Solomon. The books of Samuel and Kings show a general impartiality in which the Chronicles are wholly wanting. All the dark events which sully these two reigns are carefully hushed up by the last work. In it we read nothing of David's civil war during his reign in Hebron over Judah; nothing of his cruelty towards Moab and Edom; nothing of his deeds of adultery and murder; nothing of Amnon's brutality, or the fierce revenge and wicked rebellion of Absalom; nothing of the immolation of Saul's sons, or of the revolt of Adonijah and his slaughter by Solomon; nothing of the crimes and the punishments of Joab, of Abiathar, or of Shimei. On the other hand, we have a great deal in the Chronicles calculated to magnify the religious zeal, and especially the devotion to the Levitical system, displayed by David, of which the earlier history takes no notice. So too the Chronicler suppresses all mention of the disgust of Hiram, of the idolatries of Solomon, and the reverses of his later years; of the insurrectionary movement of the prophet Ahijah, and the cause of Jeroboam's flight into Egypt. In short, it will record nothing but what tends to glorify this prince, the great establisher of the priestly dignity. Accordingly it imputes his building of his queen's palace to a scruple of conscience as to this child of idolaters dwelling in the house of the pious David: "because (said he) the places are holy, whereunto the ark of Jehovah hath come." A few differences of this kind might be honourably accounted for; but a general review puts it beyond reasonable doubt that the Book of Chronicles is not an honest and trustworthy narrative, and must be used with great caution as an authority, where anything is involved which affects Levitical influence.

APPENDIX to CHAPTER IV.
On the Chronology.

THERE is no difference of opinion among chronologers, that the date of the capture of Samaria by Shalmaneser is B.C. 721; but when we reckon the times backward from this, various inconsistencies are discovered. It is not requisite here to reiterate what has been so often treated. What we have particularly to remark is, that after making the corrections which are usually approved, two great gaps still remain in the Israelitish history, which have been called *Interregnums;* the one of ten years, between the death of Jeroboam II. and the accession of his son Zachariah: the other of nine years, between the death of Pekah and the accession of his murderer Hoshea. In the text we read simply, "Jeroboam slept with his fathers, and Zachariah his son reigned in his stead:"[1] and "Hoshea slew Pekah and reigned in his stead, in the twentieth year of Jotham son of Uzziah."[2] It is manifest that the compiler had in neither case the remotest idea of an interregnum, and we therefore ought not to interpolate so serious an event merely in deference to figures, which are easily corrupted, and often in these books undeniably faulty.

Hitzig has rightly remarked, that the second interregnum vanishes, if we properly interpret the reign of Jotham, who began to exercise royal power before his father died. Yet when we have no new facts for Pekah's reign, it is hard to approve of lengthening it by eight years, which indeed involves more alterations than are enough. It suffices instead to correct the age of Hezekiah[3] by deducting ten years; by which indeed we make Ahaz twenty or twenty-one years older than his son, while Hitzig computes nineteen only. In the common chronology there is but ten or eleven years between them, which is obviously absurd. Accordingly in the following pages, we follow a reckoning which reduces the dates of Uzziah, Pekah, and his near predecessors, by nine or ten years, which is the imaginary interregnum between Pekah and Hoshea.

As for the other gap, we have to choose between length-

[1] Kings xiv. 29.   [2] Kings xv. 30.   [3] Chap. xviii. 2.

ening by ten years the reign of some Israelitish king, or shortening by a like sum that of a king of Judah. If the former plan be approved, we find one reason for lengthening that of Jeroboam; namely, that one correction then suffices: for the number 27 in 2 Kings xv. 1, must on other grounds necessarily be altered, and is not here to be reckoned. Yet as Jeroboam has already a reign of forty-one years, we shrink from increasing it to fifty-one; a length of time which, though possible, ought hardly to be obtruded by conjectural emendation. Instead of this, to lengthen the reign of Menahem from above, though we have then three alterations to make in xv. 13, 17,—might still be better than the former change.

If we follow the general belief, that the same Hosea who composed the last eleven chapters of the book which bears his name, wrote his first chapter in the reign of Jeroboam II., we can scarcely doubt that the received chronology is in this part much too long; for as his last chapters date from the *siege of Samaria*, it assigns to him full sixty years of prophesying. Isaiah and Micah also were believed by the ancient compilers of their works to have written under four successive kings of Judah, which is another hint to us that they held a shorter chronology. On the whole, then, we see reasons for preferring the alternative of deducting ten years from some Jewish reign.

When we endeavour to pick out the particular reign, we find that there is danger of lowering too much the excess of age of father over son. On this ground, Amaziah and Uzziah are the only two reigns to be thought of, unless we choose to encounter the need of several other changes. Their ages exceed those of their sons by thirty-eight and forty-three years respectively. Yet we cannot thus deal with Uzziah (whose accession we have already lowered by nine or ten years) without making Jotham die before his father. It remains therefore to deduct ten years from Amaziah's reign,[1] and to suppose that he was only twenty-eight older than his son Uzziah. From these changes we finally bring out that the death of Solomon was in the year B.C. 955.

The reigns of Solomon, of David, and (according to St

---

[1] For this we must change twenty-nine into nineteen in 2 Kings xiv. 2, and fifteen into twenty-five in v. 23. This imputes an error which is no mere accident of transcription, but that is perhaps in any way inevitable.

Paul in the Acts of the Apostles) of Saul likewise, are forty years each. This does not appear too long a period in itself, either for Solomon or for David; yet the number has so many mythical associations as to lessen our confidence in its having historical foundation.
A chronological table may here be suitably added.

Chronological Table from the Death of Solomon to the Fall of Samaria.

Queen Mother.	Accession of king in Jerusalem.	B.C.	Accession of Israelitish king.
Naamah.	Rehoboam	955	—Jeroboam.
Maachah.	Abijam his son	937	
(Maachah.)	Asa his son	935	
		934	—Nadab his son.
		932	—Baasha.
		909	—Elah his son.
		908	Zimri, Tibni, Omri.
		904	Omri (alone).
		897	Ahab his son.
Azubah.	Jehoshaphat his son	894	
		877	Ahaziah his son.
		876	Jehoram his brother.
	Jehoram with his father ..	872	
	(Jehoshaphat dies)	869	
Athaliah.	Ahaziah his son..........	865	
	(Queen) Athaliah	864	Jehu.
Zibiah.	Jehoash (under Jehoiada)	858	
	alleged son of Ahaziah	835	—Jehoahaz his son.
		820	—Jehoash his son.
Jehoaddan.	Amaziah his son	818	
		804	—Jeroboam II. his son.
Jecholiah.	Uzziah his son	799	
		762	—Zachariah his son.
		761	Shallum, Menahem.
Jerusha.	Jotham with his father....	757	
		750	—Pekahiah son of M.
		748½	Pekah.
	(Uzziah dies)....	748	
[Unknown]	Ahaz his son	741	
		729	Hoshea.
Abi.	Hezekiah his son	726	
		721	Samaria captured.

From the Fall of Samaria to the Razing of the Walls of Jerusalem.

Queen Mother.	King in Jerusalem.	B.C.
Abi	Hezekiah	726
Hephzibah.	Manasseh his son	697
Meshullemeth.	Amon his son	642
Jedidah.	Josiah his son	640
Hamutal.	Jehoahaz his son	609
Zebudah.	Jehoiakim his brother....	609
Nehushta.	Jehoiachin his son	598
Hamutal.	Zedekiah son of Josiah ...	598
	Destruction of Jerusalem	588

Nearly to recover the common system of chronology, we must add 10 to the numbers from Uzziah to Pekah inclusive (*except Jotham*, to whom 1 only is to be added), and then add 20 to all higher dates.

CHAPTER V.

FROM THE DEATH OF SOLOMON TO THE ACCESSION OF
OMRI, B.C. 955—904.

WE have seen how the headless body of Saul was buried at Jabesh Gilead, and was afterwards removed to his own private estate in Gibeah of Benjamin. David, on the contrary, had been interred in that part of Jerusalem which was emphatically called the City of David, the fortifications of which his son enlarged and completed. In the same spot was a royal burying-place now solemnly established, into which the successive kings of this line, when they *slept with their fathers*, were for the most part carried. Solomon accordingly was here entombed with royal ceremonies, and his son REHOBOAM prepared to step into his place.[1]

We have no ground for believing that the foreign bodyguard, which was so prominent in the reign of David, was kept up through that of Solomon. Of Cherethites, Pelethites and Gittites we hear no more, nor are they replaced by any other foreign names. The throne of the Hebrew king was now to be supported by its own popularity and by its native army; and (following perhaps the advice of his father's counsellors) Rehoboam thought proper to hold a constitutional assembly of the tribes, and formally to accept of the royal dignity in their presence. For this purpose he convened a meeting of all Israel at Shechem, a very ancient and venerated town of Ephraim. But so decisive was the general disaffection and the determination to enforce new principles on the administration, that the tribes immediately sent for Jeroboam from Egypt, who had the boldness to appear publicly at Shechem, there to confront the new monarch. Becoming (as may appear) the spokesman of the national will, he positively demanded a remission of the oppressive taxes, and on this condition proffered loyal service to the son of Solomon. Three

[1] B.C. 955.

days were taken for deliberation; after which Rehoboam, following the advice of his young companions against that of his father's counsellors, gave a haughty and contemptuous refusal, which was intended to terrify all into submission. Instead of this, all the northern and eastern tribes unanimously revolted from him, and took Jeroboam for their king: none adhered to Rehoboam but his own tribe of Judah and the contiguous one of Benjamin,[1] which in any case could scarcely refuse to follow the fortunes of Jerusalem. Rehoboam did not believe the full extent of his own misfortune, and sent one of his officers to superintend the usual collection of the tribute; but the people stoned him to death, upon which the king was glad to escape in haste to Jerusalem. His first thoughts were to recover his dominion by war,[2] but Shemaiah the prophet, by his vehement and positive prohibition, deterred him from so hopeless an enterprise.

Thus far Rehoboam acted as a prince who had but just emerged from the harem; and it is quite probable that this was his actual position. David had suffered by conspiracy from two of his own sons. This fact Solomon was not likely to forget; and we may well believe that he guarded against a similar occurrence by shutting up his only son (at least from his thousand wives only one son is named) within the walls of his seraglio. But the sharp lesson which Rehoboam had received in this first experiment of ruling, appears to have been very wholesome in its effects; for all the rest of his reign was prudent, though not religiously laudable. His mother's name was Naamah (or, *lovely one*), an Ammonitess, and it was not to be expected that he would deviate from his father's example of honouring his mother's god. The tribe of Judah everywhere consecrated high places and images to Jehovah, without a suspicion that this could deserve censure; nor only so, but deadly Canaanitish immoralities are specified with the rites of Astarte, as established in

---

[1] The old narrator seems even to comprise Benjamin in Judah: " I will give *ten* tribes to thee, but he shall have *one* tribe for my servant David's sake;" 1 Kings xi. 32.

[2] The record says, "He assembled 180,000 *chosen warriors*," which perhaps indicates no more than that the writer estimated the tribes of Judah and Benjamin to contain this number of males within the military age.

DIVISION OF THE MONARCHY.

the land under pretence of religion.[1] Thus the worldly prosperity of David and Solomon appeared to have had no other result than to give to the Hebrew metropolis, both outwardly and in reality, a large share of pagan superstition.

Meanwhile JEROBOAM was far from fulfilling the hopes of the prophet who had so unadvisedly fired the train of insurrection; but before we name any details, it will be appropriate to review the foreign results of this schism. The nations which owned subjection to Solomon were no longer likely to obey either of his successors. In the north all foreign dominion had already been lost (we can scarcely doubt) by the rise of Rezon in Damascus. The Ammonites appear to have effected their liberation from Israelite power, but the Moabites to have remained tributary. The Edomites, in the early reigns of the kings of Judah, may have still paid a nominal homage, but we find no marks that it was more than nominal. Cut off from the Tyrians and from the maritime Israelites, and deprived of the greater part of his exportable surplus, Rehoboam must perhaps in any case have found the ports of the Red Sea quite unserviceable. Nothing but the apparent ease with which one of his successors[2] resumes the power of the throne of Jerusalem over Idumæa, leads us to believe that his sovereignty was not in these times formally disavowed. As to the Philistine conduct, it is peculiarly difficult to draw inferences from our scanty materials; since we do not even know to how many of their towns the jealousy of Solomon may have permitted walls, nor what facility existed of holding their citadels by Hebrew garrisons. In the reign of Rehoboam's grandson, we find the Philistine town of Gibbethon twice endure a siege from kings of Israel, while the king of

---

[1] 1 Kings xiv. 23, 24. The Chronicles omit everything so shocking against a son of Solomon; and only indicate that in his fifth year he forsook Jehovah, and was immediately chastised by Shishak's invasion, which brought about his repentance. The *sin* is probably a mere inference from the *visitation*.

Among the images erected and consecrated by some kings of Judah, which remained until the reign of Josiah, are particularly named certain *horses dedicated to the Sun*, at the very entrance of the house of Jehovah, as likewise *chariots of the Sun*. Later writers perhaps mistook every image for an idol. Bishop Colenso identifies " the Sun " with the *Syro-Phœnician* deity called Jehovah.

[2] Jehoshaphat.

Judah remains apparently unconcerned. Since the tribe of Dan clearly must be reckoned among the ten[1] which are said to adhere to Jeroboam, it may appear that circumstances unexplained (such as the disaffection of Hebrew garrisons to Rehoboam) gave to the kings of Israel the sovereignty (whether more or less severely enforced) over the Philistine towns which were nominally the portion of Dan. On the other hand, the way in which Jericho is afterwards named implies that that fertile lowland, which is counted as a part of Benjamin, fell to Jeroboam, to whose region its physical position naturally united it. Thus the Israelite territory closed round that of Judah on the north-east and north-west, and cut it off almost entirely from the sea.

But Jeroboam had far too much on his hands to make him willing to attack his rival. A more urgent care was to fortify the city of Shechem as his capital, and next, the town of Penuel near the brook Jabbok beyond the Jordan, in order to confirm his authority over the eastern tribes. Having provided for military defence, he made regulations concerning religion. His sacerdotal censors suppose him to have been chiefly moved by the fear that all Israel would go up to Jerusalem to sacrifice to Jehovah; and this may certainly have entered his calculations. Yet it is clear that not even Judah and Benjamin were disposed to do without local sanctuaries, to which, as every other nation in the world, they were all too much attached; nor had any parties such an idea of centralized religion as after-times conceived. It is enough therefore to believe the Israelitish king actuated by the same motives as Rehoboam. During his residence at the court of Shishak he had become familiarized with the outward forms of Egyptian idolatry, and it is even possible had been struck by the resemblance of some of their sacred symbols to the mystic cherubim. In the Assyrian visions of Ezekiel and

[1] Although his kingdom (which is called *Israel* in contrast to that of Rehoboam, which is called *Judah*) is always said to contain *ten* tribes, it may seem to be difficult to find so many, for the tribe of Simeon was swallowed up in Judah, and had no territorial existence, or at any rate can in no way be made out to belong to Israel. The song of Moses omits Simeon, and makes only eleven tribes besides Levi. If however we regard Manasseh east of Jordan and Manasseh west of Jordan as separate tribes (as in fact they were), the full number may in this way be counted.

in the Apocalypse, the forms of a man, a lion, an eagle, and an ox are found in strange combination as religious emblems; and the images erected by Jeroboam for worship, if not identical with any of these, were, according to the severity of our Decalogue, neither more nor less idolatrous than they; though *his* images were displayed to the public eye, while the cherubim in Solomon's temple could be seen only by the priests. Those of Jeroboam, however, are derided by the name of *golden calves*, and it is sufficiently remarkable that (as if to identify his offence with a legendary sin of Aaron's) he is represented to use Aaron's words of exhortation:[1] "Behold thy God, O Israel, who brought thee up out of the land of Egypt." The images were set up peculiarly,[2] not in Shechem (which would have been done if the object had been to rally Israel round Jeroboam's new capital), but at the two ends of the land,—at *Dan*, the northernmost town, and in the sacred city of *Bethel*, where Samuel had held his sessions, on the very frontier of Ephraim and Benjamin. It does not appear that any foreign god was here adored, or any moral impurities introduced: on the other hand, we have convincing casual evidence that the Hebrew people were habitual image-worshippers, before and after Jeroboam. An isolated fact which comes out is here pregnant with meaning. Down to the time of king Hezekiah, or more than two centuries and a half later than Jeroboam, the people subject to the house of David continued to burn incense to a certain brass serpent as to a god.[3] Towards the close of the monarchy this was believed to have been an image made by Moses in the wilderness to work a miracle by; but we have no means of learning whether that belief was shared by the worshippers, or whether, in adoring it, they fancied they were pleasing Jehovah. The serpent is a well-known emblem in various pagan superstitions.

That the idolatry introduced by Jeroboam was *meant* to be a monotheistic ceremony is clear, not only from the language put into his mouth, so like to that of Aaron, but

[1] 1 Kings xii. 28, De Wette's Translation.
[2] Though the golden calves were at these two towns, temples were consecrated on high places in all the chief cities; 1 Kings xiii. 32, 33. In Amos we find *Gilgal* named as an idolatrous sanctuary.
[3] 2 Kings xviii. 4.

still more from the very different behaviour of the prophets, when Ahab really imported foreign religion. Nevertheless, in much later times the worship at Bethel and other high places became at length full of demoralizing practices, and called out against it the keenest attacks of the extant prophets, Amos, Hosea, and Micah; and this led the later compilers of the history to take the blackest view of Jeroboam's character, who has earned with them the unenviable epithet, "the son of Nebat, *who made Israel to sin.*"

Yet they do not conceal that their grand quarrel against Jeroboam is a ceremonial one. No moral evil, in fact, is imputed by them; his offence was, that he ordained priests, not from the Levites, but from the tribes promiscuously; and this "became sin to the house of Jeroboam, to cut it off and destroy it from off the face of the earth."[1] He likewise neglected their sacred days, making a solemn feast on the fifteenth day of the eighth month, while in Jerusalem they held the feast of Tabernacles just one month earlier. As Christians have raved concerning the time of Easter, so did the later Levites against "the day which Jeroboam had devised of his own heart."[2]

Where our earlier and better record is satisfied with noticing the fact, that Jeroboam did not employ Levites as his priests, the Chronicler superadds a great migration of Levites from Israel into Judah, abandoning all their worldly prospects. With them, he says, came many of all the tribes of Israel, for the satisfaction of living in communion with Jerusalem.—Yet the prophets came *not;* and with good reason, when the idolatry established there by Solomon and Rehoboam was so much fouler than that of the calves at Dan and Bethel. It can hardly be doubted that the Chronicler *assumed* there had previously been Levites dispersed in Levitical towns over all the land during David and Solomon's reigns, and then *inferred* that

[1] 1 Kings xiii. 33.
[2] If we could believe a legend which manifestly gained its final shape in the reign of Josiah, a man of God went to Bethel to withstand Jeroboam, and predicted that a child named Josiah should be born in the house of David, who should burn on that altar the bones of dead priests. To accredit his word, the altar was rent and its ashes poured out; and when Jeroboam put out his hand against the man of God, it was miraculously shrivelled up. Again it was restored at the prayer of the man of God. Yet the miracles produced no result whatever.

they must have been expelled by Jeroboam. On the contrary, it is not credible that this prince found any large body of Levites in his dominions; and that is probably the sufficient reason why he did not make priests of them. It has been already remarked, that the Levites cannot have lived by *tithes* in cities of their own during the tumultuous period of the Judges. To put them into possession would have been for David or Solomon a most arduous operation, either very violent and oppressive to individuals, or effected by an enormous sacrifice of public revenue. In either case some historical notice of such a proceeding would be left to us. If therefore the Levites were already become in Jerusalem a strictly hereditary caste (which is highly uncertain), even so it would seem that Jeroboam could not have selected them for the public ministrations without making petition to his enemy, and introducing among his people those who might have been dangerous to his power. If his spirit was in reality that of "the man Micah" in earlier times, who preferred a Levite for a priest when he could get one, but ordained his own son as priest when no Levite could be had,—still, when the result was, that a non-Levitical priesthood arose, this incurred deep condemnation in the days of sacerdotal rigour; much as a Presbyterian church is censured by high Episcopalians. And especially when the worship at Bethel more and more assimilated itself to the impurities of Paganism, the accumulated guilt of the whole system was made to rest on the head of Jeroboam.

In any case, through the absence of the Aaronite order, important results ensued. Nearly as in modern continental Protestantism, so in Israel the priests fell under the control of the kingly power, and never grew into any such strength as to be able to resist and modify its despotism. But for that very reason, neither were they able to strengthen the crown when it was weak, and to support a fixed dynasty in the succession of the throne. They had little hold over the mind of the people, and could neither inculcate sacerdotalism with effect, nor resist foreign superstitions; nor in fact, as yet, even in Judah had the whole ecclesiastical body at all attained strength for either enterprise. On the other hand, from the absence of Aaronite priests, the prophets had so much the clearer field for their action in

Israel. By the great numbers of them found there some fifty or more years later, it appears certain that they must have multiplied under Jeroboam and his immediate successors. From the hints given us it may be inferred that they now dwelt in communities, under the superintendence of some older prophet, and laboured together for their scanty sustenance, like the monks of certain Orders in the middle ages. Bethel itself was one of their seats. While the prophet stayed in Israel, there can hardly have been any adequate moral reasons to induce Levites and the pious part of Israel voluntarily to emigrate into Judah.

Of these prophets the most celebrated was that Ahijah the *Shilonite*, by whose agency the division of Israel and Judah was brought about. His residence was at the sacred town of *Shiloh* in Ephraim, where the ark and Eli so long tarried; and he appears to have retained the veneration of the king to the last years of his long life. It was not to be credited that such a prophet had not vehemently denounced the wickedness of Jeroboam, as well as deplored his golden calves. Accordingly, those who compiled the records of these times with a knowledge of the after-events, represent Ahijah, when the wife of Jeroboam came to consult him on her son's health, as uttering a stern and exact prediction of the ruin which should overwhelm the house of Jeroboam, and the captivity of Israel into countries beyond the Euphrates; as the only comfort to the anxious mother, he informs her that her son shall immediately be taken from so evil a world, because there was some good thing in him towards Jehovah the God of Israel. Whatever Ahijah said, Jeroboam and his queen did not resent it: the aged and now blind prophet went to his grave in peace.

Long before this event Rehoboam had had to struggle with difficult circumstances, but not from his rival's hostility. The territory to which he succeeded was not onefourth of the Israelitish land, yet in actual power he very nearly competed with Jeroboam. He enjoyed the great advantage of compactness in his dominions, and as the grandson of David he was secure in the loyalty of the tribes which held to him. At the old centre of government he found a completeness of organization which must long have been wanting to Jeroboam; and, what was not less important, he was master of Solomon's chief treasures. If we can believe the account in Chronicles, the exertions now made by Rehoboam in fortifying his kingdom and garrisoning his castle were prodigious. Undoubtedly he had cause to fear, especially from Egypt, for of the hostile temper now active there he can hardly have been ignorant; and many of the towns said to be fortified by him might seem to be intended as defence from that quarter. But putting Egypt out of the question, it was requisite to prepare for attack from the Philistines and the Edomites. Among the latter the spirit of Hadad can hardly have been dead; and the former, who persevered in uncircumcision and heterogeneous habits, were an intestine foe, hardly less dangerous when free than if under Jeroboam. But as Jeroboam remained on the defensive, and Shishak delayed his meditated inroad till Rehoboam's fifth year, the Hebrew king successfully repressed all farther hostile tendencies, and appeared to be securely seated, though with diminished lustre, on his father's throne.

But in his fifth year he was overwhelmed by a flood of invasion, which is so concisely described in one record and so hyperbolically in the other, that it is hard to conjecture the exact truth.[1] The king of Egypt rushed in upon him, to seize his destined booty;—the plunder of the temple and of the king's treasure-house. The spoiler came and went, like a dream, leaving no other trace of his irresistible march than this one particular result. He was but a meteor shooting over the sky of Judæa, baleful to the imagination, but harmless in fact. He did not dismantle the castles, carry off the arms and munitions of war, plunder the towns of their valuables and the country of its cattle, so far as is stated or can be traced. Had he acted as those who make invasions for the sake of spoil generally act, the throne of David must have fallen for ever, or have been preserved only by an intense and lingering struggle. On the contrary, for anything that ap-

[1] 2 Chron. xii. 3. Shishak brings in "1200 chariots, 60,000 horsemen, and infantry *without number.*" To gather such a host, pass and repass the desart with it, and maintain it till disbanded, would be so enormously expensive, that to save himself from great loss, Shishak would have needed to plunder the whole of Rehoboam's little kingdom. His infantry are described as "Lubim, Sukkiim, and Ethiopians."

pears, Rehoboam's power remains unimpaired; and he leaves his kingdom to his son in a high state of organization and efficiency, if at least the Chronicler has not grossly misrepresented the truth in spirit as well as in details. The loss of the battle before Ramoth in Gilead by Jehoshaphat cost Judah severe and long-continued suffering from the assaults of the Edomites, Arabs, and Philistines; yet the occupation of Jerusalem itself by Shishak leads to no result that has deserved to be recorded. This is a problem involving to us some measure of perplexity.

The most direct hypothesis is that of bold incredulity. Is it not apparent (it might be said) that the invasion of Shishak is a *Deus ex machinâ* to account for one solitary fact, the disappearance of certain treasures from the temple and palace? And if these treasures ever existed, who is so likely to have used them as Rehoboam, while struggling to preserve the remnants of his father's power? And if our historians could imagine or invent an inroad of a million Ethiopians[1] half a century later, in order to aggrandize king Asa, why may they not have equally invented in this reign the countless host of Egyptians, to screen the sacrilege of Rehoboam? And in truth, if this invasion, like that of Zerah the Ethiopian, were named solely in the Chronicles, such incredulity would not be excessive. But when it is remembered that our historians in no other instance shrink from avowing how the best monarchs made free with the treasures of the temple for political ends, we find in this no adequate motive to them for so strange an invention. Moreover, the hostile movement of Shishak is in perfect keeping with the position which he had previously held towards Solomon, whose enemy Jeroboam he then sheltered and now leaves unassailed.

A second inquiry might be started, whether in fact the forces of Shishak were not called in by Rehoboam himself and voluntarily paid by him out of his father's treasures. But we may still ask—why then should not this have been stated, as frankly as in the case of Asa and Hezekiah? On the whole, therefore, no better explanation suggests itself than the following,—which however cannot be more than conjectural. The king of Egypt, full of the hostile feelings which Jeroboam had infused or cherished,

[1] 2 Chron. xiv. 9.

marched against the son of Solomon with the intention of pillaging Jerusalem. The Jewish prince, knowing his own inferiority, was prudent enough not to resist; and received Shishak into his capital. By the personal interview thus obtained, he convinced the invader that it was not his interest to make Jeroboam too powerful: that unless he chose to advance the Egyptian frontier beyond the desart, and hereby expose himself to a thousand contingencies, true policy dictated that he should keep the balance between the two Hebrew princes, and carefully avoid to weaken Rehoboam too much. Shishak was made to see that since the days of Solomon the wings of the Jewish eagle had been effectually clipped; and changing his own views, was contented to take all the gold treasure of Jerusalem as the indemnification of his march. He then retired home in an orderly manner,[1] throwing the weight of his influence with all the neighbouring peoples into the scale of Rehoboam.[2]

In this or in some such way, the dynasty of David was saved through the dangerous transition, which, from lords of a united and conquering nation, reduced his descendants to petty princes dependent on the forbearance of a powerful neighbour. But the desart ordinarily removed all fear from the side of Egypt, and against nearer nations the king of Jerusalem and Judæa was well able to defend himself. Between him and Jeroboam there was no amity,[3] yet neither was there active or dangerous war; nothing at least of their warlike exploits has been deemed worthy of remembrance.

Although unable to vie with his father in the splendour

[1] Some have imagined that the pillars set up by Sesostris in Palestine, which Herodotus says he saw, must have been really the work of Shishak. But of these nothing is known beyond what Herodotus tells us.—Near Beirut sculptures are found, not on pillars, but on the natural rock, which are judged to be partly Persian and partly Egyptian; and, in the hieroglyphics of the latter, Dr Lepsius says that the name of Sesostris is found twice. But these can in no way be identified with Shishak's invasion of Judah.—Expounders of the hieroglyphics tell us that pictures represent *the king of Judah* (with his title added) brought bound to Sheshonk. This can only be pictorial. [Colonel Rawlinson thinks the letters on the Beirut sculptures to be " Medo Assyrian:" Journal of Asiat. S. vol. x. p. 27.]
[2] It perhaps may be added, that the Edomites had as yet imperfectly recovered from Joab's wholesale massacre. By the time of Jehoshaphat and his son their numbers had again increased.
[3] 1 Kings xiv. 30.

of his seraglio, he inherited the belief that to indulge in
many wives was a peculiar privilege of royalty.. Our
later authority alone states this, and assigns to him 18
wives, 60 concubines, 28 sons and 60 daughters. The
names also of three wives, descendants of Jesse, are
given; but they are none quite free from difficulty.[1] His
favourite wife was Maachah, who seems to have been
granddaughter to David's son Absalom, by his beautiful
daughter Tamar; and her son Abijam was selected by
Rehoboam as his successor. His other sons he dispersed
as governors through the fortified towns, intending hereby to strengthen his dynasty. He died after a reign of
eighteen years,[2] and having been buried in the royal
sepulchres, was succeeded without commotion by his son
ABIJAM.

Abijam's reign was short, and in no respect memorable.
His mother Maachah was given to superstition as much as
his Ammonitish grandmother; and he is commemorated
by our elder historian for nothing else but for his disgraceful support of foreign and impure ceremonies. It is
added, that like his father, he persevered in hostility to
Jeroboam;[3] but we have not a single trustworthy detail

[1] 2 Chr. xi. 18—22, xiii. 2 ; 1 Kings xv. 2. The mother of Abijam is
variously called Maachah daughter of *Abishalom*, Maachah daughter of *Absalom*, and *Michaiah* daughter of *Uriel* of Gibeah. Abishalom is probably Absalom, and Michaiah a corruption of Maachah: if so, it is likely that *daughter*
of Absalom is a loose expression for granddaughter. For as Absalom was slain
when Solomon was a mere boy, Absalom's own daughter can scarcely have been
Rehoboam's wife. But Absalom's daughter Tamar (2 Sam. xiv. 27) may have
been married to Uriel, a kinsman of Saul, and have become mother of Maachah. Even so, there is a new difficulty, in Maachah being also called mother
to king Asa ; but this will be presently observed upon. Another wife of Rehoboam is Abihail *daughter* of Eliab, David's eldest brother; where daughter
may seem less proper than *great-granddaughter*. For Rehoboam came to the
throne 110 years after the birth of David ; and perhaps 130 years after the
birth of Eliab. A third wife is Mahalath, daughter of Jerimoth son of David;
which is possibly correct, if Jerimoth was a son of old age to David.

[2] B.C. 937. Shemaiah the prophet and Iddo the seer are referred to as
writers of the acts of Rehoboam. Iddo wrote visions which he had seen against
Jeroboam, and is an authority also for the close of Solomon's life, and for the
whole of Abijam's.

[3] The Chronicler (2 Chr. xiii.) has thought it necessary to give some particulars of this war. Abijah (as he calls him) leads out 400,000 chosen men ;
Jeroboam sets in array against him 800,000 chosen men and mighty men of
valour. Abijah makes a pious and highly sacerdotal harangue to his troops,
and after it slays 500,000 of the enemy. Upon this he recovers from Jeroboam
the towns and districts of Bethel, Jeshanah, and Ephrain. Yet it is evident that
Bethel remained with the kings of Israel. Some have wished to divide the

surviving. He was taken off by a premature death,[1] and was honoured with the usual royal burial. His youthful son Asa succeeded him.

As for Jeroboam, though he outlived both Rehoboam and his son, our meagre historians furnish us not with a single additional fact, or any true insight into his character. It is unreasonable to doubt, that his anti-Levitical arrangements (which alone the historians care to record) formed the least part of the cares and concerns of his government. It is not likely that so vigorous and able a man lost the Israelitish sovereignty over the Ammonites without a struggle, or that the Moabites continued in payment of tribute to him without a difficult war; and if we could recover the true chronicles of his reign, we might find that these foreigners, with the Philistines of the Danite territory, next to the general organization of, his kingdom, required all the activity of his mind and body. Concerning his relations with the king of Damascus, not a hint remains even to guide conjecture. Our materials only enable us to assert that Jeroboam built himself a palace at Tirzah, a lovely spot, where his successors also held their court. He died the year after Abijam,[2] and left his throne to his son Nadab.

Geographical knowledge fails us as to the accurate site of the Philistine town of Gibbethon, to reduce which was the sole object of Nadab's reign. The book of Joshua assigns this town to the tribe of Dan, and it is generally supposed to be south of Ashdod or Azotus. If so, this will confirm our belief that the northern towns of Philistia had fallen into the hands of Jeroboam, and that the Israelite dominion was beginning to hem in Judæa from the west, and almost entirely cut it off from the sea. Neither on this occasion, nor twenty-five years later, when the attempt was renewed, does the prudent and energetic king of Judah attempt to succour the town of Gibbethon; which certainly appears to show that he did not regard it as belonging to his crown. The siege under Nadab was cut short by a lamentable deed, which began endless con-

---

large numbers by 10; but this is to overlook the whole spirit of the book. In fact the Chronicler has converted the son of Rehoboam into a pious man, instead of the impure pagan which he appears in the other record.
[1] B.C. 935.   [2] B.C. 934.

fusion to the throne of Israel,—the assassination of Nadab himself by BAASHA son of Ahijah,[1] of the house of Issachar, who proceeded to usurp the royal dignity.[2] We are not informed whether Baasha was actuated by revenge, or by simple ambition : if by the latter, it cannot be alleged that Nadab or his father had earned such a retaliation. Jeroboam did not rise against the life of Solomon or of his son : he had been the free choice of a willing and attached people, who summoned him out of Egypt to espouse their cause; and in his conduct he left no precedent which should lessen our indignation and hatred at this violent deed. The murderer knew that half-measures would only rob him of his hire, and cruelly extirpated every living soul of the house of Jeroboam; by which he certainly earned for himself an undisturbed reign, but set an example which was repeated against his son's life and throne. The ferocious manners still prevalent, notwithstanding all that the reign of Solomon might be imagined likely to effect, are indicated in the prophetical formula of denunciation, which must have been copied too faithfully from real life :[3] "Him that dieth of Jeroboam in the city shall the dogs eat, and him that dieth in the field shall the fowls of the air eat." Such, we must conclude, was the brutal treatment of the innocent members of the royal house.

As the succession in the kingdom of Israel is often broken, it will be well for the reader to examine the chronological conspectus (at p. 139 above) of the dynasties from Jeroboam to the accession of Jehu.

It appears on a glance at the table, that there are three dynasties in Israel in this period, while the realm of Judah enjoyed the great advantage of an undisputed throne. Indeed, besides the commotion attending the murder of Nadab, a civil war lasting four years followed the destruction of the next dynasty, and must of itself have so weakened this kingdom as to free the house of David from fear of its power. Both these convulsions took place during the long reign of Asa, a monarch whose

---

[1] Of course not the prophet Ahijah the *Shilonite*.
[2] B.C. 932.
[3] 1 Kings xiv. 11. The formula is repeated for Baasha, 1 Kings xvi. 4; for Ahab, 1 Kings xxi. 24.

wise administration first infused real energy into the kingdom of Jerusalem, after the disasters with which for many years it had had to struggle.

Asa, having entered upon royal cares at an early age,[1] in the very opening of his reign showed a totally different spirit from either of his three predecessors. With the discrimination of the best kings of this race, he allowed the worship *of Jehovah* at the high places,[2] and on no account confined all public sacrifice and burning of incense to the temple at Jerusalem; but he put down with a high hand the impurities which Solomon, Rehoboam, and Abijam had established or permitted, and removed all the idols[3] which they had set up. We now learn by a casual expression, what might have been conjectured from the position of Bathsheba towards Solomon, that in the little kingdom of Judæa, as afterwards in the mighty court of Persia, the king's mother enjoyed a peculiar title and rank,—which we ill translate by *queen*,—with higher privileges than his wife. In ancient Persia it is known that the king might sometimes adopt a mother for political reasons;[4] and if ever the mother of the king's father continued to receive the title and honours of the Chief Lady, it is probable that she was named "the King's Mother." This perhaps may account for our finding Maachah, mother of the deceased king, now spoken of as queen and *mother* of Asa. In the two preceding reigns, she had gone along with the degrading superstitions of the court, and had herself set up an idolatrous image of Astarte. Young Asa accordingly took the bold and painful resolution of deposing his grandmother from her queenly rank; destroyed her idol and burnt it by the brook Kedron: hereby proclaiming most distinctly that neither relationship to himself nor any station should be

---

[1] B.C. 935.

[2] 1 Kings xv. 14, is most express on this point, and the words are repeated in 2 Chr. xv. 17. The statement *seems* to be contradicted in 2 Chr. xiv. 3, which is either an exaggeration, or to be explained to mean "the high places *of strange gods*." In 2 Chr. xv. 17, *Israel* is carelessly used for *Judah*.

[3] The horses consecrated to the Sun (if already in existence) were perhaps not worshipped, and therefore not regarded by him as idols, though a later age stigmatized them as such.

[4] In the abridgement of Ctesias we read that Cyrus, upon conquering Astyages, *adopted* Amytis (or Mandane) as his mother, in order to win the easier submission of some parts of the empire not yet subdued.

allowed to shelter these detestable immoralities. The act was not less faithful than politic. He at once rallied round himself the enthusiasm of the sound-hearted worshippers of Jehovah, in whom the peculiar national patriotism was concentrated; and with no small reason was he regarded as the first worthy descendant of David. And he had need of all their support; for Baasha, the new king of Israel, however unprincipled, was not wanting in energy or in policy.

Baasha's first measure appears to have been to establish himself in Tirzah as the centre of his government. Jeroboam had been popular in Shechem, and it is probable that the usurper did not dare to trust himself to its inhabitants. Thus Tirzah, which had been a palace under the old dynasty—perhaps already a fortified one—under the new gathered around it an imperial city. Next to organizing the government in his new capital, his most weighty care was to secure the alliance of the newly risen and formidable power of BENHADAD, king of DAMASCUS. As, from this time forth, this king and his successors exceedingly influence the fortunes of Israel, it seems proper to add a few words concerning the site of Damascus and its facilities for empire.

Damascus lies on a highly fertile and moderately elevated plain, celebrated for its gardens and orchards, immediately to the east of the lofty ridge called Anti-Libanus, the southern point of which is Mount Hermon. From these heights run down many streams, the greatest of which were named Pharphar and Abana. Pharphar appears to be the river now called the Barrada, which runs through Damascus itself. Numerous canals distribute the water of the streams over the whole country, and maintain the luxuriance of vegetation in the hottest season. Even so, much water runs to waste into an internal lake which spreads out towards the eastern desart. Syria itself enjoyed a high measure of civilization and physical culture from the earliest ages, and at that æra was already an *old* country, teeming with cities and population. Its climate is moderated by the height of the plains, and by the breezes from the mountains; and taken as a whole, its advantages were such, that whoever became master of it, reckoned amongst the foremost

powers of the early world. From the city of Damascus
access is afforded to Emesa on the north and to Bashan
on the south, without ascending any formidable elevation :
so that while the fertile soil is able to support both men
and horses in great numbers, a force of cavalry or even of
chariots finds there great facility of action over a broad
expanse of country. From Emesa, returning southward,
we ascend gradually into the loftier plain of the Hollow
Syria, between Libanus and Anti-Libanus, of which
Baalbek was the chief city ; thus if these ridges cannot be
crossed by armies of horses, yet the entire plain of Syria,
by a circuitous route, is accessible to them from Damascus.
In the times of which we treat, chariots appear to have
been the principal or the most dreaded force of the
Damascenes; and in fact we may trace a greatly increased
use of them among the Hebrews. This circumstance is
important, as it explains how much more formidable an
enemy Benhadad was beyond Jordan than in western
Israel; for his chariots could come into Ephraim only by
crossing the Jordan, or by a long journey through dangerous country; and while there, were always liable to get
entangled in unfavourable ground.

Mention has already been made of that Rezon, who in
the later part of Solomon's reign established himself in
Damascus. Of his after-fortunes and those of his successors we know only thus much,—that he was followed on
the throne by Hezion,[1] he by his son Tabrimon, and
grandson Benhadad, with whom Baasha now made a
league; and that before the arms of these princes the
kingdom of Hamath and all Hollow Syria gave way, and
became absorbed in the power of Damascus, whose king
is now called king of Syria. It is probable that a good
part of Bashan was already Benhadad's, and that he
pressed close upon the land of Israel. With such a
potentate either alliance or war appeared inevitable, and
it was a piece of good fortune that Baasha was able to
obtain the former.

When the king of Israel had thus, as he hoped, secured
himself from the attack of an encroaching neighbour, he

[1] Many regard Hezion and Rezon as the same name corruptly written. This
is possible, but cannot be proved. The chronology does not refute the opinion,
but it is not very favourable to it.

commenced more active operations against the house of
Judah than either of his predecessors. It is possible that
Israel now recovered whatever small losses had been incurred by the attacks of Abijam, and by confirming its
predominance over the northern cities of Philistia, justified
the general feeling that (what was called) the tribe of Dan
formed part of the Israelitish territory. But no other details of this war have been deemed worthy of preservation,
than one of such critical importance, that all the rest
vanished in comparison with it. Baasha indeed must already have had encouraging success, or must have possessed unusual military enterprise, to adopt so bold a
policy.[1] The town of Ramah lay about six miles to the
north of Jerusalem, on the way to Bethel, and in the heart
of the tribe of Benjamin. It is situated on a hill, and
looks down upon Gibeah of Saul on its east. This spot
Baasha occupied and began to fortify;[2] by means of which
he would have been able to intercept communications
from all the richest part of Benjamin to Jerusalem, and at
every moment threaten the capital of his enemy with surprise. Asa could not fail to be at once sensible of the
danger constantly impending from such a fortress,[3] and
resolved at any price to free himself from it. Perhaps he
had already had experience of his adversary's superior
military talents or greater force (although our partial
historians are here silent); for he did not venture on a
direct attack until he had betaken himself to a measure
which must have been adopted very unwillingly. He
sent an embassy to Benhadad king of Syria, entreating

[1] Asa, according to the credulous Chronicler, had an army of 300,000 heavy-
armed troops, and 280,000 light-armed (2 Chr. xiv. 8), "all mighty men of
valour."

[2] The Chronicler (2 Chr. xv. 19, xvi. 1) commits the extraordinary error of
stating that Asa had no more war down to *the 35th year* of his reign, but that
in the 36th year Baasha fortified Ramah against him. But Baasha was already
dead in Asa's 26th year. Some therefore wish to alter the text; but an
arbitrary and double change is then needed. It is clear from the book of
Kings, that Baasha was in continual war against Asa, until all was wound up
by the affair of Ramah; but the Chronicler, who disapproves of Asa's alliance
with Benhadad, tries to thrust it off to the end of his life, in order to give him
a long period of purity and glory; and into this early part he then interpolates
a fictitious invasion by Zerah the Ethiopian with a *million* men.

[3] Such a castle was what the Greeks called an ἐπιτείχισμα, or *offensive fortress*, like that of Deceleia in Attica, or Pylos in Messenia during the Pelopon-
nesian war. Arnold often comments on this mode of warfare in his Thucydides
and elsewhere. See also Thirlwall's Greece, *passim*.

him to break his league with Baasha and attack the kingdom of Israel: and as an inducement to so discreditable a deed, presented him with all the silver and gold, whether in the form of treasure or of vessels, which he could command; sparing r⋅' ⋅he precious articles of his own palace, nor the offerıu͏̈ dicated by himself and by his father to the house of Jehovah. Undoubtedly Asa, like all ancient kings and states so situated, argued with himself, that if *he* spared the treasure, his victorious enemy would not; while if he survived the war, he would be able to replace it with interest.[1] His message to Benhadad softens the violence of his proposal, by asserting or implying that there had been a league between their two fathers; a fact of which nothing appears. It is however credible, that Abijam had sought the alliance of Tabrimon, though no result, beyond compliment, came of it. The ambassadors of Asa would probably magnify to Benhadad the wickedness, ambition, and power of Baasha, so as to furnish the Syrian prince with some pretext of conscience for now adopting the course which interest and ambition suggested. Nor were they unsuccessful. Benhadad accepted the bribe from one king, and sent his generals to despoil the other. Ijon, Dan, and Abel-beth-maachah are named among the Israelitish cities which they captured or plundered, besides "all Cinneroth (or the country of the sea of Galilee), and all the land of Naphthali." Assailed by so powerful an enemy on the north, Baasha was forced to draw off his attention from the south. Asa then, profiting by the important moment, made a general proclamation through his dominions, to assemble the able-bodied population in mass; who made a universal rush against the fortress of Ramah. Its fortifications seem to have been not quite complete, or its garrison retired through fear; and the men of Judah without delay demolished every part, and carried off the very materials of

---

[1] We not only have no ground to suppose that his contemporaries or successors disapproved of Asa's conduct, but it is not censured in the book of Kings. Only the Levitical Chronicler thinks it necessary to make a prophet rebuke him, and Asa then so angry as to imprison him. The prophet is made to declare, *from henceforth thou shalt have wars*, which appears the reverse of truth; for hitherto he had had war, but henceforth he enjoys quiet, and suffers nothing but the gout in his old age; finally the Chronicler reproves him because he consulted physicians *and not Jehovah;* that is, "and not the priests."

stone and timber. With these, Asa now fortified the little towns of Mizpah and Geba on his frontier. The site of the latter is uncertain, but we know that it is a theoretic northern extremity of the kingdom of Judah, as Beersheba is the southern point: there is however reason to think it north of Bethel, and in the actual dominions of Baasha.

No further account is given of the reign of Asa. We are only told vaguely " of his acts, and his might, and the cities which he fortified." But as he survived Baasha fifteen years, and no more war with Israel is mentioned,[1] we may assume that it was a time of peace. Indeed the internal convulsions which the northern kingdom speedily underwent, changed the whole policy of the house of Judah. It became manifest, that no longer Israel, but Syria, was the enemy to be dreaded, and that it was requisite for Judah to strengthen Israel, lest Syria should swallow up both. That the latter part of Asa's reign was one of repose and security, may be probably inferred from the great increase of strength which we discern in Judæa in the early years of his son's reign. His destruction of heathenish and impure rites may for the time have caused disaffection in one party as well as have excited enthusiasm in the other; but after the generation had passed by, which remembered and regretted these evil orgies, a more entire unanimity probably existed, and the throne of David had a stronger support in the heart of a united and flourishing people, than it had known since the early days of Solomon. The house and family of Asa was in favourable contrast to that of his predecessors. The numerous wives of Abijam, as well as of Rehoboam and Solomon, are markedly commented on; as therefore nothing of the kind is dropt concerning Asa, who in fact (as far as we know) had but one son, we could almost believe that he respected the sanctity of woman, and contented himself with his wife Azubah. At any rate, a decided check seems to have been given to the extrava-

[1] The Chronicler alludes to "cities of Ephraim which Asa had taken," 2 Chr. xvii. 2; but that is likely to have been, if correct, in the time of Baasha. The book of Kings also says that "Jehoshaphat *made peace* with Israel" (1 Kings xxii. 44); but this, in the connexion of that fragmentary summary, seems to mean *made alliance;* and does not imply that Asa had active war with Omri and Ahab.

gant abuse of polygamy. Asa died[1] after a reign of forty-one years, leaving his kingdom to his son JEHOSHAPHAT, then thirty-five years old.

We return to the kingdom of Israel. The energetic and warlike Baasha could not make the prophets forget the crime by which he had attained his kingdom; but the dread of his power and vehemence perhaps suppressed during his life any direct remonstrance. After he had been forced to abandon Ramah by the attack of Benhadad, no details of his war are given us; but it is clear that he was enabled to patch up a peace, though perhaps at the cost of the towns already captured; for we presently find his son so far freed from fear of Syria, as to resume offensive operations in Philistia. Of Baasha no more is recorded than that he died in the twenty-fourth year of his reign, and was succeeded by his son ELAH.[2]

This Elah, to judge by the slight but emphatic notice of him, was addicted to voluptuous excesses. Instead of heading his armies in person, as his father and all the kings of this age, he sent Omri, captain of his host, to conduct the siege of Gibbethon, from which the Israelites had retired some twenty-five years before, in consequence of the murder of their king. Elah himself remained at Tirzah, indulging his luxurious inclinations. His despicable character seems to have stimulated the prophet Jehu, the son of Hanani,[3] to a vehement and public denunciation of Baasha and his guilty house, which he declared by the word of Jehovah should be utterly cut off and destroyed. Nor was it long before his words were verified. ZIMRI, captain of half the chariots,—whether aware of the prophecy or not,—while Elah was at a drunken banquet in the house of his high steward at Tirzah, slew him and assumed the royal station. Without a moment's delay he took advantage of his position at the royal palace to seize and murder every living re-

---

[1] B.C. 894.   [2] B.C. 909.
[3] 1 Kings xvi. 1—5, 7, 12.—The position of v. 7 implies a denunciation uttered after Baasha's death; the incoherence however of the narrative makes the time doubtful. Altogether, since the compiler wrote in much later time, with full knowledge of the results, these prophecies become very doubtful, even when recorded in the book of Kings. Jehu, full forty years later than this, compiled the life of Jehoshaphat. He may seem to have been too young to act in the lifetime of Baasha and Elah.

lative of his late lord, and left the house of Baasha utterly desolate.[1]

But the army at Gibbethon, on hearing the tidings, was indignant that the kingdom should be thus seized behind their back by a traitorous and inferior officer; and forthwith, in the midst of the camp, they by acclamation raised to the throne their own general OMRI; on whom the acceptable duty immediately devolved of revenging his slaughtered master. Once more was Gibbethon saved from Israelitish attack by the murder of a king; for Omri without delay broke up his camp and marched straight back to Tirzah, where he besieged Zimri with very superior force. Into the *city* of Tirzah he soon forced his way; whereupon Zimri retired into the *palace*, which is likely to have been a citadel to the town; but finding escape impossible and his case desperate, he burned the palace over his head, and perished in the conflagration, only seven days after his ruthless murders.

Great as are the evils which the perversion of the idea of Legitimacy has brought on modern Europe, they are decidedly less than result from the extirpation of royal houses in a country destitute of constitutional organization. These promiscuous massacres left to Israel nothing around which they might rally. A section of the nation was averse to Omri, or disliked the precedent of the army electing a sovereign. In consequence, a strong party favoured the pretensions of TIBNI, son of Ginath, to the crown. Of this person nothing is known, save that for four years he continued the contest with Omri. In some civil wars a principle is involved, and a result of permanent importance is at last purchased, if dearly. But unhappy Israel suffered to no purpose, except to the aggrandizement of Damascus, until at length Tibni was overpowered and slain, and Omri left sole claimant of the throne.[2]

[1] B.C. 908. [2] B.C. 904.

CHAPTER VI.

THE HOUSE OF OMRI, B.C. 904—864.

OMRI, though founder of a new dynasty, ascended the throne, like Jeroboam, without crime. If Zimri had been less bloody, and had left alive any of the sons or grandsons of Baasha, the character of Omri might have come down to us less unstained; but by his war against Zimri he gained only credit, and for his civil conflict with Tibni, however disastrous to the nation, it was difficult to blame him. The centre of his power was at first at Tirzah,[1] but when his competitor had been removed, he determined to found a new capital. Tirzah had originally been selected only as a pleasant abode. The case with which Omri had himself stormed the city may have disinclined him to trust it for the future; and as the palace had been burnt, there was perhaps less to lose by removal. He accordingly selected a hill suitable for a new city, and purchased it of its owner, a man named Shemer; from whom the place was called *Shimrón*, or in its Greek modification, *Samaria*. The judicious choice of Omri is attested by the lasting importance of this celebrated city, which is regarded as having great advantage, even over Jerusalem, in strength, as well as in fertility and beauty. From the accounts of modern travellers, the following careful picture of the site has been compiled by one who has laboured meritoriously on the geography of Palestine :—[2] "The hill of Samaria is an oblong mountain of considerable elevation and very regular in form, situated in the midst of a broad, deep valley, the continuation of that of Shechem, which here expands into five or six miles. Beyond this valley, which completely isolates the hill, the mountains rise again on every side, forming a complete wall around the city. They are terraced to the tops, sown in grain, and planted with olives and figs.

[1] We have not a hint where the chief strength of *Tibni* lay. It may have been in the tribes beyond Jordan.
[2] From the pen of Dr Kitto, art. *Samaria*, in his Biblical Cyclopædia.

...... The hill of Samaria itself is cultivated from its base, the terraced sides and summits being covered with corn and with olive-trees. About midway up the ascent, the hill is surrounded by a narrow terrace of level land, like a belt, below which the roots of the hill spread off more gradually into the valleys. Higher up too are the marks of slight terraces, once occupied perhaps by the streets of the ancient city. The ascent of the hill is very steep." We may add that it is a little to the north of Shechem and of Mount Ebal. Samaria was the principal or sole work of Omri's reign; a durable and splendid monument which he bequeathed to a distant posterity.

He may have been moved to this great undertaking by military motives not indicated to us. The king of Syria appears not to have been slow to discover the weakness which civil contention entailed on Israel, and pressed severely upon the new ruler. Considering that the Benhadad who attacked Baasha took from him the towns of Dan, Ijon, and Abel-beth-maachah, we may probably infer that the military object of the Syrians in this stage of their progress had been to possess themselves of all the towns which commanded the passes from Hollow Syria and the proper land of Damascus into the Israelitish territory. Omri had not the advantage of such a frontier on the north as Judæa had on the south: and it would appear that he was forced to submit to high claims on the part of Benhadad. We learn incidentally that the latter took various cities from Omri, and forced him to assign streets in Samaria for his use.[1] In fact, the king of Israel was now open to invasion at any time convenient to his powerful rival, and appeared likely before long to become a mere vassal of Damascus. Omri accordingly, to save

[1] (1 Kings xx. 34:) Either for trade or for the residence of the Syrian representative, who would more or less control Omri's conduct. So the English make native princes in India accept a British resident, and have demanded "English streets" in Canton.

The king of Syria who attacked Omri is father of the Benhadad who assaults Ahab, and is generally regarded as identical with the Benhadad who took the frontier towns from Baasha. The chronology however rather countenances the idea that the first Benhadad is grandfather to the second, and that the antagonist of Omri is an intermediate prince, *possibly not named Benhadad*, but Tabrimon, Rezon, or some other name of that dynasty. It does not appear to have been usual for a king to bear the name of his immediate father.

himself and his people, sought alliance with the Phœnicians.

Immediately on becoming sole king of Israel, he obtained the hand of JEZEBEL,[1] daughter of Ethbaal king of Sidon and of Tyre, for his young son Ahab. Let not those who know the after-career of this notorious woman, be too quick to censure Omri for what he could not foresee. Indeed the position of the princes of this northern kingdom, in contact with an ambitious, advancing, and overpowering neighbour, was peculiarly difficult. There were two things which wisdom would exhort them to maintain; the pure faith of the nation, and its independent existence. The latter appeared a condition indispensable to the former; and if intrinsically of less value, yet was certainly that which was felt more peculiarly to be under the care of the kings. One object however was perpetually interfering with the other. When in danger of losing their national monotheism with their nationality itself, to remain isolated was to court destruction; yet to form alliances with heathen powers was to risk alloying their religious superiority;—a superiority which we believe to have been real, however much it may have been exaggerated by unwise partisanship. It is much easier for a prophet or a divine to *say*, that by disowning human alliances and trusting in Jehovah, the nation would have been saved; than for a king or statesman, on whom the responsiblity rests, to *act* on such a theory: and to inveigh against Omri and Ahab is too much in writers[2] who cannot spare a word of censure for Solomon's gratuitous heathen marriages and heathen abominations. Of Omri there is no more known than that he died B.C. 897, and was succeeded by his son.

AHAB appears to have been rather a weak than a wicked man. His evil name has been chiefly earned for him by his wife Jezebel; and *he* can scarcely be regarded as responsible for the marriage which his father contracted for him. It was impossible to cement his alliance with Tyre and Sidon without tolerating the superstitions in which

[1] Ahaziah, king of Judah, grandson of Ahab and Jezebel, was twenty-two years old in the year 865. He was therefore born in 887. Allowing his mother Athaliah to have been only sixteen at his birth, Jezebel's marriage cannot well have been later than B.C. 904, which is the year of Omri becoming sole king.

[2] The compilers of the Chronicles.

the daughter of Ethbaal had been reared; and the immediate result of tolerating them, was to arouse against himself the whole influence of the prophets of Israel. Solomon's son and grandson had indeed done as much as Ahab, and still more, without encountering the same opposition; but under Solomon the prophetical schools had not at all attained the same growth, nor the same exclusive power over the people, as now in Israel: after Solomon, in Judæa, it is probable that they had been greatly discouraged by the results of Ahijah's interference, which can have been in no respect advantageous, in the estimate of either prophet or priest. As we now read the tale in the books of Kings and Chronicles, the monotonous condemnation passed on Jeroboam and all his successors is apt to blind us to the fact, that in spite of the predictions ascribed to Ahijah and Jehu son of Hanani, no real and vehement opposition on the part of the prophets against the throne began in Israel before the reign of Ahab. And with good reason. For previous kings of this branch had avowed support to no religious rites but those of Jehovah. They had sanctioned worshipping him by emblems, but so did orthodox [1] prophets and priests of those days: they neglected the Levites of Jerusalem; but at that time the Levites seem not yet to have been a race or caste of men, but only a very humble profession. These kings had not defiled the character of Jehovah by ascribing to him, and annexing to his worship, immorality and cruelty; nor had they given honour even to the name of a strange god. A totally new thrill of horror passed through the bosoms of true Israelites when Jezebel brought in the obscene rites of Baal and Astarte,[2] with the tumultuous fanaticism of her priests; and the universal opposition which thereupon arose from the prophets of Jehovah presently made her their inveterate and dangerous enemy.

If we give the least credit to the hostile historian, we cannot refuse to admit that Jezebel, in the course of her

---

[1] I have already referred to the *Teraphim* and *Cherubim* in proof.
[2] It is believed that Baal and Astarte were originally personifications of the sun and moon. Baal (*lord*) is also probably indentified with Molech (*king*). The Hebrew writers use the latter term chiefly of the god of the Ammonites, the former of the Phœnician god; but other authorities call the Tyrian and Carthaginian god *Melcarth*, whose name and bloody worship are identified with those of Molech.

JEZEBEL PERSECUTES THE PROPHETS.

feud with the prophets of Jehovah, became a fierce and cruel woman; yet, rightly to appreciate her character, we must remember that they on their part did undoubtedly consider it a meritorious act, to kill the priests of Baal: and a remarkable legend extols the piety of the great Elijah, who on an eminent occasion instigated the people to seize and massacre 450 prophets of Baal and 400 of Astarte, who ate at Jezebel's table. We may hesitate to believe the story to the full, since a credulous admiration of Elijah would lead to great exaggeration of his exploit: yet it would be unreasonable to doubt that these prophets deliberately approved of slaying the priestly votaries of superstition, or that Jezebel had a clear insight[1] into this side of their principles. With her therefore it was a struggle of life and death. To judge of her by other Pagans, she would have tolerated Jehovism, if it would have tolerated her; but as she quite understood that they would kill her priests, and probably herself too, whenever they had the power, she pursued them with implacable enmity. Being a person of stronger will and passions than her husband, she was able to work him into compliance with her claims. Having built a temple to Baal in Samaria, with a high altar, and public images of Baal and Astarte,[2] he in his own person performed worship to his wife's deities. Nor was this all; but yielding into her hands the power of the sword, he allowed her to chase them down and put them to death.

Now commenced the Martyr Age of the prophets in Israel. As they had multiplied all over the land, there were many to be persecuted, and their extermination was not the work of a day. And besides the natural instinct of mercy, they were greatly reverenced by numbers of the people. One man alone, by name Obadiah, in the high station of *governor of the house* to Ahab,—(Mayor of the Palace might have been his title in Europe),—is stated

---

[1] A critic who pretends to believe that the Pentateuch is Mosaic, replies, that Jezebel could not have learned that Jehovism was intolerant, until *after* Elijah's massacre of the priests! Intolerance probably grew up with just zeal for pure monotheism. It is the course of human infirmity.

[2] In 1 Kings xvi. 33, as in many other places, the received English version following the LXX. darkens the sense by rendering Astarte by the word *grove*. See 2 Kings xxiii. 6, 7, for a strange instance. [I now see that Colenso interprets it of a certain obscene symbol.]

to have hidden 100 prophets of Jehovah from the rage of Jezebel, and to have maintained them secretly. This cannot have been an exceptional case; and though many were slain, it is probable that a majority were concealed and protected. The crisis called forth two great prophets in succession, Elijah and Elisha; whose adventures and exploits have come down to us in such a halo of romance, not unmingled with poetry of a high genius, that it is impossible to disentangle the truth. The account of these occupies twice as much space as the history of the kings of Judah and Israel together, from the death of Solomon to the accession of Ahab; but as their deeds are nearly all prodigies, attested to us only by a writing compiled three centuries after these events, and having no bearing that can be traced on the real course of the history, we are forced to pass them over very slightly. The ascription however of miraculous powers to these prophets is a notable circumstance, as being altogether new in Jewish history. To find anything analogous, we must run back to the legendary days of Moses. One general inference may be drawn,—that the danger and importance of the struggle worked up the minds of Jehovah's worshippers into a high enthusiasm and intense belief of his present energy to aid his prophets. The after-tale also shows, that here, as elsewhere, persecution made its victims bigoted, undiscriminating, and ruthless in their turn.

A great drought endured by the land at this period for three years together distressed Ahab, and made it difficult to find fodder for the beasts. Elijah was believed to have predicted its occurrence, and likewise to have announced its termination, having on each occasion met Ahab face to face. The prophet himself was miraculously fed; first by ravens, who bring him bread and flesh morning and evening; afterwards, when the brook at which he drank is dried, an inexhaustible barrel of meal and cruse of oil[1] are shared with him by a widow of Zarephath, a Sidonian town. In gratitude for her hospitality, he raises her child from the dead by prayer to Jehovah. When after this he presents himself to Ahab, the king

[1] This miracle is reproduced with variation in the story of Elisha, who also raises from the dead the son of the Shunammite woman who had fed him: 2 Kings iv.

(though counting him an enemy) displays no personal rancour against him, and at his request even gathers the prophets of Baal and Astarte for a trial of miraculous power against Elijah. The issue is so triumphant to him, that, as we have stated, he is enabled to massacre the 950 misbelievers: but hereby he awakens such fierce zeal against him in Jezebel that he is forced to escape for his life into the kingdom of Judah, whence he first proceeds to Beersheba, and, then supported by a miraculous cake to which an angel points him, travels forty days and forty nights till he reaches the awful solitude of Mount Sinai. From hence he is sent back with a reproof, and with a secret commission to choose Elisha as his successor. No more is heard of him during the reign of Ahab. But Ahab's successor, enraged at a hostile message from him, sends soldiers to arrest him. Two companies of fifty men with their officers are consumed by fire from heaven at Elijah's calling: a third company is saved only by pious submission. After this, Elijah is carried up to heaven by a whirlwind in a chariot of fire with horses of fire, while Elisha stands wondering and sorrowing. Yet, later still, according to the Chronicler,[1] Elijah writes a threatening letter to Jehoram, second son of Ahab.

Our narrative passes abruptly from the religious to the temporal affairs of Israel, but without any distinct note of time, and with the same unhistorical and excited spirit. The great topic is the Syrian war. In attempting to narrate this, we have a very difficult task; because, while our existing materials cannot be thought mere romance or epical invention, they are yet too much disfigured by obvious exaggeration to allow of our accepting the details. It remains for us to follow the invidious and rather arbitrary plan of selecting those prominent facts which combine well with the entire course of the history, and interpreting what is left doubtful by the geographical and military necessities of the case. The Syrian hero is BEN-HADAD, apparently grandson of the Benhadad who assaulted Baasha. In the reign of Ahab we presume he

[1] 2 Chron. xxi. 12. This was *after* the revolt of the Edomites, v. 8; which is placed *after* the ascent of Elijah and the coming of his spirit on Elisha; 2 Kings iii. 10; viii. 22. For this inconsistency however the book of Kings is not chargeable; nor indeed is the Chronicler inconsistent with *himself;* for he does not allude to the ascension of Elijah.

must have been young, since he carries on an inveterate war against the son of Ahab also. The great idea with which he seems to have been long possessed, was, to advance directly against the city of Samaria, as a certain means of reducing all Israel: perhaps also regarding it as having been specially designed by its founder to defy the Syrian power. Nor did the plan of warfare appear unwise, since he evidently had the frontier fortresses in his hand, which enabled him to march in at pleasure with very superior forces.

The campaigns of this Benhadad against Israel alone are all contained in a narrative evidently of the same tone and genius, which we can scarcely be wrong in describing as a part of some prophetical story of the *Acts of Elisha*, transmitted for a while orally in the schools of the prophets. But there is one campaign in which the king of Judah is joined, and this has all the marks of more sober chronicling, although not without slighter improbabilities:[1] the latter document may be safely referred to the court records of Jerusalem. The difference of spirit is very striking. While Israel and the prophets have the war to themselves, all is marvellous:—extreme danger, divine interposition, and stupendous victory, from which no ultimate results are derived: but when the king of Judah aids, we read of historical battle and victory resting with Syria. Having warned the reader of the nature of our materials, we resume the narrative.

The force in which the Syrians at present most trusted, was that of war-chariots; and in plain open country these were highly efficient, ridiculous as they are apt to seem to us, who are accustomed to enclosed fields and paved high roads. Even over the rough ground of ancient Britain the native chariots offered a highly respectable opposition to the veteran infantry of the first Roman invader; and it is evident in ancient history,[2] that chariots of war were exceedingly feared until discipline and tactics

---

[1] 1 Kings xxii. The more legendary accounts are in 1 Kings xx., and 2 Kings vi., vii.

[2] According to Herodotus, the Garamantes of Africa used to hunt down with four-horse chariots the Troglodyte Ethiopians, the most swift-footed of men; apparently to make slaves of them.—Because of the iron chariots of the Philistine district (Judges i. 19), the men of Judah could not succeed on the plain, though they conquered the hill-country.

among foot-soldiery reached their highest point. The Syrian chariot did not, like that of the Homeric Greek, carry a single hero armed with sword and spear, but, like that of the Egyptians, one or more archers, perhaps armed likewise with swords. But besides the efficacy of the chariot in actual battle, it may be conjectured to have served for the more rapid transport of infantry on march. Uniting solidity with lightness, lowness, and breadth, it could traverse any country which was not enclosed—(and in Palestine the hedge and ditch were undoubtedly unknown[1]),—and might possibly carry several infantry soldiers with their scanty equipage, as well as the warriors who were to fight from it in the battle. We may possibly conclude, that wherever 100 chariots went, not less than 400 or 500 infantry were carried likewise; who thus might traverse in one day a two-days' march, and at the end be nearly fresh for immediate service. By help of the chariot 200 horses might thus transport 600 men, while in cavalry service each horse carries but one man. If there be any weight in these considerations, it follows that against a large force of chariots it was difficult to move infantry with such rapidity as to concentrate them against the attack of an invader.

Two separate campaigns of Benhadad against Ahab in Samaria are reported to us. In the former, the Syrians drove in with overflowing might, as it were sweeping the country before them, while no one dared to offer resistance. But they paused at no inferior town, and made straight on for Samaria. Ahab, finding himself shut up by very superior forces, and the resources of the kingdom cut off, was terrified into the offer of absolute surrender and vassalage; but (according to our only authority) Benhadad sent so outrageous a message as to the full use which he intended to make of this surrender, that Ahab was steeled into despair. The elders of Israel to whom he appealed exhorted him to firmness and vigour, and the prophets came forward to animate Israel and the king to brave and faithful resistance. Ahab indeed personally did not deserve favour from the prophets; but they could not look on tamely and see Jehovah's Israel

[1] The sacredness of the *landmark* implies this; besides, the ground was too precious, and estates too small.

become the spoil of the stranger. While Benhadad was full of triumph and insolence, banqueting in his splendid pavilion with the thirty-two vassal kings whom he had brought with him,[1] the Israelites made a sudden attack on a part of his chariot force which had ventured upon rough ground, and so discomfited it, with danger so imminent to the whole host, that Benhadad, rising from his banquet, thought nothing better than to mount a fleet horse and escape. The whole army poured after him and got away with as much haste as they could, and no doubt with much disorder and slaughter of the hindmost.

While this success gave great additional courage to the Israelites,—who might now remember the decisive victories of David over the chariots and horse of Hadadezer,—on the other hand, the Syrians did not find reason for discouragement. They imputed their loss entirely to an error of judgment, in having ventured their chariots on to hilly ground;[2] and the captains assured the king that by avoiding this mismanagement, they should conquer Israel in another campaign. Accordingly, next year they repeated their invasion, and entered the country as far as the town of Aphek, which seems to have been on the broad slope of Esdraelon. If this is the Aphek intended, the Syrians, to avoid hilly districts, must have come along the coast near the Phœnicians, and would seem to have entered the land by the remarkable defile through which the river Leontes flows down from the lofty plain of Hollow Syria. This time however the spirit of the Israelites was very different from what it had been in the former campaign. The national pride was roused by self-confidence; and while the Syrian host poured over the plain, the bands of Israel kept collecting on the hills, watching and following its motions for six days together. The Syrians were probably so resolved not again to venture off the good ground, that they could not take full advantage of their own numbers, and prevent their army from getting separated into portions, each weaker than the enemy. Be this as it may, the Israelites made a brave

[1] This may seem only to be a romantic version of the thirty-two *captains* named in the more historical account of 1 Kings xxii. 31. Not but that Benhadad was likely to have vassal kings with him.

[2] In the religious phraseology of antiquity, this is expressed by saying that "the gods of Israel are gods of the hills, and not of the plains."

and successful attack, by which (either in the battle, or in the town of Aphek after the battle) the person of king Benhadad himself fell into the hands of Ahab.

If we could believe our authority, we should now state, that, besides the great slaughter of the last year's army, Benhadad this year lost 100,000 men slain in one day on the open field of Esdraelon, and 27,000 more, crushed to death by the fall of a wall in Aphek. If this were real history, disasters so enormous, besides the repeated loss of a most luxurious camp, would have shattered the entire empire of Damascus. Revolt in all parts would have followed, and Israel would have had no more danger to fear; just as it afterwards was, when the loss of a single great army broke up the colossal empire of Assyria. On the contrary, the very next notice which we have of this kingdom represents it in a formidable and victorious attitude towards Israel. We are therefore forced to make immense deductions from the account transmitted to us.

It is more probable, that though by bravery and good fortune the Israelites had captured the person of the Syrian king, the greater part of his host was untouched and still dangerous. If Ahab had gratified the suggestions of anger and revenge by slaying his foe, a new king might have been chosen in the camp, and the war would have been renewed. To kill the king was as it were to set the king free, and lose the advantage which had been gained. Besides, the temper of Ahab appears to have been yielding and amiable; as want of firmness has been judged his chief defect. Accordingly, he treated the captive monarch with much respect; entitling him his "brother Benhadad," and inviting him to sit by his side in his own chariot. After this, he made a treaty, by which Benhadad bound himself to restore all the cities of Israel which he held (hereby disabling himself from future invasion by the same route); and to make "streets" for Ahab in Damascus, whether for the purposes of commerce, or to flatter his pride. So moderate an arrangement kindled the indignation of a fanatical Israelitish prophet,[1]

[1] The prophet bids a man to wound him; and when the man refuses, declares that a lion shall kill him for disobeying the voice of Jehovah: of course a lion *does* kill him. The prophet then succeeds in getting another man to wound him; after which he spreads ashes on his face, and goes thus wounded and disfigured to deliver his message of woe to the king.

who severely rebuked Ahab for having "let go a man whom Jehovah had appointed for utter destruction." Yet the king, though vexed, was afraid or unwilling to show resentment against the undeserved and unseemly invective.

Benhadad thus withdrew himself and (we need not doubt) the best part of his army, unhurt, and faithfully restored the northern towns; but his pride was deeply engaged to recover his lost honour; for which he next chose a different mode of attack. From Damascus southward towards the Ammonites are wide and open plains, on which the eastern tribes of Israel could offer no effectual resistance to a Syrian army. The outlying towns, such as Astaroth Karnaim, were perhaps already in Benhadad's power, if indeed he had not subdued the Ammonites, who in these times are not heard of as an independent nation.[1] Some years after his ill-success west of Jordan, he came up against southern Gilead, and possessed himself of the important town of Ramoth, south of the brook Jabbok. From this post he could at any time cross into the plain of the Jordan, and even make a sudden attack on Samaria, as well as on the eastern tribes, northward or southward.

The western bank of the Jordan was in itself too valuable to leave undefended, and had by this posture of Benhadad become a sort of frontier to the capital. In it there were two considerable cities, Bethshean and Jericho; the former undoubtedly fortified: but the latter had remained without walls from an early æra until the days of Ahab. For defence against the Syrians its fortification was clearly desirable; and the work was (probably in this stage of the war) undertaken by a man of Bethel, named Hiel. That the territory was regarded as Ahab's, we infer from the mode in which the fact is named,[2] as likewise since

If Jehoram, the young son of Ahab, was present during this denunciation, he must afterwards have been much puzzled when Elisha laid down to him the direct contrary principle, and a much more humane one—"Wouldst thou smite those whom thou hast taken captive? Set bread and water before them, etc., etc.," 2 Kings vi. 22.

[1] They are noticed in the Chronicles during the reign of Jehoshaphat (in a passage which will need remark), and again in the reign of Uzziah, after the power of Damascus is broken.

[2] Hiel is said to fortify Jericho *in Ahab's days*, 1 Kings xvi. 34; not in *Jehoshaphat's* days.

Bethel was in Ahab's kingdom;[1] while, in the want of a northern frontier to the plain of Jericho, we cannot wonder if Rehoboam was forced to surrender this highly fertile district to his rival, though it formed a part of the possessions of Benjamin. Indeed Bethel and Jericho are on another occasion coupled together[2] as chief seats of *Israelitish* prophets under the son of Ahab. We may gather that Hiel undertook the fortification from his own resources, under the condition that he was to be hereditary governor and prince of Jericho. He fulfilled his task successfully; but a great domestic calamity befell him. The Indian climate of Jericho (it seems) was fatal to all his children; of whom it is said, that the eldest died when the foundation of the walls was laid, and the youngest when the gates were set up. In vain had he spent his private fortune in the work; in vain might Ahab grant him an hereditary princedom; when, alas! there were no heirs to enjoy it. Men then called to mind an ancient spell ascribed to Joshua, who, "when the walls of Jericho fell flat before the blast of his trumpets" (as some old poem declared), pronounced in the name of Jehovah this very curse on the man who should rebuild the walls :—

<blockquote>With his firstborn shall he lay the foundation;
With his youngest shall he set up the gates.</blockquote>

However, the city was the stronger for its fortifications, and Israel now needed the benefit; for king Benhadad beneath the walls of Ramoth could look down on the whole plain of Jordan. At the same time, Ahab was called to be always on the alert, to defend the eastern tribes from a twofold attack.

But a great change of feeling and of policy had for some time passed over the cabinet of JERUSALEM; where JEHOSHAPHAT, as we have stated, ascended the throne in the vigour of mature manhood.[3] Like his father Asa, he was a strict worshipper of Jehovah, and exerted himself to repress every demoralizing practice which sheltered itself under the forms of heathen religion: yet the burning of incense to Jehovah at the high places he steadily upheld, if indeed there was as yet any one to oppose it.

[1] *Gilgal* also, in the time of the prophet Amos, belonged to Israel; which seems to be decisive.
[2] 2 Kings ii. 3, 5.
[3] B.C. 894.

Such a king must have felt very painfully the relentless conflict between the prophets of Baal and Jehovah which was for awhile going on in the neighbouring kingdom, and nothing but an urgent sense of duty and necessity would be likely to lead him into close alliance with Ahab. But before he had been six years on the throne, he became thoroughly convinced that to support Israel against the attacks of Syria was a paramount object, and took a decisive step,[1] from the consequences of which he never flinched through all the rest of his life. He united his young son Jehoram[2] in marriage to the equally youthful Athaliah, daughter of Ahab and Jezebel.[3] Perhaps he imagined that a maiden of the tender age of fifteen could import no moral evil into his palace, and he believed it a duty to cement the two branches of the house of Israel, which had been made unnaturally hostile with results so calamitous to both. Jehoshaphat was still more respected by the priests and prophets than his father Asa, and the determination of the later sacerdotal party to make him one of their great heroes, has thrown a false light over his whole reign. The account of him given in the Chronicles is evidently to so great a degree an ideal picture, that it is unsafe to believe anything on that testimony alone. Yet the scanty facts deposed in the other record justify important inferences. His predecessors, it is supposed, had succeeded in keeping the nominal homage of the Edomites, and had perhaps been able to enforce the claim to give them kings or regulate the succession to the throne.[4] Under Jehoshaphat however this remained no barren ceremony of state: before half his reign was ended, he even fitted out a fleet on the Red Sea, and prepared

[1] The chronology would allow us to believe, that one object which Jehoshaphat bought by the marriage was a toleration of the prophets of Jehovah in Israel; for we have no proof that the persecution continued after that time.
[2] As Jehoram is thirty-two years old when he is said to come to the throne, and reigns eight years (2 Kings viii. 17), he dies at the age of forty; but he dies in 865; therefore he is only seventeen in b.c. 888. Now his son Ahaziah is twenty-two at his accession b.c. 865, and was therefore born b.c. 887. This gives seventeen as the age of Jehoram at his marriage, when Athaliah may have been fifteen.
[3] She is called daughter of *Omri*, 2 Kings viii. 26; 2 Chron. xxii. 2. If this were accurate, it would disturb our chronology. But 2 Kings viii. 18, induces everybody to explain daughter as *granddaughter*.
[4] It is not certain whether the statement in 1 Kings xxii. 47, as to the viceroy in Edom, applies to Jehoshaphat's reign alone, or to former reigns also.

for a voyage to Ophir. In building ships at so distant a port, and in planning such a voyage, very much indeed is implied. He must have held so complete a command over Idumæa, as to be able to superintend the cutting of timber in Edomite forests (which do not seem now to exist), and sending all needful supplies to the harbours of Elath and Ezion Geber. He must also have had a sufficient command of the Philistine sea-coast, to furnish him with a maritime population and experienced shipbuilders; for he built and manned his fleet without aid from the king of Israel, or (as far as we can learn) from any foreign quarter. Finally, he must have been able to provide for the security of his caravans in going and returning; and must have had a large disposable surplus of light merchandise, which would bear the expense of carriage on camels' backs to the Red Sea. Even in our older compilation, the tone in which he is spoken of implies a military greatness beyond his predecessors. Out of such substantial realities, the Chronicler has built up a fabric of romance. He furnishes Jehoshaphat with an army of 1,160,000 disposable troops under four great generals, "to wait upon the king," besides the garrisons in the fenced cities. The Philistines pay him tribute of silver, and the Arabians present him with 7700 rams and 7700 he-goats. So great prosperity must have been a direct reward from Jehovah on his piety; hence his piety must be described as even exceeding that of David. He gives order to his princes to teach in the cities of Judah, and sends out Levites and priests with the Book of the Law, who taught the people everywhere. But as half of this tale is an obvious invention, we cannot put any trust in the rest, which is unknown to our better authority, and wholly unparalleled and uncountenanced by all the rest of the history.

In the present day, a ravine close beneath Jerusalem itself is called the valley of Jehoshaphat, but there is no proof that the name was so applied in ancient times. Yet it is generally supposed that there *was* a valley so called,[1] identical with that which had received the name Berachah or *Blessing*, because in it Jehoshaphat, after a great victory over the Edomites and other allies, there offered solemn

[1] According to a received interpretation of Joel iii.—But it seems more probable that the name in Joel is mystical and not geographical.

thanksgivings to Jehovah. The name (as so often happens) appears to have generated a legend concerning the nature of the victory, which however does not contain a single circumstance that can commend itself as historical.[1]

While the Chronicler's accounts of Jehoshaphat are not admissible, we yet cannot doubt that, except towards the end of his reign, he was a prosperous prince, and that the wisdom with which he followed up the measures of his father was crowned with high success. One or other of the two had reduced the southern cities of Philistia, and gained access to the sea, with facilities for Mediterranean navigation and commerce, which afterwards suggested to renew the southern voyages of Solomon. The neighbouring Arabians felt the benefits of traffic with him, and willingly paid him homage, and his sway, as we have said, became real and vigorous over the Edomites. In about the fifteenth or sixteenth year of his reign, a definite proposal was made to him by Ahab to unite in rescuing Ramoth in Gilead from the grasp of king Benhadad. Jehoshaphat acceded to Ahab's request with a cordiality which shows that he looked on all Israel as one people, and sincerely desired its entire union and joint prosperity. Nevertheless, it might be wrong to think his conduct disinterested, which might indeed lessen our idea of his prudence; rather, for the sake of his own kingdom, it was inevitable for him to feel the greatest anxiety from the position of the Syrian monarch in Gilead. From Ramoth as his sallying-post, Benhadad was almost certain, sooner or later, to subdue the eastern tribes; and by crossing the Jordan he might invade Judah almost as easily as Israel. Against a force so superior and so near, if once allowed to root itself there, neither kingdom could hope permanently to stand; and it might seem the part of wisdom to act with an enterprise bordering on rashness, before the eastern tribes of Israel had learned submission to a Damascene master.

The two kings accordingly marched in company against Ramoth, and found the Syrians assembled round it in force so great, as may even imply that they were on the point of invading Israel, and that the sole question had been, whether to meet them across the Jordan, or to re-

[1] See Note 3, p. 183.

ceive their attack in the heart of Ephraim. The force more particularly specified now, as on other occasions, is that of chariots, over which the king of Syria had set thirty-two captains. An obstinate battle was fought, and lasted till the sun went down; in the course of which Ahab received a mortal wound with an arrow. He died in the evening; and so confessed was the defeat of the Hebrews, that a general order was sent through their bands for each man to save himself by night, as he best could.[1] After so entire a failure, we might have imagined that the whole territory of the eastern tribes would at once have been lost to the dominion of Samaria. The Syrians however must themselves have suffered severely in so hardly-contested a field; and they may have found that they had no longer strength to spare for encountering any new enterprise.

Such an overthrow, in the first battle fought by the united kings of Israel and Judah, was in itself memorable and disastrous. The moral effect on the surrounding nations,—Edom, Moab, Philistia,—was a severe wound to the Hebrew supremacy, which now appeared finally to be sinking before the star of Damascus. It was made still more impressive on the imagination by the death of Ahab, the first Hebrew monarch since Saul who had been slain in war. In consequence, the event has been transmitted to us with details which must be received with caution and a measure of distrust. Benhadad is said to have ordered his men to neglect all other objects in comparison with that of killing Ahab; which, since Ahab is not reported to us to be anything as a general, savours of personal enmity, not military policy. But by a strange coincidence, Ahab, without knowing of this order, disguises himself in a common garb, but persuades Jehoshaphat to appear in his usual royal robes; for which no reason whatever is assigned. Hence Jehoshaphat narrowly escapes being slain, as the Syrians mistake him for Ahab. The death of Ahab is imputed to a *chance-shot*, which perhaps only means[2] that the archer was supposed not to know that it was

---

[1] The Chronicler dissembles the disgraceful rout of the army, as indecorous to Jehoshaphat; 2 Chron. xix. 1.

[2] If we interpret it, that the archer *shot at random*, how was the writer to know that?

Ahab at whom he was aiming. While this account contains nothing impossible, the coincidences are odd, and certainly not easy to receive from an unknown compiler distant in time from the events.

But this is not all. That so pious a king as Jehoshaphat, and one previously so successful, should fall into such a calamity, needed to be accounted for. Had he gone forth without consulting Jehovah by Urim? or without encouragement from Jehovah's prophets? or had he even disobeyed them? Our narrative undertakes to reply to these questions, and yet in fact leaves them unsolved. Jehoshaphat, after promising to join Ahab, is seized with scruples, and suggests to inquire of Jehovah. Ahab produces 400 prophets, who reply that Jehovah shall deliver Ramoth into the hand of the two kings. But the king of Judah is still uneasy, and inquires whether there is not yet, *besides* these, some prophet of Jehovah. Ahab confesses that there is one more,—whom he does not like,—Micaiah, son of Imlah; and at Jehoshaphat's request, sends for him. Micaiah strongly forbids the expedition, and predicts the worst results: Ahab is incensed, and throws him into prison. Yet Jehoshaphat goes up with Ahab against Ramoth, as if uncertain whether the single prophet or the four hundred spoke the true word of Jehovah.[1]

There are nevertheless in this account some points of theological interest, which must not be passed over. Micaiah is the only prophet of Israel (except Hosea, who wrote much later, when that branch of the nation was near to its final ruin,) of whose doctrine we have any characteristic specimen. When asked whether the two kings shall go up against Ramoth, he first replies, "I saw all Israel scattered upon the hills as sheep that have not a shepherd: and Jehovah said, *These have no master: let them return every man to his house in peace.*" When Ahab expressed displeasure at this rebuke of his indecisive character, Micaiah resumed his address: "I saw Jehovah sitting on his throne, and all the host of heaven standing

---

[1] Among the earlier Romans we see distinctly how any great defeat is apt to be imputed to a neglect of the auspices. Even so late as in the invasion by the Cimbri and Teutones, they ascribe some of their severest losses to the incontinence of the Vestal Virgins, who are tried and cruelly killed as guilty of the public disasters.

by him on his right hand and on his left. And Jehovah said, Who shall persuade Ahab, that he may go up and fall at Ramoth of Gilead. And there came forth a spirit, and stood before Jehovah, and said, I will persuade him. And Jehovah said, Wherewith? And he said, I will go forth, and be a lying spirit in the mouth of all his prophets. And Jehovah said, Thou shalt persuade him, and prevail also: go forth and so do."

It is quite a secondary question with us whether these words were so spoken, then and there, and whether such a prediction damped the hearts of the Hebrew soldiers and contributed to their defeat: all historical reality in the address may be doubted, and it will remain not the less certain that we have here a faithful view of the belief and forms of imagination then current concerning Jehovah's throne and court. These are quite in harmony with the representations of Isaiah and of the later prophets, in the general analogy presumed between the externals of divine and human sovereignty. That which is here peculiar and instructive is the agency of *lying spirits* under Jehovah's immediate mission. The false prophets who mislead Ahab are conceived of, probably, as in some sense guilty; yet they are not the less Jehovah's prophets, speaking by the direct dictation of the spirit which he has sent. The Persian doctrine of an Evil Spirit in avowed conflict with the Good God, does not seem yet to have found its way into Israel. The times were rude enough to feel no impropriety in the God of Truth working out his own ends by lying ministers; and the ingenious methods by which a later philosophy sought to disentangle its own web were unknown and unwished for. At the same time, it becomes apparent that in Israel (as at a later time in Judah), when the prophets were admitted to give political counsel, their influence was apt to be neutralized by one another, and by this doctrine of "lying spirits."

But to return to the history. The position of the Syrians in Gilead gave them the undisputed command of the plains of Moab along the east bank of the Jordan, down to its junction with the Dead Sea; and by thus intercepting all communication between Israel and the Moabites, led the latter to disown their homage to the former.

The annual tribute which they had paid is estimated as 100,000 lambs and 100,000 rams, with the wool, which was of course withheld, now that the king of Israel could not fulfil a single duty of a sovereign. AHAZIAH, eldest son of Ahab, succeeded to his father[1] on a weakened and unenviable throne.

One circumstance alone, of political interest, is casually named as happening in his reign. Jehoshaphat had recently been making his great experiment of renewing the navigation to Ophir; but, perhaps through want of skill in his shipwrights or sailors (for he was shut up to the narrow coast of Philistia for his supply), the enterprise failed, the fleet being shattered by a tempest almost before quitting its harbour. Ahaziah appears to have imputed the misfortune to want of seamanship; for he immediately proposed to send on the next voyage subjects of his own, who occupied a sea-coast of five times the length, and had a far greater maritime experience than any Hebrews of the kingdom of Judah. But Jehoshaphat was too much discouraged to repeat the experiment. It must have been exceedingly costly, and he was no doubt already convinced that he was grasping at what was beyond his powers; he therefore positively declined the friendly offer.[2]

In a few short months Ahaziah met with an accident fatal in its result: he fell out of an upper window in his room at Samaria. Sympathising with his mother's religion, he sent to the Philistine town of Ekron to inquire of their god[3] whether he should recover. For this impiety he was believed by the prophets of Jehovah to have died shortly after. As he had no son, his brother JEHORAM succeeded him in the next year.[4]

The calamities which seemed still to beset Israel were not without their effect on the new king. Jehoram could hardly avoid imputing them to the evil influence of Baal,

---

[1] B.C. 877.
[2] 1 Kings xxii. 49. It is extraordinary to see how broadly the Chronicler contradicts this account. He represents that Ahaziah's men *had been* on board the ships, and that *to punish this alliance* with so wicked a man as Ahaziah, Jehovah destroyed the fleet by a tempest (2 Chron. xx. 35—37).
The writer likewise commits the blunder of supposing that ships could sail down the Red Sea to *Tarshish*, or Tartessus, in Spain. Tarshish was a port much frequented by the Tyrians; Jonah i. 3; Ezek. xxvii. 12.
[3] Whom the Hebrews name Baalzebub (*lord of flies*).
[4] B.C. 876.

whose worship Ahab had introduced; and (possibly not without the instigation of the monotheistic Jehoshaphat) he took the decisive measure of removing the image of Baal which his father had made. We may probably infer that in other matters also he refrained from encouraging heathen ceremonies, although respect for his mother Jezebel forbade his taking active measures against them. After this he engaged Jehoshaphat to aid him in enforcing from the Moabites the tribute which they had been accustomed to pay to Ahab; and as it was no longer possible to conduct their armies across the Jordan because of the Syrians, it was determined to lead them through the land of Edom, which was now entirely subject to Jehoshaphat. The particulars of the campaign form a part of the wonderful deeds of Elisha, and it is difficult to elicit substantial facts. The viceroy (here called *king*[1] of Edom) accompanies them; their army suffers from want of water; Elisha calls for a minstrel,—begins to prophesy,—orders them to dig ditches. They obey, and find water in abundance: the Moabites, when the sun shines on the water, mistake it for blood, and fancying that the two armies have massacred each other, make a rush for the Hebrew camp to despoil it. The Israelites meet and slaughter them with ease; then (as eager not for future tribute, but for present vengeance) they beat down the cities, cut down all the good trees, stop up all the wells, and cast each man his stone on every good piece of land. The king of Moab is filled with chief rage against the king of Edom, and with 700 chosen swordsmen makes a fierce, but vain attack on him. He then sacrifices his eldest son on the wall of some city: but with no result, except that the Moabites[2] "feel great indignation against Israel." The armies return home, and Moab is left neither subject nor tributary.[3] As no effect what-

[1] As we are distinctly informed that at this time *there was no king in Edom* (1 Kings xxii. 47), the title is here indicative of vague knowledge in the original writer of this account.

[2] Mr Robert Mackay, in his able and remarkable work, "Progress of the Intellect," which seldom agrees with the views of this volume, says (vol. ii. p. 407) that it was not the *Moabites* who felt indignation, but *Jehovah*, who was fancied to be affected by the charm of the sacrifice.

[3] The Chronicler appears to have thought this campaign not honourable enough to Jehoshaphat, for he has dropt it out and put into its place, in nearly the same point of time, a different war, which he tells as follows (2 Chron. xx.) The Moabites, Ammonites, and Edomites, a great multitude,

ever of this campaign is pretended, and we cannot imagine a miracle wrought solely to enable the Hebrews to inflict misery on an innocent population, it is most probable that the want of water, which is mentioned as a difficulty encountered by them, really caused the failure of the whole expedition.

We now enter on a yet more perplexing narrative, in which the unhistorical tone is far too manifest[1] to allow of our easy belief in it; although it is impossible to doubt that there was a real event at bottom which deeply affected the national feelings. This event is the siege of Samaria by the king of Syria. The invasion had only been delayed for some years by the spirited attack made on his forces at Ramoth by the allied kings; and now, under Jehoram son of Ahab, the Israelitish army with their king was hemmed in at Samaria. So successfully did the Syrian forces cut off their communications, that a dreadful famine arose in the town; and not only were the vilest substances sold at a great price for human food, but a woman was believed to have boiled and eaten her son.[2] Yet when the suffering was becoming unendurable, and a little more would have led to unconditional surrender, the Syrian army withdrew, and vanished of itself in the night.

Such a catastrophe is *à priori* very improbable, but is by no means impossible. Many conjectural causes might be assigned, far from absurd. The besieger may himself invade the land of Judah, entering along the west shore of the Dead Sea. Jehoshaphat prays a public prayer: a Levite becomes inspired and encourages the nation: Jehoshaphat marches out with religious singers in front of his army to praise Jehovah. As soon as they begin to sing, Jehovah sends mutual fury into the adverse host, who, before the Hebrews can come up to them, kill one another, "so that not one escaped." Abundance of spoil,—riches and precious jewels,—are found with the dead bodies, so much that the favoured army is employed three days in gathering it. On the fourth day they publicly bless Jehovah in the valley of Berachah, and return to Jerusalem with psalteries, harps, and trumpets to the house of Jehovah.

As to the date intended for this fable, it is distinctly declared to be after the death of Ahab (xix. 1, xx. 1); and it might seem by xx. 35 to be during the life of Ahab's successor. But at v. 31 of this chapter the connexion is broken, and the writer loses all chronological clue.

[1] The siege of Jerusalem by Titus is described by Josephus in perhaps a still more overwrought and romantic style; yet Josephus was a contemporary, with excellent means of information.

[2] Dramatic pungency is added to this by representing *two* women *contracting* that each in turn shall contribute a boiled child to their common meal: one of them eats the other's child, and evades to give her own; and she who has fulfilled her part of the contract appeals to the king against the other's injustice.

have suffered want of supplies, or he may have been drawn off by the attack of some enemy at home when the siege lingered beyond expectation,—as the Gauls, while blockading the Roman Capitol. Large and luxurious armies are likewise liable to unaccountable panics; and there were in this case circumstances which may have conduced to such a thing. It has been observed by a Greek writer,[1] that the Persians so dreaded a night-attack on their cavalry, that that species of force never passed the night at a shorter distance than six or seven miles from the enemy. Every horse needed to be pegged to the ground by each of his four feet. If the army was surprised by night, the time required to get the horses free and accoutre them for action was so great, that a total defeat might be first sustained. A force of chariots must have been still more liable to this disaster. Moreover, as king Benhadad had once before fallen into the hands of the Israelites, he may the more easily have taken alarm on the occurrence of a tumult which was supposed to be a hostile attack. Noises in the night are heard to a great distance, and are easily misinterpreted; and the host was probably dispersed, so as to block up all the critical approaches to Samaria, without venturing on the rough ground.

The authority from which we draw our whole information says, therefore, nothing incredible in assigning a *night-panic* as the reason for the sudden disappearance of the Syrians; but the particular ground of alarm[2] attributed to them does not exhibit the writer's acquaintance with the times in a very favourable light. It goes on to represent the Syrians as leaving their entire camp, with abund-

[1] Xenophon in his Anabasis, iii. He elsewhere, in the same work, mentions that even the Greek army, under the veteran officer Clearchus, suffered a rather dangerous night-panic, which was stilled by Clearchus bidding his loud-voiced crier proclaim a reward of a silver talent to whoever *would tell who it was that let the ass loose into the camp;* Anab. ii 2, 20. They had themselves, just before, unawares inflicted a panic on the king of Persia, which made him decamp in the night.

[2] The Syrians are stated to dread an attack from the kings of the Hittites and of the Egyptians. No Hittite kings can have compared in power with the king of Judah, the real and nearer ally, who is not named at all; and the kings of Egypt (if there were really more than one) were at a weary distance, with a desart between.

In the whole narrative, from 2 Kings vi. 8 to vii. 6, the title "king of Israel" occurs twenty-two times, yet his name never slips out, nor that of the lord who is trampled to death; nor is there a single mark of acquaintance with the contemporaneous history.

ance of food and every sort of wealth, to be plundered by the Israelites; and such, it declares, was the profusion of the supply of fine flour and of barley (the horse-food of those parts), that the dearth in Samaria was suddenly converted into cheapness.[1] A lord who had disbelieved the possibility of this, when predicted by Elisha, was trodden to death in the crowd, in fulfilment of the prophet's denunciation upon him.

The general result remains clear: Samaria, after great suffering, escaped for the present; but the power of Syria continued to threaten it with force most disproportionate. Jehoshaphat (if still alive)[2] was getting old, and possibly was daunted by the ill-success of his two expeditions in company with kings of Israel; but age had stolen over Benhadad also. He was shortly laid up with a painful sickness, and (after an interval perhaps of a few years) died. It is not stated whether he left any natural representatives, and we only know that he was succeeded on the throne of Damascus by Hazael,[3] one of his great officers.

Jehoshaphat, under growing infirmity, had recourse to the method, hitherto unpractised except by king David, of raising his son to the throne during his own lifetime. Some doubt rests on the date of this; we have

[1] The liveliness of the narrative is here quite equal to poetry. *Four leprous men* venture out into the Syrian camp, and enjoy all its good things before any of the rest have discovered the flight of the huge host. Considering the height of the hill of Samaria, it might have seemed that the state of the enemy's camp would be seen (at least in most parts) from the town itself.

[2] We cannot tell whether Jehoshaphat or Jehoram sate on 'the throne of Judah during the siege of Samaria, so little has it of real connexion with the history; yet judging from the affairs of Syria, we should suppose it to be while the two Jehorams were reigning.

[3] Hazael is stated to have murdered the poor old man in his sick bed, by spreading a wet cloth on his face. But when a man is so near to death that this will kill him, he may so easily have died of himself, that we need good evidence to show that such a story is not vulgar scandal. *How* the Israelitish writer got so accurate information of what went on in the king of Syria's bedchamber is not apparent.

In order, it seems, to give honour to Elisha, this prophet is made to utter a prediction which in a just view was highly disgraceful. Hazael brings him a present of *forty camels'-load* of all the precious things of Damascus, to inquire, in Benhadad's name, whether he is to recover of his malady. Elisha replies that he *will not* recover, although he *might* recover; but Hazael will become king of Syria, and will perpetrate every kind of cruelty on the Israelites. Hazael is shocked at the prophecy, yet on reaching home murders his master. If Elisha had wished to incite him to the murder, he could not have tempted him more diabolically. But the whole tale is apocryphal.

followed the opinion that it was B.C. 872, about three years before the old king's death. It was not to be questioned that he felt the calamities which were befalling the northern kingdom to be severe shocks given to the whole Hebrew sovereignty. Now that the tribe of Reuben, with Ammon and Moab, were lost to the throne of Israel, it was impossible that the Edomites should very peaceably submit to the yoke of Judah. A strong and vigorous hand was wanted, and age must have now disabled Jehoshaphat for the active exertion of warfare. These reasons will account for his taking so unusual a step.

That the name of his son, JEHORAM, was the very same as that of the king of Israel, is generally ascribed to the matrimonial alliance between the two families; an opinion which is confirmed by the circumstance that *this* Jehoram's son and the *other* Jehoram's brother were both named Ahaziah. Yet as both Jehorams appear to have been born in Omri's reign, it is remarkable to find such intimacy between the fathers already commenced, as to lead to their giving the same names to their sons.[1] No event at all is recorded as occurring during the joint reign of Jehoram and his father. Jehoshaphat died[2] at the age of sixty, leaving his kingdom in an anxious position, through no fault of his own, but through the irresistible growth of Damascus, which he had so long foreboded, and in vain struggled to check.

The great event of his son's reign was the revolt of the Edomites, who now set over themselves an independent king. The king of Judah did not yield up his sovereignty without a conflict; and going out with a force of chariots, he made a night-attack on the Edomite army with much slaughter. Nevertheless, though he might win a battle, he could not recover his dominion; and Edom was lost to the house of Judah about a century and a half after its conquest by David. A revolt of the strongly fortified town of Libnah in Judæa is mentioned as happening about the same time; and it is possible that the necessity imposed on Jehoram of returning from Edom to put down rebellion in his own dominions, helped to shorten the Edomite war. We should seem to know the reasons of

[1] Some may conjecture that the system of taking *royal* names was already acted on.   [2] B.C. 869.

this internal rebellion, if we could give unhesitating credit to the details which our second authority has added to the reign of this king. His father Jehoshaphat, we are told, had seven sons, whom he established as princes in various fenced cities of Judah; but no sooner did Jehoram find himself sole master of the kingdom, than, in the jealousy of power, he slew all his brothers, and with them many other noble persons. Such a massacre would necessarily produce discontents, which might well break out into rebellion at Libnah.

The Edomites had now learned their strength; and the hope of revenge kindled a clear memory of the bloody deeds wrought upon their nation by Joab and Abishai. Although they could have no thought of conquering Judah, they from this time forth, with little intermission, harassed it by inroads, in which they carried off the population to sell into slavery. Allusions to the suffering thus caused are frequent in the earliest extant prophets; yet no incursions were on a sufficiently large scale to be entitled *a war*, or to find a place in the general history.

A notice however has been preserved to us of a very daring inroad of *Philistines*, aided by tribes from the Arabian peninsula; who surprised Jerusalem itself, and carried off (it is even said) the wives of the king. The general fact is in perfect agreement with the course of the history and the references made by the prophets;[1] but we find mingled up with the narrative much that is erroneous or justly suspected,[2] so as to inspire the belief, that an

[1] See especially Joel iii. 4, 5, which at first sight seems to say that the Philistines (with the help of Tyre and Sidon?) pillaged the temple.

[2] It states (2 Chr. xxi. 20) that as a stigma on his wickedness he was buried in the city of David, but *not in the sepulchres of the kings;* while in our better authority we read, that "he was buried *with his fathers* in the city of David." The Chronicler brings up against him Philistines, and Arabians *that were near the Ethiopians*, who plunder his palace, carry off his wives (although Athaliah, his chief or only wife, was not carried off), and slay all his sons, except his youngest son Jehoahaz—for so Ahaziah is called in ch. xxi. 17. (The name Ahaziah reappears in xxii. 2, and, in another form, Azariah, in v. 6.) The Chronicler makes Ahaziah 42 years old when his father dies at the age of 40. This *forty-two* might indeed be a corrupt reading for *twenty-two*, as we read in 2 Kings xviii. 26; but even so, it is absurd to imagine Ahaziah to be only 18 years younger than his father, and yet to be the youngest son born from many wives. Again, as the Chronicler represents all the *brethren* of Ahaziah to have been killed by the freebooters, he turns those who are called "forty-two men, *brethren* of Ahaziah" (in 2 Kings x. 13, 14,) into *sons* of the brethren of Ahaziah; so that Jehoram, dying at the age of 40, left 42 grandsons who are called

undue prejudice against the son of Jehoshaphat had biassed the Chronicler, by whom this king is depicted in far blacker colours than by the earlier compiler. Jehoram died in the prime of life, of an acute attack in the bowels, which, coupled with the depressing events of his reign, in contrast to his father's greatness, led to the idea that a judgment from God had overtaken him, and that he was a sinner above other men.

His son AHAZIAH[1] had already reached the age of twenty-two, and lost no time in following up his grandfather's policy of withstanding the power of Damascus. No circumstances survive to us that might explain the only fact of which we are informed. Hazael had succeeded Benhadad on the throne of Syria. Had his accession been accompanied with any internal disorders? Had Benhadad left sons, against whom Hazael had had to contend? or had Jehoram of Israel, after the retreat of Benhadad from Samaria, obtained any fresh successes during the last illness of the old king? We cannot tell what emboldened the two Hebrew princes anew; we only know that Ahaziah, in the first and last year of his reign, joined Jehoram in another attempt to recover Ramoth in Gilead from the Syrians. King Hazael fought a battle against them, in which Jehoram was severely wounded; but the Hebrew armies kept the field, and continued in the neighbourhood of Ramoth. The Israelitish king had returned to his palace at Jezreel to tend his wounds, when a dreadful calamity exploded on the heads of both the royal houses. But before detailing this miserable event, we must cast a retrospect on the life of queen JEZEBEL.

We have seen that the palace of Tirzah found no favour with king Omri, the founder of Samaria. As the arduous work of erecting a new capital is likely to have fully occupied him, we may probably ascribe to his son Ahab[2] the

men. That Elijah the prophet wrote a letter to Jehoram, as stated in 2 Chr. xxi. 12, is irreconcilable with the chronology of the book of Kings. *Both* these records are prejudiced against the son and grandson of Jehoshaphat, because of their relation to the house of Ahab, in whose sins (they vaguely say) both walked. But when they go into details of irreligion, we find no imputation worse than "the high places," 2 Chr. xxi. 11. The son of Ahab had in fact renounced the worship of Baal.

[1] B.C. 865.
[2] We hear also of an *ivory house* which Ahab made (1 Kings xxii. 39), which may be compared to the *ivory palaces* of Ps. xlv. It is credible that all

building of the new palace at Jezreel for his wife Jezebel. Jezreel is identified with the modern village of Zerin, on an elevated part of the table-land called Esdraelon[1] by the Greeks. To the north-west the brook Kishon runs down into the bay of Carmel. Horne (in his Illustrations) describes the plain of Jezreel as "surrounded by hills on all sides; by the hills of Nazareth to the north, those of Samaria to the south, the mountains of Tabor and Hermon to the east, and by Carmel to the south-west." By general agreement, the site was worthy of a palace. It has been carefully recorded that David, when he needed the threshing-floor of Araunah the Jebusite, paid fifty shekels of silver[2] as the price of it with the oxen. Omri bought the hill of Samaria of its owner Shemer with two talents of silver; Ahab likewise was under a necessity of purchasing such land as he needed in the neighbourhood of Jezreel. It so happened that a man named Naboth had a vineyard which was wanted as a kitchen-garden to the palace; but although the king offered him whatever equivalent in money he thought reasonable, Naboth positively refused to sell it on any terms. The narrative is of interest, as showing us, that the despotism apparently vested in these kings was never understood to supersede private and social rights. In time of war they exercised so arbitrary an authority, that Saul could threaten his son Jonathan with death for disobeying a capricious order; and over their own officials, especially those under military rule, the public feeling seems to have permitted them a very unlimited sway. But their power over private men, although the constitution had not invented any mode of controlling it, was not to be exerted with wild or selfish wilfulness: usage, and respect for public opinion, demanded the observance of certain forms of justice, in a case which involved private interests. On the present occasion the refusal of Naboth greatly annoyed Ahab, who neither dared to use violence, nor conceived the idea of it. But his wife Jezebel, enraged that any one should thwart

its *ornamental* part was executed in ivory. The "houses of ivory" in Hosea iii. 15 are named in company with real dwelling-houses.

[1] Esdrael is a mere corruption of Jezreel, a word which in Hebrew means *seed of God* (or, sowing-place of God?), as indicating the great fruitfulness of the plain.

[2] 2 Sam. xxiv. 24.

and mortify her royal consort, immediately took on herself to arrange the matter of Naboth. Having written letters in Ahab's name and sealed them with his seal, she accused Naboth of the undefinable offence of "blasphemy" against God and the king,[1] and by suborning false witness, effected his condemnation; upon which he was put to death by the cruel method of public stoning. At her instance, Ahab then took possession of Naboth's vineyard, although with a bad conscience and without enjoyment of it; for when severely reproved by Elijah the prophet, he humbled himself,—rent his clothes and wore sackcloth,—and showed no resentment against his faithful rebuker. Such is the account, as we have it; and even if it be not wholly correct, it is of value, as showing a very early belief current in Israel. If we reject it, we can put nothing into its place, as we cannot hope to amend it in detail. It certainly gives us a blacker view of Jezebel's character than any other facts which are stated; and the thought may occur, whether this is anything but a story to which her murderer, in self-justification, gave currency. That is possible; and yet the crime imputed to her is only too consistent with the mother of Athaliah.

In her palace of Jezreel the queen of Ahab was still residing, and here too lay her royal son, now almost convalescent from the wounds he received at Ramoth. It does not appear that any violence on Jezebel's part had been renewed against the Hebrew national religion since the great drought which had afflicted Israel. We read that prophets of Jehovah moved freely in the camp and in the court during the Syrian invasions, and used great liberty with Ahab and his son, without encountering danger; and when Ahab joined with Jehoshaphat to go against Ramoth, we have seen that about 400 men are spoken of as prophesying in the name of Jehovah before both the

[1] The Hebrew phrase is, "Naboth did *bless* God and the king." The word *bless* is expounded to mean *say adieu*, and hence, *curse*. It may seem strange to find *God*, and not *Jehorah*, in this formula; and since in days when various idolatries were established in Israel, a purely theological punishment seems impossible, the suspicion might intrude, that this *stoning for blasphemy* is a sacerdotal notion of later days here imputed to the times of Ahab. Yet it may be that the phrase only imports *treason*, and that the word *God* inserted before *king* is mere verbiage, like the malice and wickedness which our legal formulas so liberally ascribe to defendants. That stoning was practised in Israel, we saw in the case of Rehoboam's luckless tax-collector.

kings. Jehoram, son of Ahab, had renounced the worship of Baal, and might personally have seemed to deserve some consideration and some mercy from those who dreaded or hated his mother. He was barely recovered from wounds received against the public enemy. But Jehoram's zeal, or perceptions of public duty, did not, like Asa's, mount so high as to steel him to forbid his mother's religion: the priests of Baal were still supported by her, and the temple of Baal remained in Samaria. Elisha (if we can trust our narrative) waited his time to strike a blow against Jezebel, far more ferocious in conception, and proportionably more deadly in its result, than the address of Ahijah to Jeroboam had been. He sent a young prophet with secret orders to Ramoth, where JEHU, son of Jehoshaphat son of Nimshi, one of the chief captains of the host of Israel, was abiding with the army to watch the Syrians. Having asked a private interview with Jehu, the youth took out a box of oil and poured it over his head, declaring that Jehovah anointed Jehu king over Israel, that he might cut off every male of the house of Ahab and avenge the blood of the prophets at the hand of Jezebel. After thus delivering his message, he fled and disappeared. Jehu was not slow to announce what had been done; and the other captains accepted it as a voice from heaven. He was at once proclaimed king by the army, and before the tidings should reach Jezreel by any other messenger, he hastened to carry it himself. It so happened that Ahaziah king of Judah was come to visit his wounded uncle; and when the watchman announced from his height that a man was seen rapidly driving towards the palace, who apparently must be Jehu, captain of the host, the two princes, moved by an inexplicable impulse, at once drove forth in their chariots to meet him. But on their coming near, Jehu shot Jehoram with an arrow through the heart; and overdoing the prophet's commission, sent his servants to slay Ahaziah also, who fled on discovering the treason. He was chased so closely as to receive a mortal wound,[1] though his chariot

[1] The wound is specified as received "at the going up to Gur, which is by Ibleam" (2 Kings ix. 27). But the Chronicler gives a different and irreconcilable tale (2 Chr. xxii. 8, 9). After slaying the princes of Judah, Jehu seeks for Ahaziah, and *catches him hid in Samaria.* He is slain and carefully buried

bore him off to Megiddo, west of Jezreel, beneath the mountains of Carmel. Here he died,[1] in the second year of his reign and twenty-third of his age. He was carried by his servants in his own chariot to Jerusalem, and buried in the royal sepulchres.

But this was the mere beginning of a great and historical tragedy. Jehu continued his course to Jezreel; but the news of his murderous enterprise arrived there before him, and Jezebel had full notice of her danger. With masculine spirit, she prepared to meet him boldly, showing herself out of a window which overlooked the gate of the palace. As he drove in through the gate, she called aloud to him with the significant question, "Had Zimri peace, who slew his master?" but Jehu, without deigning to reply, commanded the eunuchs who stood at her side to throw her out of window. They did not dare to disobey so fierce and relentless a man, and hurled her down in front of him. All mangled as she lay and bespattered with her gore, Jehu, as if glorying in cruelty, drove his horses and chariot over her body, and left her to live or die, as chance might determine. Those who handed down the account were careful to remark, that the corpse of Jehoram had been cast out by Jehu on the vineyard of Naboth, and that while Jehu was dining in the palace of Jezreel, the dogs devoured the flesh off the body of Jezebel.

From Jezreel, Jehu wrote letters to Samaria (where Ahab had seventy male descendants, many of them children under tutors), and commanded the elders and authorities[2] of the city to behead them all, and send the heads to him forthwith at Jezreel. The knowledge that the army was with him and that both kings were dead, terrified them into submission; and the seventy heads of the innocent men and children were sent him in baskets,

by Jehu's people, "because, said they, he is the son [grandson] of Jehoshaphat, who sought Jehovah with all his heart."

[1] B.C. 864.
[2] There is an obscurity in the phrase: "he wrote to Samaria unto the rulers of Jezreel." In fact, vv. 11 and 17 of 2 Kings x. do not well harmonize with 1—10: for in 1—10 Jehu slays Ahab's sons in *Samaria*, in v. 11 they are called "those of the house of Ahab in *Jezreel*," and afterwards, in v. 17, he still has to slay "all who remained to Ahab in Samaria." The original narrative appears to have been interpolated; but it is perhaps impossible to separate the newer parts from the older.

and placed in two heaps by the palace-gate. After this he massacred all persons of distinction whom he regarded as the partisans of Ahab,—" all his great men, and his kinsfolk, and his priests, until he left none remaining." These things must have been done with a rapidity almost miraculous, if the next tale of horror has been accurately reported. Journeying, it is said, to Samaria, he fell in with forty-two princes of Judah, brothers[1] of the late king Ahaziah, who, having heard nothing of these events, were on their way to visit the young princes of the house of Ahab. The taste of blood had only whetted the appetite of this tiger of a man, who at once gave orders, which were too faithfully executed, to slay them all on the spot. Truly he understood, that having treacherously murdered two unoffending kings, it was not wise to leave any one alive who had a family interest in becoming their avenger: nor have we reason to doubt of the main fact of his massacre, however questionable the circumstantials may seem.

Continuing his progress, he took into his chariot a man whose name had become proverbial in the days of Jeremiah the prophet, for the singular law[2] which he imposed on his descendants—Jonadab the son of Rechab. Entering Samaria with him, he assumed the character of a devout votary of Baal; proclaimed a great sacrifice on a certain day, and ordered, under pain of death, that every priest and every worshipper of Baal should assemble to celebrate it. Having thus filled the temple, and made all requisite arrangements by the help of Jonadab,

---

[1] It has been already noted that these are called by the Chronicler "*sons* of the brethren of Ahaziah;" because he has said that the *brothers* of Ahaziah were all slain by the Philistines. But as the father of Ahaziah, if still alive, would only have been forty-one years old, there is no room to doubt that the other record is right; except that the word *brothers* may include first-cousins, and even uncles, if we reject the account that Jehoram slew his own brothers, sons of Jehoshaphat. Ahaziah was probably the eldest son of Jehoram. But 2 Chr. xxii. 1—7 appears to be a fragment of different origin from xxi., and follows a different chronology. It is no accident that at once makes Ahaziah forty-two years old, and gives him so many nephews.

[2] The Rechabites were a tribe or family who lived in Arab fashion, being under oath not to build houses nor plant the ground. This is identical with a Nabathæan principle, and is evidently a barbarous endeavour to uphold liberty by avoiding to root oneself in the soil. The Rechabites were supposed to be descended from this Jonadab, and to have adopted their institutions at his command.

at an appointed moment he gave the signal for killing all that were within. When this order had been executed, he joined his guards in the temple of Baal, had all the images[1] broken and burned, the temple itself pulled down, and its site converted to the vilest purposes. Thus were the prophets of Jehovah at last avenged and gratified.

But the Fury of murder, who rioted thus perfidiously in profane Samaria, spread her contagion to holy Jerusalem. Jehu's example stimulated the daughter of Jezebel to deeds still more unnatural, if not more ferocious. In the court of Jehoshaphat, ATHALIAH from her earliest youth had seen no images to Baal or Astarte. For twenty-four years she had lived in a monotheistic atmosphere; and, but for Jehu, she might perhaps have passed without crime and without reproach to her life's end. But her mother's blood was in her veins, and now that her son and all his brothers were slain, she saw the throne of Judah within her grasp, if only she removed the young children,—the sons of her son,—who stood in her way. As mother of the king, she enjoyed high privileges, and had many servants at her bidding: at this moment there was none but she to administer the supreme government in Judah. Seizing the opportunity, she put all her grandchildren to death, and occupied the throne as QUEEN in her own title and without a rival.

Such is the train of atrocities which Elisha's message entailed on both the Hebrew kingdoms. A third time was the royal house of Israel extirpated, and now likewise that of Judah. That the Jewish writers can gloat over such funereal events, so deadly to their own people, is sufficiently wonderful. That men called Christians can read them with calm approbation, is still more melancholy, for this is the training of mind which steeled all Europe to cruelty under the name of religion. This has lit up hell-fires in Christendom; this has perpetrated treacherous massacres unknown[2]

---

[1] It was before stated that Jehoram " put away the image of Baal which his father had made;" but not that he actually destroyed it.

[2] The slaughter of the Magians at the accession of Darius son of Hystaspes, is the only event of antiquity which might seem analogous to St Bartholomew's eve. The more spiritual the forces of a religion, the more deadly is their perversion; and precisely because the old Persian belief is too pure to be called Paganism, it is credible that its persecutions may have shared in Christian atrocity. But in truth we do not know the details of the Magophonia

to Paganism; this has bequeathed, even to the present age, a confusion of mind which too often leads those who are naturally mild and equitable, to inflict hardship, vexation, degradation, and loss on the professors of a rival creed. Until men learn that Jehovah neither does, nor ever did, sanction such enormities as Elisha commanded and Jehu executed, they will never have a true insight into the heart of Him who is the God of the Pagan as well as of the Jew.

sufficiently to reason minutely about it. Certainly it was not a contest of pure opinion, but also a contest which of two races should possess imperial power.

In reply to the gross attacks on my good faith by a reviewer, I affirm that nothing in antiquity, known to me, approaches the Inquisition in conception or in consequences, as an organized, treacherous, cruel system of punishing secret conscientious opinion. Paganism has abounded with atrocities; and certainly I have nowhere disguised them: but no Pagan teachers *could* have infused into Christianity the horrible mischiefs which the consecrating of Jewish history has superinduced. As for the persecutions by Pagan Rome, they were totally different in character;—the earlier ones being the arrogant cruelties of mere despotism, while those from Trajan downwards were open attempts, increasing in violence, to dissolve an *organized* society, which was sincerely believed (and as the result showed, most justly believed) to be dangerous to the State.

CHAPTER VII.

THE PERIOD OF THE HOUSE OF JEHU, B.C. 864—762.

THE improvised epilogue by which Queen ATHALIAH crowned the murders of Jehu, transferred to Jerusalem the worship of Baal, as soon as it was suppressed in Samaria. However hearty the zeal of Jehu to slay every priest and votary of Jezebel's god, yet without the organized experience of a Spanish *Inquisition*, a radical destruction was physically impossible : and to whom else would the survivors flee but to the daughter of the murdered queen ? Nor, if her furious passions had allowed her to debate what part she should choose, was it now well possible for her to avoid professing to be her mother's avenger. As a princess of Israel and of Tyre, she had no claims on the allegiance of the house of David ; she could hardly hope to conciliate the Aaronite priesthood, all whose greatness had sprung from the supremacy of that house ; nor could she affect to avenge the princes of Judah, when she had herself slain the heirs to the throne. She could therefore only appear as the champion of Jezebel, of Baal, and of the slaughtered house of Ahab. Ill-omened and frightful as such a vixen must have seemed on the throne of David and Solomon, the people were too panic-struck, too much afflicted with calamity, to move against her. The royal race having been cut off, whom could they set up as king ? and what new murders might not arise from displacing her ? While therefore they submitted in silence, she put forward the priests of Baal into high station, and perhaps before long flattered herself, from the public inaction and tranquillity, that all were contented with her sway.

But the lapse of a century and a half had been preparing the PRIESTHOOD of Jerusalem to act an independent part. Its pusillanimous behaviour under the early kings, like that of the English House of Commons under the Tudors, had saved it while its strength was immature ; and the honours it received under Asa and Jehoshaphat confirmed its veneration among the people, without awakening the jealousy of their two departed successors. The Priests and the Levites were now knit together in Jerusalem by very close bonds, and their influence was beginning to pervade social life. The *Priestly* system indeed may be described as already adult; but that of the *Levites* was quite in its infancy. Their chief business was still to attend on the temple service; and our older compiler seldom names them in the places where the more credulous and less candid Chronicler gives them great prominence. This may nevertheless be the place to explain the position towards which the Levites were tending, and which they at length attained.

Like the Brahmins of India and the Sacerdotal Caste of Egypt, they included many whom we should call Professional or Learned men; as also many whom we name Civilians in the State, by way of contrast to the Military. The ascendency of sacerdotalism in Judæa was therefore in part similar to the ascendency of civil over military power in European government. The difference is this, that in Israel the scribes and notaries, judges, lawyers, attorneys, and all literary men, gradually came to be united by the bonds of religion; after which they may be said to have had two watchwords,—*worship Jehovah only;* and *worship him by the intervention of Priests and Levites.* By intermarrying principally with themselves, they became at last almost a hereditary caste: what they were originally it is impossible to say. The only Levite of whom a particular account is given in the times of the Judges, is described as of Bethlehem, and of the family of *Judah*.[1] In Greek and Roman history, nothing is commoner than to find organizations of men, united by religious rites, which imply their descent from a common ancestor, the hero or demigod of the clan, when there is nevertheless every ground for believing that adoption has furnished more members than natural increase. Nor is it possible to trust the alleged genealogies from ancient patriarchs, when it is most manifest that they are incomplete and erroneous even in those times, the chronology of which we know. Although a High Priest existed at

[1] Judges xvii. 7.

Jerusalem without breach of continuity from Solomon to Josiah, there is not a single priest named in the course of the history whose pedigree is satisfactorily made out;[1] yet undoubtedly those of a later period were very anxious to establish their descent from Zadok. The head of the order, at the time of Athaliah's usurpation, was named Jehoiada; of whose ancestry nothing whatever is known.[2] The kings of Judah dealt with the temple-patronage much as the kings of Europe have done with bishoprics. They bestowed it according to their inclination or judgment, —public opinion confining their choice within certain limits,—but on no account did they follow the hereditary principle. With the gradual development of sacerdotalism the families perhaps became fewer and fewer out of which a choice could decorously be made; and at last the line of Zadok obtained a celebrity with which no common Aaronite could compete.

At the time of which we are treating, the course of events itself assures us of the high political consideration which the priests (though not as yet the Levites) enjoyed. In the absence of any representative of David, there was nothing else round which the nation could rally; so that Jehoiada at this moment was little less than an Eli to it. Fortunately Athaliah, as a woman escaped out of the harem, had no suspicion how the ecclesiastics or the people were minded; and she left Jehoiada and his associates in the entire enjoyment of their dignities. The votaries of Baal did not revenge on the *priests* of Jehovah the violence which they had suffered from Jehovah's *prophets*; which at this crisis they perhaps could have done. But Jehoiada and his friends were saved by that in their predecessors, which we hardly know whether to censure as lukewarmness, or (in comparison with the prophets) to approve as humanity. Hitherto at least, it would seem that the priesthoods of Jehovah and of Baal, when alike enjoying state-establishment, had lived in decorous mutual toleration, in contrast to the fierce enthusiasm displayed by the prophets, the Puritans of that age. If however this was a stain on Jehovah's priests, the time

[1] See Appendix to this chapter.
[2] The same name is given (by the Chronicler) to the head of the "Aaronites," who came to join David at Ziklag.

was now come for their representative to wipe it off, though without such frenzy as Elisha had displayed.

Athaliah had reigned six years when Jehoiada's plans of revolution were complete. He had gained the queen's guard and the captains of some other military bodies; and having brought them into the temple, took an oath of them and opened his plot. He informed them that the late king Ahaziah had a young son yet alive, saved by the princess Jehosheba, sister of Ahaziah. At the time of the massacre the child had been but a year old, and had ever since been hidden in the house of Jehovah. He then produced the boy, whose name was JEHOASH. In the temple (as we now incidentally learn) a number of shields and spears, called king David's, were kept hung up, as in many temples of the Greeks and Romans. A sufficient number of the guards were brought into the temple unarmed, and were at the critical moment furnished with these; then, having sounded the trumpet and proclaimed Jehoash king, they slew Athaliah as soon as she came out to see the cause of the rejoicing. Jehoiada next held an assembly, at which he induced the people to bind themselves by a public covenant to Jehovah, to be His peculiar nation. From this the transition was not great to an attack on Baal and his priests; which, however, our record ascribes to "all the people," without stating that Jehoiada distinctly urged it. The temple of Baal which Athaliah had built was pulled down; the images and altars were thoroughly broken; and the chief priest Mattan was slain in front of the altars. If these two lives were alone taken, it was a singularly bloodless revolution.

There are several points of detail in the narrative, which would bear more comment than can here be afforded. The day on which the slaughter of Athaliah is said to have been perpetrated, was *the sabbath*; a word which we now meet for the first time in the history of the monarchy. That on every seventh day there was at the temple special service to which the people flocked, and sacrifices of greater splendour, cannot be reasonably questioned. The sacrifices and other offerings formed a large part of the food of the priestly and Levitical families in attendance on the temple; for which purpose they were cheerfully contributed by the pious, as well as provided by public money. By the great concourse of people to the temple on this day, Jehoiada's plot was facilitated; which in itself implies that there were as yet no such scruples about sabbatical observances, as grew up after the times of Nehemiah.

We are farther told, that upon proclaiming Jehoash king, they set a crown upon his head, and presented him with the *testimony*, or as others render it, with the *law*. This appears to be a continuation of the primitive constitutional practice, recorded of Samuel, who, when he installed Saul into the royalty, " told the people the manner of the kingdom, and wrote it in a book, and laid it up before Jehovah." Some written document was certainly presented now to Jehoash, describing the duties, rights, and powers of the king; which, we can scarcely doubt, tended to define and limit the prerogative, to mark out the claims and privileges of the priestly order, and secure a more constitutional government than had hitherto prevailed. At the same time, the earnest genius of the Hebrew religion assures us that the book contained moral rules and laws for the real executing of right between man and man. In the Pentateuch itself we have several fragmentary systems of law,[1] which clearly formed parts of earlier books; and it is quite a possibility that the very code which Jehoiada delivered to his young charge, has been incorporated with our modern Bible.

That when the ancient Hebrews spoke of the " Book of the Law," or even the " Law of Moses," they did not intend anything so voluminous as the four books which we name Exodus, Leviticus, Numbers, and Deuteronomy, or even the same with the omission of the historical parts, is very clear from a narrative in the compilation which we call the book of Joshua. We there read[2] that Joshua built an altar of *unhewn* stones, and wrote upon the stones *a copy of the law of Moses*; and afterwards read aloud all the words of the law, " *even every word which Moses commanded*," to the whole congregation, with their women and little ones. To write upon unhewn stones may ap-

---

[1] Such a system is Exod. xxi., xxii., xxiii. 1—19; which ends with a fragmentary decalogue. Such again is Levit. xix.; also Levit. xxvi.
[2] Josh. viii. 30—35.

pear an arduous task, but it admits of explanation from Deut. xxvii., which makes virtual reference to the passage already quoted. The stones were to be first plastered over with cement, by which a smooth surface might be obtained. Still, with the rude alphabet of antiquity, the largest altar that we can conceive to have been intended would take in but a few chapters of a modern Pentateuch; which by the compactness of our stereotype editions beguiles men into forgetting how cumbrous and unreadable a book it (as a whole) practically is to the mass even of an educated nation.

Nevertheless, there are circumstances which make it not improbable that the earlier books of the Pentateuch were composed, or their most important materials compiled, not later than the regency of Jehoiada; although (as will afterwards appear) extreme difficulties lie in the way of supposing that the commands and threats against having graven images, high places, and some other things, were as yet read in any avowed and authoritative form. But about three generations later unequivocal proofs appear that the outline of history, as presented in the modern Pentateuch, was generally received.

It is impossible to attain grounds for any confident opinion whether the young Jehoash was or was not a real son of Ahaziah; though there are general topics which may incline us to disbelief. Cruelty and jealousy are very keen to discover their victims. Athaliah knew perfectly the number of her son's sons; and must have been aware, if the last-born infant had escaped her sword. The age being accurately known, to bring the young child up "in the temple" under her very eye would be peculiarly difficult. On the other hand, those who guaranteed the truth of the story, of whom the *king's mother* Zibiah must have been not the least, had everything personally to gain by deception, and every possible facility of deceiving. The nation itself would rejoice to believe; and all prudent men who suspected something wrong, would in very patriotism hold their peace. Even had rumours of distrust been noised abroad, no whisper of them was likely to find its way into the pages of our historians. If we could believe, with the Chronicler, that the princess Jehosheba was the wife of Jehoiada,[1] the probability on this side would be still further enhanced; and it might even be surmised that the boy was their son. But in any case they would probably select for the throne a child of the line of David.

The king being only seven years old, Jehoiada became sole regent during the long minority. In these years of unchecked sacerdotal power, it might have been imagined that the Law of Moses would be closely enforced as regards the "high places." But we have here the vindication of all the kings of Judah against the incessant complaints of a later age:—*even the zealous and applauded Priest Regent acted in this matter exactly as the Kings.* During the time of the young king's dutiful submission, it is still recorded,[2] "The high places were not taken away; the people still sacrificed and burnt incense in the high places." As no effort on the part of the Priest is alluded to, nor any opposition on the part of the people, it may seem doubtful whether the Levitical body themselves had yet conceived the ambition of forbidding all local sanctuaries and all worship over which *they* did not preside.[3] The High Places were clearly beyond their jurisdiction: in fact we have not a particle of contempo-

[1] We have no right to dislocate this statement from another, that Jehoiada was 130 years old when he died, 2 Chron. xxii. 11, xxiv. 15. This makes him full ninety when Ahaziah was slain, aged twenty-three. Ahaziah, being only eighteen years younger than his father, could not well be younger than his sister. Thus the priest would be about seventy years older than his princess; which makes the marriage itself, as well as any issue from it, incredible. Both the royal affinity and the wonderful age of the priest seem to be fictions of the Chronicler to glorify his greatness.

[2] 2 Kings xii. 1—3.—The Chronicler (2 Chron. xxiv. 1, 2) copies word for word the two first verses, and wilfully omits the third, as less honourable to the priest! This is literary dishonesty quite disgraceful. It is more like to conscious falsehood than to mere party prejudice.

From 2 Kings xxiii. 13, which shows the buildings of Solomon to Astarte, Chemosh, and Milcom still standing, we infer that Jehoiada's zeal was limited to practical exigencies, and did not spend itself on buildings as such.

[3] The worship at the high places *implies that the people did not assemble at Jerusalem for the passover;* for it is distinctly stated that it was celebrated at the high places by the separate priests, 2 Kings xxiii. 9.

It will be seen that *afterwards* the worship at the high places became more corrupt, and it was suppressed for other than ceremonial reasons. "Hold to the Levites," then became the cry of good men, as "Hold to your Bishops," in the ancient Christian church. In avoiding the immediate evil, the far greater evil of destroying freedom and individual energies was overlooked.

rancous or otherwise trustworthy evidence, that even in
Judah the Levites were at this time settled in cities
through the land. We have the fullest proof which is
possible for a negation, that neither Priests nor Levites
were as yet a body of *local religious teachers*. The worship
of Jehovah still consisted in singing of hymns and in external pageantry,—such as burning of incense and offering sacrifice; and centuries had to pass before Public
Prayer, with Reading and Teaching of the Law, was
systematized.

One consequence of the revolution which expelled the
worship of Baal,—not noted in the history, but discover-
able in the extant prophets,—was the alienation of Sidon,
Tyre, and all the Phœnician confederacy, from the two
Hebrew kingdoms. Their rapid growth in wealth and
civilized art during the whole reign of David, and the
former half of Solomon's reign, had mainly depended on
the good understanding kept up with Tyre. Under the
immediate successors of Solomon, no breach of amity
with Judah can be traced, although intercourse was more
difficult while Philistia was a precarious possession. But
now that a Tyrian princess and her daughter had been
slaughtered, and the worshippers of Tyrian deities exter-
minated, no Phœnician merchants would be likely to
venture their persons into the Hebrew territories, and the
uniting influences of commerce ceased. In fact, commerce
itself became a source of enmity; for Tyre and Sidon were
among the greatest slave-marts of the world; and when
Philistine marauders succeeded in carrying off (as became
very common) whole troops of miserable Jews, the
Tyrian merchant was at hand in the Philistine ports, to
ship off the captives to the coasts of Greece, Italy, or Car-
thage.[1] Another course which the slave-trade took, is
imperfectly explained to us;—the captive passed from the
hands of the Philistines or Tyrians through those of the
Edomites,[2] probably to the East.

But we must revert to the affairs of Samaria, where JEHU
reigned ingloriously. It had been easier to turn the national force against unarmed and unsuspecting princes and
priests, than to repel the foreign foe against whom his
murdered master had stationed him. In fact, the same

[1] Joel iii. 4—6.   [2] Amos i. 6, 9.

voice of the prophet which called away Jehu from before
Ramoth of Gilead, laid open the whole land beyond Jordan
to be overrun by Hazael's chariots. A usurper, intent on
exterminating royal houses and entire religious sects, needs
to gird his own throne with his most trusted guards, and
has little strength to spare against the foreigner. No one
can wonder to hear that the king of Syria, whose position
at Ramoth had already intercepted the tribe of Reuben,
now not merely established his dominion over that tribe,
but conquered all Gilead and Bashan, and shut Israel up
to the west of Jordan. Two-fifths of his territory, and of
his available fighting men, were lost to the king of Samaria by this severe and irretrievable blow. No help could
be expected from Judah. In the first six years, while
Athaliah was there in power, the queen probably rejoiced
at the calamities falling on her mother's murderer and the
persecutor of her religion : and after her fall, the prudent
priest who swayed public affairs remembered too well the
unhappy result of Jehoshaphat's campaign with Ahab. A
feeling had probably diffused itself in Judah, that an alliance with Israel was unlucky ; for nothing of the kind is
again attempted down to the capture and ruin of Samaria.

King Hazael found eager and fierce auxiliaries against
the unfortunate Israelites in their eastern neighbours the
people of Ammon.[1] The old controversy about the limits
of their land, which they had mooted against Jephthah,
was not yet forgotten ; and the horrible destruction of their
nation by David seemed to make revenge, when within
their reach, a pious duty towards their murdered ancestors.
A peculiar cruelty, shocking to name, is more than once
alluded to in this implacable war, as suffered by the towns
of Israel;—their pregnant women were sought out, and
slashed open by the malignant victors. The people of
David were thus to learn, that crime begets crime, and
that its punishment too often falls on a comparatively innocent generation : yet their prophets always allude to
the atrocities of Edom and Ammon against Israel, as if
utterly unaware that it had been provoked by David,
their pattern-prince.

No more is told us of Jehu, than that he reigned twenty-
eight years. On referring to the chronological table in p.

[1] Amos i. 13.

139, it will appear that 143 years elapse from the accession of Jehu to the destruction of the Samaritan monarchy; of which period the house of Jehu held the kingdom 103 years. So long a tenure of power,—long, in contrast to the other dynasties of Samaria,—is stated by our better historian[1] to be a reward from Jehovah to Jehu for his massacring the descendants of Ahab. And it may be thought that the house of Jehu continued for three generations on an excellent footing with the whole body of the prophets, when we find Jehoash, grandson of Jehu, address the aged Elisha in terms of more than devoted filial respect.

The son of Jehu, by name JEHOAHAZ,[2] was naturally still more helpless than he against the Syrian monarch; inasmuch as Hazael's power on the east bank of Jordan enabled him to invade the western country by crossing where he pleased. Although no particulars are given of his inroads, the general summary is perhaps only the more trustworthy. We learn that he left to Jehoahaz only fifty horsemen, ten chariots, and 10,000 footmen;[3] words which seem to mean, that he kept the king of Samaria in a certain dependence, dictating to him what military force he should be allowed to keep up. It will presently appear that Hazael also exercised the right to march through the country when he pleased; so that, on the whole, the first steps to entire dominion were taken. Israel was, in some sense, become a province of the Syrian empire, governed however by its native king, who paid homage and undoubtedly tribute to the great monarch. This result was not brought about without severe struggles and immense loss on the part of the Israelites, of whom it is said, that "Hazael had destroyed them, and had made them like the dust by threshing." The calamity of war, in the reigns of Jehu and his sons, was aggravated by other causes.[4] A great drought and a dreadful plague of locusts fell within this period. Famine also and pestilence are named,

[1] 2 Kings x. 30. [2] Accession in B.C. 835.
[3] A real army of 10,000 infantry is far more than we can believe Jehoahaz to have *kept on foot*. But the historians are so accustomed to large enumerations, that, in comparison, this appeared little. On the other hand, he must have had very much more than 10,000 men *of military age*, if that interpretation be attempted.
[4] Amos iv. 6—10.

which indeed may well have been a result of the war itself.

As the "dispersion of Judah" began with the revolt of Edom and the marauding incursions of Edomites and Philistines which followed it, so the "dispersion of Israel" began, but on a greater scale, with the wars of Hazael. When that prince found that the Israelites were too high-spirited and too uncongenial to be turned into obedient subjects, our knowledge of all antiquity, and of the conduct of the other Asiatic monarchs, justifies the inference, that upon storming various towns of Israel, great numbers of the inhabitants were sold by him into slavery. Whole families of the more educated Israelites, who thus found their way to the rich and cultivated nations beyond the desart, would be likely to communicate from time to time with their lost country; and this accounts to us for the comparatively familiar acquaintance, which, two generations later, we find to have been current in Israel, with the great cities of the Tigris. And so sweeping had been Hazael's conquests, that the fear of a general transplantation of the whole nation was already rising before the minds of thoughtful men. The depression of Israel continued through the whole life of Jehoahaz, concerning which nothing else has come down to us.[1] But before passing to his son's reign, we must resume the history of Jerusalem.

About 130 years had passed since Solomon first built his celebrated temple; in which time, even under the dry climate of Judæa, some external dilapidation of a building may have occurred, enough to make repairs requisite. Moreover, the feet of multitudes may have greatly worn away the cedar floors. Jehoiada at least thought the state of the sacred edifice reasonably to demand his care; for it cannot have been without his instance, that the

[1] In 2 Kings xiii. 4—6, three mysterious verses occur, which may be a later interpolation. 1. They so break the connexion, that they can hardly have formed part of the original writing. 2. They represent Israel to have been delivered from Syria at Jehoahaz's repentance and prayer; without hinting that the deliverance did not take place in his lifetime. This is opposed to v. 22 of the same chapter. The vague mention of *a saviour* who delivered them from Syria, cannot reasonably be referred to the king Jehoash; and, on the whole, looks like the writing of a man who had no accurate acquaintance with the history. The unknown antagonist, who crippled the power of Benhadad, is possibly intended.

minor king ordered collections to be made from the pious, with the express object of repairing it. The funds to be appropriated to this object seem to be described as three-fold:—1. Dedicated gold, whether stamped or unstamped, which existed in the temple. 2. The money levied on the people, like our church rates. 3. Additional sums, which might voluntarily be paid into the temple treasury. But when it is added that the priests are "to take the money, every man of his acquaintance," it is left doubtful whether this is identical with the third source of supply, or whether (as the Chronicler has enlarged and expounded the words) the priests were to perambulate the land and make special collections everywhere.[1] Be this as it may, the account is clear, that years and years passed, during which the priests continued to receive money from the people,[2] but totally neglected to apply it to the repairs of the house. Such unfaithfulness need surprize no one. The priestly body had risen in political position, but without an increase of pecuniary resources proportioned to their advanced rank; and every corporation of men thus vested with power finds the temptation to peculation irresistible. Nevertheless, as time went on and the neglect continued, the king could at last endure it no longer. It was not until he had attained the age of thirty years,—having nominally reigned twenty-three,—that he gained strength of mind for personal conflict with his benefactor, tutor, and regent; and having called for Jehoiada and the other priests, he pointedly asked what had been done with

[1] 2 Chron. xxiv. 5, 6. Indeed the Chronicler, as usual, thrusts *Levites* forward, when the book of Kings knows only about *priests*. He also represents *the law of Moses* to have supplied the pattern: but nothing like it appears in the other record.

[2] The Chronicler dishonestly omits the fact, that the priests *actually received the money*, and lays upon them no other guilt than that of *neglecting to make the collections*. He also imputes the "breaches of the house" to the wilful act of "the sons of Athaliah, *that wicked woman,*" who had also "bestowed all the dedicated things upon Baalim." But Athaliah's sons would have been sons also of her husband Jehoram, unless we impute a most bold adultery to her as queen (and indeed in her earlier days), and suppose that she could dare now publicly to bring forward her spurious offspring. To interpret *her sons* as meaning any mere votaries of Baal, appears like an evasion. In any case, they were not likely to make half-work with the temple. If they had wished to dilapidate it, they would have chosen to ruin it, and would not have left Jehoiada in his place.

As the book of Kings is silent, the whole statement must be looked on as a fiction of hatred.

the money. Finally, a compromise was made; the past was not inquired into; in future the priests were to receive no moneys for the purpose of repairs; but by the side of the altar was set a box with a hole in its lid,[1] into which the people cast their offerings. From time to time, the king's own scribe, conjointly with the high priest, took out and counted the money, and with it employed carpenters and masons to execute the necessary repairs. The funds thus obtained were barely sufficient for the work in timber and in stone: nothing remained to spend on gold and silver vessels;[2] a fact, which, as we shall see, may have soon become even matter of congratulation.

The affair just narrated exhibits the priests in no favourable light, and might furnish matter of triumph, alike to those who suspect or hate all religious profession, and to those who believe all priesthood to be priestcraft. But happily we now come upon the domain of contemporary literature, which gives a new aspect of the ecclesiastical body then ruling at Jerusalem. Although Israel abounded in prophets more than Judah, yet those of Israel appear to have been men of action rather than of books. Jerusalem furnished an endowed priesthood, and therewith the opportunities of literary leisure; consequently, from it has come down to us the first extant prophetical writing,[3] the production of JOEL, son of Pethuel. It has been conjectured that he was himself a priest of Jerusalem; at least his whole tone is thoroughly sacerdotal,[4] and implies that he stood in the most intimate relations with the priests, between whom and his school no one can imagine any diversity of feeling to have existed. His prophecy is remarkably fluent and finished in style, so as to indicate

[1] This substitute for the method before used, seems to prove that the order to *perambulate* the country is the Chronicler's invention.
[2] Nothing can be clearer than 2 Kings xii. 13, but it is *directly contradicted* by the Chronicler, in xxiv. 14, who thought it a bad example to later times, to confess that the collections had not been very liberal.
[3] The English reader is exposed to the greatest disadvantage by the extreme defects of the English translation of the prophets, besides the confused order and erroneous divisions. The references made in this work will not always appear quite to the purpose in the common Bible.
[4] Thus ii. 14, the very first use to which a starving people is to apply the renewed fertility of the soil is, to make *a meat-offering and drink-offering to Jehovah their God*. We do not find in him any of the indignant disclaimers of sacrifice, which are met in other prophets. See Amos (v. 21, 22), his next extant successor.

that such writing had already received great cultivation; and although the paucity of political allusions makes it impossible to fix its date with nicety, there is much reason to believe that it was penned during the ascendency of Jehoiada. This beautiful and striking composition tends to give us a very high opinion of the best men among the contemporary Jerusalem priesthood. So far is it from the narrow Levitical bigotry, which would appropriate all religious eminence to a certain race, that it boldly and rejoicingly anticipates a time when the spirit of Jehovah shall be poured forth over *all flesh*: when young and old, male and female, shall enjoy the same direct communion with God, which he was believed to impart by dreams and visions to his most favoured servants. That time (it declares) will indeed only be ushered in by awful physical convulsions, such as earthquakes and volcanos are known to produce, yet in the midst of these the "remnant" shall be saved, who seek to Jehovah in Mount Zion and in Jerusalem.[1] Although we know distinctly that the worship of Jehovah at the high places, without Levites, was at this time practised in Judæa, Joel drops no word of disapproval concerning it, nor can we find out from his writing that anything approaching to idolatry was apprehended by him in the land. This decidedly confirms us in the belief, that Levitical ambition had not yet developed itself. The sacred duty of supporting the altar is indeed strongly inculcated by this prophet; yet not more strongly than the utter vanity of all lip-service and outward show of religion. "Turn to me, saith Jehovah, with all your heart, with fasting, weeping, and mourning; and rend your heart, *and not your garments*, and turn unto Jehovah your God: for he is gracious and merciful, slow to anger, and of great kindness, and repenteth him of the evil."

The particular cause which called forth this eloquent prophet was a prodigious descent of *locusts*, which so devoured the crops as to cause wide-spread famine. According to his statement, every species of plant suffered. At least he enumerates the wheat and the barley, the vine and

---

[1] It is remarkable to find, in this first extant outburst of prophecy, the idea of an *elect people* in the midst of Israel itself, thus distinctly formed already.

the fig, the pomegranate, the palm-tree,¹ the apple. Meat-offerings and drink-offerings could not be furnished for the altar. The barley-grass and the barley having been destroyed, the cattle had no fodder: and as a general *dry season* conspired with the other calamity, the flocks of sheep found no pasturage, and the very beasts of the wilderness pined for their accustomed streams of water. The locusts are described in a highly poetical, yet an impressively correct similitude, as an army of horsemen from the north, ravaging the land, hiding the face of the sun, clambering over the walls, leaping in at the windows; and the people are called upon to see and acknowledge Jehovah's own mighty hand in this unavoidable calamity. Where human exertion has no place left for it, he suitably calls on them to make it a time of peculiar supplication to their God: not indeed with the stupid conceits which under such an infliction a Greek imagination might have devised, nor with the ferocious sacrifices for which Italians and Gauls would have called; but with the outpourings of pure hearts and the lamentation of simple souls. The priests, as ministers of Jehovah, are called upon to take the lead in the public sorrow, and the nation is comforted by the assurance that their God will not thus afflict them for ever. The result of restored prosperity is to be, that wide diffusion of Jehovah's spirit among the whole nation, before alluded to, and a concussion of all nature, through which the pious and chosen ones shall nevertheless be preserved. From this topic, the prophet passes off to the judgment on foreign nations, especially Tyre, Sidon, and Philistia, for driving off into slavery the defenceless Hebrew population, who are sold to the Greeks for a trifling price. The violence of the Edomites also is denounced,² who have shed innocent

¹ It grew principally in the plain of Jericho, but there may have been a few other favoured spots.
The fourth verse of the prophecy has been understood to mean that the palmer-worm, canker-worm, locust, and caterpillar were the plagues of four successive seasons; but the best interpreters regard these words as descriptive of the locusts at different ages; so that the whole is only declarative of the long duration of their ravages, beginning from the month in which they are as caterpillars, and lasting until they are full-grown.
² Egypt likewise is threatened, but the words leave it doubtful whether they are regarded to have helped the inroads of the Edomites.

blood in the land. For these sins a day of vengeance is predicted, when Jehovah shall gather all the nations to the place where he will judge them—(by name, the valley of *Jehoshaphat*, perhaps an imaginary place; for the word means "Jehovah is Judge"),—while Judah and Jerusalem shall dwell for ever in holiness, separation, and prosperity.

In this prophet we see strikingly the tender influences of adversity. He has neither the self-glorifying tone which a too successful career often gives, nor the fierce desire of revenge which personal sufferings from enemies excite; but as one who endures more from God than from man, and knows that love is at the bottom of all the chastisement, he is melted, and not hardened by it. While he contemplates with desire and hope the coming destruction of all the men of violence, there is nothing in his writing to nourish malignant passion, or give just offence to Charity.

We return however to king Jehoash. In spite of his general respect for his instructor, his discovery how the moneys collected from the people had been appropriated, appears to have commenced feelings of distrust towards the advisers of his boyhood; and at length a positive feud arose between the royal and the priestly party. It did not break out in its full violence until after the death of Jehoiada; but there can be no doubt that the king had conceived a bad opinion of the priests, and had become uneasy in his trammels. When it was clear that they had been abusing their power, it was inevitable for him to consider farther that this power was a recent and accidental result of his unhappy orphanhood; and he would look upon it as a usurpation, which it was his duty to put down. Thus instead of a joint constitutional action between King and Priesthood, a violent struggle for supreme power commenced.

Before this could work out its results, Hazael, king of Syria, marching at will across the territories of the prostrate king of Samaria,[1] made his appearance entirely on the other side of Jerusalem,—in the country of the Phil-

From this time forth, the "bringing back the captivity of the people," or recovering them from slavery, is a constant burden of the prophets.

[1] Jehoash, son of Jehoahaz, appears just to have come to the throne.

istines. Here he besieged and captured the important city of Gath; after which he prepared to march upon Jerusalem. The physical strength and riches of Judæa were undoubtedly impaired since the time of Jehoshaphat. As for the ravages of locusts, they, though very severe, are indeed temporary. But the battle at Ramoth had been to Judah what that of Leuctra was to the Spartans. Though the loss was trifling, its moral effect on the subject states had been great. The Edomites and Philistines, with other marauders, had ever since looked on Judæa as their spoil, and far beyond the direct wounds they inflicted, must have been the damage done by hindering cultivation. Neither Jehoiada nor Jehoash were warriors; and the blood-feud against Edom, which David had provoked, forbade the reign of piety and mildness to be one of peace and happiness. Nevertheless, there had been a great multiplication of forts,[1] which, like the walls of Aurelian, though denoting conscious weakness, served as protection from the barbarian. Under Jehoiada and Jehoash the land had enjoyed (it would seem) prudent government; and if the people had been united, they might perhaps have offered a successful resistance to such an army as Hazael had with him before Gath.[2] But Jehoash felt the priestly schism to palsy the hearts and hands of his people; and as one reared in the temple, and living always in his own court, he had no enterprize for war. He adopted therefore the more prudent plan of pacifying the Syrian king by gifts of homage. The treasures of the temple had not been used for the repairs of the building, nor put into the hands of the priests. Since the day when Asa emptied the sacred store-room to gratify the first Benhadad, new accumulations had taken place, both during the brilliant reign of Jehoshaphat, and during half a century since. Sparing therefore neither royal nor sacred treasures,[3] the king sent them off

[1] See 2 Chron. xi. 5—12; Hosea viii. 14.
[2] Yet on the contrary, the better success of this prince in war may have been owing to his *not* using so large and pompous armies as his predecessors. The Chronicler speaks contemptuously of the smallness of his force, 2 Chr. xxiv. 24.
[3] According to 2 Chr. xxi. 17, the Philistines in Jehoram's reign rifled the *royal*, but not the *sacred* treasures. But this account must be received with some uncertainty.

to make his peace with Hazael; and the Syrian monarch, whether really satisfied and soothed, or conscious that his army was unequal to the task of reducing Jerusalem, marched away without farther hostility.

But the conduct of Jehoash, if we can trust our informer, must have kindled into fury the priestly dissatisfaction. The pride and the dignity of the body were alike concerned in the splendour and wealth of the temple, which it is every way probable that the late priest Jehoiada had sedulously fostered and augmented, but which their own king had now lavished away on the public foe. Although not yet old (for his age was forty-seven), he was in a bad state of health. A conspiracy was formed against his life, and he was slain on his bed by two assassins,[1] whom our more sacerdotal authority describes as avengers of the priestly cause.[2]

The general account which we have here given of the progress of the feud, depends principally on the facts furnished by the book of Kings. But these appeared insufficient to the later historian, who states that immediately on Jehoiada's death, the princes of Judah came and ingratiated themselves with the king, and obtained his leave to worship images of Astarte and other idols; that when prophets from Jehovah in vain protested, Zechariah the son of Jehoiada (a priest full eighty years of age) was filled with the spirit of God, and publicly rebuked the people; that thereupon a conspiracy was made, and the people, by the king's command, stoned Zechariah to death in the very court of Jehovah's house. In punishment for this murder, Hazael was sent up by God against Jehoash, and his own servants presently slew him. Such is the addition made by the Chronicler; but it is far more like-

From Joel iii. 5, it appears that the Philistines and Phœnicians had plundered "silver and gold" from Judœa, and dedicated it in their own temples. The words might naturally mean that they had plundered *the temple at Jerusalem*; but perhaps this is not necessarily implied.

[1] As if, after all, ashamed to put upon any true Jew the unpleasant work of king-killing, the Chronicler curiously informs us, that the mothers of the assassins were, one *an Ammonitess* and one *a Moabitess*.

[2] B.C. 818. One of my critics who professes a belief in the verbal inspiration of the Chronicles, is displeased that I here believe the Chronicler. I confess it is from the wicked Gibbon that I have learned a mode of investigating truth which my critic seems to think malevolent, viz. to lean towards believing all the evil which men tell of their own party, and to believe all the good which they tell of their adversaries.

ly that this is an invention to exculpate the priestly party from having *commenced* murder, than that the older compiler should have omitted facts so important to a Jehovist, so heinous, and so characteristic. Indeed, the general applause[1] bestowed by him on Jehoash appears fully to justify our refusing belief to any part of the story.

The murder of their king betrayed, in the priestly faction, not only moral turpitude, but a conscious weakness. Unsupported by territorial Levitism, they were not an order, or even a party in the state, but (from their fewness) merely a respectable or formidable *coterie*. They were certainly not yet equal to a direct contest with the royal power, which was strengthened by the atrocious deed which their best members must have deeply regretted. AMAZIAH, the son of Jehoash, found no difficulty in ascending the throne without the aid of the priests,[2] and having buried the murdered prince in the royal sepulchres,[3] took vengeance on the murderers.[4]

Both in Samaria and in Jerusalem a young king now reigned, each of higher spirit than his predecessors, and in more fortunate circumstances. Amaziah, in his early prime (for his age was twenty-five), finding himself master of the kingdom of Jehoshaphat, proposed to chastise the marauding Edomites, and recover them to the yoke of Judah. In some respects reminding us of Jehoshaphat (to whom however he was inferior in prudence), he strictly confined himself to monotheistic worship, tolerating no pagan impurities. The priests either feared his energy, or applauded his heroism and uprightness; and the people must have rejoiced in the hope of checking the cruel Edomites. The peaceful and priestly

---

[1] 2 Kings xiv. 3. "Amaziah did that which was right in the sight of Jehovah, *according to all things as Jehoash his father did.*" The qualification, "yet not like David his father," is a stereotype reservation of primacy to David, but not implying such guilt as the Chronicler imputes to Jehoash.

[2] B.C. 818.

[3] 2 Kings xii. 21. This is distinctly denied by the Chronicler, 2 Chron. xxiv. 25, as in the similar case of Jehoram.

[4] It is added, that in obedience to *the law of Moses*, Amaziah *did not put to death the children of the murderers;* for which the compilers quote Deut. xxiv. 16. It is a pity that Elisha had not the same advantage of reading Deuteronomy as these writers had, for perhaps he might have then spared the innocent descendants of Ahab.

exterior of the last reign was superseded once more by
martial tumult. That a powerful host was really assembled
we cannot doubt; but it is tedious to quote the
monstrous exaggerations of the Chronicler.[1] Idumæa
however was invaded. In the Valley of Salt,—the old
battle-ground of Joab and Abishai,—an obstinate conflict
took place, with total defeat of the Edomites, whose loss
was estimated at 10,000 men.[2] It is difficult to deal with
such numbers. Whether it is worth while to compromise,
and say that *dispersion* was mistaken for *slaughter*,—is
very uncertain. Since however the Jewish king got
possession of his enemy's metropolis, the strong and
rocky town called Selah,[3] it is clear that the victory,
whether more or less bloody, was really decisive. The
Edomites still maintained themselves in Elath, on the
coast of the Red Sea; but as in the prophet Amos their
chief seats are alluded to as in the distant cities of Bozra
and Teman, we must suppose that these events helped
once more to unpeople Mount Seir. Thus Idumæa itself
was for the time under the power of the victor, and the
immediate fear of Edomite incursion was removed.

Meanwhile JEHOASH, the king of Israel, who ascended
the throne two years before Amaziah, had met with still
more unlooked-for successes. From causes wholly unexplained,
the power of Benhadad, who had succeeded to
the throne of his father Hazael, shrank into sudden insignificance.
In fact, for more than half a century the
power of Damascus vanishes with Hazael from the Hebrew
horizon, as if annihilated by some great revolution. We
must not too hastily attribute this to the prowess of king
Jehoash and of Israel. If they had struggled successfully,
crippled as they already were, against the undivided

---

[1] He gives Amaziah "300,000 choice men, handling spear and shield," and makes him hire "100,000 mighty men of valour out of Israel for 100 talents of silver." In David's wars he made the Ammonites hire 32,000 *chariots* with 1000 talents of silver; 1 Chron. xix. 6, 7. Some unhappy students take these numbers as valuable statistical information.

[2] A single 10,000 does not satisfy the Chronicler's largeness of heart: he likes to improve a story. He therefore makes Amaziah fling a second 10,000 from top to bottom of the rock, "so that they were all broken in pieces."

[3] Selah (*the rock*) is believed to be the remarkable city called by the Greeks Petra, under Mount Hor. It is about half-way between the Dead Sea and the Gulf of Akaba. Bozra is commonly placed in the Hauran, but perhaps wrongly; Teman is supposed to be on the east of Idumæa.

power of Syria, it would be strange indeed that no other memorials of such a war of freedom should survive than our extant dry notices. Some personal weakness in Benhadad may have assisted the result, but the action of foreign powers upon Damascus must surely have been the moving spring of the whole. Had Hamath rebelled, and withdrawn from Benhadad the power of Hollow Syria? or did war with Northern Syria or Mesopotamia hamper him? Or was the might of Nineveh thrusting in this direction, and its arm already long enough to clutch at the provinces of Benhadad?[1] Whatever the cause, it was shortly discovered by the Israelites that the new king of Damascus was a very different antagonist from his father.

A single phrase[2] hints to us the condition of the eastern tribes of Israel under the power of Hazael. They were not properly conquered, but were kept down, and cut off from the rest of the nation. The Syrians had overrun the country and possessed themselves of all the unwalled villages, nor could the Israelites freely *rove about in tents*, as was natural to grazier tribes; but the principal cities had held out, like so many garrisons, and preserved the name and hope of Hebrew independence. The land of Bashan, though open and exposed to an inroad of cavalry or chariots, had only so much the more carefully been furnished with strongly-walled towns. Sixty cities, with high walls, gates, and bars, were celebrated as in the land of Og, the giant-king; and even the exaggerations of legend are likely to have had a basis in the existing features of the country. Such fortresses remaining unsubdued, a rapid revolution might at any favourable moment overthrow the Damascene power. Where the first shock was received is uncertain, as is the whole course of

---

[1] Since the above was written, Colonel Rawlinson's partial decipherment of the Nimrood Obelisk adds to the probability that the last is the true hypothesis. Zoba and Hamath are both named, as attacked by the Assyrian king, in Rawlinson's translation; but the chronology is still highly uncertain.

[2] 2 Kings xiii. 5. "The children of Israel," when delivered from Syria, "dwelt in their tents, as beforetime." That is to say, while under Syrian oppression they did not dare to move about in tents, but remained shut up in their cities.

This is in a passage which has been already noted as a probable interpolation; yet it must be very ancient, and shows the view taken of their position by an early writer.

events, both as to space and time. As far as can be made out, the first struggle took place on the west of Jordan, for cities which Hazael had taken from Jehoahaz. When Benhadad came, as usual, with chariots, and selected a favourable position, previously well-known, near Aphek, on the slope of Esdraelon, Jehoash encountered and defeated him. In two other unfavourable engagements Benhadad lost all the cities west of Jordan, which had been gained in the preceding reign, but (as appears) still held his ground on the opposite side of the river.

Meanwhile, the king of Jerusalem, exulting in his triumph over Idumæa and confident in the bravery of his troops, indulged the fancy that he was to recover the empire of Solomon over all Israel; and in a chivalrous spirit sent a message of defiance to Jehoash, inviting him to battle. The disdainful retort of the Israelitish monarch has deserved preservation, as illustrating the still homely and quaint spirit of the nation. He replied to the king of Judah,—"The thistle that was in Lebanon sent to the cedar, saying, Give thy daughter to my son for a wife. Then a wild beast of Lebanon passed by, and trode down the thistle." But accepting the challenge, Jehoash marched down upon his rival, and encountered him near Bethshemesh of Judah. A battle took place, in which the Jewish army was entirely worsted; and Jehoash, following up his success, captured the unfortunately boastful king, and entered Jerusalem itself without farther opposition. He then pulled down the fortifications of the city for a length of 400 cubits; plundered whatever gold and silver was to be found, not sparing consecrated vessels; and having taken as many hostages as he pleased, returned to Samaria.[1]

Jehoash, dying in the meridian of life,[2] left to his youthful son JEROBOAM II. a kingdom animated to a new consciousness of vigour. The victories achieved over the

[1] The Chronicler does not know how to imagine such misfortunes occurring to Amaziah, except as a punishment for *pagan idolatry;* hence he interpolates a tale, that after the conquest of Edom the king had brought back the Edomite gods and worshipped them. A prophet, of course, rebukes him, at which Amaziah is angry: the prophet predicts woe coming on him, &c.

But all this is set aside by the emphatic statement in the Kings, "He did that which was right in the sight of Jehovah," &c.; 2 Kings xiv. 3, and especially 2 Kings xv. 3, written on a retrospect of his reign.
[2] B.C. 804.

Syrians and over the conqueror of the Edomites stimulated the Samaritan power to a belief in its high destiny; and the first object proposed was to recover the trans-Jordanic possessions of Israel. Who then wielded the sceptre of Damascus is wholly unknown. The son of Hazael, if alive, must have been aged, and no successor is named.[1] One thing only is certain, that when Jeroboam crossed the Jordan, the eastern tribes, which had not in the course of two generations forgotten their Hebrew feelings and connexions, gladly shook off the Syrian yoke. The short notices left us concerning the "very bitter affliction" of these tribes, while beneath the Syrians, may suggest that (as so often in ancient warfare) the masters of the open country perpetually distressed the dwellers in the cities by carrying off their cattle, cutting down their fruit-trees, and burning whatever crops (although generally pastoral people) they might happen to raise. But by such methods the Syrians, if in many cases they forced surrender, yet left behind a spirit of enmity, eager for retaliation. Accordingly, the work of Jeroboam seems to have been very easy. The whole land was recovered, from the defile of the Leontes to the Dead Sea, and not a single city of Israel was left under Syrian rule.

Nor was this all. So prostrate was the Damascene power, that Jeroboam conceived the idea of attacking it at home, and taking vengeance for its long oppression of Israel. He met with entire success. Entering Damascus as a conqueror, he marched through the land of Hamath (or Hollow Syria?) and was fondly believed by his people to have re-established the glories of David. The men of Jerusalem desired to appropriate a part of his renown; and the historian, who has concisely handed down the facts, ingeniously observes, that "Damascus and Hamath were won back *for* Judah[2] *by means of* Israel."

A fragmentary notice, by a contemporary prophet, of Jeroboam's war against the Moabites has perhaps been recovered by the acuteness of a modern expositor.[3] Isaiah has subjoined to it an epilogue of two verses, and by this

[1] Amos (i. 4) speaks only of Hazael and Benhadad, although he wrote full seventy years after the accession of Jehu, when Hazael must have been in the prime of manhood.
[2] 2 Kings xiv. 28, De Wette's Translation.
[3] Hitzig. He believes the prophet to be Jonah, son of Amittai.

accident it has been preserved with his compositions (xv., xvi.) From this dirge of battle it is dimly made out, that during Hazael's occupation of Ramoth-Gilead the Moabites moved northward over the Arnon, and became masters of a large part of the tribe of Reuben; but that Jeroboam (*though this is the uncertain point,—*WHO *is the conqueror*) not only expelled them from Israelitish ground, but assailed them at home, stormed their two chief cities, Ar and Kir, in the night, and (it would seem) pushed his frontier to the southern limit of the land, where Idumæa was supposed to begin. The prophet recommends the miserable Moabites to put themselves under the protection of Jerusalem, where a merciful and righteous king reigns in the tabernacle of David, and to send tribute of lambs from Selah in Edom; implying perhaps that the Moabites were to occupy the land which the Edomites had evacuated. It is, however, intimated that Moab is too proud to accept such terms, and that more slaughter still will come on those who have escaped. The time of this is not certain; but in the chronology which we have preferred, the righteous king of Judah must probably mean Uzziah. This prophecy is vigorous and massive, but wanting in all religious interest. The name of Jehovah is not found in it, and but for the ethical description of the king of Jerusalem, it might have been written by a mere heathen.

The very meagre notice which we have of this long and important reign is happily filled out by the far more valuable writing of the contemporary prophet Amos. The contrast is most striking between Amos and his only extant predecessor, Joel. The latter exhibits the more finished cultivation of Jerusalem, and writes in his own free and fluent diction, as is habitual to an educated man. But Amos, even when his thoughts are his own, is fain to borrow words from another. As if from some inaptitude in beginning and ending his paragraphs, he is too apt, like a Homeric rhapsodist, to chant out the burden of his heart in a stereotype monotony. Nevertheless, he is to the historian a more serviceable informant than his predecessor. Joel indeed writes as a pious priest of Jerusalem, acquainted only with the domestic affairs of his people: but Amos is a man of the world, whose eye travels over distant countries; who meditates on the cities of the Tigris and "Hamath the great," even in the midst of his religious anxieties. The personal history of Amos, as picked up from himself, is of interest. He had been a keeper of cattle in the wilderness of Tekoa, a southern district of Judæa, and a dresser of sycamore-trees. He was neither a prophet nor reared among prophets, but while following the herd in this southern district, he felt himself called by the Most High to migrate into the kingdom of Jeroboam in order to prophesy against its sins. In reproving these, he gives us a great insight into the actual condition of the people.

It may be suspected that the violent suppression of Baal-worship by Jehu turned the current of impure superstition into the channel of the still-supported state-religion. Those who would have been Baal's avowed votaries if they had dared, now insinuated their favourite practices into the sanctuaries of Bethel and Gilgal;[1] so that, by the time of Amos, the calf of Bethel was an idol almost equally demoralizing with the images of Baal and Astarte. If this had been the case at Jehu's accession, the vehemence of the prophets could not have flamed out so exclusively against Baal; we must therefore believe the result to have come about during the century of Jehu's dynasty.[2] As soon as a national religion has become a source of corruption, the worst prognosis of the public disease may be justly formed: the Greek proverb here applies—When water chokes, what must one drink after it? Nevertheless, other causes had conspired to bring mischief upon Israel. The "war to the knife" which they had carried on against Ammonites and Syrians must in itself have been very brutalizing, particularly to the eastern tribes, who had suffered longest and worst from it. In the general distress, the poor had been driven to the necessity of borrowing from the rich: the rich, hardened by their own losses, exacted their debts mercilessly,

---

[1] *Dan* is not named, but Gilgal takes its place. Bethel (house of God) is often called, in this prophet and in Hosea, by way of contempt, Beth-*aven* (house of vanity).

[2] In 2 Kings xiii. 6, is a remarkable statement, that in the time of the son of Jehu "there remained Astarte in Samaria." Is it possible that Jehu can have rooted out Baal and left Astarte? Had not this stolen back in the second generation?

and often used their legal power to sell the debtor into slavery.[1] "Ye have sold the righteous for silver, and the poor for a pair of shoes," is the prophet's reiterated complaint. We might almost believe that the wealthy creditors, whom he stigmatizes as *kine of Bashan* (i. e. pampered cattle), had become rich by usury: for in such times of trial neither law nor custom will make men lend on any but usurious terms. The prophet however accuses them of fraudulent dealings in general. On the whole it is clear, that the attacks of the Syrians had broken down the middle class of the nation, and left a wide gap between the wretchedly indigent and the rich, whom he describes as building mansions of hewn stone, planting for themselves pleasant vineyards, treading down the poor, and taking from him burdens of wheat; lying on beds of ivory, chanting to the sound of the viol, drinking wine in bowls, and anointing themselves with precious perfumes. Nor is it probable that the victorious wars of Jeroboam did anything to relieve the pressure on the poor. We have no ground to imagine that any system existed for paying soldiers an adequate hire, and it may be presumed that the poor man, as in ancient Rome, left his field untilled while forced to march into a foreign land. The valuable booty of war is likely to have been seized by the king and his chief officers, while the common man was consoled by the free leave given him to rob and kill the enemy from whom he had suffered. At the end of a successful campaign the poor would come home poorer, and the rich richer, than he had gone forth. The prophet gives a retrospect of the calamities by which God has chastised Israel: famine,—drought,—blight and locusts,—pestilence,—slaughter by the sword (of the Syrians and Ammonites?),—and finally, earthquake, which is probably

---

[1] Arnold (Hist. Rome, vol. i. p 135) draws a pleasing contrast between the cruelty of Roman law and custom against innocent debtors, and the mild wisdom of the law of Moses. Unfortunately we are without the means of ascertaining how far the Mosaic law (as *we* read it) was either observed or known by the Israelites of this date. Of the liberation of Hebrew slaves after seven years, and restoration of land at the jubilee, we hear nothing in the prophets.

The prohibition of all interest, which Arnold admires, is not so wise as it was well-intended. Men who are hard-hearted enough to extort from another's necessities a really unfair rate of interest, will not be so liberal as to lend for nothing but the chance of loss. Such a law prohibits any from *lending* who are not generous and rich enough to *give*.

the same as that of king Uzziah; but as these have been unavailing to correct—(having, no doubt, been on the contrary great causes of moral evil),—he threatens them with a yet severer attack from a great nation in the distance. There is no question that he meant the growing power of Nineveh.

And this leads us to notice the light thrown upon foreign nations by the prophecy of Amos. He opens, as might be expected, against Damascus, but adds nothing to our knowledge. He speaks of it as independent of Jeroboam, and threatens it (as indeed every other nation mentioned)[1] with captivity and utter destruction. Gaza and the other towns of Philistia are next rebuked, and after them Tyre,[2] for carrying Jews into captivity and selling them to the Edomites. On Edom, Ammon, and Moab, a like denunciation falls; and here we learn, that a fierce war had taken place between Moab and Edom. The Moabites had captured the king of Edom, and "burned his bones into lime;" in recompense of which the prophet threatens fire in their palaces and slaughter to their people.

Against Judah he has somewhat to say. The town of Beersheba was held a sacred spot from the earliest times; and undoubtedly there was always a sanctuary there, at which Jehovah was worshipped as at the "high places." Amos, perhaps because of the sight which he had had of the corrupt worship in the Israelite sanctuaries, speaks more severely against Beersheba (which he couples with Bethel and Gilgal) than the historians do. He taxes Judah with despising the law of Jehovah, and threatens the same fire on its palaces as on all the rest. Yet it is hard to think, against the testimony of the historians, that under Uzziah any *strange* god was worshipped in Judah, or any neglect of Jehovah avowed.

It appears from Amos, that king Jeroboam held his

[1] The moral weight of these prophets is often hurt, by the unvarying destruction which they pronounce.

[2] Tyre is chided for *not remembering her brotherly covenant* with the Hebrews. Can this mean that there had been any recent covenant? Since the time of Jehu, such a thing seems out of the question; and Israel appears first to have cut the bond. So too, when the prophet complains that Edom "did pursue *his brother* with the sword, and cast off all pity," we cannot but regret that such merciful topics are urged only by the weaker party. Obadiah follows on the same track, equally ignoring the history of the feud, 10—14.

court at Bethel, where he had a royal chapel and a high-priest named Amaziah. He also offered sumptuous sacrifices to Jehovah, and musical chantings; of both which the prophet expresses entire contempt. The king had a winter and a summer palace, one of which perhaps was at Bethel. Ivory houses also are named, such as Ahab had introduced; but whether belonging to the king or to the wealthy, is not clear. This prophet alludes to the forty years' wandering in the desert, after coming out of Egypt, and perhaps also to the flood which drowned the Egyptians on trying to pass the Red Sea; which makes it probable that the account of the Exodus, just as we now read it, was already familiar to the nation. He concludes his prophecy by predicting a time when the house of David shall recover its sway over all Israel, and over that "remnant" of the Edomites which had escaped the arms of AMAZIAH.

To the reign of this king we must now go back. During the events which have been narrated, we have no exact synchronisms concerning the Judæan royalty. Although Amaziah had been set free by Jehoash, when hostages had been given, yet the shock to his reputation by the capture of his city, razing of the wall, and plunder of his treasure, was such, that he must have had much to do to hold his ground against the Edomites. He reigned (according to our reckoning) five years after the death of Jehoash. Perhaps that time barely sufficed him to rebuild the wall of Jerusalem, and re-establish his authority over Idumæa, which he bequeathed to his son unimpaired. Like his father, in his later years he fell into an unhappy feud with some of his own subjects, the cause of which is imperfectly indicated.[1] A conspiracy was made against him in Jerusalem, and when he fled to the fortified town of Lachish, he was pursued thither and slain, in the twentieth year of his reign, and forty-fifth of his age.[2]

His son Azariah, commonly called UZZIAH, aged only

[1] If, against the testimony of the book of Kings, we could believe in Amaziah's heathenism, we might infer that he was slain for refusing to obey the priests' orders,—from the Chronicler's words, " After the time that Amaziah *turned away from following Jehovah*, they made a conspiracy......" But it is difficult to judge whether the compiler wrote here from evidence, or by his own inference.
[2] B.C. 799.

sixteen, now followed him in the kingdom. We here meet with the formula, twice afterwards repeated when a king has been slain,—that the people of the land took Uzziah, and made him king. It seems to denote a breach of continuity in the government, which is supplied by direct popular action as in a Roman *interregnum*: but no details are known. In Uzziah's reign of nearly fifty-two years, the meagreness of our better compiler is wonderful. One foreign and one domestic event comprize nearly all that he gives; and upon these the Chronicler has built up more than we can unshrinkingly receive.[1] 1. The foreign event is undoubtedly a significant one, and is set forth as a compendium of the whole reign:—Uzziah fortified the port of Elath on the Red Sea, and occupied it as a Hebrew possession. This denotes to us how complete was now his mastery over Idumæa proper; but we are unfortunately left to conjecture to what purposes he turned the port. 2. The domestic event is, that he was afflicted with leprosy;[2] on which account he abstained from appearing in public; and, following the example of Jehoshaphat, associated his son Jotham with himself in joint and co-ordinate authority. His religious character, as a true Jehovist, is praised, with the sole qualification that "the high places were not removed." Yet we have seen that the prophet Amos looked with severer eyes on the worship at Beersheba, the southernmost town of Judah, and compared it to the idolatry of Bethel.

Uzziah succeeded in repressing the attacks of the Philistines and Arabians, if he did not actually subdue the towns of Philistia, as the Chronicler states. His general policy was that of vigorous defence. He built towers in the desart and castles on his frontier, strength-

[1] Uzziah had, forsooth, a trained army of 307,500 men, under 2600 chief officers. Side by side with such exaggerations, we cannot help being somewhat doubtful as to his conquest of Philistia and of the Arabians, and as to the homage of the Ammonites. Concerning the Ammonites, see the remarks in Jotham's reign.

[2] It was requisite to the Chronicler to invent a sin, which should *account* for Uzziah being struck with leprosy; and he finds it in the king having dared to enter the temple and burn incense, which none but a son of Aaron might do. Of this the book of Kings knows nothing.

Moreover, when he dies, the book of Kings says that he was buried "with his fathers," etc., *according to the usual phrase;* but the Chronicler tries to part him into a separate place, by the words—" *in the field* of the burial which belonged to the kings; *for they said*, He is a leper!"

ened the walls of Jerusalem, and provided himself against a siege,[1] a necessity which may have been suggested by the capture of the city in his father's reign. Both by example and by encouragement he fostered husbandry, planting, and keeping cattle; and as soon as security was better established, a rapid return of prosperity undoubtedly took place, which the ravages of one tremendous earthquake[2] in this reign did not destroy. In contrasting Uzziah and Jotham with Asa and his son Jehoshaphat, it will be observed that those earlier kings held a more powerful despotism, unchecked by priesthood; that their internal wisdom and vigour were the same; and that their foreign policy was different, chiefly because of the different attitude and power of Damascus. The two later kings must have known how, like constitutional monarchs, to yield with dignity, and to rule within fixed limits; and by a peaceful, yet energetic administration, they healed the wounds of war.

According to the Chronicler, the Ammonites "gave gifts" to Uzziah, and, it is implied, without warlike compulsion. Jotham however engages in direct conflict with them, and forces them to pay him annually 100 talents of silver, 10,000 measures of wheat, and 10,000 more of barley. How they had provoked his attack, or how it was possible for the two nations to come into contact, is not hinted. The Israelite territory, and that of Moab, intervened; and if Moab also had become subject to Judah, the fact could hardly be omitted. As the Edomites had removed from their own country so far as to Bozra (a place of very doubtful site), we might think of an Ammonite migration also; a migration perhaps into Idumæa, which was under the power of Uzziah. If this idea is admissible, it may explain why Uzziah "received gifts" as their natural suzerain, and that a discontinuance of the tribute provoked Jotham's attack. It is true that, as the Ammonites are here shown to be an agricultural people, we cannot imagine them to abandon their own land as easily as roving herdsmen might. Yet our information is

---

[1] The particular description of the engines, 2 Chr. xxvi. 15, may seem to savour of a later time.
[2] Alluded to in Amos i. 1; Zech. xiv. 5. Perhaps it is the same earthquake which threw down or swallowed up some cities of Israel (Amos iv. 11).

too incomplete to allow of asserting a large emigration to be incredible; and if the Ammonites were still in their own land, we know not how to receive the statement of the Chronicler, without believing more still;—that Moab[1] likewise had put itself under the protection of Judah.

The reigns of Uzziah and his son are practically but one, and comprise no less a period than fifty-eight years. Few as are the events recorded, it cannot be doubted that many silent changes went on in society which we can but imperfectly trace. The prophets who follow,— especially Isaiah and Micah,—afford us some important data, by which the course of events is in part indicated. The increase of mercantile wealth in an unintellectual people inevitably generates an ostentatious and rather coarse style of living, and in the wealthy females a fastidious attention to dress. The positive vice of drunkenness is alluded to, yet is not lashed so severely in Judah as in Israel: nevertheless we may believe that the contagious example of Israel had its effect in raising the standard of private luxury in Judah. As expensive habits became prevalent, and the priesthood at the same time advanced in political importance, even the priests were unable to resist the powerful tendencies towards mercenary aims. In the time of Joel we saw that the prophet and the priest were in perfect harmony; but all the later prophets abound in invective against the priests, who are described as bartering truth for money, teaching for hire, flattering the rich man, and partaking of his vices. The blacker parts of the picture belong to the next reign, or to still later times; yet on the whole we cannot doubt that under Uzziah and Jotham the priesthood became more worldly-minded, while they also consolidated their position in the state. We find also in the same prophets bitter complaints against the venality of judges; and though it may be doubtful whether this was a new evil, it is an evil which must have become more unmanageable, when a judge

[1] This may seem to re-open the question concerning the prophecy in Isaiah xv., xvi. Is it certain that Jeroboam was the assailant? or clear that Moab spurned the prophet's advice? Remembering the fierce revenge of Moab on the king of Edom, which Amos rebukes, we might believe the Edomites of Bozra to be the assailants. This will force us to delay the event till the reign of Menahem, when it was possible for the Moabites to wander out with their flocks over the land of Reuben, through the new weakness of the Samaritan power.

could not sustain the expenses incident to his rank without it, and when priests set him the example. It would also appear that the commerce with Egypt received a great development under these two kings; and, as the trade was open and no longer a royal monopoly as under Solomon, the two nations came more closely into intercourse. At least we can discern in the prophets marks of increased familiarity with Egypt, into which whole families of Jews migrated, no doubt for the purposes of trade. Desirable as this was for worldly wealth, the spiritual influence of that beast-adoring, mystery-loving, magic-ridden, and priest-led country must have been decidedly degrading to the people of Jerusalem. The *course* of the trade with Egypt can only be conjectured. If the conquests of Uzziah in Philistia are correctly reported, the direct way of the sea-coast would obviously be used; indeed peace with Philistia might have been at least as serviceable as conquest. But the port of Elath, which was retained till the third generation, afforded another, though circuitous, transport,[1] whenever the prevailing winds or Philistine enmity made the Mediterranean dangerous to the merchant. Although to build "ships of Tarshish" and sail for Ophir was too ambitious an attempt (for in the silence of the historians we may confidently infer that no such essay was made); yet small native craft[2] would, no doubt, in the fair season, easily run round to Suez, or coast along the Red Sea to some other port, by which the exchange of merchandise in fixed months would be steadily carried on. Altogether, we may conclude, that the old agricultural and more confined system was breaking up in Judah as in Israel; that the nation in general was passing through the necessary, yet dangerous, transition into the freer mercantile and polished state; unlearning perhaps many crimes and prejudices, yet acquiring also many vices: a process which may be passed through with success, if foreign influences are friendly; but which is in general fatal to a small com-

---

[1] It would be to the purpose to learn, whether wine and oil in goat-skins might be drawn *upon sledges* over the rocky soil from Judæa to the port of Elath.

[2] I cannot doubt the possible existence of such vessels, without totally disbelieving the ships of Jehoshaphat and of Solomon: and I have not yet sounded the full depth into which that disbelief would drop me. It would exhibit the entire reign of Solomon as a mist of delusion, if I rightly judge.

munity that is at the same time agitated by powerful external hostility.

Another silent change in Judæa must be suggested as having probably been brought about in this period;—an increased familiarity of the people with the art of reading and writing. The diffusion of commerce through the nation would assuredly effect this. Merchants who keep up correspondence with foreign countries must learn this art as a part of their trade. And this may be the true reason why written prophecy now becomes commoner. In Jerusalem itself, among the priests, writing had long been familiar; hence for Joel to compose his short prophecy was as natural as for others to write sacred psalms. Amos also, though he had uttered his oracles in Israel, committed them to writing a little later, and probably after his return into Judæa. Towards the end of Jotham's reign, however, the number of readers may have so much increased in all the chief towns, that a prophet had a new stimulus to written composition. The earliest essays are highly poetical. Then prosaic portions are interposed, with short narrative. In the progress of time prophecy becomes more prosaic, indicating that prose composition was now more familiar. At last, actual attempts at continuous history appear. This is an order of development quite parallel to that of the Greeks, the Arabs, and the Persians.

There is a small point observable in our historians, common to Jehoshaphat and to Jotham, which may deserve to be noted, although it is uncertain what it indicates. Every king of Judah *except* Jehoram and Ahaz have the names of the queen-mothers annexed : the exception may almost make it appear that their fathers had but one wife. It has already been observed, that a check to the abuse of polygamy was first given by Asa; we would fain believe that the son of Asa improved on his father's example : but the account given in the Chronicles, of Jehoram murdering his six brothers, if true, suggests that they were born of polygamy. It is at any rate singular, that in the two pair of kings who are in other respects exemplary, there should be room for the belief that the latter of each pair was a monogamist. Jotham died[1] sixteen years after his

[1] B.C. 741.

accession,[1] but *only seven after his father*, and was succeeded on the throne by his son AHAZ.

APPENDIX TO CHAPTER VII.,

Referred to in p. 199.

JEHOIADA in the reign of Jehoash, Azariah (according to the Chronicler) under Uzziah, Urijah under Ahaz, Azariah " of the house of Zadok " (in 2 Chron. xxxi.) under Hezekiah, Hilkiah under Josiah,—also Elishama and Jehoram under Jehoshaphat (2 Chron. xvii. 8)—are the chief priests named. We have in 1 Chron. vi. 4—15 a professed genealogy connecting Zadok with Hilkiah through two Azariahs, and a fragment of it with a slight variation and inversion in 1 Chron. ix. 11; but the impossibility which it involves can only be seen by paralleling it with the genealogy of the Kings.

David.	Zadok.	Jehoash.	
	Ahimaaz.	Amaziah.	
Solomon.	Azariah.	Uzziah.	Azariah.
Rehoboam.	Johanan.	Jotham.	Amariah.
Abijah.		Ahaz.	Ahitub.
Asa.		Hezekiah.	Zadok.
Jehoshaphat.		Manasseh.	Shallum.
Jehoram.		Amon.	Hilkiah.
Ahaziah.		Josiah.	

Hilkiah was about coeval with Josiah's father. Place Azariah parallel to Uzziah, to satisfy 2 Chron. xxvi. 20; then, since Ahimaaz son of Zadok was a strong youth during Absalom's rebellion, 2 Sam. viii. 19, and Azariah his son was a prince under Solomon, 1 Kings iv. 2, we have only *two* generations in the priests, where the kings

[1] It is the misunderstanding of this peculiarity, as Hitzig well observes, which has interposed a fictitious interregnum of nine years between Pekah and Hoshea. Yet Hitzig does not on this account shorten the chronology, but adds nine years to the reigns of Ahaz and of Pekah; in which it is difficult to follow him.

show *nine.*[1] Thus the pedigree of Hilkiah is fictitious, and that of the Azariah so pointedly called "of the house of Zadok" is not made out. But this is not all. The breach between Uzziah's Azariah and Johanan, which here suggests itself, is clear from Ezra vii., where Ezra's genealogy is traced up to Aaron through Hilkiah. From Hilkiah upwards to the Azariah whom we place contemporary with Uzziah, the pedigree agrees with 1 Chron. vi., but Azariah is made to be son of Meraioth, not of Johanan; and the series upwards runs thus:—Azariah, Meraioth, Zerahiah, Uzzi, Bukki, Abishua, Phinehas, Eleazar, Aaron, which is copied from 1 Chron. vi. 3—6 : only that there Meraioth is great-grandfather of David's friend Zadok, instead of being contemporary of Uzziah. It is then manifest that the priests in Ezra's days knew nothing of the early pedigree. Tradition or family registers traced back Hilkiah's descent as far as Zadok his grandfather only, without deviation; then some made Zadok to be son of Meraioth son of Ahitub,[2] others made Zadok immediate son of Ahitub, and continued the pedigree up to Azariah : and higher than this nothing was even reported. When one catalogue announces this Azariah as son[2] of Johanan, a contemporary of Rehoboam, and another makes him son of Meraioth, a contemporary to Phinehas son of Eli, they do but arbitrarily attach the top of a recent pedigree to the bottom of an antique or legendary one.

In fact, when we find it to be uncertain whether Hilkiah's immediate father was named *Shallum* or *Meshullam*, we might feel justified in doubting even the lower part of the genealogy.

[1] 1 Chron. ix. 11.
[2] 1 Chron. vi. 10: "Johanan begat Azariah." The words which follow: "He it is that executed the priest's office *in the temple which Solomon built*," are obscure. If "*he*" means Azariah, it implies that he was the first high priest of this race since Zadok.—I am really perplexed what to name the boldness with which one of my critics avows that there is in this genealogy nothing which the chronology refutes. At any rate one or other genealogy is false.

CHAPTER VIII.

FROM THE CONQUESTS OF JEROBOAM II. TO THE FALL
OF SAMARIA, B.C. 762—721.

IN the interval which had elapsed since Jeroboam's career of conquest, dark clouds had passed over the ever-varying sky of Samaria. Although the house of Jehu reigned for a full century, and the third and fourth princes of the line had been eminently prosperous in war, no national feeling had rallied round the dynasty, no powerful sentiment of loyalty had taken root. Men could not forget that Jehu had won his royal seat, and initiated himself in power, by a tissue of perfidious crime, which no prophet's voice[1] could hallow to the popular feeling. Nor was it easy for patriotism to cement Israel into a single whole. Ephraim, Manasseh, and Gilead sympathized but imperfectly with one another, and felt more as tribes than as a nation. No historical remembrance of David had a thrill to their hearts, rebels as they were against the heavy yoke of the son of David. Nothing perhaps but hatred of the Syrians and Ammonites united them; and this tie failed when Syria ceased to be formidable. Nor do the prophets of Israel seem to have retained with the nation any moral weight to throw (had they been ever so much disposed) into the scale of Jehu's dynasty. The regal authority continued to be the mere rule of force, unsanctified by higher principle; and the princes and chiefs, who encircled the throne of Jeroboam, were too probably aware that any of them who could displace him by crime would meet little resistance from the people. When at length the veteran warrior was removed by death,[2] his son and successor Zachariah was in the very next year murdered before the eyes of the public.[3]

The murderer was named SHALLUM, son of Jabesh, who, like Zimri, had but a brief tenure of power. One month

---

[1] Hosea (i. 4) represents Jehovah as avenging on the house of Jehu the bloodshed which the historians would have us believe that Jehovah commanded.
[2] B.C. 762.   [3] B.C. 761.

he reigned in Samaria, and was then slain in turn by MENAHEM, son of Gadi. The son of Jeroboam was thus avenged, yet no one thought any more of the house of Jehu; although we have not a hint, either in the meagre narrative itself or in any reference of the prophets, that Jehu's descendants were extirpated by either of the usurpers. Menahem indeed seems to have been a ferocious man, ready for any crime. The rather obscure expressions used may imply that the city of Tirzah,— where the first Jeroboam had his palace and Baasha his capital,—was the centre of his power. Either he was prince of Tirzah, or he commanded a body of troops stationed there: even after becoming king in Samaria, he retained Tirzah as a citadel or military post for himself. His right to the crown was disputed, especially by a town of unknown site called Tiphsah,—certainly *not* the Thapsacus on the Euphrates. The ground of their resistance to him is not named; however, by unrelenting energy and savage revenge on these first rebels, he established his pretensions over the whole land.

But he was not to remain long at ease in his new elevation. The great event of his reign is the inroad of a distant enemy, the rumour of whose terrors had already reached the ears of the prophet Amos under the reign of Jeroboam;—the first of a series of widely conquering powers, which are vaguely named the *Universal Empires* of history. It is the rapidly rising monarchy of ASSYRIA, which had NINEVEH for its capital. Of this some account will here be suitable.

Nineveh was situated on the eastern bank of the Tigris, near 600 miles in a straight line from the Persian Gulf, and therefore on a plain of some elevation; yet it is very low in comparison to the lofty country of the Kurds, whose snowy ridges and vast peaks rise at no great distance to the north of it. The modern town of Moosul marks its site approximately on the map.[1] The ruins called *Nebi Yunus* (Prophet Jonas) and *Kuyunjik* appear

[1] Layard thinks Nineveh to have been a fortified province,—of lozenge shape,—some 35 miles across in the longer diameter. I am not yet able to believe that Nimrood was part of Nineveh. It is remarkable that Xenophon gives us the name *Mespila*, where we expect *Ninus*. Possibly Mespila and Ninus were Kuyunjik and Nebi Yunus;—as Westminster and London in old days. Nimrood is conceded to be the Larissa of Xenophon.

to be the best ascertained nucleus of ancient Nineveh, still called Ninus in Roman times. We have in Diodorus an elaborate account of its vast and extensive walls; but since he makes the capital blunder of saying that it was *on the river Euphrates*, it is manifest that he had no trustworthy information, and it is hard to believe anything at all concerning Nineveh on the bare testimony of this writer.

Nineveh was separated from Palestine by the whole breadth of Mesopotamia, of the Syrian desart, and the Damascene territory. The original city was a town of extreme antiquity, whose name, like that of Babylon, peers through the clouds of legend. The native population is supposed to have talked a language deviating but moderately from that of Syria; yet this still remains to be decided, if possible, from a deciphering of the primitive monuments. Hitherto, what has been interpreted of the Assyrian inscriptions, is judged by Rawlinson to indicate a language previously unknown in literature, yet of Hebraic affinity both in grammatical structure and in elemental words: but this conclusion is apparently based on the presumption that the Assyrian language was the same as the Babylonian, and it cannot yet be received as a certainty. According to others, the wild and hardy mountaineers to the north are the nearest relatives of the Assyrians, and the language was related to the old Persian, not to the Hebrew stock. The position of Nineveh was favourable to greatness; alike from the goodness of the soil, from the supply of water by the rivers which descend from the Kurdish mountains, and from the facility of water-carriage down the Tigris. Hence from the earliest times, like other great cities on the plain of the Tigris and Euphrates, it rose to high prosperity; but (as far as can be conjectured) it was then a native kingdom only, not an empire. It may indeed have stretched its dominion northward over Armenia, or southward over Babylon: this may possibly be before long better known. But the tales reported to us by the Greeks of its early and continuous wide-spread sway are evidently mere legends.[1] We can only assert as

[1] Neither Herodotus nor Diodorus nor Justin knew anything of *two* Assyrian empires, each destroyed by a Median empire which succeeded it. This has been *invented* by Biblical students to avoid ascribing error of chronology

beyond dispute, that this city commenced a new career of conquest from nine to eight centuries before the Christian æra. The first king who showed himself as a conqueror to the eyes of Israel was contemporaneous with the vulgar date of Romulus and Remus, and was named Pul by the Hebrews.

The earliest conquests of the rising empire were undoubtedly made to the north and east. Kurdistân, Armenia, and ancient Media,—which included the modern cities of Hamadân, Isfahân, and Teherân,—formed the basis of Assyrian power : giving to it a breadth and massiveness to which no empire previously known to us in Western Asia or Europe could pretend. Although these countries afford as fine foot-soldiers as any in Asia, cavalry was the arm most important for foreign conquest: Media contained the celebrated Nisæan plains, on which were reared the most splendid horses known to the Persian kings, who used them in state ceremonies; while Mesopotamia itself furnished the same Arabian breed, whose swiftness we still admire. The Assyrians used chariots on the plains of Mesopotamia, and partly in more distant expeditions;[1] but they made a larger use of cavalry than the Benhadads had done. Their present king Pul (says Eusebius, apparently following the Babylonian priest Berosus) was *a king of the Chaldæans;* which appears to mean, that it was he who conquered the great city of Babylon,[2] with which the whole of Susiana probably fell into the empire of Nineveh. This ambitious prince must previously have turned his path to the west and south-

to the Greek reporters of Asiatic tradition. Herodotus indeed expressly says that Semiramis was only five generations before the Babylonian Nitocris, mother of Belshazzar.

For Colonel Rawlinson's genius as a decipherer and interpreter, I feel profound respect ; but supposing direct translation were completed, a vast work would remain, in settling the chronological relations, and in determining how much of these inscriptions *is to be believed.* Colonel Rawlinson seems to have an unsuspecting faith, that an Oriental Emperor's boastful inscriptions are true. If distant posterity ever decipher the court records of the late king of Persia, they will there read the name of the king of England among his humble tributaries. [New doubts are now raised by Count Gobineau.]

[1] Isaiah xxii. 6.
[2] In the year B.C. 747 begins the celebrated æra of Nabonassar at Babylon. It may be conjectured that Nabonassar and his successors in Ptolemy's Canon are viceroys of the Assyrians, and that 747 is the date of Pul's conquest of Babylon.

west, when he made his appearance before the usurper Menahem.

The Israelite well understood his own helplessness, and lost no time in propitiating the invader by the present of 1000 talents of silver, which was no doubt interpreted as tribute, and as a profession of homage. With this the Assyrian king thought fit to be satisfied, and withdrew without farther hostilities, being perhaps drawn off by more important conquests. But he did not leave the land, morally, in the state in which he had found it. Menahem had obtained the money so suddenly, only by direct exaction from all the rich men of Israel; and it was inevitable for them to reflect, that the tempest which had so lately loured would soon return and burst over their heads. Fresh and fresh extortion was foreseen in the future; nor was there the least hope that the enemy could be propitiated by anything short of total surrender. The rich men of Israel cast about to find a defender, and nowhere was he to be found but in the king of Egypt. That country could furnish them with that in which they were particularly deficient,—abundance of horses, and with every kind of military material. From the sea-coast of Israel, communication by ship to Memphis or Sais was easy; and a party arose, which was eager for alliance with Egypt, and active to promote it by argument and by intrigue. An opposite party, knowing that it was the Egyptian policy to stay at home and hold its own frontier, or having some nearer insight into the distracted state of that country, was confident that the Egyptians would never give them succour large and hearty enough to enable them to withstand the formidable power of Assyria. Hence they regarded this as a mode of exasperating their foe, and advocated the policy of cultivating his favour before it was too late. Such is the outline of the two factions which arose to distract the kingdom probably even under the reign of Menahem. With the progress of years their views became more sharply defined, and their collision more dangerous to the state.

The fierce energy of Menahem repressed all insurrection during his life. But when, after a reign of about eleven years, he left his throne to his son PEKAHIAH,[1] it soon ap-

[1] B.C. 750.

peared that no one but a military monarch could control the too great influence of the army. This predominance must have been confirmed from the time of Jeroboam II., himself a warrior, like his father. Menahem, we have observed, was probably a chieftain of Tirzah; and PEKAH, son of Remaliah, who assassinated Pekahiah in the citadel of Samaria, was a chief captain of the chariots.¹

It might seem as if it had been given to the kings of Assyria to avenge the murdered monarchs of Israel; for as Pul had appeared for the punishment of Menahem, so now TIGLATHPILESER, with still more hostile intentions, came down upon the assassin of Pekahiah. This time the Assyrian was bent on a double spoil,—plunder of the land and captivity of its inhabitants. Collateral circumstances suggest that he coveted the persons of the Israelites, not so much to make slaves of them as to people his great capital of Nineveh. The flood swept over so large a part of the ten tribes, that when its violence had subsided, the land of Ephraim seemed to remain as an island in the midst of the stagnant waters; and from this time forth, the name of EPHRAIM is used to express the entire northern monarchy. Not only Bashan and Gilead, east of the Jordan, but the whole basin of the sea of Galilee, was rent away from the sceptre of Pekah. All the booty of the land was no doubt carried off by the victor, with as many Israelites as he could seize; and it is improbable that after his departure Pekah had the means of re-establishing his authority in the half-empty and disorganized districts. Nevertheless we find no statement that at this time the Assyrian fixed any viceroy on Israelitish ground, and the events which follow decidedly prove that he made no attempt to occupy the territory even of the eastern tribes, which, as most open to his attack, it would have been easiest for him to retain. Such is the first great transference of the Hebrew population since the time of Moses. Its date is not accurately known, but we may assign it pretty nearly to B.C. 745.

This was an earthquake, which, while ingulfing so large a portion of the Israelite people, heaved up the remnant of society in lacerated and frightful masses, sometimes dangerous from their towering height. So great a con-

¹ B.C. 748½.

vulsion had scarcely before been conceived of. Joel and Amos had lamented over families of Israelites captured by roving bands of Edom or Philistia, and sold as slaves on the coasts of the Mediterranean: Hazael had swept off whole villages or towns: this was sufficient misery; indeed the individuals generally suffered a worse fate than those whom the Assyrians carried away. But the transplanting of entire tribes was a process of violence immeasurably greater in its effects. The suffering and disorder caused is not to be judged of by those actually captured; inasmuch as for every one that was caught, five would be made homeless, helpless, and desperate. The allusions of the prophets show us, that the unfortunate people who escaped the enemy were driven to violent courses, becoming a banditti that preyed upon their own land, upon one another, and upon the kingdom of Judah:

> No man spareth his brother.
> He snatches on the right hand, and is hungry;
> He eats on the left hand, and is not satisfied;
> They eat every man the flesh of his own arm:
> Manasseh devours Ephraim, and Ephraim Manasseh,
> And they together are against Judah.—*Isaiah* ix. 20, 21.

This dreadful calamity, and the contingent evils to themselves, thrilled through the hearts of the people of Judah, and drew forth in Judæa two prophets whose writings survive to us. Of these, by far the greater is Isaiah; the other is of unknown name, but we may call him the *elder* Zechariah,[1] because his short prophecy has been accidentally mingled with those of Zechariah son of Berechiah. Without their writings we should indeed be able to conjecture in general much concerning the internal state of both kingdoms, but our conjectures would want confirmation. Isaiah (as he informs us in a writing of about this date, ch. vi.) had had a call from Jehovah in sacred vision a few years earlier, in the year of Uzziah's death,[2] and at that time had received an announcement of a great captivity of the land. It does not appear that he had as yet actually committed anything to writing; but soon after

[1] Matthew names him *Jeremiah* in a well-known quotation. To call him the *pseudo*-Zechariah is offensive, as seeming to imply that he has pretended to be another than himself. Bertholdt supposes the author to have been *that* Zechariah, son of *Jeberechiah*, who is named in Isaiah viii. 2. The similarity of the father's name is certainly striking. See also 2 Chron. xxvi. 5.

[2] B.C. 748.

these events he put forth four (or five) impassioned yet artificially composed strophes, lamenting over Ephraim.[1] Each strophe concludes with a sort of chorus :[2]

> For all this, his anger is not turned away;
> But his hand is stretched out still.

To understand, and therefore truly to sympathize with them, we should read with a distinct realization of the crisis for which they were written. Mention however is made in them of an important personage, who must now be introduced to the reader, REZIN king of Damascus.

Damascus seemed to have vanished from the history for a full half-century, since its downfall under the son of Hazael. We do not know whether in the interval it had become an Assyrian province; but it must at least have been overrun sooner than Israel. Immediately after Tiglathpileser had withdrawn from that inroad, it is possible that a general insurrection of the nation, headed by Rezin, took place. Certainly, at this crisis Damascus bursts out into short and energetic life, the reasons of which, by combining the historical facts with the allusions of the prophets, we can conjecture with some probability. The personal character of the king, Rezin, may have had much to do with it, but the position of affairs still more.

Damascus now stood in the foreground, to bear the brunt of Assyrian attack; and after the recent manifestation of the power and unsparing violence of Tiglathpileser, all the states which were behind desired to uphold Damascus as their shield. If Hamath had previously been disaffected or hostile, concord now was re-established. Tyre and the whole Phœnician confederacy are likely to have tendered to Rezin pecuniary support, armour, arms, and other material of war. Besides this, in all the neighbouring districts crowds of ruined men were set loose from restraint just as in Bashan and Gilead. To say that such events gave to Rezin actual facilities, is but a conjecture; yet it is certain that he does suddenly appear at the head of powerful armies; and Isaiah, while writing the

---

[1] Isaiah ix. 8 to x. 4.
[2] This is found also in ch. v. 25; which has suggested that vv. 25—30, ch. v., really form a part of this prophecy: and this is Ewald's judgment.

elegy to which we have referred, imagined *Israel* to be
the game at which the Syrian would spring:—

> Jehovah shall set up Rezin's cruel ones against him (Ephraim),
> And shall cover his enemies with mail,
> The Syrians before and the Philistines behind;
> And they shall devour Israel with open mouth.—*Isaiah* ix. 11, 12.

But events took quite a different course. From the
cloud indeed which had gathered along the Syrian frontier, a fearful squall came down, as Isaiah had foreseen;
but its rage fell on the fair ship of *Jerusalem*, which was
gliding on in summer trim, after two generations of
peaceful repose. The wolf-hearted Rezin was not disposed to eat up the lean sheep of Israel, when the fat
kine of Judah were so near; and he chose to have Pekah
as an ally, rather than as an enemy. Their position was
very similar. Pekah was doubtless embarrassed by multitudes of houseless Israelites, who, to avoid the Assyrian
chain, had thrown themselves on the charity of the
Ephraimites and their king. Barbarian war required no
superfluous wealth or organized supplies: poverty and
despair, wielding arms easily made, afforded all the needful materials of an army. Perhaps it was an obvious resource with Pekah to prey upon the sister kingdom,
which had been in thriving progress, but never in amity
with Israel, since the war between Jehoash and Amaziah.

Before public hostilities had visibly become inevitable,
the prophet whom we have named *the elder Zechariah*
composed the earlier of his pieces, which is found in our
Bibles as Zech. ix., x. Although confessedly obscure,
especially in the English translation, yet if viewed as
written at this epoch, many points become clearer, and it
gains a real historical interest. It opens as a declaration
against several countries which may seem to have been in
league:—

"The utterance of Jehovah's word against the land of
Hadrach;[1] and upon Damascus it alights (for Jehovah
has an eye upon men, and upon all the tribes of Israel);

---

[1] This poetical title is not understood. Whether Hadrach is a mythical patriarch, a real king, or a god, is uncertain; as well as what land is intended. If it be *not* a synonym for Damascus, we may think of the *Hauran*, as geographically probable.

and also against Hamath, which borders thereupon; (against) Tyrus and Sidon, because it is exceeding wise."[1] Yet the most severe declarations are against Tyre and the Philistines; and we gather that the slave-trade by which these two states carried away the Jews and sold them into the Ionian cities of Asia Minor, was still (as in the days of Joel) the point which Judah felt most sensibly. The prophet proceeds to declare that Jehovah will defend his house (the house of Judah?) against hostile attacks: that a mighty King shall appear in Zion, meek and having salvation, riding on an ass, like the ancient judges; who will make away with all the apparatus of war, and speak peace to the nations; will reign from the coast of the Mediterranean to the Dead Sea, and from the brook of Egypt to the farthest end of the land. But before that happy time, Jehovah shall appear fighting for his people. Their prisoners shall be delivered from the odious dungeon. Judah and Ephraim shall be united in battle, and shall victoriously recover all the captives from the sons of Ion. Israel had indeed suffered chastisement for listening to idols, and the goats had been punished for the shepherds' fault;[2] but Judah had been greatly exalted by Jehovah,[3] and made as the goodly horse in the battle. In the farther progress of events, Judah shall be strengthened and Joseph shall be saved. Their God will gather back from far countries—especially from Egypt and Assyria—those who have been dispersed, and will plant them again in Gilead and Lebanon.[4] The pride of both these heathen powers shall be brought low, and Israel shall be strong in the name of Jehovah.

The distinct notice here given of the large number of Israelites already resident in Egypt is important; so also is the clue to an alliance between Damascus and Tyre, though it is remarkable how Damascus vanishes from the prophecy. Of still greater moment is the proof that the idea of a Messiah had already received such sharpness. It will be observed however, that He is distinctly re-

[1] De Wette's Transl.
[2] The *people* for the fault of the princes or *nobles*. This appears always to be the sense of *shepherds* in this prophet.
[3] Namely, during the prosperous reigns of Uzziah and Jotham.
[4] Whence Tiglathpileser had driven the population. *Lebanon* clearly is a poetical phrase for Galilee, as in xi. 1.

garded as having the land of the twelve tribes as the limits of his proper sway. He is to be at peace with the heathen, but is not to rule over them; and their power is to be so beaten down that they dare not attack him. The severe tone against Egypt—a highly friendly land— is to be imputed to its grovelling idolatry, as well as to the remembrance that it was the ancient house of bondage to Israel.

It is not to be imagined that the growth of Rezin reached its full height in a single year. It is more credible that support came from his allies just in proportion as he became stronger, and apparently more able to screen them from Assyria; so that his resources increased *after* his first successes against Judah. Jotham still sate on the throne of Jerusalem when the two confederates commenced this eventful war.[1] The course of it, and the nature of the case, may persuade us, that their first measures were to possess themselves of the frontier fortresses, and of such other castles as were important for securing their safe passage across the country. Judæa, especially at this time,[2] abounded with strongholds carefully fortified; and during the life of Jotham the allied kings may have found enough to do in these preliminary occupations. A second and angry piece from the elder Zechariah appears now to have been put forth,[3] which bitterly condemns the nobles of Ephraim, while boding fresh misery to the people. Under the symbol of breaking two staves, he represents Jehovah as breaking, *first*, his own covenant with Israel, and *next*, the brotherhood between Israel and Judah. The prophet, personating Jehovah, forswears his office as Shepherd of Israel; and after breaking the shepherd's staff, receives from Israel the pay of thirty shekels for his past services, and casts the money into the treasury[4] of the house of Jehovah.

[1] 2 Kings xv. 37.   [2] Hosea viii. 14.
[3] Zech. xi. To the same period we may refer Isaiah's prophecy, contained in Isaiah xvii. 1—11, which threatens Damascus and Israel as combined powers; yet without indicating that they have *as yet* effected any mischief against Judah. (At least, if we rightly follow Ewald in adding vv. 12—14 to the following chapter.)
The prophet declares that "Damascus is *taken away from being a city*, and shall be *a ruinous heap*." If Damascus, instead of being among the most flourishing towns of Turkey, were at present suffering the same desolation as Babylon, a succession of treatises would dilate upon the fact.
[4] The passage is unintelligible in the common versions, which ridiculously

The opening lines are highly poetical, and betoken something like exultation in the devastations inflicted on Israel by Tiglathpileser:—

> Open thy doors, O *Lebanon*,
> That the fire may devour thy cedars.
> Howl, O fir tree;
> For the cedar is fallen, the mighty is spoiled.
> Howl, O ye oaks of *Bashan;*
> For the steep forest is come down.
> There is a voice of the shepherds' howling;
> For their glory is spoiled:
> A voice of the roaring of young lions;
> For the pride of *Jordan* is desolate.

Jotham perhaps, as a prudent and experienced man, remained carefully on the defensive against the superior power of the invaders, or death happily removed him at the premature age of forty-one, before calamity came on his people. He left his kingdom at a most critical moment to his son AHAZ, who was only twenty years old.[1] We do not know how soon the resolution was taken of encountering the allied kings in the open field; but when the country began to be ravaged, the cry to oppose them would swell from all sides, and an inexperienced youth[2] was likely to rush into the unequal conflict in such a cause, even if not impelled by the popular voice. Two battles, each unfortunate, were fought by the armies of Ahaz against the two kings separately.[3] Rezin took a great number of prisoners, and sent them off as slaves to Damascus, but Pekah inflicted more slaughter than Rezin. The account is, as usual, exaggerated beyond credibility by our informant, nor is it possible to divine the truth. According to him, Pekah slays 120,000 men in that one day,[4] and carries off from the country 200,000 persons,

render this word *the potter.* The LXX. translate it by χωνευτήριον, the melting-furnace or foundry; which was far better. The two Hebrew roots -y- *to mould,* and -צר *to treasure up,* have been confounded.

[1] B.C. 741.
[2] *Perhaps* to this period we may refer the prophecy of Isaiah which is contained in ii., iii., iv.
[3] 2 Chron. xxviii. 5, 6.
[4] It is added, that a mighty man of Ephraim in this great battle slew Maaseiah, son of king Ahaz. But Ahaz being barely twenty-one years old, cannot have had a son in the battle. Hitzig indeed, by elongating the reign of Ahaz, adds eight or nine years to his age, but this is insufficient. We are forced to proceed with him to condemn 2 Kings xv. 37, as erroneous; we must next postpone the battle till Ahaz shall be at least forty years old, that is, to B.C. 730,

with much spoil, to Samaria. The prophet Oded forbids their enslavement, and the chief men of the Ephraimites second him warmly. Hereupon the captives are fed and clothed, the feeble among them are set upon asses, and all are conveyed safe to Jericho, and there delivered up safe to their brethren from Jerusalem. We may gather that Jericho was now looked upon as the frontier city of the Jews on that side. They may have perhaps regained it since the fall of the house of Jehu.

Nevertheless, the war continued in all its rigour. The allies now hoped for a real conquest of the country, and (probably to avoid the danger of quarrelling over their booty) resolved to set up a new king, their own puppet, in Jerusalem; a man of unknown name, the son of *Tabeal*. When their united armies marched against Jerusalem and presented themselves under its walls, the dismay occasioned was extreme; yet the Jews defended their city pertinaciously, and no progress was made in the siege.

Meanwhile Rezin undertook a remarkable exploit, which gives us an instructive view of the reach of his power. He attacked the distant town of Elath on the Red Sea, which was still held by Jews of Jerusalem. The earlier Benhadads in the prime of their might could hardly have ventured on such an enterprise; and we may safely assume that Rezin had the goodwill and active assistance, not only of the Edomites of Bozra (who are likely to have suggested the attack), but of the Ammonites and Moabites, who lay on his route. At Elath the Jews were wholly unprepared, and finding resistance impossible, probably took to their ships,[1] and escaped into Egypt. The Syrians kept possession of the empty town. After this success it cannot be doubted that the Edomites were encouraged to claim the whole country of Idumæa as their own once more; though no particulars are preserved to us, nor do we even know whether the important city of Selah (or *Petra*) remained in the power of the Jews. According to the Chronicler,[2] an irruption of Edomites

and then no room is left for half the events. (Hitzig has not, that I know, tried to uphold this statement of the Chronicler.)

[1] It is said that Rezin "drove out" the Jews, not that he captured or slew them. Unless they escaped by sea, they could hardly avoid being captured.

[2] 2 Chron. xxviii. 17.

against Judah now took place, by which severe distress was inflicted, and masses of people carried into captivity. Indeed if we receive the prophecy against Idumæa, contained in chapters xxxiv., xxxv. of Isaiah, as the genuine writing of that prophet, we can scarcely question that the Edomites at this time proved, as of old, most deadly enemies to Judah. *Bozra* however and *Teman* (not Selah) continued to be at this period their chief cities.

In the course of these disastrous times, the Philistines, taking advantage of the weakness of Judah, invaded the low country, and took possession of six towns with their villages. These are enumerated as Bethshemesh, Ajalon, Gederoth, Shocho, Timnah, and Gimzo ; all of which they retained, as Ahaz had no force to spare against them.

The threat of setting up a new king in Jerusalem, not of the line of David, if it terrified the royal circle by its very novelty, still more shocked the ecclesiastical body by its profaneness ; and the prophet Isaiah came forward to re-assure the desponding Ahaz. In the vision which first called him to be a prophet, Isaiah had been informed that *a remnant should return* of those who were carried away into captivity : and to indicate his firm faith in this, he had bestowed on his son the name *Shear-jashub*, which expresses that statement. Taking this son with him as an emblem of his own conviction, he came before Ahaz, affirmed on the word of Jehovah that the confederates would fail of their object, and that "within sixty-five years Ephraim should be no more a people." As a sign to Ahaz, he added, that a certain young woman should bear a son, who would be called Immanuel (or *God is with us*), and that before this son should be old enough to know evil from good, the land should be desolated, by whose two kings Ahaz was affrighted. It is not essential for the historian to discuss this prophecy from a theological point of view. It at present suffices to observe, that in the sense in which alone it was any sign to Ahaz, some young woman[1] then alive must have been intended, and

[1] Although it is not stated that Isaiah was accompanied by his *wife* as well as by his son Shear-jashub, yet when we read viii. 1—4, it is difficult to resist the persuasion that she was pointed at in the phrase " *the* young woman." She is *the prophetess* who bears to Isaiah a child, of whom nearly the same is predicted as of Immanuel. He is indeed called Mahershalalhashbaz ; but so Solomon was called *Jedidiah* at his birth by the prophet Nathan, 2 Sam. xii.

the child Immanuel must have been looked for within a year from that date. The period of sixty-five years first assigned was thus shortened into ten or twenty, according as we may be disposed to fix the age at which young persons know good from evil. In point of fact, Samaria was captured and Ephraim was no more a people, in *less* than twenty years from this time.

Whether the siege of Jerusalem was continued or not, it is evident that Pekah and Rezin commanded the open country, and no farther attempt was made to oppose them in the field. There is no question that they made war support itself, and that the whole land was put under severe demands to maintain and to gratify the hostile army. It is remarkable that Isaiah, both now and at other times, remembers brotherly feeling towards Israel. He scarcely prophesies more severely against it than against Judah, even in the midst of public hostilities; and in his very next piece which survives to us, he is as full of the sorrows of Jacob—Naphthali, Zebulon, Galilee—as of Judah and of Zion. This may arise from his viewing the whole land as Messiah's kingdom, and believing that all the tribes will (as Hosea (i. 11) had predicted) be hereafter won back to Judah. Yet if we are disposed to believe that many Jewish captives had really been sent home by the Ephraimites safe and unransomed, another influence aided this mild and wholesome feeling.

Upon the birth of Isaiah's second son, who, like the first, had been made a sign and had received a remarkable name, the prophet uttered a new declaration, that the Assyrians should despoil Damascus and Samaria, and overflow into Judah. But from this afflicting topic he passes over into comforting ones. The districts of Israel which Tiglathpileser has ravaged (the circle of the sea of Tiberias, the farther side of Jordan, and Gentile Galilee)

25. Such names might be multiplied *ad libitum*. Isaiah speaks of *his children* as signs, viii. 18.

With regard to the Messianic aspect of *Immanuel*, it deserves remark, that no other blessing is promised to Judæa from his birth than deliverance from the hostile league; and the land is, even so, to be desolated *by Assyria and Egypt making it their battle-field*, vii. 17—25. How sagacious an anticipation that was, we see by the sufferings of Palestine in the warfare of the Ptolemies against the kings of Syria; yet, in fact, no contest between Assyria and Egypt ever took place on Jewish ground, nor did the Egyptians tread upon it till the last days of Josiah, when the Assyrian monarchy had vanished.

ISAIAH ENCOURAGES AHAZ.

shall hereafter be made honourable. Light and joy shall dawn on the nation. The yoke of slavery shall be broken; the hosts of enemies shall be slaughtered and burned up: "for unto us," says he, "a child is born, unto us a son is given, and the government is on his shoulder: and his name is Wonderful, Counsellor, Mighty God, Everlasting Father, Prince of Peace." He will rule happily and righteously on the throne of David, to establish it for ever.—Such is Isaiah's first, and perhaps his most splendid prophecy concerning a future Messiah. It is very strange that the Alexandrine translators[1] so mistook the sense as to make the most important passage useless to the Christian Church. Concerning the right translation, indeed, there is not yet perfect agreement; and there are some who maintain that Hezekiah (who may have been just born) is intended. Yet the words are too like those of the elder Zechariah to be understood of any lesser personage than the great son of David, and Isaiah elsewhere does not anticipate the day of Messiah as about to dawn immediately.

But the most ardent hopes of futurity could not do away with the present reality of suffering. The pressure of the allied armies[2] at length drove the unfortunate Ahaz to a step which appears to have marked him with posterity as a profane and wicked king. He sent ambas-

[1] They have "Messenger of great counsel; for I will bring peace upon rulers, and health to him:" in place of, "Wonderful, Counsellor, etc........ Peace." Reading from a text of unpointed Hebrew, they seem to have been unable to add the vowels aright. The text Isaiah ix. 2 is applied in the New Testament to Jesus preaching in Galilee, etc.; therefore the rest was likely to be used by the Fathers, if they had understood it as we do.

For " Mighty God," almost the first German scholars prefer " Strong Hero ; " but Hitzig will not concede this, and says that the word God is used with oriental laxity. De Wette also maintains our common version.—" Everlasting Father" has alarmed some, as supporting the heresy of the Patripassians; but it is interpreted "long-lived father *of his people*," according to the formula, " Oh king, live for ever!" On the contrary. Hitzig renders the phrase " Father of booty," and explains it of a warlike king who distributes booty to his victorious army. This certainly agrees with vv. 3—5 which precede, however opposed to our old feelings.

[2] At this time Isaiah's *first* chapter may have been written. The moral description suits this reign better than that of Hezekiah, nor can it be inferred from the project of setting up "the son of Tabeal" that the allies were not at last provoked to commit fierce ravages. The " strangers" of v. 7 may be very well understood of the Damascenes, whose speech the Jews did not understand ; 2 Kings xviii. 26.

sadors to Tiglathpileser, whose power had already been so cruelly experienced by the two confederates; and with the profession of homage, presented the silver and gold from the house of Jehovah and his own royal treasures, entreating the great king to deliver him from the arms of Pekah and Rezin. So the account is handed down to us. It may seem extraordinary that the treasure reached its destination safely, when the Philistines were hostile and cut off access to the sea, and the allies had full command of the surrounding land: this may indeed suggest that that part of the tale is an involuntary fiction. If Ahaz sent an ambassador to tender homage, the historian would *infer* that he sent the sacred and royal treasures also.[1] Not that this concerns the question. Ahaz, if his conduct was precisely what has been stated, did no more than the pious Asa had done before him; and in any case the Assyrian knew how to remunerate his own services. He was ready at the call, and perhaps would have paid this second visit without invitation. The hour of Damascus was arrived, which Amos had anticipated and Isaiah recently announced. Tiglathpileser came down upon it with overwhelming force, slew king Rezin in battle, and captured the city. Its delightful country was too valuable to neglect; it probably became an Assyrian province. The people (it is said) were carried away and planted in Armenia, and nothing remained of the great empire of old so brilliant and just now so formidable.[2]

---

[1] The words of the narrative appear quite like a *formula:* "he took the silver and gold which was found in the house of Jehovah, and in the treasures of the king's house," etc.

Josephus, to evade the difficulty of conveying the treasure to Tiglathpileser, *postpones* the gift; and perhaps he is right.

[2] We should be glad to know whether history has here been made out of prophecy, as so often in later times. It is with some doubt that we receive the statement that the Damascenes were carried to Armenia; since the historian may have inferred it merely from the prophecy of Amos. Historically, it appears improbable that the country of Damascus was emptied of population.

Perhaps there is no crisis of the history to which we may so plausibly refer the production of the remarkable prophecy, Isaiah xxiv.—xxvii., *if genuine*, as to that before us. The " lofty city," over the destruction of which the prophet moralizes, is in that case Damascus.

Certain peculiarities of doctrine, as in xxv. 21, xxvi. 19, are alleged to prove that it was after the captivity. But Assyria, and not Babylon, is described as the power which has inflicted exile on the people (xxvii. 13), and the mention of Moab in xxv. 10 implies that petty struggles were still going

FALL OF DAMASCUS.   249

We may approximately fix this catastrophe to B.C. 738 or 737.

The king of Israel, bereft of his ally and threatened once more by the dreadful Assyrian close at hand, gave Ahaz no farther trouble. The remainder of his life is a blank in the history, but we may conjecture that internal broils, almost amounting to civil war, ensued. Murder is a crime peculiarly denounced by the prophets of the day. He was slain in the twentieth year of his reign,[1] and the twelfth of Ahaz,[2] by Hoshea, his successor; and as no particular blame is fastened upon Hoshea, but even a measure of praise beyond what might have been expected, it was perhaps no assassination, but death in open battle, and not necessarily by Hoshea's own hand.

Ahaz, being thus rid of his most formidable enemies, might seem free to repel and punish the Edomites and Philistines, to whom the Jews were ordinarily more than equal. But there was here some secret difficulty. It may be that he was thoroughly cured of military enterprize by his first disastrous essays; but it is at least as possible that the tribute demanded by the Assyrian kept his treasury empty, and that he could prosecute none but a strictly defensive and cautious war without stopping the payments to this dreadful patron. In hope either to gain some remission or to procure some direct military help, and otherwise to show respect, Ahaz paid a visit in person to Tiglathpileser when he was at Damascus. If the great king's troops escorted him from the lower Jordan, after he had crossed it opposite Jericho, the journey was now quite safe. Nevertheless, his pains were to no purpose. He gained nothing from Tiglathpileser,[3] and in-

on against neighbour states. What can be more likely, than that after the successes of Pekah and Rezin, the Moabites may have in turn taken their fling at the helpless Ahaz? It may be suspected that the Moabites grew stronger by the captivity of Gilead, as that invasion does not seem to have reached them, and afterwards by the capture of Damascus. At any rate, Isaiah xvi. 14 proves that from *some* cause they had again become powerful after their great calamity.

[1] Pekah came to the throne in the year of Uzziah's death, and reigned twenty years (both facts are stated): he therefore died *in the twentieth year after Jotham became sole king.* By haste of expression, in 2 Kings xv. 30, this is converted into *the twentieth year of Jotham.*

[2] B.C. 729.

[3] This seems to be the ground of the Chronicler's broad statement, that "Tiglathpileser *distressed him* and *helped him not.*" The uncandid writer con-

curred new contempt with the more zealous of his own subjects.

All consideration of the religious character of Ahaz has been purposely deferred, in order that the whole may be viewed together. Both the historians are severe upon him; but the Chronicler, as usual, exaggerates the accusations of his predecessor. By far the worst charge against him is that he devoted one or more of his children to Molech. This is expressed in the older narrative by saying, that he "made his *son* to pass through the fire,"[1] confining it to one son, and leaving it doubtful whether life was actually sacrificed. The later statement is that he "burnt his *children* in the fire," multiplying the number, and making their destruction a certainty: it adds also, that he "*made molten images for Baalim.*" The one states that he admired the form of a Damascene altar so much, as to set up one in Jerusalem after the same pattern: the other converts the tale into sacrificing to *the gods* of Damascus. The one drily notices that he altered the *great basin* of brass by cutting away the pedestal with the brazen oxen; the other (who would have represented this in a Jehoshaphat as zeal for the law of Moses, which forbade such sculptures) modifies the story as follows:—"He gathered together *the vessels* of the house of God and *cut them in pieces.*" The one says that he made an alteration in the two entrances into the house;[2] the other that *he shut up the doors* of the house, and *made him altars in every corner of Jerusalem*. There is a greediness of scandal here, which suggests, that, if the story

ceals the fact that Tiglath had done Ahaz the essential service of drawing off his enemies, and had perhaps saved the line of David from total extinction. This was a tale with a bad moral; so forsooth it was to be suppressed.

[1] It is believed that one or more bonfires were lit, through which the unfortunate child had to run, and that the ordeal was so severe as to be almost necessarily fatal. But in *this* form of the rite, time would assuredly modify it. Except in a crisis of great public danger, when men's superstition becomes gloomy and cruel, the fires would be made smaller and smaller, and parents would hope for the *merit* of the sacrifice without incurring the *loss*. But in the other form of it, when the child was sewn up inside a wicker idol and burned alive, or first slaughtered and then burned, there was no power of softening it at all. Josephus represents Ahaz as making a "whole burnt offering" of his son.

[2] The obscurity is in the words, "for the king of Assyria;" 2 Kings xvi. 18. It seems to have been done to please him, yet no one would suspect him of caring about it.

against Ahaz grew so much between the æras of our two
narrators, it may also have grown not a little between the
time of the events and the earlier compiler. And other
circumstances persuade us that this was the case.

It is a presumption in favour of Ahaz that the chief
priest Urijah (who is selected on one occasion by Isaiah as
a "faithful witness to record," viii. 2) promptly agreed to
his architectural innovations[1]—a fact which the Chronicler
dishonestly conceals. Nor did any feud arise between
Ahaz and the prophets of his day, as soon after with
Manasseh: Isaiah and Micah, his contemporaries, both of
whom outlived him, are totally silent as to any of these
charges. Isaiah's genuine writings abound with elaborate analysis of the sins of Israel and of Judah. He speaks
of men having idols of silver and gold, of being soothsayers like the Philistines, of seeking to wizards who chirp
and mutter, as well as of immoralities and crimes of
various dye; but he does not accuse Judah of worshipping
foreign gods, of making molten images to *Baalim*, and
much less of sacrificing their children to Molech.[2] The
deed of Ahaz cannot have been a solitary one; and if
Isaiah feared to rebuke him personally for it during his
life, he might have rebuked others, at least after Ahaz's
death. Micah has a passage (vi. 7) in which a man is
supposed to ask the prophet whether Jehovah requires
such a sacrifice: the prophet simply denies it, without a
word to imply that such things actually went on at Jerusalem. When it is considered, that if Ahaz was a man
who deserved no positive commendation from Isaiah, the
prophet could not anticipate these scandalous imputations
and directly deny them, his marked silence appears enough
to acquit Ahaz. In fact, in no place does he charge this
king with anything worse than want of "faith;" which
meant, want of confidence that Jehovah would support
him against enemies without human help. The vindication of Ahaz will seem to be complete, if we can account
for our historians being so prejudiced against him; and
that we are able to do. According to the principles of
both (and eminently of the later one), misfortunes imply
wickedness: the people of Jehovah *could not* be conquered
in war, except because of their sin; hence when their de-

[1] 2 Kings xvi. 26.   [2] In contrast, see Jerem. vii. 31.

feat is notorious, the historians must find or feign proportionate iniquity. Thus the Chronicler represents the defeat of Ahaz by Rezin to be a punishment for burning his children to Molech; which is evidently fanciful, as the things have no relation of cause and effect, by which the Divine Government is carried on. The power of Rezin rose out of widely different causes, and must have been felt by Jotham had he lived, except so far as prudence might have shielded him. At the same time it is highly doubtful whether at that period Ahaz can have had any children to burn. In short, his great crime was, that at the age of twenty he could not withstand the simultaneous attacks of Damascus, Israel, Philistia, Edom, and perhaps Moab; and that he sought for aid to the great Assyrian power, which shortly carried Israel into captivity. But neither Isaiah nor these historians themselves tax him with violence, tyranny, or unconstitutional conduct, nor with any of the crimes which stain David and Solomon. His sculptural innovations, however tasteful, may have been unwise; yet he had the sanction of the high priest. His later career was not unprosperous. At least he left his kingdom to his son HEZEKIAH neither decaying nor disorganized,[1] but re-invigorated by repose for a fresh struggle. Nevertheless, the Chronicler pursues him even in death,[2] asserting (against the better authority) that he was *not* buried in the sepulchres of the kings.

As, unfortunately, the history of the Assyrians by Herodotus has not come down to us, we cannot trace with certainty the order of their successive conquests, nor even of their monarchs. Yet, looking to the intervals of time,[3] it appears most credible that SARGON, king of

[1] B.C. 726.
[2] We have seen the same thing in the matter of Jehoram, Jehoash, and (with modification) of Uzziah. The Chronicler wishes to accustom his readers to the belief, that over the race of David in Jerusalem, nearly as over the kings in Egypt (Diodor. i. 72), the priests, supported by the popular voice, had power to decide concerning the deceased monarch's burial-place. He says "kings of *Israel*," by carelessness, for kings of *Judah* (2 Chron. xxviii. 27), nearly as in xv. 17.
[3] Between Tiglathpileser and Shalmaneser we reckon ten clear years unoccupied (B.C. 738—728), and the interval *may* have been greater. Between Shalmaneser and Sennacherib we can barely command *three* (B.C. 716—713), and those appear to be all needed for the siege of Ashdod.
It must be confessed that Rosenmüller, Gesenius, Winer, and all leading authorities, interpose Sargon in the latter interval. Perhaps they would not

Assyria, who is alluded to only once,[1] followed Tiglath-pileser on the throne. The order of time and place alike suggests, that after the conquest of Damascus, the next movement of the Assyrians would be against Tyre and the Phœnician confederacy; which, as we have seen, had possibly, by assisting Rezin, given some plausible ground of war to the victor. The Phœnicians were wholly unable to resist so formidable a foe, and in spite of the determinate resolution of the city of Tyre itself (which, being on an island, was inaccessible to the land forces), the chief cities of Phœnicia professed allegiance to the Assyrians, including the old city of Tyre on the continent. The Assyrian general, whose name, or rather name of office, was *Tartan*, then proceeded into Philistia, and demanded homage. The only city whose resistance is recorded is Ashdod, or Azotus, which in the next century endured a siege of wonderful length from the king of Egypt. How long it now resisted is not distinctly asserted, but Isaiah is understood to imply that it was for three years or more. Yet neither Philistia in general,[2] nor Tyre, was yet reduced. King Sargon so quickly vanishes from our sight, that we may conjecture his premature death to have occasioned a sudden withdrawal of the Assyrian forces. Besides, the attack on those fortresses of Philistia which commanded the passes into Egypt began to alarm that power in earnest:[3] the Philistines had the highest expectations of support from thence, and Gaza[4] was looked upon as almost impregnable.

Nevertheless, the Philistines after a time began to suffer severely from the Assyrians; possibly from the garrison of Ashdod, but no particulars are given us. In their distress the Jews rejoiced, and no doubt began to meditate expelling the Philistines from the six cities of Judah. In the year of the death of king Ahaz,[5] Isaiah composed a short ode of triumph (xiv. 29—32), telling Philistia that

do this, did they not assume that the *two* expeditions of the Assyrians into Phœnicia, quoted by Josephus from Tyrian history (Ant. ix. 14, 2), are both by Shalmaneser, and both after the capture of Samaria. But why may not the former be according to the narration here ventured?
[1] Isaiah xxi. 1.   [2] Isaiah xx. 6.   [3] Isaiah xx. 5.
[4] See the siege of Gaza by Alexander the Great, in Thirlwall's Greece, vol. vi. p. 204.
[5] B.C. 726.

she had no cause to rejoice in the breaking of Judah's sceptre, for her Assyrian master was, after him whom she had shaken off, as a flying dragon compared to a serpent. Meanwhile the poor of Judah fed their flocks in safety, and lodged by night in the open field; while the Philistines suffered famine and desolation from the constant alarms in their country. He then calls on every gate and every walled town in all Philistia to howl for fear of the Assyrian host, which was soon about to march down upon them. What reply then shall Zion give to the Assyrian ambassadors,[1] who come to remind her of allegiance and tribute? She will tell them (what Philistia cannot reply) that Jehovah hath founded her, and that her poor put their trust in this.—The ode, of which the above is the substance, seems to indicate that revolt from Assyria was already decided on in Jerusalem.

But Isaiah did not anticipate that Assyrian ambition could pause at Philistia. The struggle for those towns which were to a northern invader the key of Egypt, made it manifest to him that the tide of war would shortly overflow into that country. Its great wealth, its antique wonders, and its universal celebrity, were certain to invite attack: and if the stronger power cared for a specious cause against the weaker, that would be found in the aid which the Philistines had asked, and perhaps obtained, from Egypt against Assyria. Since the æra of Shishak, Egypt had been often contested by kings from Ethiopia. The Israelite emigrants had already made their countrymen well-acquainted with Pathros, or Upper Egypt, and it was familiar to a Jew of that day to think of Ethiopians and Egyptians together,[2] whether as constituting the same or allied powers, or as fighting in the same ranks. Accordingly, in the very year when Ashdod was attacked by Sargon's general,[3] Isaiah received a vision against Egypt and Ethiopia which took a singular form. He believed Jehovah to command him to unloose the covering from his loins and the sandals from his feet, and walk about publicly barefoot and " with his buttocks exposed,"—whatever the

---

[1] The words of the original are obscure: " What shall *one* then answer the messengers of *the* nation ?"
[2] Besides Isaiah xx., see Nahum iii. 9; also Isaiah xliii. 3.
[3] About B.C. 733 ?

full meaning of the words. This the prophet obeyed without scruple, and continued it for three years; apparently until Ashdod was captured. The symbol was then expounded to mean, that in this shameful plight the king of Assyria should lead away the Egyptians and Ethiopians prisoners. We learn historical facts from the prophecy, although we know nothing concerning its fulfilment. The Assyrians were not yet at leisure for attempting the conquest of Egypt, and when they took it in hand, they failed.

In the twelfth year of Ahaz (as was stated), HOSHEA having slain Pekah, established himself in Samaria.[1] Although he is included by our historian in the general censure of all the kings of Israel, it is with the remarkable qualification, that he did *not* do evil as the king who had preceded him. This comparative praise suffices perhaps to show that no peculiar weakness or baseness in Hoshea precipitated the ruin of his people; but the day was at hand which neither wisdom nor energy could avert. The first incident preserved to us after his accession is, the invasion of Israel a second time by the new king of Assyria, whose name was Shalmaneser. To this period we may probably refer the storming of the stronghold of Beth Arbel, which the prophet Hosea feelingly mentions. Beth Arbel was a small village of Galilee, which gave its name to certain fortified caverns in the side of a rock. By reason of their great strength, they are not likely to have been left empty during the desolation of Galilee, whether their tenants were now a mere banditti, or acknowledged the authority of the king of Ephraim. To drive men out from such a place was a great exploit even in the days of Herod, and with the advice of Roman soldiers; but Shalmaneser succeeded, and massacred all the inmates, without distinction of sex or age, by hurling them down the face of the rock. Perhaps it needed not this demonstration of power to lead the helpless Hoshea to promise allegiance and yearly tribute to the great king; who, accepting the presents tendered to him, withdrew his forces, and vanishes for a little while from the eye of the historian.

Now was a very perplexing time for Ephraim. We

[1] B.C. 729.

have an echo of the distractions of the land in the last eleven chapters of the prophet Hosea,[1] which appear to have been composed now or a little later. The Assyrian party in Samaria was very powerful, and kept up a constant communication with Nineveh; but the commercial relations with Egypt gave advantages to the Egyptian party. The calamities manifestly impending added perhaps a stimulus to superstition, and the impure ceremonies of the heathen were practised shamelessly. Gilead, half-desolate and disorganized, was infested with banditti; gross drunkenness and sensuality prevailed over Israel; people, priest, and prophet were involved in common iniquities. Emigration to Egypt kept increasing. The national bond was so broken up, that no wise prince could hope to rally round himself the hearts of the nation for a struggle against the overpowering stranger.

Very soon after, a change took place in Jerusalem, which may have acted unfortunately on the mind of Hoshea, and incited him to defy the power of Assyria. Ahaz, as was above stated, was succeeded on the throne of Jerusalem by his youthful son HEZEKIAH.[2] As the father terminated his career at the premature age of thirty-six, we cannot well regard the son as older than fifteen.[3] The counsellors of Ahaz struggled of course to retain power, and appear to have been at variance with the prophetical party.[4] We know the name of but one only, Shebna, who was "over the household,"—a very high office. But either by the temperament of the young king, or by the genius of Isaiah, the decisive influence lay with those,

[1] The first three chapters of Hosea are of a totally different genius, and (whether or not from the same author) belong to a very different time, about forty years earlier. The unfortunate augury of a great battle to be fought on the plain of Jezreel,—by which the house of Jehu is to be destroyed, Judah to be made glorious, and to be elevated once more as head of the twelve tribes,—seems to assure us that this portion is really as ancient as Jeroboam II. The writer follows in the steps of Amos, but by venturing on specifications has gone astray.

[2] B.C. 726.

[3] He is called twenty-five by the historians, which is probably an old corruption for fifteen. This places his birth somewhere in the second year of Ahaz, the year in which we apprehend the prophecy (Isaiah viii., ix. 1--7) to have been delivered. Hitzig sees in Isaiah xxxviii. 12, an insuperable obstacle to this reduction of the age of Hezekiah; but that verse does not seem to mean that Hezekiah was then an old man, only that he was on the point of death.

[4] Isaiah calls them, "Ye scornful men, that rule this people in Jerusalem;" xxviii. 14.

who, in the faith that Jehovah would protect his people, refused submission to the foreigner. The prophets became for the time as predominant as the priests had been during the minority of Jehoash; and they signalized their power at once by the decisive measure of removing the high places,[1] which (by the contagion perhaps of the increased corruption in Israel) had now become seats of foreign idolatry. At least we find not images only, but *Astartes*[2] named as objects of worship there; which may imply that the line separating the worship of Jehovah from that of inferior and base beings had (as is usual in the progress from image-reverence to image-worship) been overstepped. The brazen serpent to which "down to those days" incense was burned,[3] was now destroyed; and in all other matters the law of Jehovah, as understood and expounded by the prophets and by the most eminent of the priests, was observed and enforced more diligently. A people thus devoted to their God, it was believed, might defy the foreigner; and the tribute was forthwith withheld from Shalmaneser. Nor only so, but active measures of war were commenced against Philistia; perhaps with the very money which had been destined as tribute to Nineveh. The Jewish towns appear to have been without difficulty recovered, and the land of their weak but high-spirited neighbours was ravaged from end to end.

Hoshea no doubt envied the freedom and success of his youthful brother-king, and in an evil hour resolved to imitate it.[4] He did not however design to be so imprudent

[1] 2 Kings xviii. 4, 22.
[2] 2 Kings xviii. 4. The silence of Isaiah leads to a suspicion that this is exaggerated. Or had "an Astarte" become a term for a graven image of a certain kind, without reference to the form of worship? The *Astartes* in Micah v. 14, seem to have been in Israel: so do the *Astartes and images to the Sun*, in Isaiah xvii. 8; xxvii. 9. Private idols (see Isaiah ii. 8, 20. and more particularly x. 10, which is of later date) could not be suppressed; but they did not imply a renunciation of Jehovah.
[3] "Unto those days, the children of *Israel* did burn incense to it;" 2 Kings xviii. 4. Is this a lax phrase for the people of *Judæa?* Or does it imply that Israelites also came into Jerusalem or Judæa to worship it? [One of my critics reproaches me with concealing the fact, that the worship of the serpent *was not tolerated*, though it existed. What does he mean?]
[4] We do not certainly know the year of Hezekiah's revolt; but the order of the narrative in 2 Kings xviii. 7—9, implies that it was before Hoshea's seventh year and Hezekiah's fourth, and therefore the probability is, that it took place

17

as to expose himself without allies to the brunt of an Assyrian invasion; but the time was now come when he might hope for aid in earnest from Egypt. That power, we may infer, had at last been roused by the capture of Ashdod, and felt that she had no longer any breakwater against Assyrian force. The king therefore gladly listened to Hoshea, and concerted projects of revolt. But the party within Ephraim itself, which from prudential reasons favoured the Assyrians, could not be kept in the dark as to what was going on; and Shalmaneser received notice of it. If we rightly interpret the very concise account given of these events, he ordered Hoshea to come in person and explain his conduct; especially as the yearly tribute was no longer punctually paid. Hoshea, it appears, not being ready to declare his revolt, hoped to dissemble, and obeyed the summons; but the Assyrian monarch, dissatisfied with his explanation, shut him up in prison,[1] as a contumacious vassal. Here the captive king was exposed to slavish indignities, if to him the words of Micah are meant to apply, "They strike the judge of Israel with a rod upon the cheek." When Shalmaneser soon after marched into the land and besieged Samaria, no help arrived from Egypt, the untrusty ally. This need not be imputed to treachery or fickleness. The scorn and vehemence with which not Isaiah only, but the Assyrian ambassadors to Hezekiah, predict that Egypt will betray those who have expectations from her, indicate their belief in some internal embarrassments of that country. And here the Greek historian Herodotus may assist us. If So, king of Egypt, is the same whom he calls *Sethos*, he was priest of Vulcan (or *Pthu* of the Egyptian mythology), and came to the throne[2] against the will of the military caste, with whom he was in political feud, and whose lands he endeavoured to dimin-

as soon as the internal parties of Jerusalem had re-adjusted themselves after the death of Ahaz.

[1] This sudden disappearance of Hoshea may be alluded to by the words, "I will be thy king. I gave thee a king in my anger, and took him away in my wrath," Hos. xiii. 11; and in x. 7, "As for Samaria, her king is cut off as the foam upon the water." If so, the later chapters of Hosea were written after the war had broken out. Indeed xiii. 16 anticipates far worse than the Assyrians inflicted.

[2] Mr Kenrick, in his erudite and comprehensive volumes on Ancient Egypt, regards it as proved that the king of Egypt *might* be elected from either order, priests or military; and that the sons of priests were not necessarily priests.

ish. This was so violently resented by them, that a little later he could not command their services, even to repel invasion. Much more must he have been hampered in his wishes to send forces out into Palestine. With money indeed he may possibly have assisted the Samaritans; unless the arrest of Hoshea disconcerted all his plans. Be this as it may, Samaria by her natural strength, or because the enemy was simultaneously engaged with other places, held out to the third year. In fact this city, though of all the most important, had no *exclusive* interest for Shalmaneser, who was intending and executing the extensive project of removing the mass of the unfortunate population from all the towns of western Israel into the far east. At last however the blow fell upon Samaria herself; though it cannot be doubted that many of the inhabitants, as indeed from all Israel, had previously escaped into Egypt. The Assyrian policy seems to have been similar to that which induced Darius, son of Hystaspes, to carry off the whole nation of the Pæonians, and Alexander the Great to plant great military colonies. He desired to break up national associations and prevent dangerous revolts; to secure his distant provinces, and to bring a greater population into the less-frequented districts near home. While he sent the Ephraimites to dwell " in Halah and at Habor,[1] the river of Gozan, and in the cities of the Medes," he brought men from other parts—from Babylon, Cuthah, Ava, Hamath, and Sepharvaim—to supply the gap. The order was executed by an officer who is called in the book of Ezra " the great and noble Asnapper" (iv. 10), in a passage where the new inhabitants of Israel are specified as from Dina, Apharsathcha, Tarpela, Persia, Arach, Babylon, Shushan, Deha, and Elam.[2] Many of these names are obscure; but those which cannot be mistaken are useful in showing us the wide grasp of Assyrian domination at this time; being such as the world had not yet seen, unless we believe in the half-legendary empire of Rameses or Sesostris. The

---

[1] There is no unanimity as to these places. Gozan is speciously held by Major Rennell to be the district of the river *Kizil Ozien*, which runs from Kurdistan through Azerbaidjan into the Caspian.

[2] Many are led by Ezra iv. 2 to suppose that Esarhaddon planted this colony. He no doubt planted a later one; but he never held sway over the nations here named, and cannot have brought them into the land of Samaria.

whole of modern Persia, from the Caspian to the Persian
Gulf, Susiana and Babylonia, Kurdistan and Armenia,
Mesopotamia and Syria, were all prostrate under the sceptre of Nineveh, before which the little kingdom of Judæa
now stood helpless.[1]

The Jews had no doubt watched with intense anxiety
the progress of the war and siege in the sister country.
We have two extant records of the workings of thought
at that time in the foremost minds of Judæa; if we rightly
believe that the prophecy of Isaiah, which we register as
chapters xxviii. xxix., and part at least of the Book of
Micah, were composed in this interval. Isaiah opens more
grandiloquently than usual, denouncing ruin on "the
crown of pride, the drunkards of Ephraim." The sin of
drunkenness which is again and again charged on them
(even on the priest and prophet) is declared in words so
plain and coarse, as cannot be explained metaphorically:
and we are led to believe that the Ephraimites, when
thus oppressed by an irresistible foe, like the Bœotians
sinking beneath the Ætolians, tried to drown shame and
sorrow in feasting and excess of wine.[2] But the firm belief that Jehovah has everywhere an elect people, and that
"a remnant shall be saved," cleaves here, as everywhere,
to this great prophet, and streaks his darkest pictures
with gleams of light and beauty. He turns away rapidly
from his moralizing over Israel, to warn[3] the proud nobles
of Jerusalem of impending danger: a siege of Jerusalem
itself,[4] he declares,[5] is coming, by the multitudinous nations which fight in the Assyrian host; but they shall miss
their prey when they think to devour it. He describes
the leaders and wise men of his own people as strangely
unable to read the signs of the times and understand
Jehovah's call to devotion of the heart, not of the lip.
But a total upturning of everything is to come; new
times, in which the deaf shall hear the prophet's words,
the blind shall see, the meek and poor shall rejoice in
Jehovah. *Then* old Jacob shall no longer be ashamed,
nor shall his face turn pale; but he shall see his children,

---

[1] B.C. 721.
[2] In fact, this seems to have been the case at Jerusalem when attacked by Sennacherib: Is. xxii. 13. [3] Is. xxviii. 14, etc.
[4] Which he entitles *Ariel*, Hearth of God. [5] Is. xxix. 1—8.

and they shall glorify his God, and all who have erred shall be brought back into truth. The words in which the prophet describes the confidence of the Jewish nobles, sounds like an oblique imputation on them of keeping up a secret correspondence with Assyria. "They fancied," he says, "that when the scourge passed over the land, it would spare *them*; for they had hid themselves in lies and falsehood." And we have reason to suspect that Shebna, who was in a manner prime minister to Hezekiah, was of the Assyrian party.

The prophecy of Micah, though simple and grand, does not add enough to the historical picture to justify our analyzing the whole. His rebukes upon Israel are in substance identical with those of Hosea and Isaiah; but two points may be noticed as peculiar to him. The other prophets do not on *this* occasion venture to predict a return to Israel from her Assyrian captivity and a rebuilding of Samaria; but it appears pretty distinctly in Micah vii. 11, 12, etc.[1] In regard to his Messianic expectations again, he is more impatient than Isaiah. While taking for granted that the Assyrian inroad must overflow into Judah, he announces that from the birthplace of David shall come forth Israel's rightful ruler, whose origin lies in the dim foretime. Until His mother shall have borne Him, Jehovah will yield up his people to suffering; but when He, the great Deliverer, arises, he shall rule them in the majesty of Jehovah his God. He shall be mighty to the ends of the land, and shall give it peace and security when the Assyrian makes his invasion, and treads in the Jewish palaces. Against the intruder seven "shepherds" and eight anointed persons shall then be raised up, who shall waste with the sword the land of Assyria

---

[1] Hitzig regards this chapter as written *after* the capture of Samaria; and there is much appearance of it; yet when Micah augurs that the Israelitish flock, which now dwells solitarily in *Carmel*, shall hereafter feed in *Bashan* and *Gilead*, as in the days of old;—does it not suggest that Israel has not yet been rooted up from both sides of Jordan, but from the east only?

The passage of Micah, which (with deference to expositors) we cannot but suspect to betray a later hand, is from iii. 8 to the end of iv. This seems like a mere cento from other prophets, compiled during the Babylonish captivity. The chiming of Jacob and Israel, and confounding both with Zion, is like the *later* Isaiah, ch. xl —lxii, and iii. 12, which at first seems to assure us of the genuineness of the passage (cf. Jer. xxvi. 18), may, on the contrary, have been suggested by Jeremiah.

and the frontier of Nimrod. So shall Messiah deliver Judah from the Assyrian, when he comes upon their land and treads on their borders. Then the remnant of Jacob shall be among many people as a dew from Jehovah, as showers on the grass, as a young lion among the flocks, who rendeth and none can deliver. Such were the glowing anticipations of Micah.

During the last period of Samaritan nationality, whatever prophets may justly say concerning the demoralization of the people, it ought not to be forgotten, that the worst of it was caused by overwhelming calamity, and by the fierce parties which so agonizing a position engenders. Nor can the prophets of Israel, as a body, escape their own measure of censure. After their voice had armed Jehu against his unfortunate king and Ahab's innocent house, we have no trustworthy evidence that the school of Elijah and Elisha did anything good or great for their nation, spiritually or politically. According to our extant prophetical writers, these monitors of Israel sinned equally with the people and with the royal priests. Amos was urged in spirit to leave his rustic occupations in Judæa, and migrate into the country of Jeroboam, there to protest against iniquities which the seers of Jericho and Bethel ought to have sufficed to denounce. How are we to account for this? Had the Honey Bee of prophecy, by playing the part of the Wasp, madly stung forth its own life? Had the sacred fire died out for want of fuel, when every antagonist element hid itself away from Jehu's violence? Or had the mist which loured over the whole land, clouded the eye of the Seer, as well as of the vulgar? All these causes may be presumed to have conspired. It is undeniable, that in the Israelitish prophets, as in the Scotch Reformers, the pugnacious principle was too much in the ascendant. There was earnestness and deep conviction, noble ends proposed, and unshrinking self-devotion to them; but nothing of the meekness of wisdom; no gentleness and sensitiveness as to other men's equal rights, and far too little scruple to combine with bad men and commit their good cause to wicked means. The prophet needed a public Sin to fight against: an Ahab called out his energy, a Jehu damped it; and when Elisha's contemporaries had been cruel in their fanaticism, it was but natural for succeeding generations to be lukewarm, and even favourable to the unhappy victims. From these extravagancies Jerusalem was saved by the mild influences of cultivation and by the prudence or worldliness of an established priesthood. There, the prophet and the priest had lived in harmony, and had tempered each other's besetting faults. But besides this, it does appear that the wars against Syria and Assyria, which demoralized the nation, degraded the prophetical schools also; much as the Christian church sank into dotage, when the surrounding world became whelmed in barbarism. Even in contrasting the representations given of Elijah and Elisha, we perceive a gravitation towards meaner notions and low superstition. The forty-days' fast of Elijah, his journey to the solitary Horeb, the stormy wind, the earthquake, and the fire, in which Jehovah was not; with the still small voice in which Jehovah was found; are a noble poem. But Elisha, sitting in Samaria, and miraculously revealing the plans of Benhadad's campaign and the words which he speaks in his bed-chamber, is far less dignified, and reminds us of tales of magic. When Elijah twice calls down fire from heaven, and slays two bands of fifty soldiers sent to arrest him, he is severe and terrible; but when Elisha curses a troop of young children in the name of Jehovah, and brings two bears out of the wood who devour forty-two of them, because they mocked at his bald head, he is ludicrous as well as savage. Elijah, who assembled the prophets of Baal, and after vanquishing them in a public trial of miracles, incites the spectators to slay them all, commits a semi-heroic crime; but Elisha, who by proxy incites a captain with an army at his back to kill his wounded and confiding master, and make away with Ahab's children and little grandchildren, besides being barbarous, is cowardly and deceitful. Elijah appears before Ahab face to face, to threaten him bitterly for the murder of Naboth; but Elisha, when the king is angry with him, and seeks his life, has supernatural intimation of it, and gives orders to shut the door in the messenger's face, while others arrest him outside. Elijah predicts a drought to Ahab, and again predicts rain, in simple words; but Elisha, when about to spell warlike successes to king Jehoash, makes them depend on a piece of luck. He bids him to take his arrows and shoot upon the ground. The youth (who lavishes appellations of honour on the aged prophet)[1] intends to obey, and shoots three times. But Elisha is enraged that he has not shot five or six times, because (as he now reveals) Jehovah had decreed to give him as many victories over the Syrians as the times he should shoot. Finally, when Elijah's hour of removal is come, he is carried up to heaven in a chariot of fire; but when Elisha dies and is buried as other men, his bones have a like virtue to those of a dark-age Saint:—they raise to life a strange corpse, which by accident touches them. These may be sufficient indications that young enthusiasm was spent, and legend was beginning to drivel, when the second set of tales first gained currency. It may deserve remark, that Bethel, the head-quarters of superstition in the day of Amos, was, with Jericho, a great centre of the prophetical alumni under Elisha.

Of the extant books of prophecy, one only has come from an Israelite,[2]—that of Hosea; and his fire seems to have been kindled at the hearth of the Jewish Amos. Nothing properly Messianic appears in him. It is peculiarly honourable to Hosea, that he possesses in a high degree the tenderness of spirit in which Elijah and Elisha were so deficient. It was not his fault that invective and lamentation were alike too late, and that neither patriotism nor religion had materials left for saving Israel. Clinging still to hope against hope, he ended his solemn appeals by auguring a time when Ephraim should abandon his idols, cease to supplicate Assyria or trust in horses, and should flourish high and deep under the favour of Jehovah.

[1] "My father, my father, the chariot of Israel, and the horsemen thereof!" Elisha was better to Jehoash than chariots or horsemen.
[2] Concerning Jonah nothing distinct can be asserted. The book called by his name is evidently not written by him, though the prayer in it may be his composition. The story of the whale in which it is imbedded, appears to have grown out of a frigid misinterpretation of his prayer; and the whole account is to us nothing but an echo of the low esteem in which the Jewish writers held the prophets of Israel.

If Jonah is, as Hitzig ingeniously opines, the author of the ode upon Moab in Isaiah xv., xvi., it does but make us regret his dearth of spiritual sentiment. Yet the invitation to become subject to Judah, and the high praise of the king of Judah, is against the belief that the writer was an Israelite.

APPENDIX to CHAPTER VIII.

In filling up the history, much depends on the chronological order assigned to the pieces of extant prophecy; and even where this cannot be decided so as to exclude all controversy, it becomes necessary for the historian to form a probable theory. A list is added of the approximate dates here imagined for the earlier prophets; partly in order to stimulate to their intelligent perusal (although the defects of the English version are a great drawback), and more especially that the reader may be able to check the narrative.

Approximate dates of the Earlier Prophecies.

B.C.	
858	Accession of Jehoash under the priest Jehoiada.
840	Plague of locusts and drought.
	Prophecy of Joel.
818	Death of Jehoash.
804	Accession of Jeroboam II.
780	Ode against Moab, Is. xv. xvi.
770	Prophecy of Amos.
763	Hosea's first three chapters.
762	Death of Jeroboam II.
748	Uzziah dies. Isaiah has his first vision, ch. vi.
745	Captivity of Gilead and Naphtali by Tiglathpileser.
744	Isaiah ix. 8 down to x. 4.
743	Zech. ix., x.
742	Zech. xi. ; Is. xvii. 1—11.—Pekah and Rezin invade Jotham.
741	Accession of Ahaz. He loses two great battles.
	Isaiah ii.—iv. Isaiah vii.—viii. 1, 2.
739	Isaiah viii. 4—ix. 7. Isaiah i.
738	Damascus falls by Tiglathpileser. Isaiah xxiv.—xxvii. ?[1]
733	Sargon (or his general Tartan) attacks Phœnicia and Philistia.—Is. xx.
739	Hoshea slays Pekah.
	Sufferings of Philistia.
726	Death of Ahaz. Isaiah xiv. 28—32.
723	Shalmaneser invades Israel the second time.

---

[1] But for the phrase "a palace of strangers" in xxv. 2, one might be tempted to explain these four chapters as Isaiah's *dirge over captured Samaria.* The fall of Damascus appears less likely to have called out so much feeling, than this nearer event: and so also we should see more force in the whole conclusion concerning Israel, xxvii. 6—13. But the real difficulty is to account for the prominence of Moab in ch. xxv.

B.C.	
723	Hosea's last eleven chapters. Isaiah xxviii., xxix. Micah i.—iii. 7, v.—vii.
721	Samaria taken.
720	Tyre besieged by Shalmaneser for five years.
717	Isaiah xxiii.
714	Isaiah v. ?
713	Sennacherib invades Judah. Is. xxx.—xxxii. Is. x. 4—xi. Is. xvii. 12—xviii. (and xiv. 24—27 ?) Is. xxii. Is. xxxiii. Is. xxxviii. 21—35.
712	Hezekiah is sick.
708	Isaiah xix.

CHAPTER IX.

FROM THE FALL OF SAMARIA TO THE DEATH OF JOSIAH,
B.C. 721—609.

As soon as the armies of Shalmaneser had effected their whole work on the hapless people of Israel, it was only to be expected that Judah would be the next victim. They had committed the same offence, and might be taxed with peculiar ingratitude; but Israel had never received any favour from the Assyrians. During the three years' war it is likely that considerable plunderings of Jewish territory took place;[1] but no formal attempt was made to reduce the strongholds; and even when Samaria had fallen, a new object intervened to give farther respite to Judæa.

Shalmaneser was looking beyond Jerusalem to the rich land of Egypt, and felt the importance of having all Phœnicia at his command, for the sake of its maritime aids. But of this he could not be sure, while the insular Tyre continued to defy him: its freedom was a perpetual stimulus to all Phœnicia to revolt. Expecting perhaps to capture it by a momentary exertion of force, he deferred his attack on Judah till he had accomplished it;[2] and ordered the subject Phœnicians to prepare 60 galleys and furnish them with rowers, intending to land his troops on the island.[3] Against these, the Tyrians, abandoned by all their confederates, had only 12 to oppose; but these 12 were animated by an eager spirit of liberty, while the 60 were filled with Assyrian landsmen, and with Phœnicians engaged in a cause which they detested. The little Tyrian squadron gained a brilliant victory and captured 500 Assyrian warriors; whereupon Shalmaneser endeavoured to reduce the town by guarding the whole coast so as to cut off the supplies of water. The Tyrians, notwithstanding, persevered, and dug wells for themselves in their narrow

---

[1] If this was the epoch of the composition of Isaiah i., more than mere plundering of the country was endured; for many cities were then consumed by fire. But see note 2, page 247.
[2] Josephus, Antiq. ix. 14, § 2.   [3] B.C. 720?

island. How much water they thence obtained, and how much they imported in spite of all precautions, rests entirely on conjecture; but they lasted out until the fifth year; after which we are left in uncertainty by the historian whether the blockade was given up, or the besieged were forced to yield.[1] The king cannot have superintended it in person for so long a time; his presence must have been needed elsewhere; and probably in the year B.C. 716 he was cut off by death. Such was the first great siege endured by this heroic yet peace-loving people, against the foremost power of the world. A second was sustained successfully against Nebuchadnezzar.[2] Sidon made a like brave resistance to Darius Ochus, and when betrayed by her own king, fell with horrible self-sacrifice. Finally, Tyre stood at bay for seven months against the great Macedonian hero,[3] and then at last the mole which he constructed against the island, by turning it into a peninsula, spoiled for ever the advantages of the site.

It is unpleasing to find the prophet Isaiah (ch. xxiii.) exult in the dangers which came upon this noble city, while standing in the foreground for freedom, and really shielding Jerusalem from the common oppressor. We here see the evil element of exclusive patriotism, which, when imbibed by those who had not Isaiah's other great qualities, made the Jew to appear as *a hater of mankind*. In the ode itself there is no intimation that Tyre was hostile to Jerusalem: the slave-trade is not named, nor the alliance with Philistia or Syria. But here, as elsewhere, the Hebrew prophets show a narrow-minded abhorrence of worldly art, skill, and science, as producing merely wealth, pomp, luxury, and pride. This illusion is perhaps a necessary result of limited experience, in those whose moral principle has full ascendency over the rest of their nature. Dread and grudge were felt against Tyre, "because she was exceeding wise."[4] Jehovah was believed to share the same sentiment,[5] and to be jealous of every-

[1] Since the above has been out of hand, Grote's third volume of Greece has appeared, in which he treats it as certain that the insular Tyre was *not* reduced by Shalmaneser: p. 428.   [2] Ezekiel xxix. 18.
[3] See Thirlwall's Greece, vol. vi. pp. 195—202, on this deeply interesting siege. The fate of Sidon is in p. 138 of the same volume.
[4] Zech. ix. 2.
[5] The only sin charged against Tyre is the extensiveness of her honourable and gainful traffic.

thing grand and high. To the end of his dirge the prophet subjoins rather dark words of comfort. Tyre is to be forgotten seventy years; after which she is to take a harp and sing as a harlot; she shall turn to her harlotry with all kingdoms, and her merchandise and her hire shall be holiness to Jehovah. While stigmatizing mercantile traffic by the contemptuous name of harlotry, Isaiah could not help admitting that even merchandise might be holy,[1] when it was spent upon the food and clothing of the priests or prophets of Jehovah. As regards the result here predicted, as well as the period of seventy years, it does not appear that they answer to any historical reality. Indeed, as this is the period assigned by Jeremiah for Babylonian domination, some critics find in it a confirmation of their suspicion that the whole chapter belongs to an author of a century later.

Out of the ruins of the kingdom of Ephraim many families must have taken refuge in Judæa, and, under the circumstances, were open to strong impressions of Jewish religion. Such as had never been present in Jerusalem at any of the great feasts, would attend the Passover there now with a peculiar feeling; and their presence could not fail to produce some excitement in Judah. Perhaps it was a simple event of this nature which the Chronicler has exaggerated into the account of a remarkable Passover celebrated by Hezekiah,[2] to which he specially invited

"Who hath taken this counsel against Tyre, the crowning city, *whose merchants are princes, whose traffickers are the honourable of the earth?* Jehovah of hosts hath purposed it, *to stain the pride of all glory, and to bring into contempt the honourable of the earth*" (xxiii. 8, 9). So ii. 12—16. Compare Herodotus vii. 10, § 5. "Seest thou how God striketh with his thunderbolt all tall creatures, but the little ones fret him not at all? Seest thou how he hurleth his darts alway at the loftiest buildings and trees; for God loveth to lop shorter whatever is towering."

[1] "(Her wealth) shall not be treasured nor laid up; it shall be for them that dwell before Jehovah, to eat sufficiently, and for durable clothing." This is very mean and tame; and more than any other sentiment in the ode, would help our acquiescing in the belief that the whole is of later origin.

It may be well to remark that v. 5 of this chapter in the English version gives the impression that the prophecy was written *after* great calamities on Egypt, such as the Persian conquest; but De Wette, Hitzig, and Ewald agree in rendering it, "When the news reaches Egypt, it shall be terrified by the report concerning Tyre." The notice of the *Chaldeans* in v. 13 is very puzzling. Ewald cuts the knot by altering the word into *Canaanites*: "Behold the land of the Canaanites! This people is no more; the Assyrian has made it a wilderness." This is a very bold, but perhaps happy conjecture.

[2] He seems to represent it as *before* the fall of Samaria (xxxi. 1). But it is

all the members of the northern kingdom. That the event can have been so important and striking as he represents, the total silence of the older historian (who is not at all wanting in sympathy for religious interests) makes it extremely difficult to believe. Yet there are a few points deserving remark, as implying that the religious zeal, which was kindled in this reign, introduced ceremonies before unpractised. The Levites were the movers in them, and the priests were reluctant.[1] The latter wished to adhere to the established practices; the former to introduce what they found written in the compilations which professed to give the most precise directions. This is the first trace which we find of Levitical zeal for ceremonies outgoing that of the priests; and this is the first occasion on which the word *Passover* is used in the historical books. We find also in a phrase of Isaiah,[2] reason to believe that the fundamental points in that feast were already observed. According to the Chronicler, this was a *peculiar* Passover, as celebrated by Hezekiah once only in his reign. Had it even been otherwise, we might easily understand that by reason of the destruction of the High Places, the country people had in considerable numbers attended the Passover at the central city : on which ground it is every way probable that under Hezekiah the Jerusalem Passover became a more imposing ceremony.

During the gallant struggle of the Tyrians, the counsellors and people of king Hezekiah had abundant cause to rejoice with trembling. An interval was gained, if they had been disposed to use it, for storing and strengthening their fortresses ; yet even the walls of Jerusalem itself were left in imperfect repair. This can be well explained. The revolt had been decided by the ascendency of the prophetical influence, not by worldly wisdom. The prophets looked for success to superhuman power, and thought more of moral defence by piety than of the phy-

so little credible that Hezekiah could " throw down the high places and altars in Ephraim and Manasseh " while Hoshea's kingdom stood, that this might alone warn us not to trust the details of the narrative.

[1] " The Levites were more upright in heart to sanctify themselves than the priests " (2 Chr. xxix. 34). This refers to empty *outward* purifications, which it cost the apostle Paul much labour and suffering to reduce to their real insignificance.

[2] Is. xxx. 29; xxxi. 5.

sical bulwark of walls.[1] Reasoners of a commoner sort judged by the examples of Damascus and Samaria, not to speak of Ashdod, that to resist the Assyrians without the help of Egypt was utterly an infatuation; hence all are likely to have been languid in preparation for war, unless that help could be secured. If any bold patriot were found to hold that the fortresses of Judah would suffice to repel the enemy, he would soon be convinced by the despondency of others, that there was no heart in the nation for so intense a struggle.

A new monarch ascended the throne of Nineveh, about 715 years before the Christian æra, by name Sennacherib;[2] and his accession perhaps deferred yet a little the fearful moment, in expectation of which the hearts of Judah quivered. At length his expedition was determined upon, and his great army began to assemble. As this could not be done in a day, and the chief part of the host was infantry, rumour would precede it by several weeks, and a short tumultuous time still remained to the Jews. Embassies to Egypt now began in earnest. Drowning men will cling to a straw, and the fate of Samaria did not deter them from trusting in this empty power. It does not indeed appear that the king himself despatched any such embassy; but the nobles sent off camels and asses laden with treasure,[3] humbly to ask aid from the venerable name of Pharaoh. Cavalry and chariots were the great want of the Jews for defence against the Assyrian foragers, and for this species of force peculiar entreaty was made.[4] Now at length also some decided measures of defence were adopted. The weak parts of the wall of Jerusalem

[1] Is. xxii. 11; xxxiii. 15, 16.
[2] According to the account of the Babylonian priest Berosus, extracted by Alexander Polyhistor, and preserved for us by Eusebius (see Fynes Clinton, Fast. Hell. vol. i. p. 270, on the Assyrian empire), Sennacherib was preceded on the throne of Nineveh by his *brother*. This may perhaps be claimed as favourable to the belief that a short reign of Sargon is to be interpolated between Shalmaneser and Sennacherib. But if Sargon's armies had been engaged in Philistia *after* Hezekiah's revolt, we should surely have some notice of their attacks on Judah, which indeed would be an earlier object; and that Hezekiah had revolted before the siege of Samaria, appears beyond reasonable doubt. The book of Tobit (i. 15) makes Sennacherib son of *Enemessar*, the king who carried Naphthali captive (2). This identifies Enemessar with Tiglathpileser, and appears to make Shalmaneser, Sargon, and Sennacherib his three sons. But in truth the worth of the book of Tobit is not much above that of Judith.
[3] Is. xxx. 6.   [4] Is. xxxi. 1—3.

were mended: a second wall was added, where chiefly necessary, and by turning off the waters, the moat between the two walls was filled. At this crisis one heart at least in Judah remained unshaken, although expecting severe trial. Isaiah did not repent of the revolt, and did not approve of asking help from Egypt. Not that he would have spurned real aid sincerely proffered (for we shall see that he thought well of the Ethiopian ambassadors), but he had an intense conviction that no succour would come from Egypt. At this time, while the Assyrian was marching upon the land, but had not yet entered it, Isaiah appears to have composed chapters xxx., xxxi., xxxii. of his prophecy. The great subject of them is scorn of Egyptian expectations. He announces that the strength of the people must be in quietness and confidence; that if they trust in Jehovah, he will fight for them; will smite down the Assyrians without human sword, and prepare a huge funeral pile in the valley of Hinnom to burn up his carcases. The prophet's mind glances far forward more than once, to a mysterious blessed future, when the righteous shall have an inward teaching such as Joel spoke of, besides outward instructors. In that day the earth shall be more fruitful, the cattle shall flourish, the moonlight shall be as sunlight, and the sunlight sevenfold; the idols shall be cast away; a righteous king shall reign, princes shall give just judgment, and bad men shall be degraded. We cannot fail to recognize in this the golden age of Messiah. Yet the prophet cannot stay on this joyful topic: he sees misery impending; he predicts even to the pious that they shall have "water and bread of affliction," —scant supplies in the time of siege,—that women shall mourn over the ravaged fields and unmilked cattle; that thorns and briers shall come up over the pleasant palaces, that the forts and towers shall be dens for ever,[1] and a place of wild asses' pastime, until the Spirit is poured from on high, and the blessed age arrives. He seems to strive in vain to lift himself into the happier anticipations; scenes of desolation recur to his mind, and he ends abruptly, in a rather incoherent strain.

By what route the Assyrians marched we are not posi-

[1] The English reader must beware of obtruding on the prophets our ideas of *eternity*, when this phrase is used.

tively informed; but as they brought chariots with them, it may be conjectured, that, like the second Benhadad, they came from Damascus along the breadth of Israel, and so entered the plain country of Judæa. It is indeed quite credible, that a prophetical piece of Isaiah[1] represents to us exactly their track,—crossing the border of the Jewish territory at *Aiath* or *Ai*, passing on to *Migron* and *Michmash*, lodging at *Geba*, in the neighbourhood of Ramah and Gibeah of Saul, and ravaging the country from *Gallim* to *Anathoth*. At *Nôb* he remains one day, and "shakes his hand against the hill of Jerusalem." But the invader did not intend to attack the strongest town first, but passed on to lick up all that was good in the land and whatever could be secured with least effort. His chariots were outnumbered by the clouds of horsemen, and his horsemen by the multitudinous infantry; among whom the most interesting to us are the Armenians, Medes, and Persians, who for several years proved themselves truly formidable soldiers. Besides these were masses of mere rabble, who, though useless in fight, were valuable in sieges, where every hand could help to raise a mound. When the vast host came before the frontier fortresses, their mounds rose so quickly, that they could soon walk up to the top of the walls. In other places they erected water-wheels worked by the foot, and pumped off the streams which supplied the besieged. Such appear to have been the only modes of attack used;[2] and their efficacy depended on the number of hands and feet which the besieger could set to work. In their own methods the Assyrians had had great experience, and were now, as heretofore, successful. Castle after castle was rapidly taken, or surrendered to save its crops.

Meanwhile ambassadors came to Hezekiah from the distant power of Ethiopia, which had been stirred up by alarm at the great king's approach; and to clear, as far as possible, this rather dark subject, a digression is here

[1] Isaiah x. 5—xi. The 11th chapter is wholly Messianic, and in magnificence second to none concerning the glorious age. It closes with predicting conquests over the Philistines, Edomites, Moabites, and Ammonites; a bringing home of the Israelites from Assyria, as also from Egypt (by a renewed miraculous passage of the Red Sea), and a permanent union of Ephraim and Judah.
[2] The Assyrian sculptures, like the Egyptian paintings, denote a *knowledge* of the arts of siege nearly equal to anything that the Romans ever attained.

needed concerning the relations of Egypt and Ethiopia. It has been already stated that the Ethiopians had for more than two centuries contested the possession of the land of Egypt. The country immediately intended by Ethiopia appears to be that which the moderns call *Sennaar*. This is a large triangle formed by the Nile on the west, the *Tacazze* (a tributary of the Nile) on the east, and the highlands of Abyssinia in the south. The junction of the two rivers is the vertex of the triangle, and is the most northern point of the country. The Greeks conceived of the region as an island, and called it Meroë: between it and Egypt the Nubian desert intervenes, and the rapids of the river make navigation extremely difficult. Sennaar, or Meroë, is thus naturally a distinct country from Egypt. Its monarchs however had often held possession of all Upper Egypt; indeed of all except that which was called *the marshes*, the capital city of which was Sais. According to Herodotus, the Ethiopian king Sabaco was induced to abandon Egypt by terrible dreams which ordered him to slay all the priests. It is impossible to divine the historical truth here veiled, if we scruple to accept the statement literally; but as in Meroë it is well known that the priestly power was at its height, we get some clue as to the internal conflict of society by combining all the accounts. For we find that when the Ethiopians retire, the military caste of Egypt is unable to retain the throne for one of its own body; but an Egyptian priest, named Sethos, becomes king, and endeavours to despoil the military of their landed possessions. For all warlike purposes he is exceedingly weak, because of the disaffection in the soldier-caste; and this (we apprehend) disables him from succouring Samaria or Jerusalem. It is farther believed that Tirhakah,[1] an Ethiopian successor of Sabaco, reigned in the Thebais, or Upper country; and that the Ethiopians did not retire from all Egypt, but only from the central or *Memphitic* region. In the Hebrew history this Tirhakah is found ready to meet Sennacherib in Palestine, so that he evidently had power of passage through Egypt, and far greater ability to make war than Sethos. This may suggest that there was not merely a close alliance between the two powers at this time (which

[1] Tirhakah is in Manetho's list of Ethiopian kings *of Egypt*.

seems undeniable), but that the priest was kept on his throne by Ethiopian influence; which, though now in the background and avowedly withdrawn, pursued its own policy of aggrandizing the sacerdotal caste in Egypt at the expense of the military. We thus get a new insight into the union of the Egyptians and Ethiopians by Isaiah, in his prophecy after the siege of Ashdod (ch. xx.).

Tirhakah manifestly was more on the alert than the armies of Sethos to guard the approaches into Egypt against Sennacherib, and sent ambassadors to Hezekiah to advertise him of his approach, as also to concert measures. Of this embassy we learn only through a prophetical piece in Isaiah, the extreme difficulty of translating which has given rise to the greatest diversities of opinion. The rendering however of the most recent expositor of high reputation[1] (who perhaps has scarcely his equal in knowledge of the Syro-Arabian languages) is eminently consistent with the general probabilities of the war. According to him, the piece begins with ch. xvii. 12, continues through ch. xviii., and should probably have annexed to it the fragmentary passage, xiv. 24—27, which is at present clearly out of place. The prophet opens with calling out to the "multitudes of rushing nations,"—the host of Sennacherib,—whom God shall rebuke and chase as the chaff of the mountains:—" Behold! at eventime trouble; and before the morning, the enemy is no more! Such is the portion of them that spoil us, and the lot of them that rob us." This indicates that the ravaging of the land was already begun. But in the second stanza he proceeds to address the Ethiopian ambassadors in words of honour:—" Oh land of winged boats, beyond the rivers of Ethiopia,[2] which sendest ambassadors by the sea, and in bulrush-vessels over the water: return, swift messengers, to a people tall[3] and slim, to a people terrible ever since it first was; a nation of vast strength and treading down; whose land rivers intersect." The prophet ends his third stanza by declaring that hereafter " *a present shall be brought to Jehovah* from the people tall and slim ..

[1] Ewald: Die Propheten des alten Bundes.
[2] Sennaar was to a Hebrew *beyond* the Nile and the Tacazze.
[3] The tallness of the Ethiopians, as well as their longevity, was proverbial in ancient times.

.....," which implies no such repugnance towards their aid as he may seem to express concerning the Egyptians.

While the Assyrians pressed their sieges and overran the country, great activity prevailed in Jerusalem to get the walls into the best condition for defence, and bring out the arms from the arsenal; for it became very clear that the capital itself would soon be invested. Meanwhile a large part of the people, seized with despair, resolved to enjoy their wealth and freedom while it lasted. In the midst of the tumult of arming, digging, and building, while the prophets' voices were calling to mourn and to fast, the shout of festivity rang through the city: "Let us eat and drink, for to-morrow we die."[1] Like the "drunkards of Ephraim," Judah was disposed to drown his sorrows in the wine cup; and Hezekiah saw too plainly how little he could depend on such subjects to bear the miseries of a siege. Hence, when a portion of the Assyrian army presented itself, the heart either of the king or of his counsellors fainted. It was resolved to surrender before the invader should be made implacable: Hezekiah confessed his offence, and humbly declared that he would bear whatever punishment should be imposed.[2] The terms exacted of him appear to be lenient, especially in being wholly pecuniary: he was required to pay 300 talents of silver and 30 talents of gold. In seeking to raise this moderate sum, he had not merely to sacrifice all the available treasure, sacred or royal, but to cut off the gold with which he had himself overlaid the doors and pillars of the temple; nor is it stated that even so he was able to satisfy the demands of the Assyrian.

The Jews in general, with the fate of Samaria before them, must have anticipated nothing less than expatriation or personal slavery; and if the war had continued, they would have been exposed to famine, pestilence, and casualties innumerable. That the insulted majesty of Nineveh should be satisfied with a pecuniary fine, which touched principally the honour of the king and scruples of the priests, appeared good news beyond hope. Universal gladness

[1] Isaiah xxii. 8—13.
[2] This important event is omitted by the Chronicler *as dishonourable to Hezekiah:* such is his way. It is similarly omitted by the compiler of Isaiah xxxvi., and is the more marked because he otherwise adheres closely to the very words of the book of Kings.

broke forth everywhere into mutual congratulations. The terror of battle had turned into pomp and parade, and all Jerusalem peered from the housetops to see the splendid array of the Assyrian army[1]. The quivered Elymæans[2] mounted in chariots or on horses, the shield-bearing Armenians, and other previously unknown people, might now be gazed at as curiosities. While the thoughtless were thus indulging in national joy, Isaiah was filled with shame for the disgrace of Zion, and every cry of exultation caused him a pang. "Her slain," says he, "are not slain with the sword; her rulers have been captured without drawing the bow; look away from me, labour not to comfort me." Nor was this all. He now took a most unusual step, in fact without parallel, either before or after, among the prophets of Judah: in the name of Jehovah he uttered an oracle concerning the displacement of the king's prime minister by a worthier rival, which took the form of a vehement attack by name on Shebna, who was at present Treasurer and governor of the House. We can scarcely doubt that this person had been a principal adviser of the recent treaty, and probably his whole policy leant towards the Assyrians. In punishment for his mal-administration, Jehovah was about to drive him from his high station, and carry him away into a distant captivity. He had proudly hewn out for himself a family-sepulchre in the rock, imagining that his name and posterity would abide in Jerusalem; but on the contrary, he himself should die in a far land. In his place should be raised up a faithful servant of Jehovah, Eliakim the son of Hilkiah, to enjoy the full and unrestricted powers of government, and become a true father to the people and founder of a noble family.[3] Such a panegyric clearly indicates that Eliakim held Isaiah's

---

[1] Isaiah xxii. 1, etc.
[2] We hear of Elymæans of the mountains and Elymæans of the plains in classical authors. (See Long's map of Persia, published by the Society for the Diffusion of Useful Knowledge.) It is here natural to understand the latter, who are in Lower Susiana.
[3] The meaning of the last verse of the chapter is contested. Although Hitzig says the sense generally assigned is *impossible*,—viz. that it goes back to Shebna, who is "the nail *which is to be pulled down*,"—Ewald, who has written since Hitzig, adheres to that view. It is certainly difficult to believe that Eliakim can be meant. Of Shebna's captivity we know nothing.

policy, and was bent upon inveterate opposition to the Assyrians.

The publishing of this invective must have made a deep impression on the king, whe sincerely venerated the prophet. But what was to be done? To disgrace Shebna for no ostensible crime, merely because he had been thus denounced, appeared to be unjust: to retain a man as prime minister against whom the voice of Jehovah had been uttered, was ill-omened and fearful. Hezekiah pursued an intermediate course. Without dismissing Shebna from his service, or putting needless ignominy upon him, he lowered him to the position of *scribe* or secretary, and promoted Eliakim to the high posts of Treasurer and governor of the House. How soon this took place will perhaps be questioned; but unless we abandon our best guide,—the compiler of the book of Kings,—all was begun and ended while Sennacherib was still at Lachish.[1] This implies the change of ministry to have followed so speedily on Hezekiah's surrender, that it would appear to the enemy as in immediate consequence.

Since no Assyrian historian has expounded to us his master's policy, it can but be conjectured from the feeble outline of facts preserved. A great and sudden change in Sennacherib's conduct followed: there is an evident chasm, which we cannot confidently fill up. So much may perhaps give a clue. A century later Pharaoh Necho obtains as tribute from Jerusalem the sum of 100 silver talents and *one* only of gold. The demand of Sennacherib is so very large in comparison, that we may doubt whether the whole sum had been raised when new events kindled fresh thoughts in the invader. He had not actually received the submission of all the towns of Judah. Lachish

---

[1] The popular chronology puts three years between v. 13 and v. 17 of 2 Kings xviii.; which proceeds upon an assumption that xx. 6 must have been uttered *before* the destruction of Sennacherib's army. This is by no means certain; but if it were, we still ought not to do violence to the narrative in order to force the scattered chronological notices into harmony. Such an army as Sennacherib's could not have been in the land a second year without absolutely starving the population. The probability is that it entered in the early summer, and perished in the autumn. We here agree with Clinton, that Hezekiah reigns from B.C. 726 to B.C. 697; Sennacherib invades him in his fourteenth year (B.C. 713); and his sickness is either in the same or in the following season, when he has fifteen full years (or less than sixteen) more to live.

appears still to have been resisting, and it is certain that Libnah was not in his hands.¹ As he was preparing to invade Egypt, he chose to hold these strong forts himself, and not to leave them in his rear; and when he met with refusal, doubts of Hezekiah's sincerity would of course suggest themselves. As he had demanded no hostages, what security had he against revolt as soon as he was departed? He had left the fortifications of Jerusalem untouched; and the resistance of Lachish and Libnah showed that the capital city might defy his arms disastrously, if aided by Egypt and Ethiopia. If in the midst of such thoughts the news arrived that Hezekiah had displaced Shebna, who negotiated the treaty, and had put forward into chief power Eliakim,—a partisan of a certain Isaiah, a fanatical opponent of the Assyrians,—what else could he infer but that revolt was intended at the first convenient moment? If the stipend required had not been all paid, he would seem not to be bound, even by the letter of a compact, against fresh hostilities: or supposing the whole payment to have been made, still under the new circumstances he could hardly do otherwise than insist on hostages as a guarantee of future good conduct; yet if this came to Hezekiah as a new demand, it would appear to him perfidious, as though the Assyrian were stripping him under pretexts of peace before destroying him by war. From some such causes, hostilities flamed out afresh.

To impute simple *treachery* to Sennacherib as an adequate account of his conduct, is wholly unfair while we have the narrative of one side only, and that so imperfect. It is evident that a violent fit of passion against Hezekiah personally had at this moment seized him, for he now sent his messengers to Jerusalem with words of exasperation and insult, of which there is no trace in the former mission. Hezekiah's trust in the king of Egypt and in Jehovah are alike topics of his scorn. Nevertheless, towards the Jews themselves he is not harsh, but frank. He demands that they will pay homage to him by a present, in which case he will leave them to enjoy their own comforts " *until* he comes (after his conquest, no doubt, of Egypt) to take them away to a land like their own land; a land of corn and wine, a land of bread and vineyards, a land of

¹ 2 Kings xviii. 14, 17; xix. 8.

oil-olive and honey, that they may live, and not die." Such was exactly the spirit of Darius, son of Hystaspes, in carrying away the Pæonian people. However violent and cruel in detail and in its secondary results was the proceeding of each invader, yet the end at which they aimed was (in their own conception) humane and good; and we have no reason to doubt that they meant to treat the population well, which they chose to transplant nearer to the centre of their power.

This message came with three great officers, of whom Rabshakeh was the chief spokesman, from Sennacherib at Lachish. A large army accompanied them, and when they could get no reply from the Jewish ministers (for such had been Hezekiah's order), we can scarcely doubt that it began an unsparing ravage in the immediate neighbourhood of the capital. At this crisis it is probable that Isaiah composed his thirty-third chapter, which opens,—

> O thou that spoilest, though thou wast not spoiled;
> O thou that dealest treacherously, when none dealt treacherously with thee.

He describes the "sinners" and "dissemblers" in Jerusalem as in great alarm of the devouring fire and unquenchable burnings (which the Assyrian host was inflicting?), yet declares that the righteous

> ...... shall dwell in a lofty place:
> His stronghold shall be a fortification of rock:
> Bread shall be given him, his waters shall be sure:

that is to say, the Assyrian siege shall not prevail against *him*. In short, Isaiah was still steadfast in the belief that Zion was "a tabernacle which should not be taken down," and the temple (as he before said) "a tried stone, a precious corner-stone, a sure foundation;" and accordingly he exerted himself to the utmost to support the drooping spirits of the pious but less ardent king. Meanwhile Rabshakeh returned to his master, whom he found besieging Libnah. Just then the news arrived that Tirhakah king of Ethiopia was on his march to repel Sennacherib; news which stirred him up to fresh rage against the Jewish king, as having merely sought to gain time by pretended submission while secretly negotiating with the Ethiopians. Yet he made no new attempts against Jerusalem farther than a war of words, in which he was decidedly inferior; for his repeated message of defiance was met by a splendid piece of eloquence from Isaiah, which we still read with interest and admiration.[1] The more formidable attack to be expected from the Ethiopians, and Sennacherib's desire to possess himself of all the fortresses on the frontier, forbade his concentrating his force on Jerusalem. And his career in Judæa was almost closed. The very next fact preserved to us is the dissolution of his formidable host without the hand of man. In the emphatic description prompted by devout gratitude, "the ANGEL OF JEHOVAH went out, and smote in the camp of the Assyrians 185,000 men." So marvellous a drying-up of the flood, which had almost swept the land bare, even had it not been predicted, must have seemed a supernatural mercy, brought about by miraculous agency; and if the received explanation is correct, that *Pestilence* was the secondary cause, this could scarcely be held to make the event less mysterious, if the words of Isaiah had been stereotyped on the day of delivery.[2] According to the traditions reported by Herodotus, the town-population of Egypt had become so alarmed by the obviously impending invasion, that the priest-king was at length enabled to make up an army of artisans, who marched out against Sennacherib. But before they could reach the foe, an unseen hand had done the work of destruction; whether panic smiting his people's hearts by night, or pestilence while he was sitting before Libnah, or the hot wind of the desert, or the quicksands of the Serbonian bog, while he was essaying to march into Egypt. Whatever was the cause, the army was no more: the Egyptians ascribed glory to the god of Memphis, and Hezekiah to the God of Zion. On the arrival of the news, all the dispersed detachments of the ruined

[1] 2 Kings xix. 21—34.
[2] This may lead on to a simple remark of perhaps no little importance. *We are apt most unduly to assume that a prophet wrote his speech the same day that he delivered it.* That may sometimes have happened, but it often was otherwise. We know by Jeremiah's own statement (xxxvi. 1, 2) that he did not commit his prophecies to writing till twenty-two years after he began to deliver them. It is equally possible, and indeed probable, that Isaiah did not write down his utterances against Sennacherib during the turmoil of the war; and if they received their final shape from his pen after the event, he would almost *inevitably* (*without consciousness of it*) give point to all the predictions. It is well known that preachers never write a sermon exactly as they recited it from notes. Peculiar difficulties in orations of Cicero, and perhaps of Demosthenes, are solved by simply remembering that the date of speaking and the date of writing are not the same.

invader of course consulted for themselves, so that Hezekiah's territory was instantly freed from the presence of an enemy.

The gratitude of Judah burst forth into various hymns of praise, several of which are extant. There seems at least to be little doubt that the 76th,[1] 46th, and 48th[2] are commemorative of this great event, and there can have been few in the land who refused, for once, to become religious. But while glory was given for a little while to God, a more permanent glory accrued to men, to Hezekiah among foreign powers, and to Isaiah among his own countrymen. The latter may seem now to have been at the height of his greatness. For ten years together he had held the same invariable language; indeed from the commencement of his public career as a prophet he had proclaimed a doctrine similar in tone, and now crowned by success. The seal of the Most High appeared to have been put upon his testimony; and during the remainder of his tranquil old age he must have enjoyed universal veneration from his own people. Yet when from this distance of time we endeavour to gather up the general lesson which was to be learned, when we ask, not, what did Isaiah allege concerning Jerusalem and the Assyrians? but, what does he teach for generations to come and for future conjunctures? we find it hard to extract a moral worthy of the God who alone can suspend the course of nature,—a moral justified by experience or by Christianity. Did the prophet teach that no righteous city can be captured by an unrighteous power? Nay, but that is untrue; nor in fact did he himself hold Jerusalem to be righteous, for he stigmatized it as a Sodom and a Gomorrah,[3] whose time of holiness was all in futurity.[4] But did he then teach that Jerusalem, irrespectively of the holiness of its people, was secure against hostile attack, on account

---

[1] The poetical name *Salem*. for Jerusalem, is alleged by Ewald now to appear for the first time, Psalm lxxvi. 2. It appears to glance back towards Melchisedek.

[2] Verse 7 in Psalm xlviii. is rendered by De Wette and Ewald, "by means of the East Wind, which shatters ships of Tarshish." If this were a professed account of the destruction of the army, it would seem to mean a hot east wind, blowing when it began to march through the desert. We can hardly think that it means shipwreck, for there is no hint that Sennacherib *took ship* against Egypt.

[3] Isaiah i. 10. Also xxx. 9, xxxi. 6, etc.   [4] Isaiah i. 26.

either of Jehovah's oath to David or Abraham, or of the sacred temple on Mount Zion? This is indeed the doctrine imbibed out of the psalms which celebrate this wonderful overthrow. The stream of Siloah, which makes glad the city of God, is henceforth a sufficient defence for Judah. Mount Zion, beautiful in situation, the holy seat of Jehovah, dwells under His protection; her towers are unassailable, her palaces perpetual abodes. And out of this root sprang the fanatical confidence of Jeremiah's prophetical opponents, who believed that the holy Jerusalem was able to defy Babylonians as easily as Assyrians. Nor is it clear how to resist the force of their argument, except by questioning whether the God of the hurricane and the simoom more peculiarly revealed his thoughts of human deeds when he destroyed Sennacherib's host, than when he breathed a deadly blast on the army of Cambyses. Such events should warn proud monarchs and armed states of mortal weakness and the treacherousness of mere force; but they do not in themselves express a divine purpose against him who falls, or in favour of those who reap the advantage.

Sennacherib himself returned safe to Nineveh; and since he, of all others, on every moral[1] estimate, should have fallen by the destroying angel, our confidence is somewhat shaken as to the universality of the destruction. If so much of the army was lost that all disappeared, all would be supposed to have perished: the obvious probability is that the king did not go home unaccompanied, but like Xerxes from Greece, carried back a fragment of his force, not intrinsically despicable, though small in comparison to that which had marched out from Assyria. Nevertheless his ignominious return roused the highspirited nation of the MEDES, who had hitherto been the main strength of the Assyrian armies. Disdaining to serve any longer under one whom they began to despise, they unanimously revolted,[2] and inflicted a far severer blow on the power of Nineveh than that received on the

[1] That is, *if* the destruction of the army was by a *special* interference, and not by general law. This I add, because one of my Reviewers has, willingly or unwillingly, missed the sense.

[2] About B.C. 712. Herodotus's chronology is very nearly correct, if we count Deioces's reign from the revolt. Indeed it is quite improbable that a man who wins a throne by peaceful methods can sit on it fifty-three years.

plains of Philistia. The Median territory consisted entirely of highlands. It stretched from the great ridge of Zagros on the south-west, or the mountains of modern Louristân, to the chain named by us Elborz, which fences off the Caspian Sea. From north-west to south-east its limits are less defined; yet it seems to have pressed upon lake Van in Armenia in one direction, and on the Hollow Persia in the other. So great a tract of country, with so advantageous a frontier, could never have been subdued by Nineveh if it had been well-peopled and united. We may judge, from the anxiety of the Assyrian monarchs to plant new colonies in Media, that a large part of it was vacant; and when conquered by the Assyrians, the Medes were probably a much ruder race, and not subjected to any single sceptre. But in the Assyrian armies they had learned their own unity, as well as the arts of war, and their revolt cut away at once half of the military resources of Nineveh. Nor was this all: the ancient town of Babylon next gained courage to defy its northern master, and its ruler assumed the place of an independent king. This farther entailed the loss, not only of the Lower Euphrates and Tigris, with the rich province of Susiana, but also of the whole Persian nation, who were hereby entirely shut off from Assyrian contact. No greater proof is needed of the too rapid rise of this powerful and widespread empire than the ease with which it thus fell to pieces,—without any previous process of decay, but in the very acme of its brilliancy and strength. It had not entwined itself with the habits and associations, more than in the affections, of the subject nations: and at the moment of revolt it had no other advantage than that which organization and internal concord generally give to a central power so assaulted. The nearer and more dangerous enemy was in Babylon, where *Merodach Baladan*[1] made himself king, having slain his predecessor *Hagis*, who had kept the throne but a month. Merodach Baladan was slain in turn, after a reign of only six months, by a new usurper named *Elib*, or *Belib*; against whom at

[1] These events we hesitatingly receive from fragments, principally of Berosus, preserved in the Armenian Chronicle of Eusebius. It proceeds to attribute to Sennacherib the foundation of Tarsus, which perhaps is an error. Abydenus absurdly adds, that he built a temple for the Athenians.

length, in his third year, king Sennacherib made an invasion. It proved successful: the Babylonians were defeated in battle; Esarhaddon, son of Sennacherib, was made their viceroy, and the Assyrian empire was saved, though not in entireness. Sennacherib's whole reign was eighteen years, so that he may have lived nearly as late as Hezekiah;[1] but his end was a miserable one. While worshipping in the temple of Nisroch,[2] he was slain by two of his sons. They escaped into Armenia from the vengeance of their brother ESARHADDON, who was already king of Babylon, and now stept into the vacant throne.

The remainder of Hezekiah's life was spent in a safety and tranquillity so contrasted with the former portion, that very few events have been recorded. Soon after Sennacherib's overthrow, or possibly even before it had happened,[3] the Jewish king fell into dangerous sickness, which some have alleged to be the same oriental plague as destroyed the Assyrian host; apparently because a *boil* is named as coming out in him. The boil was poulticed with figs at the order of Isaiah, and the king was convalescent on the third day after. At this time the prophet, according to our compiler, not only predicted speedy recovery, but promised the king fifteen more years of life; and when asked for a sign of his veracity, wrought the miracle of making the shadow go back ten degrees on the sun-dial of king Ahaz. An interesting poem or psalm, composed by Hezekiah after his recovery, has been preserved, and shows the little progress which the best-instructed Jews had as yet made towards a doctrine of future personal re-existence. According to this devout king, earth is emphatically the land of life, and after death there is no feeling, no knowledge, and no piety.

> I said,[4]—No more shall I see Jehovah,
> Jehovah in the land of the living;
> No more behold man among the dwellers of the still land.
>
> * * * * * *

---

[1] The book of Tobit says that Sennacherib was slain fifty-five days after his return. But that book deserves no historical respect.
[2] I understand that Colonel Rawlinson regards *Nisroch* as the genitive case of *Assarac*, the great god of Assyria.
[3] B.C. 713 or 712.
[4] De Wette's Translation, Isaiah xxxviii.

Behold, my sorrow has been healthful to me,
And thou lovingly rescuest my soul from the annihilation of the grave;
For thou castest all my sins behind thy back.
For the underworld praiseth thee not,
Death celebrateth thee not,
Those who sink in the grave cannot stay upon thy truth.
The living, the living, he praiseth thee, as I this day;
The father makes known thy truth to the children.

And for other than personal reasons, it was excusable in Hezekiah to be grieved at the prospect of death; for it is probable that he had as yet no heir: certainly his son and successor Manasseh was not born till about three years later. The land had not yet begun to recover from the late ravages; a great distraction of the kingdom had taken place; fear of the Assyrians had as yet by no means blown over, as may appear even from Isaiah's words of comfort now addressed to Hezekiah: "I will deliver thee and this city out of the hand of the king of Assyria." The death of the king might have involved many new calamities to the people; but happily, the event was delayed. The name of Hezekiah became renowned even in distant parts, where men measured him by the greatness of the Assyrian whom he had resisted; and Merodach Baladan, the now independent king of Babylon, even sent ambassadors with a present, to congratulate him on recovery from sickness. We may also suspect that their duty was to report to their master, whether an alliance with Hezekiah against the Assyrians would add strength to him.[1] In the fifteen years of tranquillity which followed we are acquainted with no reasons which make it doubtful that the prosperity of Uzziah and Jotham returned. Countries like Judæa, whose culture depends on annual industry, not on fixed capital elaborately invested in the

[1] To this incident the spirit of moralizing (after seeing the events of a century later) appears to have attached some unhistorical particulars. Hezekiah showed "all his treasures" to the ambassadors; (but Merodach had vanished from the scene before Hezekiah had much to show:) for this act of pride Isaiah pronounces that the treasures shall hereafter be carried to Babylon, and *all which his fathers had amassed* (which must have been gone already, when he cut off the gold from Jehovah's doors to pay Sennacherib's demand); his sons also shall be carried away and made eunuchs in the palace of Babylon. —Contrasting Hezekiah with David or Solomon, the punishment might seem disproportionately severe; yet the king receives the announcement with a false resignation, which combines selfishness with silliness. "Good is the word of Jehovah which thou hast spoken! And he said: Well on! Only let there be peace and truth in *my* days!"

soil, recover rapidly from hostile ravages, if an unimpaired population and vigorous government remain. These conditions were here fulfilled; so that Hezekiah in his later years may have been master of such treasures as were afterwards believed to have excited in him too weak a vanity.

When it became fully understood that the Medes and Persians were in permanent revolt against the sceptre of Nineveh, the Assyrians ceased to be feared in Jerusalem. Meanwhile the neighbour country of Egypt was in its turn of more peculiar interest to the Jews, who had so many families fixedly established there. Its position became increasingly critical through internal struggles. The priests and military fell into inveterate dissension; the Ethiopians, who sided (it is believed) with the priests, were unable to maintain their influence on the lower Nile; and before long, a most lamentable civil war arose, which temporarily rent Egypt into numerous independent kingdoms. This state is named the *Dodecarchia* or government of twelve powers; but it cannot be ascertained whether twelve is here an accurate or a round number. Nor is the duration of this period of confusion and divided rule known; there is reason however to believe that it reached through half a century. Already was it impending in the close of Isaiah's life, who appears to have bestowed his last words on the prospects of Egypt.[1] The æra is pretty well fixed by the altered tone towards Assyria, which was no longer an object of terror. The prophecy consists of two parts, the former containing nothing but gloomy anticipations, the latter wholly cheerful. The Egyptians, it is declared, shall fight against one another, and a cruel lord shall reign over them. The river shall be dried up, the reeds shall wither, the fishers shall mourn, the workers in fine flax shall be perplexed. The princes of Pharaoh in Zoan and in Noph (in Tanis and in Memphis) shall become fools; all Egypt will stagger; there will be no work for high or low to do. In that day Egypt shall be weak as women; the little land of Judah will suffice to frighten it; all will shudder on naming it, because of the punishment which Jehovah is sending upon it. But, after such humiliation, he who

[1] Isaiah xix.

has smitten shall again heal them. In that day five cities[1] in the land of Egypt shall speak the tongue of Canaan; there shall be an altar to Jehovah in the midst of Egypt and a pillar to Jehovah on the border; they shall cry to him for a rescue, and he will send them a mighty deliverer. Then shall Jehovah become known to the Egyptians, and they shall make offerings to him and perform vows.

Perhaps it is impossible to find in previous Hebrew prophecy such words of comfort concerning any special Gentile kingdom. Egypt might seem to have deserved it, by her uniform hospitality towards the outcasts of Israel and Judah who flocked into her cities. To extend the same mercy towards Assyria, late the grim foe and blaspheming scorner, was a harder effort of charity; but the greatest of the prophets was not allowed to depart with the contracted heart of a mere Jew. His bosom expanded to embrace Gentile enemies, until his "swan-song" forgot its natural harsh note, and died away into the accents of the Gospel. In that day (continues he) there shall be a highway to join Egypt and Assyria, and the Egyptians shall serve (Jehovah) with the Assyrians. In that day shall Israel be the third with Egypt and with Assyria, as a blessing in the midst of the land; whom Jehovah of hosts shall bless, saying, *Blessed be Egypt my people, and Assyria the work of my hands, and Israel mine inheritance.*

No grander and more lovely sentiment ever came from a prophet of Jerusalem, and it is delightful to receive it as Isaiah's last bequest. Since nothing more is recorded either of him or of Hezekiah, and we now close the first great æra of Hebrew prophecy, it may be suitable to cast a general glance over its extant productions. The most important and most honourable peculiarity is their purely *moral* character. The sins rebuked by the prophets Joel, Amos, Hosea, Micah, Isaiah, are such as we still hold to be sins; such as man-stealing and robbery, incest and whore-

---

[1] Jews were already numerous in several cities; but the number *five* is not historically made out.

The prophecy about the "altar to Jehovah" led (according to Josephus) to its own fulfilment; for Onias was moved by it to entreat Ptolemy to allow him to erect an altar and temple such as Isaiah predicted in Heliopolis, and obtained ready acquiescence. Nothing is known about the *pillar on the border*.

dom, cruelty and oppression, griping treatment of the poor, impure idolatries, unnatural sacrifices, excess of wine, adultery, murder, treachery and deceit, vain and superstitious divinations, pride and confidence in human prosperity. But in these writers we read nothing about periodical fastings, ceremonial cleanliness, incense-burning, sacrifice of beasts, sabbaths, sabbatical years, jubilees, new moons, and other festivals; little about tithes and firstfruits; nothing about the genealogy of priests and Levites, threefold presentation of the person every year at Jerusalem,[1] sacrificing at Jerusalem only, unclean meats, or any other part of the yoke which neither Peter[2] nor his fathers were able to bear. We are not to infer that none of these things existed, as law or as custom; most of them probably did exist; but it is evident that they were not prominent in the prophetical view, since no one is rebuked about such matters. And when in the prophets of the second æra we find an increasing estimate of such ceremonies; when after the return from Babylon the Levitical ascendency developes itself; when finally Rabbinism and Pharisaism flourish on the destruction of simple spirituality; we cannot mistake the career of degeneracy down which Hebrew doctrine was carried. From Joel to Isaiah it had stood on so noble an eminence, that we may wonder how anything inferior could find acceptance. This however is explained by the progress of events.

Two causes may be observed to have given a new scope

[1] If those are right who hold the unity of the second part of Zechariah (ix.—xiv. inclusive), a beginning of this zeal appears in a prophet contemporary with Isaiah (xiv. 16—19); yet only for the feast of *Tabernacles*. In that case however it seems almost certain that the threatened siege of Jerusalem in xii.—xiv. was from Pekah and Rezin; and several considerations occur :—1) *Israel* in xii. 1 could not at that æra, or at least in such a conjuncture, mean *Judah*. 2) When Israel was leagued against Jerusalem, that could hardly be unnoticed in the prophecy? 3) The mourning in the valley of Megiddon, which is alluded to as *past* in xii. 11, seems to be rightly understood by Wichmannshausen of the mourning for Josiah's death there (2 Chr. xxii. 25). 4) Moreover the recent martyrdom of Urijah by king Jehoiakim (Jerem. xxvi. 20 —23) gives a good explanation of Zech. xii. 10—14; while in Isaiah's day it is hard to conjecture what martyr was intended. [" *Me* whom they pierced " seems to be an old corruption for *Him*.] These are reasons for espousing the opinion that xii.—xiv. are from a later prophet, a contemporary of Jeremiah. As for the argument drawn from the similarity of the opening xii. 1 to ix. 1, and other similarities of style, may not that in part *account* for these three chapters having been subjoined to Zechariah?
[2] Acts xv. 10.

to the priestly ambition of Jerusalem. The former was, the removal of the High Places in Judah by the zeal of young Hezekiah and his advisers; an act in which we believe the prophets to have concurred, as necessary in order to stop corrupt worship. In the retrospect, we cannot doubt that it would have been better to modify than to destroy the independence and the existence of the local sanctuaries; better, so to uphold the apostolic application of the words, "The earth is the Lord's;" and not the hill of Zion only. Few of us probably realize the violence and greatness of the revolution expressed in the words, "He removed the high places;"[1] a measure which, as we have seen, the priest Jehoiada did not venture to enforce. It was just as though all Congregational or Presbyterian ministers in Wales or Scotland were suddenly expelled from their posts. As such expulsion could hardly be effectual and permanent, unless Episcopalian ministers, under the regimen of a central power, replaced them, so in Judæa we can scarcely doubt that Levites took the place of the priests expelled from the high places. There is no crisis in the whole history, from which the residence of Levites in fixed country-towns, as local teachers in connexion with Jerusalem, can be so plausibly dated; and until better advised, we may assume this to be the real beginning of territorial Levitism under organic centralization. It is of course possible, perhaps probable, that all who followed *civil professions*, as lawyers, scribes, and learned "kadis" or local judges were already incorporated into the sacerdotal idea; and Levites, in this sense, may have been residing in all the considerable towns: but to recover the history of this Order is beyond our reach. As the ejected priests must before have lived on voluntary contributions, efforts would now be made to influence the conscience of the people to direct the same liberality towards the Levites; and the duty or merit of Levitical tithe must henceforth have become prominent in the sacerdotal mind. So also was it with the superiority of Aaronic or Levitical priests, without reference to their spiritual qualifications; concerning which the vulgar were no longer trusted to judge. Moreover as the Passover and other feasts had been held at the high places,[2] the cessation of

---

[1] 2 Kings xviii. 4.   [2] 2 Kings xxiii. 9.

this worship forced the rustic population either to neglect the great festivals, or go up to Jerusalem to celebrate them.

A second impulse to the Levitical principle came forth from the ruins of Samaria; for, in order to bring the scattered population of the northern kingdom within the sphere of Jerusalem teaching, the duty of periodical journeys to the holy city and showing honour to the high priest there, became a topic of great moment. Thus in general, what had been *custom*, more or less prevailing, whether concerning pilgrimages or tithe, was now hardened into *law*; and to give new force to it as law, it would need more peculiar inculcation. Hence the reign of Hezekiah, which exhibits the prophetical spirit in its highest and purest energy, likewise commenced a ceremonial action which was to undermine and supersede that spirit. The events of the following reign persuade us, that the religious party in Judah, having full sway over Hezekiah's affections, in the last fifteen years of his reign strained the bow till it broke. The expelled priests and their friends had perhaps spent their resistance previously. But when an exterior of religion was imposed on the nation beyond what was generally felt, those whose fears or hopes made them hypocrites, secretly longed to overthrow the growing sacerdotalism. Such appears to have been the internal state of Judah, when Hezekiah prematurely expired,[1] leaving his son MANASSEH, at the tender age of twelve, as heir to his throne.

The mystery of Manasseh's character, in contrast to that of his father and his grandson, cannot be wholly accounted for by his circumstances; much must have depended on inward actings of the spirit, of which the historian can take no cognizance. Superficial observers might have expected that the son of a pious father, surrounded by religious persons from his early youth, would go the right way and second all their devout desires. Nor is it recorded that this did not happen for a time, until in advancing manhood new thoughts and feelings arose. When Manasseh was twenty-five years old, the same outside of religion may have shown itself in Jerusalem as in the year of his birth; or rather, a still greater pretence

[1] B.C. 697.

to sanctity, in consequence of the accumulating impetus of sacerdotalism. But the voice of prophecy was nearly mute; nothing at least was uttered so living in spirit as to outlast those times; and if ceremonialism was rife, while hypocrisy supplanted sincere devotion, it is not wonderful that a youthful monarch, disgusted with the religion which fenced him round, resolved to break it down. The time when this determination burst forth is not stated; and the broad fact constitutes the sum of all that is preserved to us concerning the longest reign of all the Jewish kings. Fifty-five years was its duration; and through the greater part of it an unceasing war was waged against the worship of Jehovah, and against the influence of his priests.

Nor did the king want pleas, drawn from just and humane topics, or perhaps even sound arguments, for altering Hezekiah's system. No cruelties indeed against corrupt priests, like those of Jehu, have been recorded in the preceding reign; but the violence of the revolution which expelled them gave a precedent for a similar ejection. The hardships inflicted by their expulsion must have left rankling remembrances in hundreds and thousands of bosoms. Antiquity, and the example of every king from the commencement of the existing rule, had pleaded in vain against the innovating spirit of Hezekiah's ministers. Those who bore with impatience the new Levitism would be able to ply Manasseh's ear with the pretences of grave conservatism, such as Roman aristocrats and emperors used to pour forth upon the Senate in defence of antiquated mummery; and the young king, who was so soon hurried down the precipice of intolerance, fanaticism, bigotry, cruel and besotted superstition, may really have begun in the belief, that he was only re-establishing ancient rights and redressing the deranged balance of toleration. Such being the outline of things, we might seem able to fill it up without consulting the book. The high places were rebuilt and their priests restored (perhaps from the sons of the expelled); altars were set up to Baal and Astarte; the "host of heaven" were worshipped, as by the Sabæans. The king used enchantments, dealt with wizards and necromancers, and observed times by astrology or other methods of superstition. When he had a son old enough, he made him pass through the fire in the valley of Hinnom. So much is nearly the same as is ascribed to Ahaz and to Ahab. But in Manasseh the following points are peculiar. He set up altars to the Host of Heaven in the two courts of the temple, and introduced into the sanctuary itself a graven image of Astarte. Houses for impure men, connected with her odious worship, were built close to the temple itself, and in them the Jewish women wove hangings for the goddess. When Manasseh encountered opposition— undoubtedly from the priests and the whole religious party, —he resorted to the approved old plan of persecution, and *shed innocent blood very much, till he had filled Jerusalem with it;* deeming, no doubt, that he could do as much by the sword for Baal as Jehu had done for Jehovah. That prophets were slain with the sword in Judæa in these times, is distinctly stated by Jeremiah.[1] The object of his proceedings manifestly was to cripple or destroy the Jehovistic sacerdotalism ; which trammelled him as a king, vexed him as an unspiritual man, or excited his scorn by its frequent hypocrisy. But he did more than he can have wished : he disorganized the whole nation, which could not retain its vital union without its peculiar monotheism. Great moral corruption spread through Judah; his cruel measures accustomed the people to blood, and gave intensity to faction. At the same time we cannot doubt that the pretensions of sacerdotalism rose higher and higher by reason of the persecution, and (as among the Scotch Covenanters) divine right was claimed for every common ordinance or petty ceremony. Priests must have been angels wholly to escape fanaticism; and we may well suspect that (like Christians under the persecutions of Decius and Galerius) they imbibed some measure of guile. It appears indeed to have been a long and dreary time to the worshippers of the one God; for, in spite of the false assertions of the Chronicler,[2] we have the authority of the book of Kings

[1] Jer. ii. 30. There are positive notices in the same prophet of the existence in these times of Baal-worship and sacrifices of children to Molech in the valley of the son of Hinnom (vii. 9, 30—32; xix. 4—6). We might have equally expected Isaiah to allude to it in the reign of Ahaz, if it had then existed.

[2] He cannot bear so bad a moral, as that this guilty king should live unpunished and impenitent, and go down to his grave in peace; so he brings up

for saying, that no reaction in their favour took place, either during his reign or that of his son. It is also a fact which ought not to be passed without comment, that in the Martyr Age of the prophets of *Judah* we read of no miracle-working Elijahs and Elishas, as in the times of Jezebel. The distinction of the periods is this, that Manasseh and Amon lived in a country and age which was no longer illiterate, and much nearer to the times of the compiler. Indeed, from this time onward, all pretence to miraculous interpositions, great or small, vanishes wholly from the narrative; a phænomenon too similar to that of other histories to be neglected by well-informed and candid minds.

It is to be wished that we could accurately present an outline of the contemporaneous Assyrian history; but our information concerning it is so ambiguous, that it is hard to narrate anything with confidence. Provisionally, however, and until the decipherment and accurate translation of inscriptions shall guide us better, the following may be received as some approximation to truth. Esarhaddon, the son of Sennacherib, having proceeded from his viceroyalty of Babylon to possess himself of his father's throne in Nineveh, next undertook to reduce the revolted Medes. After a severe contest he was foiled, and was forced to submit to see a new empire rise by his side; for one effect of the war was to compress the Medes into union, and probably sufficed to make[1] any other form of government than monarchy impossible. This successful issue of the Median struggle appears to have generated the confused tale, that the Assyrian empire was destroyed by the Medes while *Sardanapallus* was king; for it can scarcely be doubted that Sardanapallus is a compound word, and that its element Sardan

against him the host of Assyria, which carries him off to Babylon. There he repents and prays. In consequence Jehovah restores him to his kingdom. Manasseh takes away the strange gods, and the idol out of the house of Jehovah, and the altars that he had built in the court of the temple, etc. etc.

This we know by the book of Kings to be untrue; for Josiah found them still there, and had to destroy them (2 Kings xxxiii. 5, 6, 7, 12).

[1] Herodotus ascribes the elevation of Deioces to the monarchy, after the repulse of the Assyrians, to his valuable qualities as a judge and magistrate. This is an echo of the fact, that after the revolutionary war crime was common, and the whole energy of the first king was directed to repress it. Hence his character was with posterity that of *an energetic magistrate*.

is identical with Esarhaddon.[1] This prince is proverbial with Grecian writers as the type of all luxury and epicureanism while in his palace, though possessed of much martial ability in the field. To him is ascribed the founding of the two cities of Tarsus and Anchiale in one day; of which the former commanded the pass of Issus, and guarded northern Syria from a western invader.[2] It seems likewise to be he, who, with very severe loss on his own side, discomfited a Grecian army collected in Cilicia. He now cast an eye on the still vacant territory of Israel, and sent a new colony into it.[3] The mixed population had suffered from the ravages of wild beasts, which had quickly multiplied over a large and empty land; and, imputing the calamity to their want of skill in propitiating the gods of the soil, they begged of the king of Assyria to send them some priest of Bethel as their instructor. Esarhaddon was able to gratify them, and a mongrel worship of heathenism and Jehovism arose, which excited the peculiar disgust of the monotheists in Jerusalem. Such is the beginning of the schism between the Jews and the new Samaritans.

A reign of only eight years is attributed to Esarhaddon in Nineveh. Of his successors nothing is certainly known; yet as the book of Chronicles represents one of them to have invaded Judah and carried Manasseh captive,—impossible as it is to believe the last fact against the silence of the book of Kings,—it may seem unlikely that the war itself was an invention. As Esarhaddon had taken pains to settle Samaria, one of his successors may well have invaded Judah, and have either ravaged it or exacted ransom; to which a dark allusion seems to be made in the prophecy of Nahum.[4] It is however here only needful to say, that the Assyrian empire, though deprived of its most martial, retained its wealthiest provinces, and was still a proud and imposing fabric. Its conquering æra

---

[1] He is called *Asordan* in the Armenian Chronicle of Eusebius.
[2] Tarsus (in the Armenian Chronicle) is ascribed to Sennacherib. It is also said to have been built after the plan of Nineveh.—On Tarsus and Anchiale see the extracts collected by Clinton, Fast. Hell. vol. i. p. 275. Abydenus, quoted by him in p. 271, makes the victory of Cilicia to have been over a Grecian *fleet*. But what he adds about "an Athenian temple" overthrows his credit.
[3] Ezra iv. 2. [4] Nahum i. 11, 13; ii. 1.

was past, and the spell of its resistlessness broken ; yet as long as Nineveh and Babylon were united, Susiana, Mesopotamia, and all Syria were likely to be obedient; and such a power seemed to have nothing to fear from Medes, Lydians, or Egyptians.

When king Manasseh died, he was buried, not in the sepulchres of the kings, but in the garden of his own house. No reason is assigned for this ; but we may conjecture that the royal sepulchres were consecrated by Jehovistic ceremonies, and that either the priests succeeded in refusing him the honour, or his son AMON, continuing his father's feud, spurned the royal tombs because of their associations. For Amon, following his father at the age of twenty-two,[1] served the same idols, and wrought the same evil. But he either did not inspire so much terror as Manasseh, or was less cautious in his despotism; for after a reign of two short years, he met his death by a conspiracy in his own house. He left a young son named JOSIAH, only eight years old, to succeed him.[2]

If, in order to ascertain the murderers of Amon, we were to apply the question of the celebrated judge Cassius, —"Who gained by the crime?"[3]—we might fix the criminality on the priests. But this would probably be wrong. Had it been so, the royalists, who had for near half a century been in possession of the government, would have been able to make some struggle against their opponents, and the sacerdotal cause might rather have been injured by its deed. It is more likely that Amon by insolence or tyranny alienated his own adherents: he was murdered by his servants and in his own house, where the priests are not likely to have had influence so extended as to conceal a conspiracy. But a faction among the royalists themselves so fierce as to end in the murder of the king, would break up the party, and help to throw

---

[1] B.C. 642. *Twenty-two* is the least age which we can attribute to Amon ; for it makes him only sixteen years older than his son. We have no check whatever on these numbers. Since Amon is now made forty-seven years younger than his father, it is possible that twenty-two should have been thirty-two; but conjecture is here uncontrolled. Reasons will hereafter be given for thinking Josiah three or four years older than our text states.

[2] B.C. 640.

[3] "Cui bono?" (a phrase commonly mistranslated). See Cicero Pro Milone, 12, § 32.

public affairs once more into the hands of the priests. As at the murder of Amaziah, a popular movement and new election was called out by the event. "*The people of the land*," we are informed, "slew all them that had conspired against king Amon; and *the people of the land* made Josiah his son king in his stead."

His early years glided away without any event which has been recorded; yet the time was one of important preparation through the land. There is no evidence that the priestly party were at first in full power; if some of them were near the king's person, they were still too weak to attempt great changes, and many important offices must have been held by nobles reared in Manasseh's regimen, whom it would have been dangerous to eject. The rites of Baal and of Molech, with all their impurity and cruelty, continued in the land unmolested by authority. But in the course of eighteen years[1] many silent changes took place. The posts vacated by death were doubtless filled by men of a new stamp; the purely Levitical notions were imbibed with ardour by the best educated youths and pious persons, who looked back with hatred on Manasseh's cruelties, and saw with disgust the emblems of his idolatry. So far then, outward circumstances were ripening for a religious revolution.

At the same time, literature was advancing: the period of prose-writing was setting in: the times were beginning to demand a written and complete code of laws. In most nations the process of code-making comes rather late. Custom generally precedes Law by a long interval. It is only in the case of colonies from civilized countries that the written code can be well coeval with national existence. As for the Jews, the century which preceded Josiah had been a time of preparation for a system of Statute Law, which should be accessible to the mass of the people. From the very beginning of the monarchy, Samuel the seer, and at a later time Jehoiada the priest, had laid up written memorials adapted to secure certain rights against

[1] The narrative of the book of Kings is here followed. The Chronicler, to increase the glory of Josiah, has made him a religious reformer in his eighth year of reign, at the age of sixteen, and *before* he had seen the book of the Law. This is refuted by Jeremiah, who did not begin to prophesy till Josiah's thirteenth year of reign; and found the worship of Baal and Molech standing at a time when the Chronicler pretends it had been for five years put down.

the crown; but this was no code accessible to the people, nor was there as yet any order of learned men to interpret it. But ever since the reign of Uzziah the intercourse with Egypt had been steadily on the increase; and the colonies of Jews and Israelites there were so considerable, that the absentees in Egypt and the exiles in Assyria are often spoken of in one breath (which indeed we have seen in Isaiah), as though coordinate and almost commensurate. Although Egyptian art perhaps was sinking, Egyptian learning must have been at its height in Isaiah's day; and wealthy Jews established in that country, where all the trials before a judge are said to have gone on in writing,[1] would necessarily gain more definite ideas of the value of a complete written body of statutes. Communication with the exiles in the cultivated cities of Assyria must have had the same tendency; and it is more than possible that the severities of Manasseh against the public exercise of Jehovistic religion turned into retired students many who would else have been its ministers. The fact at any rate is clear, that a new school of learning arose, which was in due time to expand into Rabbinism, after combining influences from Babylon and Egypt with the peculiarities of the Jew. The leaders of this school were perhaps rather Levites than Priests; for, with the development of learning, the Levite had become independent of the Aaronic order, nearly as in the middle age of Europe the lawyers or *legists* grew out of the clergy and became an order of themselves. But in the new school there must have been very various minds; some disposed to heathenism and Egyptian mystery, others simple as Moses; yet all eager for Levitical aggrandizement. Before their movement was fully ripe, political events of first-rate moment had burst forth from the dim distance of the unknown north in the earlier portion of Josiah's reign, which, after afflicting and still more terrifying the Hebrew nation, waked up anew the strain of prophecy. It is requisite here to trace back these striking phænomena, although they carry us far from the scene of Judæa.

DEIOCES, the first Median monarch after the war of independence, had been an active magistrate; by him internal order was established, and all the tribes of Media it-

[1] Diodorus, i. 75.

self united under one sceptre. His son and successor PHRAORTES in consequence felt himself strong enough to attack the Persians, and by subduing them commenced an empire over foreign nations;—which now reached southward over the modern provinces of Fars and Kerman. After this he ventured to make war upon Assyria, but was severely defeated and slain : such was the energy still retained by the empire of Nineveh. The new king of the Medes was named CYAXARES, son of the preceding; who having introduced great improvements into the discipline of his armies, overran Armenia, and extended the Median sway to the banks of Halys, now the *Kizil Irmak* in Anatolia. This district appears to have been previously in nominal homage to Nineveh: it now became a real and efficient part of the Median power. *After* this success, as is most probable,—for we cannot expect from our excellent historian any exactness in the chronology of these events,[1]—Cyaxares resumed the aggressive against his father's foes, and drove the Assyrians off the field, with a superiority so decisive as to confine them to their fortifications. But before the strife could be terminated, a " lion from the thickets " of the north (to adopt Jeremiah's metaphor) sprang out to devour both the combatants. The *lion* was a great nation of Tartary, who obtained the name of SCYTHIANS with the early Greeks. Themselves driven westward by the Massagetans, they were pressing hard upon the nation of the Cimmerians, who then occupied the country north of the Black Sea; and the struggle proved of fearful interest to the more cultivated people of the south.

Nature herself has erected a wonderful wall of defence for Armenia, Persia, and India against the wild rovers of Russia and Tartary. The great chain of Caucasus, beginning from the N.E. side of the Black Sea, throws strag-

[1] Herod. i. 103. The lengths of the reigns of the Median kings, as of their contemporaries in Egypt, with the twenty-eight years' sway of the Scythians, may possibly be squared with the Hebrew dates by such methods as Mr Clinton (an author more successful in classical than in oriental chronology) employs; but when this is with a sacrifice of historical probabilities, it seems unreasonable to yield such deference to *figures*, which are exposed to so many causes of error. Of the twenty-eight years, nothing historical can be made: the Scythian invasion *may* have been about B.C. 630. Phraortes is supposed to have been slain in B.C. 635. The Chaldæan occupation of Babylon seems to be earlier than the fall of Nineveh.

gling masses across to the south of the Caspian, whence it
stretches with nearly unbroken line to join the Hindu
Kush, and so onward to the mighty Himalayas. The
passes are very few, and can with great ease be secured
by a civilized and vigilant power against barbarian inroad.
Yet (so many have been the times of disorganization or
negligence) the barrier has been again and again broken,
and Persia has become the spoil of the Tartars. The Scythians of whom we speak, were named by themselves
Scolotians;[1] they talked a kindred dialect to the Sarmatians, whose later history is well known, and whose descendants appear in the middle age of Europe as the great
Sclavonic nations.[2] At that time the Scythians had in
common with the Medes the warlike exercise of horse-
archery, and when equal in numbers were so nearly equal
in prowess that no one could predict which would prove
superior. But they were essentially a roving people;
when they set forth, it was a nation and not an army in
motion. Their women and their cattle came with them:
hence their numbers and speed were overwhelming, when
every man was a warrior and every warrior a horseman.[3]
In beauty and swiftness the finest steeds of Media are
likely to have excelled those of Scythia; but in endurance
the Scythians had the advantage, as at present the Tur-
komân cavalry. If we believe Herodotus concerning
events so distant from Greece, in a contest which took
place between Cimmerians and Scythians north of the
Caucasus a vast body of each nation migrated southward; and while the Cimmerians passed round Caucasus on the west and entered Anatolia, the Scythians
found out an eastern circuit and came down upon
Media.

Cyaxares was called off from his Assyrian war by the
startling tidings, and hurried to engage the barbarous in-

[1] After the conquests of Alexander the Great, the word *Scythia* was extended to include Independent Tartary and even Thibet; and under the Romans the Scythia of Herodotus (or Southern Russia) was named *Sarmatia*, the Scythians having evacuated it under pressure of the Sarmatians.

[2] Prichard believed the Scythians of Herodotus to have been a Sclavonic people.

[3] Gibbon's twenty-sixth chapter on *the Huns and Tartars* is an able and eloquent description, which will apply to any ancient nation whose habits were generated on the same soil.

vader. A total defeat of the Medes ensued. The conquerors spread over the whole country, and by their numbers and violence dissolved the Median empire for the time; although their ignorance was too great to allow of their organizing a new government or taking any measures for permanent occupation. The fortified cities would generally be unassailable by them, but the open field was at their mercy. Enterprise, curiosity, or restlessness carried a large army of them far southward into the land of Israel, and even into Philistia; where the novelty of their aspect, their brutality and utter barbarism, made Jews, Philistines, and Egyptians shudder. The town of Bethshean, on the plain of Jordan, is supposed to have been occupied by them; we do not even know whether they found it empty or inhabited; but from some occurrence of this date it gained the name of the City of the Scythians. Their mark however was Egypt. Before they could cross the frontier, they were met by ambassadors from Psammetichus, then king of that country, who by rich presents and clever persuasion induced them to turn back: yet on their way northward having entered the town of Ascalon, which seems to have been then under Egyptian rule, some of them stayed behind the rest and plundered the rich temple of Astarte.[1] None of these events could be unknown to the Jews, who looked with tremor and uncertainty towards the main body of Scythians, still rioting over the wide plains of Mesopotamia and Media.

But the most permanent results of this great irruption were secondary ones. It broke the fetters of another rude northern people, whose name was known to the Hebrews from Abraham their great ancestor, a native of Ur of the *Chaldees*, though they had as yet no practical acquaintance with them. Their proper appellation seems to have been *Kardim* or *Kards*, an element which reappears in the Carduchians of Greek writers. The Hebrews named them *Kasdim*, by a well-known change of sound; while another dialect transformed the word into *Chaldim*, whence we have their European appellation of

[1] The Greeks call the goddess *Heavenly Venus*. The Scythians were subject to a singular disease, in which their men lost masculine spirit, supposed themselves to be incapable of manly exercises, and would do nothing but w' men's work. Herodotus believed that Venus inflicted this on the individuals who had despoiled her temple, and on their descendants for ever.

Chaldees. This people occupied the mountains which fringe Mesopotamia on the north, and, as the modern *Kurds*, in part wandered over, in part occupied the underlying plains. It has been much controverted, whether they were a nation of Shemitic language (who then proceeded northward and conquered a part of the mountain region), or a nation of Median relationship which spread itself southward; but the question is nearly unimportant to history, and will perhaps never be decided.[1] Enough for us, that the bands of the Chaldees vied in enterprise with those of the Scythians: profiting by the general disorganization, they set Nineveh at defiance, in whose armies they had in all probability been used to appear; and at its expense clutched for themselves many a goodly town. The first name on which we can reckon with any confidence as a king of the Chaldæans, is *Nabopolassar*, whose reign is computed from 625 B.C., according to the astronomical canon[2] of Ptolemy. It is highly probable

[1] High authorities for the Shemitism of the Chaldees are Mannert, Olshausen, Prichard, and Grote: but the weight of opinion is on the other side. The best *argument* for it seems to turn on Gen. xxxi. 47, as proving that the Hebrew writer believed Laban (who had come from Ur of the Chaldees) to talk the language now called Chaldee. The importance of the question is exceedingly overrated, nor can we confidently hope that even the deciphering of the Babylonian bricks will solve it; for what one interpreter might call Chaldee, another may claim as Assyrian or Babylonian.

Grote (Greece, iii. p. 388), resting on Herodotus and Strabo, can see nothing in the Chaldees but *Babylonian priests*. That was certainly their later position (or the later use of the name), but nothing is clearer in the Hebrew writers than that it was not so originally. Magians and Chaldees seem both to have fallen from dominant tribes into priesthoods. The prophets so familiarly speak of the Chaldees as coming from the north, that until it is proved that Babylon was their proper home, our position is, to disbelieve it. Ur was in *northern* Mesopotamia.

[2] The Canon is to be seen in Clinton, Fast. Hell. vol. i. p. 278, and contains the names of kings of Babylon from Nabonassar (u.c. 747) to Nebuchadnezzar. Its earlier portion does not at all agree with the Armenian Chronicle of Eusebius.

Nabopolassar is also named in extracts from Berosus preserved by Josephus. One extract is repeated, Ant. x. 11, 1, and c. Apion. i. 19; with the variation that he is called Nabuchodonosor, as also his son, in the Antiquities, Nabopolassar in the reply to Apion. Berosus, as a Babylonian priest, is likely to have known the Babylonian affairs of such a king: but the statements made to glorify him in this very extract are so grossly false, as to warn us against trusting the author. He represents Nabopolassar as lord of Egypt, Hollow Syria, and Phœnicia, over which whole country he has set a satrap. When the satrap revolts from him (Necho is evidently intended), he sends Nebuchadnezzar to make war against him, who captures his person, and recovers the provinces, etc. etc.—It is quite as false that Nabopolassar ever possessed a foot of ground

that this is merely the date of his becoming master of Babylon. His position made him appear as a natural ally to Cyaxares, who had already unlearnt fear of the Scythians, and was once more bent upon hostilities with Nineveh. In fact, the Scythian forces had wasted away of themselves;—from their numerous and distant excursions, heat of the climate and disease, treachery of the people of the south, who intoxicated and then slaughtered them, and other causes that may be conjectured. Cyaxares is said indeed by Herodotus to have taken some bands of them into his own service.[1] The war against Assyria was at length resumed by him; and as the Chaldees not only occupied the Lower Tigris, but by their primitive position in northern Mesopotamia cut off the communication with Syria, Nineveh was left to a most unequal contest against the Medes. Of the details of the war nothing is known, nor the date of its termination. So celebrated a city had not even the sad consolation of leaving to posterity a remembrance of her last struggle. Her sufferings are "blotted out by the sponge of Lethe;" a harder fate, says a Greek poet,[2] than suffering itself. We can only infer that *about* the year 615 B.C. her waning star dipped beneath the ocean, where it disappeared for ever. The Medes at once took Assyria Proper to themselves, but respected the right of the Chaldees to Babylonia and its dependent provinces. Events moreover drew their efforts to the far west, where they fell into conflict with the wealthy and civilized monarchy of Lydia, small but energetic: for the present therefore they seemed to have abandoned to Nabopolassar all the lower country of Mesopotamia, and whatever he could conquer of Syria.

When the Assyrians were no longer able either to threaten or to aid the mixed people of the Samaritan cities, it was natural that the king of Jerusalem should cast upon these an eye of pity and of ambition. The

in Egypt, as that Nebuchadnezzar conquered Africa and Spain, which Josephus gravely tells from Megasthenes.

[1] Herod. i. 73. The expressions of the historian here are not in harmony with the twenty-eight years' empire which he assigns to the Scythians over Upper Asia. In fact, all that we can believe is, that some detachments of them continued formidable at so late a time after the irruption.

[2] Æschyl. Agam. 1300 :—

...... σπόγγος ὤλεσεν γραφήν.
καὶ ταῦτ' ἐκείνων μᾶλλον οἰκτείρω πολύ.

events which follow show that Josiah now looked on Israel west of the Jordan as his own realm; yet there is no trace of its being gained by war. We can therefore scarcely doubt that his claim of homage was readily admitted by the scattered population which had recently felt themselves so helpless against the Scythians, and probably also against Chaldee marauders; and the greatness of Josiah's power was exaggerated to men's apprehensions by the severe sufferings of the neighbour states. Ammon indeed,[1] and perhaps Moab, profited by the emptiness of the Transjordanic plains, and extended their border considerably; but they had no hereditary pretensions to sovereignty west of the river. On the other hand, the nature of the case persuades us that a large residue of genuine Israelites must have remained on the Samaritan territory, in spite of Shalmaneser. The ease with which Josiah's pretensions establish themselves confirm the belief; and it is apparently assumed in some passages of the contemporaneous prophets, where Israel and Judah are combined or confounded.

The reverses of empire which have been described stimulated the Jewish mind, and called forth several energetic prophets: Nahum, Zephaniah, Habakkuk, Jeremiah. Nahum, in Assyrian captivity,[2] was chiefly affected

[1] Jerem. xlix. 1; Zeph. ii. 8.
[2] He is called an *Elkoshite*. Elkush is still a little town on the Tigris, near to ancient Nineveh. Ewald, moved (it seems) by Nahum i. 9. "affliction shall not rise up *the second time*," is disposed to place Nahum's prophecy in the war of Phraortes against Assyria. But we do not know whether Nineveh at that time came into any great danger. If it did, Ewald would seem to be right: if it did *not*, Nahum may have prophesied a little later, during the war of Cyaxares; and this is the more obvious supposition, though nothing can be determined. In fact, we seem to be disputing about an interval of ten years, when it is quite uncertain whether Nahum may not have polished up his poem ten years after he commenced it. Some make Nahum earlier and Habakkuk later than we here represent. If those are right who refer the book of Zechariah to *three* eras, Zechariah *the second* (or the author of chapters xii.—xiv.) is another contemporary of Jeremiah. Ezekiel also will be afterwards mentioned.

We may remark, that while in the northern kingdom the prophets are made most prominent by internal Baal-worship, in Jerusalem they are called out by times of suffering or by danger from foreigners, but are silent during the tyranny of Manasseh. Shall we ascribe it to the greater weight which legitimacy added to the crown in Judah? or to the influences of literature, which trusts more in time and milder methods, and is apt to "temporize," because here is its strength? Habakkuk may have *dwelt* in Israel, but his cultivation is from Judah.

by the approaching downfall of Nineveh; but on those in Palestine the Scythians and the Chaldees made the strongest impression; and since both came from the north, alike great equestrian nations, alike rude and fierce, allusions are found in these prophets capable of applying to either people, and possibly blending both in dimness of conception. Of the four prophets who have been just named, three belong to the old school. In Nahum, Zephaniah, and Habakkuk, we have all the raciness of antiquity, and high poetical vehemence. Jeremiah was younger than they, but was their contemporary by beginning his ministry at a very early age; he was the son of a priest and has a smack of the new cultivation, of which we have already spoken. *Nahum* and *Zephaniah*, the one in Assyria, the other in Judæa, prophesied at a very short distance of time, when the fall of Nineveh was impending. This is the sole topic of Nahum, and is glanced at by Zephaniah. The latter dwells on the corruptions of Judah in the early part of Josiah's reign, and threatens it with dreadful desolation, apparently from the Scythians. Philistia is implicated in the threat, as also Moab, Ammon, and even Ethiopia; but there is generally much vagueness spread over the gloomy predictions of this prophet. *Habakkuk* wrote,[1] when the Chaldees had suddenly made themselves known as swift and formidable marauders; and they are his main subject. He denounces them as given to excess in wine, rapacity, and cruel violence,—vices which may be expected from a rude people who suddenly become conquerors of more wealthy lands; he indicates that their ravages had been felt in "Lebanon," or the newly colonized northern Palestine, where they had laid some city waste; for which he declares the judgments of Jehovah upon them. This prophet is rather Israelitish or even Gentile than Jewish. He neither laments as past, nor predicts as future, an invasion of *Judæa* by the Chaldees; but calls aloud to all the heathen, that this nation shall " march over the breadth of the *earth*,[2] to possess the dwelling-places which are not theirs." Habakkuk knows nothing of the foreign idolatry

[1] About B.C. 620 ? The text refers especially to ii. 5—17; i. 6.
[2] The same Hebrew word means *land* and *earth;* but the whole context guides us here to understand it as earth. See also i. 17.

in Judah, nor yet of its reformation: his mind stands in no contact with the affairs of Manasseh, Josiah, or Jehoiakim, but is that of a cosmopolite Hebrew, like Paul. One might believe that he lived among the northern colonies and had suffered famine from the Chaldee inroad.[1]

Jeremiah's prophecies began to be delivered a few years after the Scythians first appeared in Media; but they were not committed to writing, in their final form, until Jerusalem had been carried captive in the eleventh year of Zedekiah, as the book states on its front.[2] It is too monotonous in its colouring to be of service for distinguishing the moral aspects of different periods in his long career; yet it is of value for the general picture of the times.

Small as was the influence of Jeremiah in his own town of Anathoth, where his extreme youth would make him unpersuasive to his neighbours, it was nevertheless probably a valuable aid to the rising school of reformers, that two such prophets as Zephaniah and Jeremiah denounced in the name of Jehovah the prevailing idolatries. Many persons still retained a high veneration for the prophetical character, and the traditions of Isaiah and Sennacherib must have been alive in every memory. There was also a prophetess named Hildah, who gave her whole influence to the cause of Jehovah; and thus strengthened, Hilkiah at last moved in the cause of religious reform in the eighteenth year of Josiah, when the king was about twenty-six years old. Either at his own thought, or at the suggestion of Shaphan the scribe, Josiah sent orders to Hilkiah to count out the moneys contributed to the temple, and apply the sum to execute necessary repairs. Shaphan returned, announcing that Hilkiah had obeyed the king's word, and had also delivered to him a book,— the book of the Law, which *he had found in the house of*

---

[1] Hab. iii. 17, 18.
[2] Jer. i. 3. See also xxxvi. Jeremiah was son of Hilkiah, a priest of Anathoth, whom some take to be Hilkiah the high priest. This is denied by others, on the ground that the latter, *being of the line of Zadok*, cannot have had lands at Anathoth, *which was the patrimony of the sons of Abiathar alone*. Neither fact alleged is clear: yet on the whole it seems probable that Jeremiah would have entitled himself " son of Hilkiah the high priest," if that had been true.

Jehovah. The scribe read the book to the king, who, on hearing it, rent his clothes with grief and terror. Hereupon he commissioned Hilkiah, with four others, "to inquire of Jehovah concerning the book," which was evidently quite unknown to him. What was the mode of inquiry which the king wished, or what questions were to be asked, is not indicated: the commissioners however proceeded to the prophetess Hildah and "communed with her." They do not appear to have asked her the first grand point, and the only one of importance to us: "what was the age of the book, and who wrote or compiled it?" nor need we charge her with evasion, that she does not touch on such matters. Her reply in fact is a mere echo of the threats of the law: "Jehovah will bring evil on this place and upon its inhabitants, according to the words of this book," etc.

The king was exceedingly affected, at learning for the first time that idolatry was a sin which Jehovah threatened to punish by his severest anger. He forthwith summoned the elders of Judah and Jerusalem, and having made a great assembly in the temple,[1] read aloud to them "the words of *the book of the covenant* which was found in the house of Jehovah." After this, he himself took a public oath of allegiance to Jehovah, to abide by the covenant of the book; and was followed herein by all who were present. Then the vessels made to Baal, Astarte, and the host of heaven, and the image of Astarte herself, were brought forth out of the temple and destroyed. The houses of the impure votaries of Astarte at the side of the temple were pulled down. The horses dedicated to the Sun, which were set up at the entrance of the temple, with the chariots of the sun, met a like fate; so too did the idolatrous altars, especially those erected by Manasseh in the two courts of the temple. The high places before Jerusalem, which Solomon had built for Astarte, Chemosh, and Molech (mere ruins probably), were defiled by approved ceremonies; as also was Tophet, in the valley of Beni-Hinnom, so as to spoil the virtue of sacrificing a child to Molech. Everywhere he sent round to overthrow altars, images, and sanctuaries of every kind, whether

[1] The temple itself would not hold a very large congregation; but the court of the temple may be intended.

nominally dedicated to Jehovah's worship, or avowedly to a foreign god. The groves were cut down, and men's bones strewed upon their site. After this, of course the priests were removed who worshipped Jehovah idolatrously at the high places; for *idolatry* was now understood to attach to the use of images, even though Jehovah was the object: much more were the votaries of foreign religion put down. But the zeal of Josiah or his ministers reached beyond the limits of Judæa; he overthrew the altar and high place at Bethel and polluted them, as also the buildings attached to the high places in the cities of Samaria. Here also was his only recorded cruelty committed: he slew the Samaritan priests upon their own altars, and burned men's bones upon them: which is the more remarkable, as nothing of the kind is implied against the perpetrators of at least equal superstitions in Judæa. Of course every kind of enchantment and necromancy, together with idolatry in every shape, was forbidden; and after such cleansing of the land, preparation was made for a general keeping of the Passover. The statement concerning this which we read in the book of Kings by implication admits that this festival had never before been rightly[1] performed, as far back as history or tradition could reach:—" Surely there was not holden such a Passover *from the days of the judges that judged Israel, nor in all the days of the kings of Israel nor of the kings of Judah.*"[2]

The very remarkable narrative, of which an abstract has been just presented, affords material for much rumination, and is indeed of extreme importance. A majority of modern reasoners are accustomed to ignore it, and speak as if our Pentateuch had been in the hands of a reading public from time immemorial, without any chasm between Samuel and Ezra. Others choose to assume that Manasseh had persecuted this sacred book, and that through his

---

[1] By *rightly*, I of course mean "according to that which the later Levites regarded as right." One of my critics has taken strange offence at the word, though his Chronicler speaks far more decidedly concerning old neglects, 2 Chron. xxix. 6, 7, 34; xxx. 3, 17, 18. The zeal with which the Chronicler recounts the killing, flaying, dabbling in blood and fat, roasting, seething in pans, caldrons, pots, etc., under Josiah, is quite worthy of old Homer:—2 Chron. xxxv. 9—14.

[2] 2 Kings xxiii. 22.

violence it had disappeared; but that under Hezekiah it had been as familiarly known as in later times. But this assumption is untenable in fact, and wants internal coherence. We cannot imagine that Manasseh had been guilty of so grave an offence, when it has not been charged upon him; an offence, which is of so new and peculiar a kind, that it must have drawn emphatic notice. But again, granting that he did so act, it is certain that he must have failed, if the book had been for so many centuries the law of the nation. Numerous copies of it must have been in the priests' hands. It must have been well known to the Egyptian colonies of Jews, to say nothing of the Israelites in Assyria, whom Manasseh's power could not reach; and immediately on Josiah's accession, the book would have re-appeared in Judæa. Nor is this all; for it is evident in the narrative, not only that it was out of sight but that no one had missed it. No nation, while unconquered, ever yet lost the sacred books of its religion,[1] and forgot their existence: much less is that possible, if the same books contain the practical code of civil and criminal law. To allege a discovery is to confess an invention. Moreover, the persevering and gross neglect of the plainest precepts of our modern Pentateuch, not merely by the less religious, but by the most applauded kings, is another mark that they knew no more of it, than young Josiah till the eighteenth year of his reign. The continuance of the high places, which drew after it the breach of so many other precepts of the law, is an eminent instance; but we may add, so is the neglect of the sabbatical year. According to Jeremiah's computation,[2] for four hundred and ninety years this institution had been violated; which is a confession that it had never been observed during the whole period of the monarchy. It is true that this may have been a mere theory, directed to verify a text of Leviticus;[3] but the theory could not have been held at all, unless the neglect had been notoriously inveterate.

There is a passage in the book of Deuteronomy, here very applicable. Every king is commanded, upon his first

[1] One of my reviewers refers me to the Lutheran resurrection of the Bible as a parallel case; as if the Bible had been *lost* before Luther; or as if the Bible contained the civil law! To have recourse to such an argument simply indicates a desperate cause.
[2] 2 Chron. xxxvi. 21.   [3] Chap. xxvi. 34.

accession to the throne, to write out for himself a copy of the law from that which is kept by "the priests the Levites." Now it is evident, that if this had been done by those who are called the pious kings,—by Hezekiah, Jotham, Uzziah, Amaziah; by the priest Jehoiada, by Jehoshaphat, Asa, Solomon, David;—by so moderate intervals do they follow, that the book could never have been lost, much less forgotten : and if a king neglected this duty, were there not prophets bold enough to remonstrate ? The solution is simple and clear; the command was unknown alike to prophet, priest, and king.

But this leads us to mention some special grounds against the antiquity of this last book of the Pentateuch. In it, Moses foresees the contingency of his people's desiring a king, and does not condemn or reprove it, but seeks to regulate it :—" When thou art come into the land which Jehovah giveth thee, and shalt say, I will set a king over me, *like as all the nations that are about me*"— (the very words imputed to them in the history)[1]—"thou shalt in any wise set him king over thee, whom Jehovah shall choose : "[2] that is, they were to allow the priests or prophets to elect the king, and all would be right. Now it is morally certain, that the prophet Samuel had never seen this law ; and that, if our narrative is correct, Jehovah never dictated it: for when the case occurred, Jehovah said to Samuel, "the people *have rejected me, that I should not reign over them.*"[3] In the same words this prophet addressed the people, "Ye have this day rejected your God."[4] But how so ? in doing that which he distinctly permits them to do ? which he foresees without expressing displeasure ? which in fine he orders to be done under the superintendence of his ministers ?

The remark has already been made, that the prophets of Israel, who stimulated to the massacre of innocent royal children for the fault of their parents, were ignorant of that humane precept in Deuteronomy, "The children shall not die for the fathers, but every man shall die for his own sin."[5]

One out of many indications that Deuteronomy is more recent than the other books is seen in contrasting the

[1] 1 Sam. viii. 5.   [2] Deut. xvii. 14, 15.
[3] 1 Sam. viii. 7.   [4] 1 Sam. x. 19.   [5] Deut. xxiv. 16.

mention of Levi in what is called Jacob's blessing and in that of Moses.[1] Jacob in fact does not bless, but curse, and involves Levi in a common lot with Simeon.

> Simeon and Levi are brethren:
> Instruments of cruelty are in their habitations.
> O my soul, come not thou into their secret:
> *Unto their assembly,* my heart, *be not thou united:*
> For in their anger they slew a man,
> And in their self-will they digged down a wall.
> Cursed be their anger, for it was fierce;
> And their wrath, for it was cruel;
> I will divide them in Jacob,
> And I will scatter them in Israel.

But what says Deuteronomy ? *Simeon is not mentioned at all;* but,

> Of LEVI he said:
> Thy Thummim and thy Urim are with thy Holy one,
> Whom thou didst prove at Massah,
> With whom thou didst strive at Meribah:
> Who sayeth of his father and mother, I saw him not;
> Nor acknowledgeth his brethren, nor knoweth his children.
> For they observed thy word, and kept thy covenant.
> *They shall teach Jacob thy judgments,*
> *And Israel thy Law.*
> *They shall put incense before thee,*
> *And whole burnt sacrifice upon thy altar.*[2]
> Bless, O Jehovah, his might;
> Accept the work of his hands;
> Smite through the loins of his adversaries,
> And of his haters, that they rise not again.

This diversity cannot have proceeded from the Divine Spirit. Both prophecies treat of the tribe of Levi, not of Levi personally, and declare the fortunes of that tribe in the land of Israel. The purpose of God was the same, and his foresight as clear, when Jacob was on his deathbed, as when Moses was about to ascend Pisgah. It remains that the former song was composed when Levi was merely scattered in Israel, without any of the dignity derived from organized priesthood; and the latter after

[1] Gen. xlix. 5—7; Deut. xxxiii. 8.
[2] In the whole book of Deuteronomy there is not a line whereby it could be learnt that a Levite was not equal to an Aaronite, for all purposes of sacrifice, etc. To the same effect is the omission of the name of Korah the Levite (whose sin consisted in pretending equality to the race of Aaron), Deut. xi. 6. Many phenomena suggest the hypothesis, that the religious revolution of which the external mark was the suppression of the local sanctuaries, was really the triumph of the Levitical over the older Aaronite party.

the last remains of the tribe of Simeon had vanished in the days of Hezekiah.

Deuteronomy, though more Levitical than the preceding books, has also a higher spirituality, and implies a more advanced stage of religious thought. Its very excellencies are cumulative evidence, that it is not from the same pen as Exodus and Numbers. Numerous other discrepancies and contrasts in detail might be pointed out, but that belongs to a special treatise. Many of them are explained away by those who have a hypothesis to maintain; but if Moses had been no more to us than Mohammed, no well-informed mind would now doubt the diverse origin of the book of Deuteronomy. Even the English reader will notice the long roll of its sentences, and the same rhetorical fulness as characterizes Jeremiah and Ezekiel, having something of the fluency of the former and of the formality of the latter. It has peculiar collections of words, noticeable even in a translation, such as "the land which Jehovah thy God giveth thee," "the priests the Levites;"—and according to the testimony of the best Hebraists,[1] its whole colour and composition fixes its origin to the reign of Josiah.

No Hebrew lore is needed to show us the absurdity of supposing that Moses wrote the account of his own death and burial, and the closing summary, that "there arose not a prophet since in Israel like unto Moses." It is impossible to say, that a book which contains such a passage, *professes* to be from the pen of Moses, or that the man who wrote the book "is an impostor, unless he was Moses himself." To cut off this chapter arbitrarily, and then pretend certainly that *the rest* is from Moses, is simple wilfulness. There is no appreciable diversity in style,

---

[1] There are respectable Hebrew scholars (not first-rate) who entirely deny the fact. We need not impute it to any deficient sensibility in their acquaintance with the language; for there are perverse modes of putting the argument, by which an Englishman may maintain that Hume's History *might* have been written by Lord Clarendon, or Macaulay's Essays by Addison. The question however is not whether such things are possible, but whether the evidence of the style does not make it improbable.

In fact, the discrepancy is so great even in the English, that on hearing a passage of the Pentateuch read aloud, one can almost always discern, by the form of the sentences and marked phraseology, whether it comes from Deuteronomy or not; while there is no such diversity between the other books.

THE PENTATEUCH A GRADUAL GROWTH. 313

and no difference in the channels of transmission, between the first chapter of the book and the last: and if the last cannot be admitted as Mosaic, we must assume the whole to be of later origin, until the contrary is strictly proved. Nevertheless, it concerns us little to be able to ascertain minutely the time and mode of composition, or to answer all possible objections; plainly, because a thousand things in the history of the past can never be explained, when no historical account has come down to us. That the book of Deuteronomy was composed in the reign of Josiah, can perhaps be no more proved positively, than in what century the Iliad was written. We must be contented with probabilities, or, if they fail, with total ignorance.

Nevertheless, it seems impossible to adopt the theory that Deuteronomy, as opposed to the other books, *alone* came to light by Hilkiah's finding. There is nothing so peculiar in it to harrow up the king's mind, which can account for the facts recorded. Its twenty-eighth chapter indeed is by some referred to; but this says little which is not already contained in the twenty-sixth chapter of Leviticus: and although the whole tone of Deuteronomy, as regards the Levites, distinguishes it from the former books, yet there are no duties towards the Levites in it so new, that Josiah can have thought he was fulfilling the law, as read in Exodus, Leviticus, and Numbers, and then have found himself condemned by Deuteronomy. In fact, the course of conduct to which he is primarily impelled is the extirpation of foreign idolatry; against which the earlier books are equally decided and severe as the last. It seems indisputable, that if Josiah upheld the rites of Baal and Molech, and left a graven image of Astarte in Jehovah's house, and while acquainted with Exodus, repented not; neither would he have repented, when Deuteronomy rose from the dead.

The four first books of the Pentateuch are to be regarded as a growth, not as a composition. Exodus, Leviticus, and Numbers did not now begin to exist, but now received their final shape, and their public recognition in that shape. That general agreement as to their history is not yet attained, is no ground for doubting the broad fact, visible on very cursory examination, that they, with Genesis, are piecemeal works, made up out of pre-existing fragments, many of which are duplicate[1] accounts of similar events or laws, and often mutually inconsistent. Indeed, commentators most zealous for the Mosaic origin and divine authority of the Pentateuch, freely confess that it has received many smaller alterations and additions in later times, which they generally assume Ezra to have made by divine injunction.

Finally, the high pretensions made for the Pentateuch are disproved by a topic which cannot be plainly stated without extreme offence, yet which it would be cowardice on that account to suppress. Its prophecies indicate a marked acquaintance with events which preceded Josiah, but nothing at all clear which needs to be referred to later times. The book is familiar with the tribes of Israel and their distribution; with the qualities which characterized Judah and Ephraim, Reuben or Zebulon. It knows well the extent of David and Solomon's empire; the conquest of Edom and its final liberation; the fortunes of the Ishmaelites, and the desert over which they roved. It knows even the numerous wives of Solomon, his wealth, and his importing of horses from Egypt. It foresees the horrible fact of a woman devouring her child in a siege,[2] as in that of Samaria by Benhadad; also the scattering of Israel by piracy and by invasion into many distant lands. It predicts not only the vanishing of Amalek from among the names of nations, but the wide-

---

[1] The duplicates are sometimes so clear that no unbiassed mind can help seeing them, as in the story of a wife passed off as a sister, twice by Abraham and once by Isaac. So of the duplicate account of the Creation and of the origin of circumcision; of the name Isaac; of the names Israel, Bethel, and Beersheba; and of the revelation of Jehovah's name. Less observed are, the twofold miracle of the quails (the latter implying ignorance of the former); the double description of the manna; the double appointment or appearance of elders of the congregation; water twice brought out of the rock, with a twofold bestowal of the name Meribah; the duplicate narrative of Aaron's death (Deuteronomy making him die before he reaches Meribah Kadesh); the twofold account of the hostilities of Amalek and the curse upon him; the double promise of a Guardian Angel; double consecration of Aaron and his sons; double (or threefold?) copy of the Decalogue; and others that need not here be stated. If some of these may have been real repetitions, no one will ever make it probable that that can have been the case with more than a few. Several of the duplicates are contrasted by the names Jehovah and Elohim.

[2] Whether this, reported as fact in 2 Kings vi. 26—29, be history or legend, is in this connexion unimportant. It suffices that it was believed in Josiah's day.

spread power of *Assyria*, which shall carry the Kenites into captivity. Nay, it is acquainted with the Cyprian force which attacked Esarhaddon from the Cilician coast, and perhaps also declares the final ruin of Assyria.[1] But the *Chaldees* are not named as a conquering nation ; nor had they yet become formidable to Judæa when the book at length came out. Knowledge thus limited to the æra which preceded its publication,[2] cannot be imputed to a divine prescience, nor yet to accident.

Whether there was, or was not, imposture in these transactions, is a question, on which there are, and will be, differences of opinion, even among those who are alike convinced that the Pentateuch in its modern form is later than Hezekiah. It is far from my intention to impute deliberate and conscious fraud to the composers of any of these books. Such an imputation appears to me every way gratuitous, and involving new and needless difficulties. Enthusiasm, inaccuracy, and a belief in dreams, appear amply to account for the growth of the narratives, which incorporated with themselves the conceptions and belief of the day, or of the school. At the same time, I confess, I cannot myself shake off the belief that here, as in so many[3] other instances, the enthusiasm of many was assisted and heightened by the fraud of a few; and though no one can say *who* were the fraudulent, Hilkiah and Shaphan seem the names most open to the charge.

In regard to this topic, a majority of reasoners start with the very unfounded assumption, that Hilkiah and others must necessarily have been truthful in the highest

[1] Numb. xxiv. 20, 22, 24.
[2] The return of the Jews from Babylon is not announced in any terms which imply prescience of that event. There is nothing but a conditional promise of restoration, *if* they repent, in words applicable to Jews in Assyria or Egypt as much as in Babylon, and as valid in the present day as at any earlier time. The allusions to the captivity or dispersion apply *better* to the earlier one of Assyria and Egypt than to that of Babylon or Rome ; for it says, "there shall ye serve other gods, wood and stone." This we know by Jer. xliv. 8 to have been true of them in Egypt, and it was probably true of them in Assyria, but certainly not in later times, to which most persons refer Deut. xxviii.
[3] A reviewer triumphantly asks me, to tell him of "any nation that was ever revolutionized by the fabrication of a ritual." I suppose he regards the Book of Mormon as a fabrication. It has gained credence under difficulties far greater than Josiah's Pentateuch had to overcome, which introduced no new religion, but only gave new sanctions to an old one.

and noblest sense; in a sense so lofty, that of those Christian bishops and statesmen, whose names are prominent in history, but a small fraction has attained the standard. To choose and devotedly pursue a purely good end, is a high and rare thing in those who stand at the head of nations: to pursue that end by none but purely good means, is a still rarer virtue, even in Christendom, in free England, under the light of publicity, and with the fear of exposure. Of the priests in Josiah's day, the prophet Jeremiah declares: "The prophets prophesy falsely, and *the priests bear rule by their means;*" in fact, his whole prophecy is one long invective against them: yet modern commentators who profess to believe that writer, treat it as absurd, profane, and malevolent, to abide by his word, except as a dead letter. Of Hilkiah's moral worth we know absolutely nothing, much less have we any proof that his veracity was more sensitive than that of a Chrysostom or a Justin Martyr, with whom Sibylline or other "pious frauds," which helped a Christian advocate, certainly met with no reproof.—What is more; neither do we know, what was the total amount of responsibility definitely assumed by Hilkiah, or by any one else; nor, in our total ignorance of the men, is it rational to found any conclusions on personal character. Our sole consideration is with *the book* and *the history.* If the evidence turns against it, then, even did it assume such a shape as to indicate the grossest conscious fraud in Hilkiah, we should merely have to adapt our view of his morality to such a state of the argument. In no case can any support whatever to the genuineness and antiquity of the book be found by declamation about the impossibility of Jewish priests and Levites perpetrating a fraud.

To recapitulate this whole event: the four books could not have been *lost* during Manasseh's reign, if they had in the preceding centuries been the public and avowed national law;—the narrative is not satisfied by supposing Deuteronomy alone to have been then first made authoritative; and the mortification to our prepossessions which that hypothesis brings on is as great as that of the more obvious interpretation. We farther find that Josiah entered into no investigation whether the documents presented to him by Hilkiah were genuine and authentic, but adopted them under a crisis of religious fervour, through the impression which the threats of the book made upon his feelings; that the prophetess Hildah, who was consulted, forbore to moot any question about human authenticity, yet was supposed by her reply to decide all that was requisite to be known. And here is the kernel of the matter. Early Christian Fathers believed the law of Moses to have been destroyed and lost in the Babylonian captivity, yet to have been *re-written* by Ezra under divine inspiration. This did not startle their imagination or embarrass their faith. Just so, with the religious men of Josiah's day the question was, not whether the pen of Moses wrote, but whether the voice of Jehovah guaranteed the book; and the latter point they settled by methods unknown to us, but satisfactory to themselves. Such topics as "genuineness and authenticity" never dawn on the minds of spiritual persons, except where a literature exists which is beyond the cognizance of the national religion. Had not a Vico and a Bentley gone first, a Geddes and Eichhorn and a Gesenius would not have appeared in modern times.

If it be thought that many a shrewd worldly man, when the excitement of the time was past, would have discerned the whole proceeding to be an imposture; it must be remembered that public opposition was unsafe; it would have been ascribed to sympathy with idolaters; and the slaughter of the Samaritan priests was a broad and unmistakeable warning to adversaries. It does not appear that the law was even now *published:* certainly it was not statedly read aloud to the people until the institution of synagogues under Ezra. That the prophets had access to it, is soon manifest in the numerous imitations of its phraseology, as in Jeremiah; but if it had been widely diffused,—if, for instance, it had found its way to Egypt,— it is difficult to think that the story of its being lost under Nebuchadnezzar could have arisen. Even if it had been publicly exposed to the cavils of objectors, we could not now expect any record of their criticism, which is likely to have dealt in sarcasm and vituperation, but to have been destitute of argument, against that which did not pretend to rest on argument. That bold unbelief did exist, and perhaps abound, the prophets assure us.

When this great external reform had taken place, Josiah appeared to be at the height of Jewish glory. His nominal sway extended over Israel and Judah from Dan to Beersheba. It was easy and even natural to ascribe this to his piety, and fondly to imagine that the reign of Solomon was about to return in greater purity. At this time it is highly probable that the beautiful seventy-second Psalm was composed in his honour, which even in ancient times was mistaken for a last prayer of David over Solomon. The Psalmist anticipates that the reign of the king (or of the king's son)[1] shall be extended to Tarshish and to the Isles; that homage shall be paid by the dwellers in the wilderness, and by the kings of Seba and Sheba; that the righteous shall flourish and peace be perpetual. At last he warms into words so high, as appear to transcend all other greatness than that of the Anointed King, of whom so many prophets had spoken. Whether the Psalmist hoped that Josiah, or the son of Josiah, was to be he, cannot distinctly be asserted: meanwhile, to turn from the ideal to the actual, the state of Judæa was by no means so satisfactory; there was in it, to a discerning eye, very much to alarm and little to give solid assurance.

Three successive violent revolutions, under Hezekiah, Manasseh, and Josiah, displacing the local clergy from the whole of Judæa, or constraining them violently into a new religious course, must have produced general effects much the same as the changes of public religion enforced on England by our Tudors and our Stuarts. A fair exterior was kept up by Josiah's measures; but Jeremiah's writings prove that unbelief, indifference, and profligacy were widely spread. Although the later king kept sedulously clear of Jehu's ferocity, the prevalent course of Jewish feeling from this time is not very different from that which we may gather concerning Israel. Internal parties arose, and became peculiarly dangerous when theoretical scepti-

---

[1] It is not clear whether *the king's son* may not be a synonym of *the king*, as legitimate heir to the immediate predecessor. Yet it is quite in human nature to anticipate such things of a child; as Virgil in his fourth Eclogue concerning the yet unborn child of Augustus.

cism concerning the national faith was superadded to the inclination for a luxurious or lascivious heathen ceremonial; and this was aggravated by the "false prophets" who now appear, as direct opponents of the true, in Jerusalem, as under Ahab in Samaria. We are left greatly in the dark as to the very critical question,—how people knew, or thought they knew, the true prophets from the false. We may however reasonably believe that men were stigmatized as *false* prophets only by the test which the book of Deuteronomy[1] furnishes; namely, by *comparing the prediction with the event*, when it arrived. It is clear that the author of that law never contemplated such a thing as prophecy concerning far-distant ages; for it is an appendix to and illustration of the command to slay every false prophet. No reason appears for doubting that the prophets Hananiah, Ahab, Zedekiah, and Shemaiah were as sincere as Jeremiah; but their predictions about deliverance from Babylon (aping those of Isaiah concerning Assyria) turned out false. They were possibly fanatical persons, yet were not the less able to attract devout belief from well-intentioned Jews. Thus did the very religion of Jerusalem fail at length to unite the people, partly because it was widely disbelieved, and partly because the religious body was divided against itself. The national bonds having become loosened, the progress of events was precipitated by foreign politics.

Once more it is requisite for a Jewish historian to touch on the dark and disputed history of the contemporaneous neighbour-kings. The last time we had occasion to mention Egypt, it had fallen into civil commotion, and broke up at length into numerous kingdoms, or the system called the *Dodecarchy* by the Greeks. One of the chief cities during this period was SAIS, in the marshes; and about

[1] Ch. xviii. 20—22. That no external signs of a "true prophet" were attainable or looked for is manifest through the whole book, and is sarcastically alluded to by Shemaiah, when he glances at Jeremiah by the phrase, "every man that is mad and *maketh himself* a prophet," Jer. xxix. 26. According to his doctrine, it was for the high priest to judge concerning true and false prophets.

It is remarkable, that even the verification afforded by the events is in another place of Deuteronomy not allowed to be in itself an adequate test of an inspired prophet. Even "if the sign or wonder come to pass," the prophet is to be stoned who persuades to idolatry, Deut. xiii. 1—5; a generous argument, ill applied to the cause of persecution.

the middle of the century a king named Psammetichus reigned there. His position on the coast threw him into acquaintance with the Greeks, and overcame his Egyptian prejudices. Perceiving the great superiority of the Greek tactics and defensive armour, he took into his service a large mercenary body of Carians and Ionians, and by their aid subdued all his fellow-kings, so uniting all Egypt once more under a single sceptre. Herodotus, our best informant on these events, is nevertheless not trustworthy as to the dates. Yet we may roughly compute the beginning of Psammetichus's reign over all Egypt from B.C. 650, and regard the civil commotions and Dodecarchy to have lasted at least half a century. This Psammetichus is he, who by presents and flattery averted the Scythian inroad. With him begins a line of policy entirely new to Egyptian monarchs, which we can scarcely be wrong in ascribing to Greek influence.[1] Hitherto, Egypt had kept at home as much as possible, avoiding maritime commerce and interference with her neighbours. Henceforth, Greeks are permanently established in Egypt, as merchants, and as the king's body-guard. Tyrians, Greeks, and perhaps other strangers, are allowed to fortify factories on the Nile. The Egyptians become mingled in foreign affairs, and covet the harbours of Philistia and Phœnicia. Psammetichus besieged Ashdod (it is said) for twenty-eight years, and at last captured it: we may probably infer that the nearer cities of Gaza and Ascalon were in his hands. His influence must also have been widely spread over the nations south and east of Judæa, to judge by the projects of his son and successor Necho.

Necho is supposed to have ascended the throne B.C. 616, and must then have already been past middle age. He endeavoured to cut a canal from the Red Sea to the Mediterranean; a measure which could not have occurred to him, unless the nautical commerce of Egypt had now become very great. He built triremes, in Greek fashion, on both seas; and sent down the Red Sea, to sail round Africa, a squadron of Phœnician vessels, which completed

[1] Finding themselves neglected by Psammetichus, a large army of the native Egyptian warrior-caste (240,000 men, according to Herodotus) migrated up the Nile into Nubia. This is likely to have been connected with the king's use of Greek mercenaries.

their circumnavigation in the third year. It is conformable with the enterprizing spirit and power of such a monarch, that he undertook to avenge the cause of Egypt against Assyria,[1] for the injuries of a past century. Nineveh was already fallen as a governing power; and its possessions, whether in Syria or on the Upper Euphrates, seemed to lie open to the first claimant. According to the Chronicler, Necho's march was directed definitely against the town of Carchemish on the Euphrates; but as it seems incredible that this can have been his final object,[2] and impossible for a mere king of Egypt to keep such a conquest, we can scarcely doubt that the fertile and beautiful land of Hollow Syria was his first and great aim.[3] The mention of Carchemish may have arisen from a confused memory of the renowned battle which took place there a few years later. That Necho should seek to possess himself of Syria was natural in itself, and was connected with another scheme of conquest: he coveted Tyre and the Phœnician cities, which his grandson soon after attacked. But by sea it was hard to become superior to them; whereas, if once mistress of Syria, Egypt would soon establish her ascendency over Phœnicia and its harbours. Such at least is the only plausible interpretation which we can give of Necho's unexpected enterprize.

A king of Egypt, designing such a campaign and possessed of a powerful marine, would hardly subject his troops to the wearisome and expensive march through the desert towards Philistia; but would transport them by ship to the most northern port of Syria, at which he could land without asking leave of the Phœnicians. The map at once suggests that he would select the bay of Accho;[4] and this conjecture on the whole agrees best with the ac-

---

[1] The old historian says that Necho was going *to attack the king of Assyria at the river Euphrates*. Unless he uses the phrase *Assyria* vaguely for the Mesopotamian power, as the Greeks say *Medes* improperly for *Persians*, we might infer that a king still reigned in Nineveh. Nor indeed do we distinctly know when Nineveh was taken; but it was probably some years before this. The Chronicler, prudently perhaps, avoids the word Assyria, and says, *the house with which Necho was at war*.

[2] The town *in itself* could not be worth maintaining even to a king of Syria, with the desert intervening.

[3] The same strife was reproduced between the Ptolemies and the Seleucidæ. Hollow Syria was the debated ground.

[4] The modern *Acca*, oftener written *Acre*.

count before us. Josiah, we may presume, received the news that an Egyptian army was landing on the coast of Israel, the destination of which was doubtful: nor is it wonderful that it should have greatly disquieted him. If upon sending to Necho, he even received a true and distinct explanation of his designs (as appears to be implied in our account), this would not reconcile him to the expedition; for what would become of the Jewish power, if Syria and Egypt both fell under the same potentate who was already master of Philistia? what chance too had Josiah of confirming his present uncertain sway over Samaria and Galilee? So much for the undesirableness of Necho's success. As to the Jewish king's ability to stop him, we can ill judge. It is possible that the Egyptian army, destined for a long march, was of picked troops, but not very numerous; and Josiah may have appeared well able to contend with it. The future war which he would thus incur, he might feel was fitly to be trusted to the overruling care of Jehovah, who would surely support a pious king of the line of David in warring for the integrity of David's land. In any case, if the Egyptians established themselves in the north, to have war against them or become subject to them would be the only alternatives proposed; and if war was inevitable, it was better to face the necessity at once, before the Egyptians could use Syria as a sallying post and centre of supply.

Such, it is believed, must have been the motives which drove Josiah to a measure, which by reason of the unfortunate result has been looked on as an infatuation.[1] He marched out with his army, resolved to attack Necho's rear, and hinder his passing through the land of Zebulon, Asher, or Naphthali. The Egyptian warned him off, with the assurance that he had no hostile designs against Jewish interests; but finding this to be in vain, he turned to meet him on the celebrated battle-field of Esdraelon, where Egyptian horse or chariots could act to advantage. Almost before the contest could begin, Josiah received a mortal shot with an arrow, and was carried off the field to

[1] The Chronicler seems to attribute a divine inspiration to Necho: "the words of Necho *from the mouth of God*," etc. (2 Chr. xxxv. 21, 22). See also Esdras i. 29, where Josiah is pretended to have acted against the express warnings of the prophet Jeremiah.

DEATH OF JOSIAH.

Megiddon. His army dispersed, and Necho did not pursue them, but resumed his march northward.

The body of the prince, cut off in the meridian of life at so unfortunate a crisis, when the greatest affairs were impending, was conveyed to Jerusalem, and buried in the sepulchres of his fathers. Universal mourning seized the state, which was now in just consternation at the power of Pharaoh, with the prospect of a young and inexperienced king to oppose him. Jeremiah composed a funeral dirge over Josiah, and a solemn unusual wailing was made, perhaps at Hadad-Rimmon [1] near Megiddon, where he received the fatal shot. Nearly the last of the kings of David's line, he is the first who fell in battle. This was in the year 609 B.C., and in the thirty-ninth year of his age, according to our authorities.

[1] Zech. xii. 11.

CHAPTER X.

CLOSE OF THE HEBREW MONARCHY.

IT is somewhat discouraging, as we step into the period of which our earlier annalist had almost contemporary knowledge, not only to find the narrative become more meagre than ever, but to encounter difficulties of chronology; a fact which tends to shake confidence in all criticism of earlier dates. According to the text of the writers, Josiah was but 14 years older than his son Eliakim, and 16 years younger than his father Amon; while Eliakim at the age of 18 is father to Coniah. Thus Amon would be a father at 16, a grandfather at 30, and a great-grandfather at 48; a result obviously incredible.

The lengths of the reigns at this late epoch are not likely to have been at all doubtful to our compiler, though his text may have been corrupted. We ought not then (without absolute necessity) to seek a remedy by tampering with these. But the ages of princes are easily mistaken. That Josiah was a boy at his accession, and Amon a very young man, need not be questioned; but if Josiah was 11, not 8 years old, and Amon was 26, not 22, such errors need not surprise us. Perhaps then we must here resort to the arbitrary method of so correcting their ages,[1] which does not disturb the received chronology.

Josiah had three sons known to us in the history;

---

[1] We thus obtain the following scheme:—

	Birth in	Accession in	Aged
Manasseh.	709	697	12
Amon.	668	642	†26
Josiah.	651	640	†11
Eliakim.	634	609	25
Coniah.	616	598	·18

The numbers marked † are in the Bible text 22 and 8. If in preference to this change we seek to lower the ages of Eliakim and Coniah, we are stopped by finding Coniah to have a seraglio of wives in his short reign of three months. See Jerem. xxii. 24, 28; xxix. 2; 2 Kings xxiv. 15. This shows that the statement in Chronicles that he was only eight years old is erroneous or corrupt.

The scheme here given makes Amon a father at 17, a grandfather at 34, and

Eliakim, Shallum, and Mattaniah, who were respectively aged 25, 23, and 10 years at his death. To these in the genealogy of the Chronicles we find a son Johanan superadded, as eldest of all;[1] if so, we may suppose him but months or days older than Eliakim, and born by a different mother. Still, the evidence of that text is the less valuable, as it makes Shallum younger than Mattaniah, which is undoubtedly erroneous.

We now return to the history. Upon the violent death of the king, the same formula is used as upon the murder of Amaziah and again of Amon:[2]—*The people of the land took Shallum the son of Josiah, and anointed him and made him king* in his father's stead. It is hence probable, that it had become a constitutional custom in Judah for the sovereign himself, after the manner of David, Rehoboam, and Jehoshaphat, to appoint a successor out of the number of his sons; although this by no means superseded the formality of a constitutional coronation, at least since the revolution under Jehoiada. But when a king had been suddenly cut off without nominating his heir, a popular election was requisite; and on this occasion, unfortunately perhaps, the people did not choose Eliakim or Johanan, the elder sons, but Shallum. This prince on his elevation took Jehoahaz[3] as a new or royal name; a practice which is repeated in the case of every king who follows him, but is mentioned in regard to none of his predecessors.[4] It is known to have been a practice of Persia; and, as used in this stage of history by the Jews, may perhaps be imputed to a growing familiarity with the East.

a great-grandfather at 52. Even this may strain our credulity. The Oriental Jews at present give wives to their sons at a very early age; so do Brahmins in many cases; and the line of David may have done the same. Some might think this not unconnected with the fact of their being so short-lived.

[1] 1 Chron. iii. 15.
[2] 2 Kings xiv. 21; xxi. 24; xxiii. 30.
[3] This appears from comparing Jer. xxii. 11 with 2 Kings xxiii. 31. "Jehoahaz" means, *Jehovah holdeth* or *sustaineth*.
[4] In 2 Chron. xxi. 17, *Ahaziah* is named *Jehoahaz;* but we find no reason to think Jehoahaz to have been the royal and current name. It is rather a transposition of the parts of *Ahaz-Jah*.

It may indeed be thought that Solomon's original name was Jedediah (2 Sam. xii. 25), and Solomon (*peaceful*) the name given him by David on appointing him king; but the plausibility of this is weakened by David's having given the name of *Absalom* (father of peace) to another son.

This election of the younger brother appears to have excited a court-cabal among the partizans of Eliakim, who may be suspected of having opened a communication with Necho, and entreated his interference. It is evident that a powerful party in Jerusalem took that side; for without any farther war which is mentioned, and much more without the labour of besieging and storming Jerusalem, Necho, three months after the death of Josiah, arranged the affairs of Judæa according to his own will. His expedition had manifestly so far at least succeeded, as to put him in possession of the entire country of Hollow Syria. We hear of him as tarrying at Riblah, a town on the northern frontier of that district, which commanded the entrance from Hamath proper, and in fact from Damascus or Mesopotamia. This place lies on the Upper Orontes, and has never before been named in the history. It is credible that Necho was occupied in fortifying it, with a view to secure his valuable and easily-won conquest; for hence he sent to Jerusalem for the young king Jehoahaz. He was brought, apparently without resistance, and there thrown into chains. Necho at once put the elder brother Eliakim on the throne, exacting of him in token of homage the sum of 100 talents of silver and *one* talent of gold. This may appear a small infliction, the least quit-rent or titular acknowledgment that could be expected, when we remember that Sennacherib demanded of Hezekiah 300 talents of silver and 30 of gold, and that Menahem gave 1000 talents of silver to king Pul; yet it was seemingly felt as a heavy burden by the people of Jehoahaz; for the older annalist notes, that the new king "taxed the land to give the money to Pharaoh; he exacted the silver and the gold of every one according to his taxation;" and the other expresses it, that "the king of Egypt *condemned the land* in a hundred talents of silver and one talent of gold." But we are now in the region of sober history; and the enormous figures with which the Chronicler entertained us in the more distant times can have no place here.[1]

Necho, returning to Egypt, carried away Jehoahaz with him as a valuable hostage for the good behaviour of the new king, against whom he could now at any time let

[1] In 1 Chron. xxii. 14, David laid up for Jehovah 1,000,000 talents of silver, and 100,000 talents of gold.

Jehoahaz loose. This was a policy which the Romans afterwards learned to practise; and the book of Jeremiah[1] shows that persons in Jerusalem speculated on the possible return of Jehoahaz through a change of policy in the Egyptian court. Eliakim, having assumed the name of Jehoiakim (or *Jehovah establishes*), commenced his reign inauspiciously enough, as obtaining his place by a sort of treason against the independence of his country. Patriots who remembered Josiah and had read of Hezekiah may well have been disgusted by this: and the Levitical party would regard his submission to a foreigner as a direct violation of a command in the book of Deuteronomy.[2] The only events which can be recovered concerning the opening years of this king, concern his conduct towards the prophets. One who was named Urijah first prophesied against the city and the land. What he said is not distinctly stated; but as it gave offence not only to the king and princes, but to "all the mighty men" or *chief warriors*, we cannot doubt that they regarded his words as calculated to infuse cowardice into the Hebrew army. Urijah escaped into Egypt from the king's anger, but Necho was readily convinced that an example was wholesome, to deter other prophets from weakening his tributary king; so Urijah was given up to Jehoiakim and put to death. Jeremiah at this could not be silent, yet he did not directly attack the king. He however called on all the cities of Judah " to hearken to the words of the prophets," otherwise the house of Jehovah at Jerusalem should be made as desolate as his tabernacle at Shiloh. The *priests and many of the prophets* now turned upon Jeremiah, and recommended putting him to death also; but his spirited replies, and the reverence felt for his character both by the elders and princes, preserved him. Especially Ahikam, son of that Shaphan who introduced the book of the law to Josiah, pleaded in his cause; so that he was only kept in prison.[3]

Nothing besides is known of the three first years of Jehoiakim's reign, during which Necho had been pushing

[1] Ch. xxii. 11, 12.
[2] Deut. xvii. 15. "Thou mayest not set a stranger over thee, who is not thy brother." This text seems to have suggested to the Pharisees the celebrated question, "Is it lawful to pay tribute to Cæsar, or no?"
[3] Jer. xxvi.

eastward, undoubtedly conquering Damascus, perhaps also northern Syria,—and pressing to the border of Euphrates, until his progress was stopped by the Chaldee power. The formidable character of this newly risen and little-known people was perhaps imperfectly apprehended by him until, in the fourth year[1] of Jehoiakim,[2] he suffered a decisive defeat at Carchemish on the Euphrates from Nebuchadnezzar,[3] a young Chaldee prince, who commanded the army of his father Nabopolassar, then fast declining in health.[4] Whatever the amount of Necho's loss in men,[5] the defeat was fatal to his schemes of foreign conquest, for he had no resources to fall back upon: an Egyptian could not recruit his army with Damascenes or other Syrians. His ambition had overreached itself by its too rapid advance; and perhaps even his person might have fallen into the hands of the victor, had not the death of Nabopolassar suddenly recalled the prince to Babylon. Yet as soon as he had secured himself in his father's throne, he resumed the aggressive; with such a rush of unchecked success, that, within the year of the battle at Carchemish, he had swept off every vestige of Egyptian power in Damascus and Hollow Syria, and showed his armies as irresistible on the eastern side of Palestine.

These events, as we have said, took place in Jehoiakim's fourth year,[6] and immediately called forth the prescience of Jeremiah, who was still shut up in prison. In a spirited ode, having much of antique raciness,[7] he triumphs over the fall of Pharaoh, and predicts that Nebuchadnezzar shall overrun and conquer Egypt itself; after which the Israelites who are scattered are to return to their own land. Nor was this all; the prophet further understood that Nebuchadnezzar was to become a universal scourge both to Judæa and to all the nations round about, who

[1] The book of Daniel (so-called) makes out, in its first verse, that Jehoiakim, *in his third year*, suffered a seige from Nebuchadnezzar; whereas Necho was master in those parts until after the battle of Carchemish in Jehoiakim's *fourth year*.
[2] B.C. 605.   [3] Jer. xlvi. 2.   [4] Joseph. c. Apion, i. 19.
[5] Josephus (Antiq. x. 6, 1) says that Necho "lost many tens of thousands of men in the battle;" but it is evident that he had no other means of information than we, and he inferred the greatness of the slaughter from the great results of the victory.
That Necho *fell into the hands of Nebuchadnezzar* (αὐτοῦ τοῦ ἀποστάτου ἐκυρίευσε) is asserted by Berosus in Josephus, but is undoubtedly false.
[6] B.C. 605.   [7] Ch. xlvi.

were to serve him *for seventy years;* and when seventy years were completed, then Jehovah should punish the king of Babylon, and the land of the Chaldæans, and make it perpetual desolations.[1] This is memorable as the beginning of a remarkable series of prophecies against Babylon, which have received a very plausible fulfilment.[2] It will be observed also, that the prophecy of Jewish captivity in Babylon *for seventy years* is but a modification and offshoot of this. Jeremiah moreover began at length to write into a book the prophecies which hitherto had been only uttered by word of mouth, and retained in his memory, for twenty-three years together. Baruch, son of Neriah, officiated as his secretary.[3] When at length the writing was finished, in the fifth year of Jehoiakim,[4] as he was himself still in prison, he sent Baruch to read it publicly in the temple courts on a certain fast-day. News of this was brought to the king's council, who sent for Baruch with his roll, and made him read it to them. Upon hearing it read, they protested that they must lay it before the king; but bade Baruch hide himself and Jeremiah too, and let no man know where they were. It may hence appear that secret orders were given to let Jeremiah escape from custody. When the king had heard a few divisions of the roll, in spite of the remonstrances of several of his princes, he cut it with his penknife and cast it into the fire. The offence which it gave him is clearly explained. It was not that Jeremiah taxed the people or princes for vices, crimes, or idolatries; nor that he threatened them with defeat, *if* they were thus guilty: but that he said, "The king of Babylon *shall certainly* come and destroy this land, and shall cause to cease from thence man and beast."[5] Such prophecies have a tendency to produce

[1] Jer. xxv.
[2] From this date (B.C. 605 or 604) to the capture of Babylon by Cyrus (B.C. 538) is sixty-six or sixty-seven years; yet Chaldæa did not thereupon become "perpetual desolations." Babylon was still a flourishing city under Alexander the Great: and *Chaldæa* collectively can hardly be said ever to have become desolate, except by comparison. Its worst desolation has been in the last three centuries, during the decline of the Turkish empire. It is evident that the connexion in Jeremiah's mind was a moral one: but the delay of the desolation is fatal to this; for it is absurd to represent the emptiness of *modern* Babylon as a punishment for the pride of Nebuchadnezzar. The true prophetical idea is much simpler: *pride and violence dig their own grave;* and that is eternally true. See in the Appendix corroborative facts, adduced by an able writer.
[3] Ch. xxxvi. [4] B.C. 604. [5] Jer. xxxvi. 29.

their own accomplishment, by the panic or languor of heart which they induce in all who believe them : nor did Nebuchadnezzar need any better aid for his schemes of ambition, than that every nation which he attacked should have a hundred Jeremiahs. Undoubtedly no English general, however pious, would, on the eve of an engagement, allow a prophet to announce to his troops, that the enemy would defeat them disgracefully next morning : a general who *should* permit it, and afterwards suffer defeat, would without fail be himself shot by verdict of a court-martial. It is therefore dealing very hardly with Jehoiakim, to condemn him, because he would not allow his people's hearts to be discouraged by Jeremiah, when attack from Babylon was impending : nor had this prophet any right to expect permission so to speak, unless he could give the king some other index to the truth of his prediction than the only one which the Pentateuch furnishes, viz. by waiting for the event. The case is the more marked, as no practical end is made prominent, except it be that of inculcating submission to the king of Babylon ;[1] which it is absurd to treat as a precept of religion. Modern reasoners generally assume that Jehoiakim was to be judged by some technical law, differing from the broad universal rules of morality : hence they join in chorus again the king, for doing that which almost all modern magistrates would regard as their clear duty.

According to the text of Jeremiah—(we know not accurately when this chapter was committed to writing),[2]—the prophet received secret orders from Jehovah to write a new roll like the former, and to add a solemn declaration against Jehoiakim, that, "*because* he had asked, Why hast thou written, saying, The king of Babylon shall cer-

[1] This is the view given by an able writer who certainly aims to be impartial. "In opposition to a strong Egyptian faction, Jeremiah *urged the impracticability of resistance to the Assyrian* [Chaldee ?] *forces already on their march.* But he spoke to deaf and heedless ears."—Milman, Hist. of Jews, vol. i, p. 320.

[2] The total want of chronological arrangement in the book of Jeremiah may warn interpreters of the vanity of assuming chronological order in the earlier prophets. It likewise shows that he *must* have revised all his writings, and *may* have introduced changes, in his latest years. Indeed there is one striking fact; he not only makes no allusion to Josiah's reforms, but there is no change of tone in any part of this volume. We cannot therefore doubt that his memory failed of reproducing accurately the utterances of years long past.

tainly come," etc., *therefore*, Jehoiakim should have none to sit on the throne of David, and his dead body should be cast out unburied. As the first part of this prophecy is not true, unless accepted with modification (for his son Coniah succeeded him for three months, and his brother Mattaniah for eleven years), we should exercise some reserve in receiving the latter part as certain. Undoubtedly, unless we suppose the facts to be erroneously represented by Jeremiah against himself, or God to judge by other laws then and now, we cannot admit the idea, that it was he who sent this message to Jehoiakim. While religious teachers confine themselves to religious topics, the case is wholly different; but when they enter the political arena and (under whatever inward convictions) so conduct themselves as to play into the hands of the public enemy, it is too much to claim for them the inviolable character of sacred persons.

No long time passed before the armies of Nebuchadnezzar appeared in Judæa; nor was any help from Egypt at hand. Necho was a very old man, now declining rapidly; and he had had a severe taste of the Chaldæan arms. Accordingly Jehoiakim had nothing to do but renounce his Egyptian connexion, and accept the terms of homage proffered by Nebuchadnezzar, whose tributary he now became; perhaps in B.C. 603. For three years he remained faithful to his allegiance; but when Necho died,[2] and his son Psammis succeeded him, new plans and hopes arose in the mind of the Jewish king. Whether he had positive promises of succour from Egypt (a power born to disappoint and betray the unfortunate Hebrews) cannot be ascertained: Jehoiakim however revolted from his Chaldee master. It would appear that Nebuchadnezzar was unable at once to come in person and chastise him;

---

[1] This is a totally different question from the general one, whether Jehoiakim was *a wicked man* or not. He may have been as bad as Jerem. xxii. 17 represents him. As he came to the throne by displacing his brother Jehoahaz, it is probable enough that he exercised many severities against his brother's partizans. These (as well as his execution of Urijah) may be the "innocent blood" alluded to. Confiscation of their estates would follow of course: this may be the "covetousness" denounced. Yet it must be remembered, that we have no evidence against this king, better than the vague words of the man whom he pursued as a political offender.

[2] B.C. 600.

but he sent up some bands of Chaldees, with orders to collect a mixed army from the neighbouring nations and prey upon the land of Judæa. These are recounted as Syrians, Moabites, and Ammonites. A harassing warfare resulted, and it has been conjectured that Jehoiakim was slain in some petty action, and that his body could not be found. A mystery however hangs over his disappearance. Both our authorities are clear enough as to the throne becoming vacant[1] in the eleventh year of his reign; but they abstain from alluding to his death. The Chronicler states that Nebuchadnezzar " bound him with fetters to carry him to Babylon," but does not say that he executed this design: indeed he makes him plunder the temple during Jehoiakim's reign, which is undoubtedly erroneous. The chasm in both the writers is so marked, as to excite speculation as to the cause. If the king died in his chamber, disappeared after some battle, or was carried off by the enemy, why did they not state one thing or other? Was it because they were unwilling to contradict the clear predictions of Jeremiah, that Jehoiakim should be cast unburied outside the gates of Jerusalem like a dead ass?[2] They well knew of the prophecy: if it was fulfilled, why did they not name it in the history?—We cannot pretend to decide in this matter. Some may even reverse the view of things; and without conceding foresight to the prophet, whose works were perhaps in his own hands to revise *after* the king's death, will think it unlikely that he exercised such self-denial[3] as to leave in his book a prophecy already falsified by fact. Such reasoners therefore will take the prophecy as an index to the history. But whatever theory is adopted, difficulties remain.

On the death or removal of Jehoiakim,[4] his son Coniah

---

[1] B.C. 598.   [2] Jer. xxii. 19; xxxvi. 30.

[3] This difficulty is not peculiar to the present passage, and may possibly be relieved by the following considerations. There is no doubt that these prophets were devoutly persuaded that the words which they uttered were Jehovah's and not their own: hence when they had once committed them to writing, they would reverence them as profoundly as their successors did; and if ever the words appeared to be falsified by fact, instead of renouncing them as Deuteronomy orders, they would probably seek for mystical interpretations and other such numerous evasions as are familiar to the ingenious theologian. Thus we have in Ezekiel, side by side, a prediction that Nebuchadnezzar shall make a spoil of Tyrus (xxvi. 12, etc.), and a confession that he got no spoil (xxix. 18).

[4] B.C. 598.

became king, and took the appellation of Jeconiah, which is also written Jehoiachin (*Jehovah foundeth*) and Joiachin. His reign lasted but three months; yet of this it is recorded that " he did evil in the sight of Jehovah, *according to all that his father had done;*" words, from which in this connexion we can hardly infer more than that, like his father, he persevered in resisting the king of Babylon, against the dictation of Jeremiah.[1] Nebuchadnezzar had now arrived in person, and the siege of Jerusalem was pressed vigorously. Jeconiah, after he had reigned three months, finding that no help came from Egypt, and that he could not hold out, proposed surrender while he might hope for better terms, and came out voluntarily with his mother and all his chief officers. Nebuchadnezzar desired to spare so wealthy a city, so favourably situated for maintaining the prosperity of the province, and thought to keep it in due homage by retorting the policy of Necho. Jeconiah, after his father, owed his throne to the Egyptians; and Jehoahaz seems yet to have been alive in Egypt, as a security for Jeconiah's allegiance. The new invader therefore set up, as king, Josiah's youngest son Mattaniah: and Jeconiah—who, though only aged eighteen, had a circle of wives—was transferred with them to Babylon, as also his mother and chief princes; partizans, it may be supposed, of the Egyptian alliance. Of course whatever treasure was to be found, in the palace or in the temple, became the spoil of the conqueror: to leave it was to leave a weapon of revolt with the new king. But when it is stated that Nebuchadnezzar "cut in pieces all the vessels of gold which *Solomon* had made," we are merely warned of the narrator's credulity.[2] In the last chapter of history appended to the book of Jeremiah, 3023 is assigned as the number of persons carried away on this first occasion.[3] In ch. xxix. 1, 2, this prophet himself

[1] Only one half-chapter of Jeremiah is inscribed with the date of Jeconiah's short reign: xxii. 20—30. No sin is there named against him, yet severe fortunes are pronounced in a tone of exasperation. The closing prediction, that *he should be childless*, did not prove true; but perhaps the meaning, in that context, is only that his children shall not succeed him on the throne.

[2] He even makes it the fulfilment of prophecy: "as Jehovah had said"! Compare 2 Kings xiv. 14.

[3] The writer carefully enumerates the total number carried away by Nebuchadnezzar: in his seventh year 3023; in his eighteenth year 832; in his twenty-third year 745; in all (he adds) 4600. This distinctly shows that there

enumerates among the captives, besides the court and
other more eminent persons, *the carpenters and the smiths,*
who are also named by the annalist. The latter writer
roughly estimates the entire number now carried away at
10,000, or 18,000 according to one interpretation, and
says that the choicest part of the army was contained
among them. It may at first sight appear that the carpenters and smiths could not have been wanted, and that
the sole motive of the removal was, to weaken the new
king or viceroy in Jerusalem. But Nebuchadnezzar was
now employed in immensely enlarging the seat of empire.
The new Babylon was a vast oblong area enclosing the
old town as its citadel, and was divided by uniform streets
parallel to the gigantic walls. The general scheme of the
city is that of a camp. A regular plan is formed by a
single mind, and its outline is executed at once, but on a
scale so enormous, that the parts are perhaps never filled
up. This is what happens when a conquering monarch
determines to have a large capital. His first work is to
make the walls and main streets; to people it is a more
gradual affair. Meanwhile, it encloses large tracts of field
and orchard, assimilating it to a fortified parish, and giving to it resources of food, beyond what mere cities can
have. Such considerations alone can explain to us the
prodigious extent ascribed to the walls of Babylon: in any
case, the magnitude of the works was such, that Nebuchadnezzar might well have peculiar need of "craftsmen
and smiths," as well as of soldiers. The princes, chief
priests, and elders, who are said to be carried away, were
of course regarded as dangerous persons if left in Judæa.
Among the more eminent captives was perhaps an elder
named Daniel, concerning whom a celebrated but unhistorical book has been written; and a young priest, Ezekiel,
son of Buzi, whose authentic and ample prophecy is extant. That Daniel was proverbial among his own people
for goodness and wisdom, is manifest in the writings of

were but three captivities; and that that pretended by the book of Daniel (i. 1)
in the third year of Jehoiakim is a fiction. Yet the exactness of figures does
not add credibility to the writer. Such accuracy is unattainable; and in fact,
the largest number 18,000 seems more probable than 3023.
    It will be observed also that he places the first captivity in Nebuchadnezzar's
seventh year. This appears more accurate than 2 Kings xxiv. 12, which
names it his eighth year.

REBELLION OF ZEDEKIAH.

Ezekiel; if indeed some earlier Daniel is not intended. No farther devastations were committed, and Mattaniah was left on the throne as a weakened and tributary prince.[1] He was only twenty-one years old, and took as his royal name Zedekiah.

For eleven years longer the national existence of Judah was preserved; but scarcely a single fact remains to the historian. According to a rather dark allusion,[2] it appears that in the fourth year of his reign, Zedekiah paid a visit in person to Babylon, in company with one of his princes named Seraiah; but neither the object nor the result of the visit is stated. In the whole course of this time, Zedekiah was distracted by the equally confident assertions of different prophets, predicting contrary things. In his fourth year, for instance,[3] the prophet Hananiah uttered an oracle: "Thus speaketh Jehovah: I have broken the yoke of the king of Babylon. Within two full years I will bring again to this place all the vessels of Jehovah's house, and Jeconiah king of Judah and all the captives of Judah." Jeremiah however contradicted him, and denounced him publicly. Such altercations must have been common, to judge by the frequent complaint of "false prophets."[4] From the nature of the case we can hardly doubt the statement of the Chronicler, that Zedekiah had made solemn oath to Nebuchadnezzar to remain in honourable allegiance to him; which would have been the right moral ground for urging Zedekiah to submit. But the topic is nowhere to be found in the ample writings of Jeremiah; nor is breach of faith ever charged by him on Zedekiah in his most pointed addresses. This prophet seems to be rather soft-hearted than tender; he melts at the prospect of suffering, and desires his people to avoid it by the shortest and safest method,—that of submitting as quickly as possible: nor does any other argument for such a proceeding ever appear in him, except the *danger* of an opposite course.

---

[1] B.C. 598.   [2] Jer. li. 59.   [3] Jer. xxviii. 1.
[4] It must not be assumed that these "false prophets" were not fully equal in moral worth to Jeremiah, and as sincerely convinced that Jehovah spoke by them, as he was in his own case. When of two contending parties one, and only one, must prove correct in the result, to brand as wicked impostors those who turn out false is highly unjust.

It is hard to call this patriotic, any more than high-minded.

The unlucky Zedekiah thought his favourable moment to be arrived, under the new king of Egypt. Psammis, son of Necho, had died after a short reign of six years, and was succeeded by his son Hophra, called by the Greeks Apries;[1] an enterprizing prince, and until his last years successful. He marched an army into Phœnicia, and fought a naval battle against the Tyrians, facts which sufficiently indicate his struggle for the whole sea-coast of Syria; and from him the king of Jerusalem might hope for aid. Zedekiah, after a secret compact with him, did at last revolt, perhaps in his ninth year;[2] and the contest that followed was slightly diversified by the Egyptians proving faithful for once. Towards the end of his ninth year,[3] Nebuchadnezzar with a formidable army appeared before Jerusalem, and built forts outside it to harass the country and repel sallies; but before he could reduce the city, an Egyptian army marched out against him, and he was forced to abandon the siege.[4] In the interval, fresh supplies were no doubt introduced; for although in the year after,[5] Nebuchadnezzar, having repulsed Hophra, was enabled to resume the attack, a tedious resistance was still made.

Within the city during this whole war, Nebuchadnezzar received faithful aid from at least one man, who believed himself the heaven-appointed instrument of weakening his own people's hearts and hands. In part, undoubtedly, the king himself was to blame for this, who displayed an irresolution common under circumstances so difficult. Having a secret belief that Jeremiah could foretell the future, he acted towards him as the heathens towards their oracles or diviners. He sent an officer to inquire of the prophet what would be the event of the war,[6] and got from him a reply which might have been foreknown. The princes were angry with Jeremiah, when they should rather have blamed the king's indiscretion; and as Jeremiah[7] had vehemently commanded all who desired safety to go over to the Chaldæans, they accused him of being

---

[1] B.C. 594.
[2] B.C. 590.
[3] Jer. xxxix. 1; Ezek. xxiv. 1.
[4] Jer. xxxvii. 5—11.
[5] Jer. xxxii. 1.
[6] Jer. xxi.
[7] Jer. xxxvii.

about to desert, when he left the city during an interval of the siege. On this charge he was thrown into prison, but was liberated by the king's interference. Yet after this again, the princes, complaining that he damped the courage of the soldiers, induced the king to consent to his imprisonment.[1] His dungeon was this time as barbarous as in ancient times such places were wont to be: but Zedekiah once more relented, and even sought a private conference with him; after which he had him removed to a milder custody. A king who showed such weakness was not likely to be able to inspire active courage into his people, whose hopes had wasted away under the constant trickling of these chilly predictions. Yet the city walls defied the besieger. He could not succeed, by any methods of attack available to him, in making a breach; but by the closeness of his blockade, he at last brought on the extreme sufferings of famine.

At the moment when the distress became unbearable (it is recorded as the *ninth* day of the *fourth* month of Zedekiah's *eleventh* year),[2] the Chaldee king was at Riblah in the land of Hamath, whither Jehoahaz had been brought to Necho. By a singular coincidence, Zedekiah also, having been caught in the attempt to escape out of Jerusalem, was led to the same place before Nebuchadnezzar. No mercy was now to be expected. His two sons were first slain in his sight; after which his eyes were put out, he was loaded with fetters, and sent to Babylon. The chief nobles of Judah were also slain. The king's palace in Jerusalem, the temple, and all the well-built houses were burned down in the following month; and the walls were laboriously demolished. Whatever of brass and copper or silver vessels remained in the temple were seized as spoil, but destruction was more thought of than booty. The common people were planted over the country, having land assigned them for vineyards or tillage. Nebuzaradan, the captain of the guard, to whom the execution of all this work had been entrusted, seems to have aimed to turn Jerusalem into a desart; for many chief men and sixty common people were sent by him to Riblah, for no other offence that is named but that of being "found in the city;" all of whom were slaughtered

[1] Jer. xxxvii. 4. [2] Jer. xxxix.

by the enraged conqueror. The numbers carried to Babylon on this occasion are reckoned in the book of Jeremiah[1] as only 832 persons; which must be immensely under the truth. No other estimate however is at hand.[2]

In the retrospect of these affairs, it is impossible to overlook the tendency of men to judge of actions by their event, without asking whether the event could have been foreseen. The resistance of Hezekiah to the Assyrians is admired; that of Jehoiakim to the Chaldees is condemned; although it was called for not only by general principles of patriotism, but by his special obligations to the Egyptians, at least in the opening of his reign. An unsuccessful king, whether an Ahaz or a Zedekiah, meets with little sympathy. Over the fall even of a Josiah men moralize and wonder; as if to suffer and to perish were not often the peculiar part of goodness and of heroism. Yet perhaps there were few materials for heroism now left in Jerusalem. It was a people divided against itself, and threatened by a superior adversary; in which case nothing is harder than to know whether to advise submission or resistance. The brave and the hopeful will maintain that by spirited counsels the nation may be roused and united: the cautious, the feeble, and the desponding will treat such a course as madness. How far the weakness of Judah was now caused by this division of opinion, is not distinctly recorded; and perhaps even the contemporaries did not know. But the general facts justify the assertion, that *if* Jeremiah had felt the national independence of Jerusalem to be as dear as Isaiah felt it; *if* he had taught that life was not worth preserving, at the expense of enslaving the people of Jehovah to the heathen; *if*, in short, those who with him abetted Babylon had bravely opposed it,—the fate of Jerusalem would have been at worst not more painful, and certainly more glorious.

If we judge of Jeremiah's position by the common laws of prudence and morality, we shall find that there were two ways of promoting his country's welfare: one, by trying to persuade the princes and the king to yield at once to Babylon; the other, by inciting the people to

---
[1] Ch. lii. 29.   [2] B.C. 588.

resist manfully, when the rulers obstinately chose that course. The third method, which Jeremiah followed, of urging individuals to flee for their lives, because defeat was certain, was not the part of prudence and patriotism, but was the highest imprudence. It was the most obvious way of distracting the nation, paralyzing its rulers, and ensuring the public ruin. It is requisite to insist on this, because writers who do not venture to say that Jeremiah was freed from the observance of common obligations, are fond of extolling him as a model of patriotism and of practical wisdom.

Nebuzaradan appears rightly to have understood the service which Jeremiah had rendered to his master's cause. Finding him at Ramah among the prisoners who were chained for transportation to Babylon, he set him free, and offered to look after his interests if he chose voluntarily to accompany the rest. Understanding that he preferred to stay behind, he requested him to go and dwell under the protection of Gedaliah, whom Nebuchadnezzar had made governor of Judæa; and so sent him away "with victuals and a reward."[1] It deserves attention that Gedaliah was son of that Ahikam who was Jeremiah's especial patron among the princes. Observing that so many of the princes were slain in cold blood at Riblah, it is impossible to doubt that Gedaliah, who was thus favoured, was regarded by the conquerors as their own friend, and must have been, with his father, the nucleus of the Babylonian faction in Jerusalem, with whom Jeremiah had so zealously been co-operating. Gedaliah now had his reward, in becoming the Babylonian satrap of Judæa; and exerted himself successfully to gather back the Jews from Edom, Ammon, and Moab, into which countries great numbers had fled. Nebuzaradan had also been so complaisant as to give up to him Zedekiah's daughters, whom Gedaliah now kept in his fortress at Mizpah. As their father was only thirty-two years old, they were no doubt very young; it is probable that Gedaliah intended ere long to make one of them his wife, and thus establish for his descendants a hereditary claim on Jewish allegiance.[2] He had also a Chaldee guard, besides the other army allowed him. But his

[1] Jer. xl. 1—6.   [2] Jer. xli. 10.

course was cut short by violence. The princes of Judah who had escaped the sword of the Chaldees regarded him as a perfidious traitor, and grudged him life and prosperity earned by courting the Babylonians. Among these was one of the line of David, by name Ishmael; perhaps a descendant of Amon; but his precise relationship is unknown. He, with ten others, had taken refuge among the Ammonites, and now came to Mizpah in the guise of friendship. Hardened to deeds of blood, and regarding Gedaliah to have set the example of treachery, they mercilessly murdered, not him only and the Chaldees whom they found about him, but all his Jewish associates, and (it is added) seventy out of eighty men who came up from Shechem, Shiloh, and Samaria with offerings and incense to the house of Jehovah.[1] But one of Gedaliah's chief officers, Johanan son of Kareah, easily resisted these princes, who had no disciplined forces or attached dependants, and forced them to escape again to the Ammonites. After this, in spite of Jeremiah's remonstrances, Johanan and his captains, dreading the vengeance of the Chaldæans for the death of Gedaliah, took Zedekiah's daughters, and all persons whom Nebuzaradan had left under Gedaliah's care, including Jeremiah himself with the Jewish population who had been re-assembled, and removed them to Egypt as the only place of safety.

This proceeding exceedingly kindled the prophet, who had already predicted that Nebuchadnezzar should ravage that country. Besides his hatred of its idolatries, he regarded the step as a fleeing into fresh dangers. Accordingly, while at Tahpanhes in Egypt, he uttered a new oracle, distinctly announcing[2] that Nebuchadnezzar should set up his throne there, should smite the land, burn the temples, and carry gods and people into captivity. It is clear that this expectation was taking a fixed hold of the prophetical school of that day. In the preceding year, just after Nebuchadnezzar had repulsed the army of Hophra which came to relieve Zedekiah, Ezekiel on the

[1] This happened after Nebuzaradan was departed: yet according to 2 Kings xxv. 9, he had already destroyed the temple; nor is it at all likely that he left it standing. It therefore seems as if this particular were invented to increase the odium against the assassins.
[2] Jer. xliii. 10—13.

river Chebar was stimulated to predict that Egypt should be made desolate " from Migdol to Syene and to the border of Ethiopia,"[1] and that her people should be scattered for *forty years;* after which period the Egyptians were to be gathered together again and brought back into their own land.[2] In this year also, Ezekiel resumed the strain,[3] and plainly declared that *Babylon* should conquer Egypt. The dirge was repeated the year after.[4] When sixteen years more had passed,[5] the same prophet enlarged still further on this destructive invasion from which no part of Egypt or Ethiopia was to be exempted. Nebuchadnezzar was to take the spoil of the land as a recompense for his fruitless campaign against Tyre, and there was to be no more a prince of the land of Egypt.[6] But happily, the grasp of the Chaldæan was more limited than human imagination. We have the contemporary history of Egypt from the pen of Herodotus, containing not the most distant allusion to a conquest of the country by the Babylonians. At that time a numerous Greek colony had been established there for the best part of a century, and commerce with the Greeks was very active. Merchants who knew nothing of the foreign politics of the Egyptians would have known too well, if Egypt had been desolated from end to end by a Chaldæan host, and if the king of Babylon had dealt as rudely with the temples and the gods, as Cambyses did

[1] Syene is the southern limit of Egypt; Migdol must be in the north (Jer. xlvi. 14). Hence this describes all Egypt, and Nubia beyond Egypt.

A most treacherous mode of corrupting truth is unsuspiciously used by many honest men,—that of making *history* out of *prophecy.* This is quietly done, for example, by a recent very learned writer (article *Nebuchadnezzar,* Kitto's Biblical Cyclopædia, p. 406; where Nebuchadnezzar's conquest of Tyre and Egypt is told in a historical tone, with reference to Ezekiel as sufficient proof. In proportion as we may have reason to suspect that historians have so acted, it becomes impossible to verify predictions. This is what Josephus seems to have done, Antiq. x. 9, 6.

Grote, vol. iii. p. 439, regards it as certain that Nebuchadnezzar did not conquer Egypt, nor lay Tyre desolate; but he infers that Tyre must have *capitulated* to him, because we hear of Tyrian princes captive in Babylonia. But this proves nothing. The Cæsars also kept Armenian and Parthian princes at Rome, and by them operated upon the politics of those nations; but that did not imply any capitulation or loss of independence, even though they sometimes descended to *ask for a king.*

[2] Jer. xxix. 1—16. [3] Ezek. xxx. 30—26; xxxi. [4] Ezek. xxxii.
[5] B.C. 572. [6] Ezek. xxix. 17—21; xxx. 1—19.

fifty years later. Had therefore the announcements of Jeremiah and Ezekiel proved true, we should inevitably have learned of it from Herodotus.[1]

Five years after the destruction of the walls of Jerusalem, when the Chaldee forces were again in that neighbourhood,—whether in connexion with the war against Tyre, which was besieged to no purpose for thirteen years,[2] or in the course of hostilities with Egypt,—Nebuzaradan made a third and final deportation of Jewish people to Babylon.[3] The land had been left without any fixed government, and was probably too desolate to repay the expense of a resident satrap; but no particulars are preserved concerning the objects of this last removal. By these events the cities of Samaria were left in a comparative prosperity, overlooking ruined Jerusalem: a large part of their population was Israelitish: they had received the Pentateuch from Josiah; and in spite of the mixture of idolaters and of pagan folly, a germ seemed to be there still preserved out of which something good might grow up.

But it was not in Samaria that the Jewish faith was destined to exert its chief energy. The tribes of Israel planted in Assyria and Babylon spread eastward and westward from city to city, like the Armenians in modern Persia, when similarly torn up from their own land. Now it was that they learned those arts of life which they have ever since retained. As the pedlar, the money-changer, the merchant, the money-lender, an Israelite was everywhere known by a peculiar character. To find scope for their employments, they of necessity colonized rapidly, and wherever they settled, a nucleus was formed, upon which the action of the sacerdotal spirit of restored Jerusalem should in after-time be exerted.

The Jews in captivity saw with pleasure before long that the Median empire became stronger and stronger, and that upon the death of Nebuchadnezzar[4] no successor

---

[1] Ezekiel in fact was equally unsuccessful in his prediction concerning Tyre, which he declared that Nebuchadnezzar should take, plunder, and destroy (Ezek. xxvi. xxvii.). Herodotus is very full and particular concerning the closing years of Hophra, who fell by domestic revolution; his successor Amasis was a man eminently Egyptian and very prosperous.

[2] Joseph. c. Apion, i. 21; Ezek. xxix. 18.   [3] Jer. lii. 30.
[4] B.C. 562.

of like spirit or experience arose. In the last decade of his forty-three years' reign, decay had perhaps already commenced. His empire was as large and as powerful in his tenth as in his last year: in fact, after Syria and Phœnicia had acknowledged his sway, he won nothing more; and his laborious campaigns against the insular Tyre, with his vast works at Babylon, must have greatly drained his resources. As with Solomon and Louis le Grand, his early successes shed splendour on his whole reign, and his domestic magnificence dazzled men's minds; but the Chaldæan armies, at his death, had been long taught that they were not invincible. Immediately after, the intestine quarrels which followed in his family presaged final ruin. Evilmerodach, son of Nebuchadnezzar, was killed by his sister's husband Neriglissar, after a two years' reign. Neriglissar dying four years later, left the throne to his boyish son Laborsoarchod, who was allowed to live but nine months longer. He was assassinated[1] by a domestic conspiracy, and one Nabonnedech, whose relationship is contested,[2] obtained the kingdom. According to Herodotus, his mother Nitocris had been queen of Babylon,—wife perhaps of Neriglissar, and daughter of Nebuchadnezzar; this will make him grandson of that great king, and nearly agree with the tradition of the book of Daniel. In fear of the Median power, Nabonnedech executed the great labour of building walls along each bank of the Euphrates, which flowed through the middle of the city. Great brazen gates closed the streets which ended on the river. A valuable interval for all such works of defence was left to the Babylonian king, while civil strife rent the rival empire apart; until the supreme power was won by Cyrus the Persian. Reaching out eastward over Bactria, to the south-east over Carmania, in the west this prince added the wealthy kingdom of Lydia to his sceptre, and overran all the lesser Asia down to the seas of Greece. No resistance is recorded on the

[1] B.C. 556.
[2] Berosus (in Joseph. c. Ap. i. 20) and Abydenus (in Euseb. Armen. Chron. p. 60) represent him as no way related to Laborsoarchod; and that is possible, even on our view, if he was son of Nitocris, but not of Neriglissar.

Nabonnedech (Ναβοννίδοχος) is Nabonnēdus in Josephus, and Labynētus in Herodotus. The word is not likely to prove transformable into *Belshazzar*, who is undoubtedly meant for the same individual.

part of Babylon to his conquest of Syria on her left, and little to that of Susiana, on her right. In the seventeenth year of Nabonnedech,[1] the arms of Cyrus folded that great city around, which lay now exposed to his attack, a victim almost as clearly destined for capture as Nineveh when environed by the Medes.

The Jews in Chaldæa were not inattentive to these events; and a variety of prophecies boded desolation to the lordly city, their fatal foe, from the arms of the Medes and Persians. Of the prophets of this æra by far the noblest and most interesting is he, whom (in ignorance of his true name) we may call *the younger Isaiah*, the author of the beautiful writings which extend from the 40th to the end of the 62nd chapter of our modern book of Isaiah. The writing is obviously that of a Jew in Babylonia during the exile; and his great subject is, the approaching restoration to their own land. He addresses Cyrus by name, as the heaven-appointed instrument of this event, and announces his conquest over Babylon. If we do not find that the results of this return equalled his magnificent predictions, it is easy to forgive the pious patriotism which dictated them: they are in fact only too splendid poetry to be fulfilled in this prosaic world. More important is it to observe the softened tone towards *the Gentiles* here pervading. Indeed the tenderness and sweetness of this prophet is far more uniformly evangelical than that of any other. His very rhythm and parallelisms generally tell of the more recent polish and smoothness. He retains moreover all the spirituality of the older school; ceremonial observances are in no respect elevated by him. The *Sabbath* alone is named, and that in a tone the very reverse of formalism, although indicating the same high reverence for that institution which Christians in general have retained. With the exception of the fall of Babylon,[2] which was the immediate means of release to his people, he does not concern himself with Gentile politics; but

[1] B.C. 540.
[2] Even in this, there is no gloating over images of blood, nor anything to indicate and excite fierce rejoicings in misery, such as pain us in so many of the prophets. [Isaiah lxiii. 1—6 is an exception, if that passage, as Ewald thinks, comes from the same writer. But this invective against Edom is quite isolated; and makes a very abrupt close to his prophecies, which terminate naturally with chap. lxii.]

dilates on the trials, sorrows, and hopes of Zion, and the promises of divine aid to her, in general terms, to which the heart of spiritualized man in all ages and countries has responded.

Some psalms also of this date are fully worthy of the older times; and the last of the prophets, in the next century, shows much of the same terseness, gravity, and pure moral spirit. But all the religious productions of this æra were not so elevated. The writings of Ezekiel painfully show the growth of what is merely visionary, and an increasing value of hard sacerdotalism.[1] The younger Zechariah is overrun with the same. Obadiah has some verses of much energy, (which have been suspected to be older than the rest,) imbedded in a rather flat complaint against the Edomites. The story of Jonah indicates a lower taste than the general literature of that day, and is perhaps of still later date. Yet on the whole, even the splendour of the second Isaiah can hardly conceal from us that the prophetical energy was declining, and giving way before the newer tendencies.

At last the shock of war from Persia reached the city of Babylon itself.[2] The Assyrians had been distinguished by chariots and horsemen, the Chaldees by cavalry alone; in horse-archery the Medes also excelled; but the pride of the Persian nation was in its infantry, which besides the bow and arrows, carried a battle-axe, two javelins, and a light wicker shield. One battle on the plains of Babylonia laid prostrate the late overwhelming Chaldee forces. Nabonnedech fled with a small retinue into the fortress of Borsippus (*Birs Nimrood*), and was there blockaded by the victorious army. Deprived of its king, Babylon appears to have made no farther active efforts, and, perhaps when at length threatened with famine, easily accepted

[1] Contrast the heavy materialism of the new temple expected by Ezekiel, with its priests, sacrifices, and prince, and its rigid observances according to the Pentateuch (Ezek. xl.—xlviii.), as tedious and unedifying as Leviticus itself,— with the splendid poetry of Isaiah lx.—lxii.; where the heart is lifted into a spiritual region, even when the words of the prophet speak of outward and material prosperity.

Although the historical temple of Nehemiah and the new distribution of the land were in many respects widely different from Ezekiel's predictions, it cannot be doubted, that they so kept alive on the minds of the next generation a belief in certain return from captivity, as to have exceedingly conduced towards the result.

[2] B.C. 540.

the terms offered by Cyrus. After becoming master of
the capital, he pressed the siege of Borsippus more closely, until Nabonnedoch, despairing of escape, threw himself on the conqueror's generosity. Nor was he disappointed; for Cyrus, with the liberal policy which
distinguished the best of his race, treated him kindly and
established him on an estate in Carmania. Such is the
account given by Berosus,[1] a priest of Babylon, who is
likely to have had access to good sources of information.[2]

When Cyrus the Great, thus becoming master of Babylon, resolved to re-establish Jerusalem, only a fraction[3] of
the exiles were willing to return. The dangers of the
enterprise were great; and none but the most zealous,
and especially those who were most attached to local religion and external worship, were likely to encounter
them. Undoubtedly few Jews of that age (if of any age)
could make light of externals without losing religion
altogether; yet a superstitious over-estimate of these
things animates men to pilgrimage more successfully than
a purely spiritual impulse; and on the whole we cannot
doubt that those who returned to Jerusalem were chiefly
persons over whose minds sacerdotal principles had a
commanding influence. Accordingly, from this time forth,
the nation wore a new character. They reverenced
ordinances more than they had before despised them.
Idolatry, and even the making or possessing of graven
images at all, became their peculiar horror. For the
Levitical priesthood they felt a profound reverence.

[1] Joseph. c. Apion, i. 20.
[2] The tale as generally given from Herodotus (whom Xenophon follows) is
far less likely; for to drain off the whole water of the Euphrates on so level a
soil is a most arduous and perhaps impossible operation for an army; but, as
the more romantic story, it would be preferred by that graphic writer.
Grote observes, vol. iv. p. 287 : "The way in which the city was treated,
would lead us to suppose that its acquisition cannot have cost the conqueror
either much time or much loss.........It formed the richest satrapy of the (Persian) empire ;........ *the vast walls and gates were left untouched.* This was
very different from the way in which the Medes had treated Nineveh,........ and
in which Babylon itself was treated twenty years afterwards by Darius, when
reconquered after a revolt."
[3] In Ezra ii. 64, they are called 42,360 persons, which is probably an enormous exaggeration : for those carried away by Nebuchadnezzar were in all
only 4600 according to Jeremiah. The immense disproportion indicates that
neither enumeration is trustworthy. But whatever the actual number which
returned, it did not alter the fact, that the Jewish race continued to be most
widely diffused : which justifies the statement in the text.

Though previously they neglected the sabbath and sabbatical year, now they observed both, although no miraculous abundance was granted on the sixth year, such as the Pentateuch promised, to supply the lost harvest of the seventh. The Lawyers, or expositors of the law, became the most important profession; and Rabbinism took firm root, even before prophecy was extinct.

It is not intended here to pursue the later fortunes of the Jewish nation. We have seen its monarchy rise and fall. In its progress, the prophetical and the sacerdotal elements were developed side by side; the former flourished in its native soil for a brief period, but was transplanted over all the world, to impart a lasting glory to Jewish monotheism. The latter, while in union with and subservient to the free spirit of prophecy, had struck its roots into the national heart, and grown up as a constitutional pillar to the monarchy: but when unchecked by prophet or by king, and invested with the supreme temporal and spiritual control of the restored nation, it dwindled to a mere scrubby plant, whose fruit was dry and thorny learning, or apples of Sodom which are as ashes in the mouth. Such was the unexpansive and literal materialism of the later Rabbi, out of which has proceeded nearly all that is unamiable in the Jewish character: but the Roman writers who saw that side only of the nation, little knew how high a value the retrospect of the world's history would set on the agency of this scattered and despised people. For if Greece was born to teach art and philosophy, and Rome to diffuse the processes of law and government, surely Judæa has been the wellspring of religious wisdom to a world besotted by frivolous or impure fancies. To these three nations it has been given to cultivate and develope principles characteristic of themselves: to the Greeks, Beauty and Science; to the Romans, Jurisprudence and Municipal Rule; but to the Jews, the Holiness of God and his Sympathy with his chosen servants. That this was the true calling of the nation, the prophets were inwardly conscious at an early period. They discerned that Jerusalem was as a centre of bright light to a dark world; and while groaning over the monstrous fictions which imposed on the nations under the name of religion, they announced that out of Zion should go forth the Law and the word of Jehovah. When they did not see, yet they believed, that the proud and despiteful heathen should at length gladly learn of their wisdom, and rejoice to honour them. In this faith the younger Isaiah closed his magnificent strains, addressing Jerusalem :—

> Behold, darkness covereth the earth,
> And thick mist the peoples;
> But Jehovah riseth upon thee,
> And his glory shall be seen on thee :
> And the Gentiles shall come to thy light,
> And kings to the brightness of thy rising.
>
> * * * * * *
>
> The Gentiles shall see thy righteousness,
> And all kings thy glory;
> And thou shalt be called by a new name,
> Which the mouth of Jehovah shall name.
> Thou shalt be a garland of glory in the hand of Jehovah,
> And a royal diadem in the hand of thy God.
> Thou shalt no more be termed Forsaken,
> Nor shall thy land any more be termed Desolate;
> For Jehovah delighteth in thee,
> And thy land shall be married to him.

349

APPENDIX.

THE DESOLATION OF BABYLON.

From "THE REASONER," *No.* 19, *November 5th,* 1854.

(*Referred to in p.* 329.)

EVERY commentator and evidence-writer since controversy commenced, has delighted in extolling the circumstantial verification of the prophecies of Isaiah and Jeremiah concerning Babylon. We shall endeavour to show that in every separate aspect of the time and causes, and of the circumstances to manifest their fulfilment to the world, the prophecies are completely falsified by history and by the actual state of the site of Babylon.

In the first place, it must be remarked that the judgments denounced were not confined to the destruction and desolation of the city alone. "The word that the Lord spoke against Babylon and against the land of the Chaldæans by Jeremiah the prophet. It shall no more be inhabited for ever, neither shall it be dwelt in from generation to generation." (Jer. l. 1, 39, 40). These predictions are positively contradicted by both the past and present condition of the rich province known as Irak Arabia (the ancient Chaldæa), forming a most valuable part of the Pashalic of Bagdad, containing the important cities of Bagdad and Bussora, the seat of an extensive commerce by land and sea, and, although not cultivated nearly to the extent of which it is capable, producing, according to the calculations of Sir Harford Brydges, a revenue of upwards of a million sterling.[1] Is this "a wilderness, a land wherein no man dwelleth, neither does any son of man pass thereby?" (Jer. li. 48).

But we will even consent to restrict our inquiries to the undoubted destruction of the ancient city. And first

[1] "An Account of the Mission to the Court of Persia," by Sir Harford Jones Brydges, Bart. Vol. ii. p. 18. London: 1834.

as to the time. Jeremiah indicates the termination of the seventy years' captivity as the epoch for the punishment of Nebuchadnezzar and his people, and for the fall of Babylon. "And it shall come to pass when seventy years are accomplished that I will punish the king of Babylon and that nation, saith the Lord, for their iniquity, and the land of the Chaldæans, and will make it *perpetual desolations*. And I will bring upon that land *all my words which I have pronounced against it, even all that is written in this book*" (Jer. xxii. 12, 13). Now the end of the captivity, and the conquest of Chaldæa by the Persians, did not mark even the *commencement* of that series of circumstances which led to the decline and desolation of Babylon. "Cyrus was not its destroyer," says Dr Keith, "but he sought by wise institutions to perpetuate its pre-eminence among the nations. He left it to his successors in all its strength and magnificence."

It is also distinctly predicted both by Jeremiah and Isaiah that the ruin of Babylon was to be sudden and final. "These two things shall come upon thee *in a moment, in one day*, the loss of children and widowhood. And desolation shall come upon thee suddenly" (Isa. xlvii. 9—11). "Babylon is *suddenly* fallen and destroyed. O thou that dwellest upon many waters, abundant in treasures, *thine end* is come, and the measure of thy covetousness" (Jer. li. 8—13). And Jeremiah, after desiring Seraiah to rehearse the prophecy in the city of Babylon, directs him to signify her approaching fate by an emphatic and expressive ceremony. "When thou hast made an end of reading the book, thou shalt bind a stone to it and cast it into the midst of Euphrates; and thou shalt say, THUS shall Babylon sink, *and shall not rise* from the evil that I will bring upon her" (Jer. li. 63, 64). She was clearly to sink under judgment suddenly as a stone thrown into deep water, and, like the stone, she was never again to rise from the abyss. Both Isaiah and Jeremiah declare that her condition shall be like Sodom and Gomorrha, which, according to Jewish traditions, were burnt by fire from heaven, and lie buried beneath the Dead Sea. Jeremiah, indeed, distinctly says "the sea is come upon Babylon, she is covered with the multitude of waves thereof" (ch. li. 42). This is incapable of even a specious interpretation. Dr Keith, indeed, in his "Evidences of Prophecy," with profound ignorance of Oriental agriculture, considers this curse to be fulfilled by the periodical overflowing of the Euphrates, which has ever been, and is now, about as great a curse to Chaldæa as the annual overflowing of the Nile is to Egypt. Dr Nelson, an American writer, in his "Cause and Cure of Infidelity," coolly asserts that the predicted "pools of water" appeared in Babylon "in comparatively modern times, in consequence of some singularly spontaneous obstruction of the Euphrates, which caused its overflowing."[1] Very singular, certainly, an overflowing which happens every year, and the cessation of which for one year would most assuredly cause a famine. Jeremiah neutralizes and contradicts this passage with two others. "I will dry up her sea and make her springs dry" (ch. li. 36). "A drought is upon her waters, and they shall be dried up" (Jer. l. 38). The predicted drought has proved as false as the predicted deluge.

And so far from sinking at once and for ever like a stone thrown into water, Babylon was the subject of seven successive sieges and conquests, by Cyrus, Darius, Alexander the Great, Antigonus, Demetrius Poliorcetes, Antiochus, and the Parthians, and survived them all. Her impoverishment was effected not by any sudden catastrophe, but by the gradual secession of her inhabitants to the neighbouring new cities of Seleucia and Ctesiphon. In the third century of the Christian æra, seven centuries after her first capture by Cyrus, the walls remained in existence. Does this accord with Isaiah? "Her time is near to come, and her days shall not be prolonged" (ch. xiii. 22).

Even now, interspersed among the remains of the ancient city, are found many detached dwellings, date gardens, cultivated lands, five villages, and a large commercial town, named Hillah, the population of which is variously stated at from 10,000 to 25,000.[2] Does this

[1] "Cause and Cure of Infidelity," by the Rev. David Nelson, M.D. Routledge & Co. London : 1853.
[2] This town is thus described in Malte Brun and Balbi's "Geography" (Longman & Co., 1844), p. 655 :—"Hillah, a large, well-built town of 10,000 inhabitants. About two-thirds of the town are on the right bank, the rest on the left of the Euphrates, with a bridge of boats between them, 450

agree with the prophecy? "It shall no more be inhabited for ever, neither shall it be dwelt in from generation to generation" (Jer. l. 39). "It shall be a wilderness, a land wherein no man dwelleth, neither does any son of man pass thereby" (Jer. li. 43). "None shall remain in it, neither man nor beast, but it shall it be desolate for ever" (Jer. li. 62). The prophets seem to be quite reckless of contradicting themselves, for although Jeremiah here says that "no beast shall remain in it," in other passages he describes it as a dwelling-place for "the wild beasts of the desert and of the islands," for owls and dragons, satyrs and lions.

Mr Rich, formerly British Resident at Bagdad, in his "Memoir on Babylon," thus describes Hillah:—"The gardens on both sides of the river are very extensive, so that the town itself from a little distance appears embosomed in a wood of date trees. The air is salubrious, and the soil extremely fertile, producing great quantities of rice, dates, and grain of different kinds, though not cultivated to above half the degree of which it is susceptible. The grand cause of this fertility is the Euphrates. When at its height it overflows the surrounding country, fills the canals dug for its reception, and facilitates agriculture to a surprising degree. Many of these irrigation canals pass among and between the masses of ruins, as also do several beaten tracks, and the high road from Hillah to Bagdad, and many "sons of men pass thereby" continually. Wellsted, in narrating Ormsby's travels, writes:—"Hillah, next to Bagdad and Bussora, is the largest town in the Pashalic; well-built mosques and extensive bazaars bespeak its opulence. The number of its

feet long, the depth of water being 18 feet at the lowest season. Hillah is situate within the precincts of Babylon, and built with bricks dug from its ruins." The following facts I have gathered from other sources. Three of the largest ruins, named Mujelibé, Al Kasr, and Amran, lie in almost straight line from north to south on the east side of the river, and to the north of Hillah. A village is situated between Mujelibé and Al Kasr, and two more villages, one on the right and one on the left bank, at a bend of the river between Amran and Hillah. The most extensive and celebrated mass, the Birs Nimrood, lies to the south-west, at a distance of about five miles from Hillah and about eight miles from Amran, the nearest of the northern ruins, and of course, on the opposite side of the Euphrates. Thus it will be seen that Hillah lies undoubtedly within the walls of the ancient city, which embraced a circuit variously stated by historians at from 48 to 60 miles.

inhabitants is estimated at 25,000. Fruit, grain, and other provisions are cheap and plentiful at Hillah, and boats are constantly arriving from various parts."

It is further predicted of the site of Babylon :—"Neither shall the Arabian pitch tent there" (Isa. xiii. 20). Mr Thomas Lumisden Strange, of the Madras civil service, mentions in a lately published work, entitled "The Light of Prophecy,"[1] that he visited Babylon in 1835, and saw indubitable signs of a recent Arab encampment near one of the most extensive ruins, Al Kasr.[2] Sir Robert Ker Porter, as quoted by Mr Strange ("Light of Prophecy," p. 10), states that he paid a visit within the limits of the ancient city to the encampment of a chieftain named Kiahya Beg, "made up of bodies of men collected from distinct tribes." He goes on to say, "we then bent our steps to the lines of an old Arab Sheikh, named Mahomed Bassani, who with his tribe had adhered invariably through all changes to the Pashalic of Bagdad. As soon as we arrived within sight of his camp, we were met *by crowds of its inhabitants.*"

It is also prophesied "they shall not take of thee a stone for a corner, nor a stone for foundations" (Jer. li. 26). The following extracts will prove that the very reverse of this has been the case with respect to the ruins of Babylon. "Lying on a spot of the vast site of Babylon, nothing was more likely than that it (Hillah) should be built out of the fragments of that great city. The town is defended by a number of brick-built towers, all the spoil of Babylon. From her fallen towers have arisen not only all the present cities in her vicinity, but others which, like herself, are long ago gone down into the dust. Since the days of Alexander, we find four capitals at least built out of her remains—Seleucia by the Greeks, Ctesiphon by the Parthians, Al Maidan by the Persians, and Kufa by the Caliphs, with towns, villages, and caravanserais without number. Scarce a day passed without my seeing people digging the mounds of Babylon for

[1] Printed and published at Bangalore at the Wesleyan Mission Press. 1853.
[2] It should be observed that Mr Strange is a "futurist," and believes that Babylon will be *rebuilt* and become a powerful city previous to the fulfilment of this prophecy. Of course the extravagance of his speculations does not detract from his credibility as a living eye-witness.

bricks, which they carried to the verge of the Euphrates, and thence conveyed in boats to wherever they might be wanted" (Sir Robert Ker Porter). "The bricks of Al Kasr are of the finest description; and notwithstanding this is the great storehouse of them, and that the greatest supplies have been, and are now, constantly drawn from it, they appear to be abundant (Rich's "Memoir," p. 22). What a commentary on the prophetic text, "they shall not take of thee a stone for a corner, nor a stone for foundations!"

The writers of the "Evidences of Prophecy" have no more right and no more reason to boast of the predictions regarding Babylon than they have of those regarding Damascus; which latter, so far from having become "heaps," and having been "taken away from being a city," contains upwards of a hundred thousand inhabitants, and is the most flourishing and beautiful town in Syria. Babylon, indeed, has become desolate, but not at the time, not from the causes, not to the extent, and without the peculiar signs, which alone could verify the circumstantial denunciations of the Jewish prophets.

Madras, 1854.

THE END.

JOHN CHILDS AND SON, PRINTERS.

www.ingramcontent.com/pod-product-compliance
Lightning Source LLC
Chambersburg PA
CBHW020230240426
43672CB00006B/476